Science and Inquiry in Social Work Practice

BEN A. ORCUTT

Science and Inquiry in Social Work Practice

CONTRIBUTORS

Linda C. Flowers
Jeffrey Seinfeld

COLUMBIA UNIVERSITY PRESS
New York

COLUMBIA UNIVERSITY PRESS
New York   Oxford
Copyright © 1990 Columbia University Press
All rights reserved

Library of Congress Cataloging-in-Publication Data

Orcutt, Ben Avis.
  Science and inquiry in social work practice / Ben A. Orcutt ;
contributors, Linda C. Flowers, Jeffrey Seinfeld.
      p.   cm.
  Includes bibliographical references.
  ISBN 0-231-07040-3.—ISBN 0-231-07041-1 (pbk.)
  1. Social service—Philosophy.   2. Social service—Research—
Methodology.   3. Science—Methodology.   I. Flowers, Linda Cox.
II. Seinfeld, Jeffrey.   III. Title.
HV40.069   1989
361.3'2'01—dc20   89-23844
                              CIP

Casebound editions of Columbia University Press books are Smyth-sewn
and printed on permanent and durable acid-free paper

Printed in the United States of America

c 10 9 8 7 6 5 4 3 2 1
p 10 9 8 7 6 5 4 3 2 1

To the Memory of My Parents
Benjamin A. and Emily Connell Adams

Contents

Foreword

Science and Inquiry in Social Work Practice makes an outstanding contribution to the advancement of clinical social work and research. For many years, Ben Orcutt has had a major interest in integrating scientific thought and research into social work practice and now shares her understanding of that process in this remarkable book. The purpose was to stimulate scientific inquiry and discovery and to integrate scholarship and research within the process of clinical social work. She assumes that scholarship and systematized knowledge draw on selected social and behavioral science theories; the values, theories, and principles of social work practice; quantitative and qualitative research; and the philosophy of science. She assumes also that social workers not only use, but also contribute to, those areas of knowledge. She integrates these components and demonstrates their implications for direct service practice and research. The theoretical approach is a broad biopsychosocial and ecosystems one that is consistent with the person-environment focus of the profession.

In the early chapters, Orcutt presents a brilliant summary of scientific inquiry that is relevant to social work. She provides knowledge, not available elsewhere in the social work literature, of the diversity that exists in philosophical and scientific thought. Just as there is not a unified theory of social work practice, there is not a unified theory concerning how scientific consensus is formulated and controversies resolved.

The evolution of empiricism is described, including the place of mathematical and statistical procedures in logical thought and research. That philosophy of science was dominant until mid-century, by which time there was growing criticism of strict empiricism with regard to conceptions about the role of observation in obtaining empirical knowledge. Challenges to empiricism have recently taken root in the literature of the philosophy of science; the natural, social, and behavioral sciences and, to some extent in social work. Varying paradigms and methodologies are available, from which the practitioner-scientist in social work may select in the search for valid knowledge. Processes of inquiry aimed at discovery of unique phenomena and building of valid theoretical generalizations should be integral components of the practitioner-scientist's role. Such advancement of practice is dependent on understanding the logic of scientific discovery to generate new knowledge as distinguished from the logic of proof. Discovery of new knowledge for social work practice requires that practitioners be committed to purpose, have a prepared mind set, be persistent, and be open to inquiry, learning, and change.

The author moves next to a consideration of what inquiry, encompassing both heuristic and validational qualities, can offer practitioners as a guide to solving problems within the social work domain. The problems for solution may be empirical or conceptual ones which concern questions about theory. She portrays the practitioner-scientist as having knowledge about and skills in the use of practice procedures and techniques along with knowledge of rational inquiry in science and a spirit of questioning.

One major contribution of the book is its exploration of types of heuristic research that is not covered in research texts commonly used in social work courses. Orcutt sets forth ways in which the philosophy and methods of heuristic research, encompassing both scientific investigation and discovery, can have wide theoretical application to social work practice. Heuristic forms of research fall within a new paradigm of subjective-objective reality that is an alternative to the logical positivism-empiricism one. The new paradigm attempts to synthesize intuitive inquiry with the objectivity of the more conventional paradigm. The new paradigm offers special possibilities for social work since "the person is construed within the paradigm as a holistic human system within its natural context." Such a view is consistent with the biopsychosocial perspective on social work practice. Although dealing with subjective as well as objective reality, the new paradigm is as concerned with rigor and validity as is the other one.

The philosophy and principles of hermeneutics, the science of interpretation and explanation, are explored by Orcutt. This material is useful to social workers in understanding and assuring the validity of their interpretations as used in clinical social work practice and in case study research or research based on interpretation of texts, taped interviews of practice, or historical materials. Through such study, new discoveries may emerge to be tested later by empirical or analytical standards. Hermeneutic activity is also one feature of a phenomenological method that emphasizes discovery and clarification of insights as contrasted with verification.

In part 1, Orcutt makes clear that there is a philosophical and scientific base for the use of numerous qualitative as well as quantitative methods in discovering and verifying knowledge that is applicable to direct service practice in social work. In part 2 her focus is on scientific practice and research in social work.

Orcutt presents a masterful historical sketch of scientific developments in social work practice, relating them to trends in the philosophy of science. She analyzes the contributions of research to practice and the emergence of the practitioner-researcher role. From this material, the reader will gain deep respect for the scientific foundations of practice. It will be useful in teaching courses on the history of social welfare as well as on the development of practice theory.

The chapter on scientific themes in the history of social work practice is followed by an equally valuable one that reviews selected major research studies focused on the process and outcomes of direct practice. These research projects fall within the overlapping categories of: case studies; predictions of continuance in treatment; classifications of interventive procedures; evaluation of outcome and effectiveness; development of models of direct service practice; applications of interpersonal dynamics and strategies to family and group modalities; surveys of needs, problems, or services; and the use of clinical judgments in practice and research. Examples of research in each area are presented. Orcutt urges evaluating and building on what has been done and suggests ways that scientist-practitioners can contribute to the science of practice and to a comprehensive network of research to advance knowledge about and the quality of clinical social work practice. The methodology—quantitative or qualitative in nature—needs to be selected according to the nature of the problem and the status of existing knowledge.

A later section of the book covers the history of doctoral education in social work, clarifying the reasons for lack of emphasis on clinical social work practice and clinical research in curricula of most schools.

Some leaders are now making strong pleas for the inclusion of content that interrelates practice, theory, and research in the preparation of scholar-practitioners. Orcutt shares her own model of doctoral education for clinical social work, including a practicum, that aims to bridge the gap between the academic and professional components of education. Other models have been proposed but the intent is similar: to prepare the student to contribute to knowledge building and research integrated with highly competent practice. She gives a clear rationale for the position she espouses and sets forth the competencies and abilities that advanced clinical scholars should have to become leaders in advancing clinical practice and research.

The final two chapters present papers, based on dissertation research, written by Linda C. Flowers and Jeffrey Seinfeld, which describe use of the single subject designs and historical analysis in scientific inquiry into practice. Flowers presents a practice model in which she attempts to incorporate behavioral techniques into a psychosocial perspective on practice and to evaluate the outcome. Seinfeld's effort is to contribute to foundational theory in applying object relations theory to the problem of rejection of practitioner's empathy by a borderline patient. The projects are thought-provoking, providing opportunity for students and faculty to debate the relative merits of different research designs.

This scholarly book has much to offer the advanced practitioner, researcher, and educator with an interest in the research-clinical practice interface. I expect the result will be that readers, particularly doctoral students and instructors of both direct service practice and research, will modify their teaching in dramatic ways. Research teaching will be more effective if it is based on knowledge of the philosophy of science with its alternative beliefs and means to discover and validate knowledge. Practice teaching will likewise be more effective if it incorporates a philosophical perspective on knowledge about practice and its outcomes and builds on the existing knowledge.

The author has achieved a remarkable linkage between the philosophy of sciences, research designs and methodology, and competence in clinical social work practice. It is clear that the subject matter of clinical practice offers tremendous opportunities for creative research and new insights into scientific inquiry.

Helen Northen, Ph.D.
Professor Emeritus
University of Southern California

Preface

Science and Inquiry in Social Work Practice integrates scientific inquiry and discovery into practice from a historical background in philosophy of science. Inquiry is considered within orthodox and non-orthodox paradigms, which allows for exploration of client-contextual or practitioner-client interactions and the use of quantitative and qualitative methods. Empirical-based practice and empirical studies are considered as well as intuitive, reflective, and interpretive methods in hermeneutics, phenomenological, and historical approaches.

The book supports the interfield linkage of social work with other scientific disciplines and helping professions, and calls for the social work practitioner-researcher to contribute toward foundational knowledge as well as further development of practice knowledge devoted to the dual focus in social work of person-environment. The influence and contribution of doctoral education to the practitioner-scholar-researcher is addressed and cooperation between the practitioner and research specialist is also urged.

The book is exploration and discovery, and provides an integrative, substantive resource in scientific inquiry for the advanced student, educator, practitioner, and researcher in social work.

A source book that encourages and integrates scientific thought and inquiry in social work practice, this book limits the scope of practice to direct or clinical practice for manageability. The practice scholar is urged to use analytical reasoning and the tools of scientific inquiry in exploration and discovery of new understanding and meaning, as well as the evaluation of practice itself. The practitioner's major objective is to help clients who may be troubled by an interplay of emotional, socio-relational, and economic stresses. However, the practitioner also must be cognizant and inquiring with respect to the use and limitations of practice knowledge. The book suggests patterns for inquiry that can be associated with the practice process, since this arena offers special opportunity for exploration pertaining to varying clients, their problems and their interrelated social systems.

Acknowledgments

I am deeply indebted to several Academic colleagues and friends, and to my many students, in the preparation of this book. I would like to express my appreciation posthumously to Florence Hollis, Professor Emerita, Columbia University, for her intellectual stimulation and generosity in providing historical information on the development and conceptualization of casework practice. I am also deeply grateful to Robert E. Comas, Max O. Hocutt, and James D. Ramer, University of Alabama; Tony Tripodi, University of Pittsburgh; George Frank, New York University; and Professor Emerita Isabel Stamm, Columbia University for their critical reading and helpful suggestions during the formative stages in the preparation of the manuscript. I am also indebted to Professor Emerita Louise G. Faircloth, University of Alabama, for her editorial contributions, and to Carol H. Meyer, Columbia University, and Paul R. Mills, Jr., formerly of the University of Alabama, for selected source material.

I want to express my deep appreciation to Jennie Flowers, librarian at the University of Alabama, for her untiring efforts in locating and making accessible the array of resource materials necessary to the research for this book. I am also most grateful to Marietta Long for her insightful clarification of ideas and to my sister, Ophelia Adams Albritton, for her unfailing support.

The book could not have been completed without the tireless and loyal efforts of Loma Simms in the typing and preparation of the manuscript. I am deeply appreciative of her contribution.

How can a man's life keep its course if he will not let it flow?

Lao-Tzu, 650–514 B.C.

The Integration of Scientific Conceptual Thought, Research, and Practice in Clinical Social Work

This book is written as a source book aimed at advancing the integration of scientific scholarship and research within the clinical practice process of social work. It defines the clinical social worker as practitioner and scholar-scientist and views the helping process embedded within a wider context of scientific inquiry.

Theoretically, clinical practice is conceptualized within a holistic biopsychosocial systems framework with the focus on the dynamic and transactional nature of the person-in-environment.[1] The systems framework allows for a holistic conception of the person (organismic) system as a dynamic, structural component of the social transactional (family-socio-environmental) suprasystems.[2] In this conception, we envision the components of any one system as interlocking with larger hierarchical systems of which it is a component part. Thus, structural arrangements of living systems are conceptualized as a fluid, dynamic order of parts and processes.[3] The conception of the person as an internally active system of biological and psychic structures in reciprocal processes of interaction and transaction with structures of familial, small group, and other social systems, suggests theoretical concepts, observations, and interventions that relate to these structural processes.

The use of a systemic transactional paradigm, or world view, consequently permits the dynamic complexities of individual parts and collective wholes to be examined in their transactions, understood in their relational dynamics, linked, and changed. Such a view is consistent with the traditional focus on "person in-situation" that theorizes psychosocial relations within an interdependent environment,[4] and with the current ecosystems perspective.[5]

This book assumes that scholarship and systematized knowledge in social work draws on and contributes to:

1. foundational social and behavioral science theory
2. practice theories, principles, and values in social work
3. scientific research of quantitative and qualitative nature
4. philosophy of science and the spirit of scientific questioning

It is recognized that these four elements for scholarship and systematized knowledge reflect different theories in current use and different spheres of phenomena (psychodynamic, organizational, structural, etc.). They have, however a common scientific aim of understanding, exploration, and prediction for the helping process.

The different theories and practice principles range in complexity, and there may be overlap, complementarity, or competitiveness. To deal with the complexity of these phenomena, we need not only to be able to predict, but to understand how explanations answer or do not answer needed questions for practice. As an example, Garfinkel lists several central questions that are important to explanation:

When are two explanations inconsistent with each other?

When are two explanations irrelevant to each other?

When can two explanations from different theories be added or joined to each other?

How does one explanation replace or supplant another?

When does one explanation presuppose another?

When are two explanations from different theories really explaining the same thing?

What could make one explanation superior to another?[6]

If one considers these questions of explanation in terms of philosophy, knowledge, and research in social work, they are either partially answered, unanswered, or not precisely explicated. The thrust of this book, therefore, is to facilitate a quality of science and scholarship in practice that asks questions, finds explanations, evaluates, and further explicates knowledge. The expectation is that there is a mind-set by the practitioner for scientific inquiry that frames the therapeutic and problem-solving activity. Conceptually, the flow of the case activity is interactive with a flow of scientific inquiry and/or case evaluation. Figure 1 visually depicts a structural framework for operationalizing activities of scholarship and science within, or associated with, the practice process.

The structural framework reflects the parallel processes in alleviation and solution to client problems and scientific inquiry as manifested by identification of the problem, assessment, or hypothesis

---

FIGURE 1 Structural Framework for the Practitioner as Scholar-Scientist

---

Feedback Loop

Alleviation-solutions

(1) The Case. Therapeutic-problem oriented (referral-request)	(2) Assessment of Case. (Ongoing-periodic) observation-assessment plan of action or intervention goals	(3) Intervention Process. Intervention or treatment process, modification of assessment or goals, evaluation
(4) Fit of theory to case		(5) Fit of inquiry/research strategy to case
(1)[1] The Case. Scientific inquiry, unknowns, presuppositions Foundations of Knowledge	(2)[1] Hypothesis-Understanding. Observation-inference, Judgment of relationships and guide to alternative action modes; explanation-interpretations, analytic scheme	(3)[1] Heuristic Investigation Process. Low-level trying-out actions, alternate modes; instrument measurement; single-case experiment/measurement; description-comparison, description/essence
Knowledge Building		Transcript understanding/interpretation

Feedback Loop

SOURCE: Adapted from Analytic Practice System, Ben A. Orcutt and Paul R. Mills, Jr., "The Doctoral Practice Laboratory," *Social Service Review* (December 1979), 53:637.

formulation, and the therapeutic, problem-solving processes, and heuristic inquiry for understanding or for evaluation. Figure 1 also identifies the practitioner-scientist as making judgments in the helping process as to the fit and adaptation of theory to the case, whereas in scientific inquiry, judgment is made as to the fit of a strategy for investigation of a selected problem or evaluation of the case process. The course of clinical intervention may suggest modification of the assessment and further intervention strategies for achieving treatment goals. Likewise, hypotheses may be reformulated and different strategies suggested for understanding, experimentation, or interpretation. It is expected with the achievement of case goals that the feedback alleviates or solves the case problem as presented. The understanding or the evaluation resulting from scientific inquiry may, in a similar fashion, be fed back as new knowledge or new insights to be tested.

The structural similarities in clinical helping and scientific inquiry depicted in figure 1 illustrate the logic of the helping process conceptualized within the wider context of scientific inquiry or as associated with it. The structural framework will be largely developed in this book from the vantage point of scientific inquiry and discovery that is linked to foundations of practice knowledge and philosophy of science rather than a focus on the direct, helping processes.

INTEGRATION OF RESEARCH AND PRACTICE

The logic and science of social work were historically grounded in "scientific charity,"[7] and as early as 1890,[8] research and statistics were considered vital to the emerging profession. The concept of the clinical scientist, articulated by Briar,[9] and the integration of research into the clinical practice process, however, has been largely a phenomenon of the past two decades.[10] The integration of research has been devoted largely to measurement of change in case process or outcome and to the facilitation of an empirically based practice. The linkages in practice-research with scientific issues, the relation to philosophy of science, and the processes in discovery and theory building (with the exception of Reid and Smith)[11] have been less well articulated. These issues are thus the major focus of this book. We want to recognize especially the extensive contributions to empirical model building and developmental research by Reid,[12] Thomas,[13]

Rothman,[14] and Mullen, [15] with respect to task-centered, behavioral, and personal models.

Integration of research within the practice process has been stimulated by well-documented empirical findings of strain, lack of relevance, and barriers to utilization of research in the practice of social work.[16] With the advent of integration of the practitioner-researcher (clinical scientist), many books and articles appearing on the professional scene have dealt with empirically based practice, single-subject design, time series measurements, and the evaluation of case outcome.[17]

Patti commented in 1981, that

the relationship of social work research to social work practice is no longer a marginal professional issue. Long the object of general hand-wringing and exhortation but seriously addressed by only a handful of academics and practitioners, the interaction of research and practice has recently emerged as a central preoccupation of the profession.[18]

However, the profession was also reminded by Gordon of his predictions some twenty years earlier, in which he stated that

if results of research were to ever strengthen practice, some social worker researchers would need to become social work scientists and develop a social work paradigm that would serve to make studies cumulative, comparable, and applicable in practice and would form a common conceptual base for both research and practice. Failing that, social work researchers would turn to social science disciplines to find an intellectual base through which to develop hypotheses and pursue their studies, which would often not be of interest or of use to practitioners.[19]

Gordon's predictions are perhaps at the root of the strain that has been observed between practice and research. During the late 1970s and the early 1980s, however, there has been aggressive movement in the direction of empirically based practice, single-case research, and model building. Blythe and Briar have recommended that practitioners begin to develop their own models within their practice, using single-case methodology.[20] Even with the acceleration of literature and technology, there has not yet been a groundswell of empirical model building and single-subject measurement among practitioners.

Recently, the professional literature has reflected some questions as to the feasibility of the practitioner's use of the experimental, controlled AB, ABA, and ABAB single-subject research designs, or other quantitative procedures, especially in the charged crisis situations of practice.[21] In this vein, Siporin has defined practice as a "scientific art," rather than a science, albeit based on valid data, with tested and verified theories, principles, and techniques.[22] Our position is that the practice arena offers immeasurable opportunity for creative research and new insights in scientific inquiry. Differential qualitative and quantitative research procedures and replication can serve as a building block for knowledge and for model- or theory-building related to more rigorous investigation. Such research can stimulate the pursuit of theoretical knowledge that is grounded in practice and can provide a complementary practitioner-researcher to the research specialist in social work. Our emphasis combines, with the technology of inquiry, the scholarship that examines scientific search methods and the conceptual foundations of scientific assumptions as in the philosophy of science. Though some general concerns have begun to emerge, there continues to be a paucity of literature in social work regarding linkages with the philosophy of science in scientific discovery and with research within case practice.[23]

It should be noted that we have used the terms *model* and *theory* and want to call attention to the fact that there is some diversity in usage of these terms. Some scholars view "theory" as fundamental explanations in science and "models" as representations of reality, whereas others view the term *model* as a synonym of "theory."[24] Reid, in referring to the task-centered model, has given an especially lucid distinction, "A theory consists essentially of definitions and propositions: it defines, explains, and predicts but does not direct. In contrast, a model prescribes what the practitioner is to do under given circumstances."[25] The model is a structural pattern. We use the two terms, *theory* and *model,* and consider *model* as particularly relevant to developmental research, where the building of knowledge is within the reality of the practice process.

INTERFIELD LINKAGES AND FOUNDATIONAL THEORIES

It is paramount that interfield linkages in the science of knowledge building and research be nurtured, especially as there is increasing scientific interdependence in the professions and in the natural and social sciences. Philosophers of science have lamented the fact that interfield connections have not been sufficiently made use of in interdisciplinary domains.[26] Clinical social work has drawn on such interfield foundational theories as systems, egopsychology and psychoanalysis, object-relations, cognitive theory, behavioral theory, social structure, organization, and communication. These foundational theories offer conceptual explanations and predictions for human individual and group behavior within a social context, but linkage between the "inner" and "outer" of human social behavior and functioning, which is a paramount focus in clinical social work, is not theoretically synchronized. Maas' description and analysis of aspects of social life that reciprocally enhance or inhibit individual and group development and effects on environment is a positive step in that direction.[27]

It is imperative that adequate foundational theories support clinical professional work and important that the social worker contribute to this basic knowledge, as well as to practice theory. Though practice theory may be a priority, knowledge that is fundamental to practice should not be totally relegated to other sciences.

Changes in scientific thought and issues regarding certainty have escalated since the mid-1950s. Debate and a shift from emphasis on formal conceptions in science to the more functional have been noted.[28] (The influence of logical positivism of the 1920s and 1930s was liberalized by the 1950s.)[29] The acceptability only of knowledge that is verified through sensory processes or that is physically observed (sense data) was under attack. The strict empirical verification, as being necessary for a proposition to have meaning, was modified by Reichenbach, who considered probability theory rather than strict verification of meaning.[30] Popper, as a contemporary of the era of logical positivism, also advanced the ideal of rational scientific method in the consideration of rules and hypothetical constructs, degrees of confirmation or testability, and a thesis of falsification.[31] The liberalization of positivism has been associated with many philosophers of science, and in current history and philosophy of science, there is the tendency toward replacement of narrow "formal conceptions and analyses of rationality by broader functional ones."[32] Toulmin contends that the current shift in "attitudes toward rationality need involve no rejection of 'rational' inquiry or action in practice; rather, it involves a re-analysis of the nature and content of 'rationality' on the theoretical plane."[33] The practitioner-scientist needs to be abreast of scientific debate on issues of rationality and investigation that makes possible an adaptation to shifting demands.

It is this view that we want to emphasize in scientific inquiry. The practice-scholar must understand canons or rules of scientific inquiry but also be open to adaptation in application and to changing thought.

The rationality of science must represent for the practitioner what is involved in processes that enable one to inquire scientifically, to find new concepts, new meanings, and possibly new methods of inquiry.

Philosophy of science, itself, is regarded as experiencing a "revolution"[34] with regard to the nature of science and knowledge, and it is believed that "the systems complexity of social life and of its interface with science will demand a greater systems awareness from philosophers of science."[35] The belief is held because of increasing need for science and philosophy of science to consider values. These currents of debate are entirely consistent with issues for knowledge development and values that confront the systems-oriented practitioner.

Some scholars in the social sciences are currently advocating a division between human science and natural science, or, at best, different presuppositions and methods. They believe that the methods of positivism-empiricism used in the natural sciences have failed to capture the more holistic understandings that can be gleaned from the dialectical, action, and participation-observation processes in human observations and interpretations.[36] In addition, advanced analyses are increasingly possible, through use of computer technology in testing models, and measurement itself is considered to be a conceptual and empirical action, giving meaning to the varying factors (variables) in theory.[37]

SCIENTIFIC RATIONALITY AND SOCIAL WORK PRACTICE

Structurally, science in social work practice refers to the systematized body of knowledge that underlies the understanding and explanations of the complexities of diverse client problems (i.e., problematic attitudes, feelings, behavior, relationships, and sociocultural conditions) confronted in practice. Science also refers to the theoretical conceptual framework, generally accepted rules, and empirically tested interventions that offer probability or predictability for prevention, support, or change. In addition to this structural delineation of science in practice, reasoning activity and scientific inquiry are also expected as an ongoing process. Practice and inquiry, therefore, form a complex of activities directed toward some end, whether the inquiry is for therapeutic change or scientific purpose, and recognition should be accorded to the systematic nature of the process.

The scientist in social work is like all other social workers, but, in addition, studies observations of clients in their structural relationships and milieu for patterns and regularities. The inquiry and analysis of case data may lead to the formulation of a network of concepts from which a more holistic conceptual framework or structure may evolve. Wartofsky has said:

The work of the scientist—both his theoretical activity and his practical research and experimentation—is guided by such concepts and made systematic by such conceptual structures, so that what he discovers here has bearing on his understanding of what he has discovered there, linked by the network of thought and inference which the conceptual framework provides.[38]

Reid and Smith, in *Research in Social Work*, have also described systematic inquiry and knowledge building in social work practice with great clarity and explicitness.[39] We refer the reader to this volume, as it is consistent with our philosophy of systematic search and knowledge building in practice.

Epistemology in clinical social work has emerged not only from theoretical concepts and propositions within foundation sciences, but from empirical and reasoned observation in clinical experience and from formalized methods of scientific inquiry.[40]

At this time, however, there is no unified theory of social work practice, only a framework for organizing its conceptual models and fundamental system of values.[41] Diversity exists in accepted methods and interlocking treatment approaches.[42] Diversity also exists in the theoretical formulations, methods, and definitions, in family therapy,[43] though Hoffman has recently attempted to develop some unification.[44] Actually, diversity has been considered by some as a distinctive attribute of social work.[45]

Turner, in his original book, *Social Work Treatment* (1974), pointed to a rapid emergence of thought systems and cited fourteen such systems in treatment; five years later, however, in his second edition, a noticeable decline in this trend had occurred. He found instead that "new developments [were] emerging from the established theories and thought systems."[46] There were new interpretations and expansion in the identified theories, rather than an emergence of new theories.

The more substantive shift could suggest further attention to conceptual analysis in scientific thought. By 1979, the National Invitational Forum on Clinical Social Work held by the National Association of Social Workers in Denver, Colorado, recognized professional differences, but was able to achieve broad common agreement on a definition of clinical social work, its mission, implementation of values, elements of process, and acceptance of diversity in theoretical sources for understanding and action.[47] In 1983, Meyer advocated an eclectic position from an ecosystems perspective.[48]

Maas, in the *Encyclopedia of Social Work*, in 1977 considered unification of theory in social work to be a formidable task that, if accomplished at all, would require years in the making.[49] He thought that generating limited theories related to identified areas of practice would be more likely to occur. Consistent with the philosophy of this book, Maas also envisioned a systems view of reality, with a broadening of the range of research methodology beyond the rigor of hypothesis deduction and quantitative methods to include qualitative methods and the investigation of subjective experience.[50] In the ten years that have followed, a systems view of reality has not facilitated wide expansion in methodological considerations, even though use of qualitative methods has increased. Our fervent hope is that through planned, cumulative research and knowledge-building efforts of committed research specialists and practitioners, the current biopsychosocial systems framework can unite and spawn theories of dynamic and contextual linkages of individual and group systems that can be fruitful and aimed toward the larger goal of unified theory. The activity will require building and testing limited theories linked inductively within a unified framework. For example, the framework of systems theory for conceptualizing biopsychosocial phenomena is largely at an abstract level, or high order of constructs, and does not yet conceptualize the dynamic interchange of the interpersonal, transactional processes with the intrapersonal (psychic) dynamic systems of persons. The practitioner must synchronize at two levels of theory, or as is often done in family therapy, focus on the structural or the cybernetic processes of interpersonal relations for promoting early problem change and then using object-relations theory and ego psychological theory for more intra-interpersonal work. What is needed is a far more complete conceptualization of interaction and transactional patterns of "inner" and "outer" forces in interlocking systems.[51] We need to continue to move from abstractions to valid interlocking concepts and principles for guiding the actions of practitioners,[52] under differing problematic, temporal, and structural conditions.

When one considers the formidable task of system level linkage and the expansion, explanation, and probabilities for prediction in accepted theoretical approaches for an understanding of multifaceted client problems and functioning, a myriad of directions for future research and knowledge development are suggested.

Given the fact that there is no unified theory for social work practice, there is also no unified theory of scientific rationality with regard to how scientific consensus is formulated relative to theories, or how disagreement and controversies are terminated.[53]

Philosophers of science from the 1930s through the 1950s tended to believe in the "Leibnizian ideal," which characterized science cognitively by a high level of agreement.[54] "The Leibnizian ideal holds that all disputes about matters of fact can be impartially resolved by invoking appropriate rules of evidence."[55] The canons of a shared "scientific methodology" or "inductive logic" were considered sufficient to resolve disagreements about matters of fact.[56] More and more evidence would eventually resolve the disagreements. Then there began to emerge the argument that "the rules of evaluative criteria of science do not pick out one theory uniquely or unambiguously to the exclusion of all its contraries."[57] Kuhn considered that the standard criteria for evaluation of theory which are shared by scientists are too imprecise to determine choice.[58] In fact, Kuhn believed that common agreement could exist in identification of a paradigm, without agreeing on a full interpretation or rationalization of it. "Lack of a standard interpretation or of agreed upon reduction to rules will not prevent a paradigm from guiding research."[59] He further noted that when scientists disagree about whether the fundamental problems of their field have been solved, a search for rules tends to be accelerated: "While paradigms remain secure, however, they can function without agreement over rationalization or without any attempted rationalization at all."[60]

In this vein—although at the aforementioned clinical social work forum, there was agreement in the acceptance of diverse psychological and social theories—arguments do exist in social work regarding scientific purpose, on the methodological rules, validity, and the efficiency of theoretical preference. An example is the current debate by Heineman-Pieper, Scheurman, Hudson, Geismar, Gyarfas, and Brekke,[61] on whether social work methodological imperatives in scientific research are obsolete. Heineman-Pieper has criticized heavy reliance on orthodox empiricism with its stringency in objectivity, operational definitions, quantification, and probability as being unable to capture the complexities of important problems in social work research.[62] Cooper has also raised concerns that practitioners yield their convictions to academicians, who misjudge the nature of science and the theory and knowledge it generates.[63] It is important to social work that these debates are taking place, as they raise professional concerns with regard to issues in science and consensus.

The scientific goals in social work and the generation of knowledge can be visualized within a "hierarchical model of justification" in scientific debates as proposed by Laudan.[64] The model consists of three levels: factual, methodological, and axiological. In level one, factual disagreements are resolved by rules of relevant evidence and standard account, such as used in a court of law. When shared factual rules fail to resolve disagreements, one needs to move up one step in the hierarchy to the level of shared methodological rules. In level two, factual disagreements are resolved by methodological rules. These rules generally are of empirical nature (independence, testability, probability, algorithms, etc.) or of comparative nature, providing evidence for support or agreement. If disagreement continues, then the methodological controversies may be resolved by moving up to the axiological level. In level three, factual disagreements are considered at the axiological level, which refers to the shared aims or goals of science. To quote Laudan, "When two scientists [or more] find themselves espousing different and conflicting methodological rules (and assuming, as the standard account does, that they have the same basic aims), they can in principle terminate their disagreement at the methodological level by determining which of the rival rules conduce(s) most effectively to achieving the collective goals of science."[65]

In criticizing this model, however, it is asserted that the scientific decision is not which theory is best supported by the evidence, but which is the "best theory they can find."[66] The formation of any consensus is then placed in a comparative mode.

In the practice of social work, one comprehensive theory may attract greater consensus within a comparative mode under selected conditions and with selected problems. But it is important to the science of social work practice that knowledge and epistemology achieve some consensus at level one, and that dissent at level two should be the object of continued study. That would insure that current methodological approaches and issues of science continue to be examined.

Considering that there may be "underdetermination" in the methodological rules for determining facts (which we will discuss later), a systems paradigm can be used in the development of explanatory systems models that are based in the descriptive facts or evidence. These phenomena are derived from observations and communications regarding client(s) problems-situations, actions, and interactions. They offer understandings and predictions of future events that can be subjected to a clinical judgment of the factual evidence and claims. It coincides with Gould's claim that "Theories are not inexorable inductions from facts. The most creative theories are often imaginative visions imposed upon facts."[67]

Schensul has recently delineated for applied anthropology an interactive action/practice model which he believes could improve anthropology's scientific nature,[68] and which is pertinent to our conception of the theoretical-research work of the social work practitioner. He proceeded from a scientific goal in the generation of a logical systems model, consisting of a set of testable propositions to be validated by future events in the social context. He noted that—similar to that of social work—anthropology's value system could structure the inquiry with attention to issues of health and welfare of the human group and the resources available to them to maintain and improve their quality of life. The process of validation would be embedded in the "application of results to those elements involved in the maintenance and change process."[69] Application of results was considered as much a part of the social scientific process as is replication in the laboratory research process. These ideas bear a resemblance to demonstrations in social work and to the action research represented in Lewin's early action model.[70] Nevitt Sanford has delineated this action model as consisting of "analysis, fact-finding, conceptualization, planning, execution, more fact-finding or evaluation—and then a repetition of this whole circle of activities; indeed a spiral of such circles."[71]

Further discussion in the text will center on inquiry within the parameters of scientific thought and the issues related to such concepts in science as pragmatism, relativism, realism, praxis, phenomenalism, and so on. It will suffice for now that concern is increasing among the social scientists who question a total reliance on the methods of natural science as the most suitable methods for studying social phenomena. There are concerns that methods of science can be specialized to the point that the most significant modes of reality can be missed. These concerns underlie our position that refers to taking a broad view of methodology, with attention to theoretical assumptions, to the nature of content, and to varying methodologies, validity of evidence, and fruitfulness of inquiry.

ISSUES IN JOINING SCIENCE AND THE TECHNOLOGY OF HELPING

There is much discussion in scientific literature with regard to limitations on science and the technology it produces.[72] The joining of science and technology in the industrial world has produced recognizably vast changes and innumerable benefits for mankind. We ask, in a positive vein: cannot the alignment of science with the technology of people-helping practice also benefit society and the quality of life for individuals and families? We think it can.

While science and technology in the material world have been joined, with resulting great advances, we know that there have emerged concomitant social problems and that there are many ethical issues to be confronted. The question arises as to whether there are higher values than the acquisition of knowledge? If so, then, must there be a consideration of restriction of acquisition at some optimal level? These value questions have emerged particularly with reference to human subjects research, DNA technology, planetary pollution, and disturbances in the ecology.[73] Debates are occurring among contemporary scientists (especially in the natural sciences) that call on human judgment for restraint, as knowledge has accelerated in scientific discoveries to the extent that human modification and destruction can be contemplated.[74] Sinsheimer has noted that our "price for freedom, for tolerance of diversity, even eccentricity . . . may require that we forego certain technologies, even certain lines of inquiry where the likely application is incompatible with the maintenance of other freedoms."[75] In our emphasis, in this book, on scientific clinical inquiry for knowledge building, we consider it crucial that the ethical value system of social work pervade the judgments made in the search for knowledge, as well as in the clinical helping process.

Science in the helping profession of social work has historically been interwoven with a system of values. From the earliest formulations at the turn of the century by Richmond and others, the goals and science of the new profession were articulated as human betterment.[76] Richmond drew on methods of science in the rational processes of inquiry with evaluation of evidence and the design of interventions which were grounded in the philosophy of "the interdependence of individual and mass betterment."[77] Franklin, a more recent historian, has noted that the early contributions to the science of practice by Jane Addams have often been overlooked.[78] She credited Addams with the "utilization of Dewey's techniques of rational inquiry and experimentation [and she] introduced the concept of research and accountability into social work practice."[79] (For a good discussion of social values and the philosophy of social work, see Max Siporin's *Introduction to Social Work Practice*.[80] Our emphases in this book on the dimensions of discovery and knowledge development, as a component of the clinical practice, is grounded within the context of ethical values of the profession,[81] and the cognitive values and standards of science.[82] In our development of ideas related to the science of social work practice, it is assumed that practice is a configuration of art and science. The configuration supports a fusion of scientific observation, inquiry, and research within the context of practice.

Historically, the art and science of practice have been differentiated. Rapoport defined *science* as concerned with how basic knowledge is arrived at, and *art* with how the knowledge is adapted and applied.[83] Chester Barnard, in a similar vein, defined the function of the arts as:

to accomplish concrete ends, effect results, produce situations that would not come about without the deliberate effort to secure them. . . . The function of the sciences, on the other hand, is to explain the phenomena, the events, the situations, of the past.[84]

Within these authors' interpretations, social work practice would be the art of doing, whereas the profession of social work would encompass the body of knowledge that underlies this art. Our position here is that the knowledge and art of doing must be laced with an eye to discovery, formulation of conceptual meaning, and—so far as is practical—appropriately integrated with a design for systematic inquiry and the measurement of outcome processes. Science, in this context, embodies systematized knowledge, and art makes that knowledge more efficient through skill and creative inquiry.

Actually, the exploratory and reflective processes in the problem-solving of practice, germane to the art and technology of helping clients, are also employed in the systematic, scientific efforts that search for clinical understandings, explanations, and predictions for change. Logically, these processes fall within the scientific purview of inquiry as research and discovery. The special case confronting the practitioner can always be viewed within the context of comparative data and the quest for systematization and generalization from data should be basic to the professional attitude.

THE DISCOVERY PROCESS

The discovery process in the science of social work practice is conceived of here in a broad sense from the incubation of ideas, through the testing of preliminary findings and hypotheses, to comparative analyses.

A long debate has existed in the philosophy of science with reference to the logic and parameters of discovery. Stemming from positivistic views during the early twentieth century, particularly those of Karl Popper and Hans Reichenbach in the philosophy of science, discovery and refutation of theory were considered separate phenomena; discovery was set outside the purview of the philosopher of science.[85] They considered *discovery* only as the early creative formulation or shaping of an idea or conjecture that preceded the formal question for assessment. Hanson in 1958,[86] and some others who followed, argued in response that discovery exhibits characteristic patterns and is at the center of rationality.[87] In other words, discovery could incorporate logical processes.

Laudan later conceptualized discovery as consistent with Hanson's view, but from a broader perspective that included a "context of pursuit." He defined the "context of pursuit" as lying between the "context of discovery" as a "eureka experience" and the "context of ultimate justification."[88] Actually, Popper was drawing a distinction in his logical analysis between psychology and logic—"between a description of how people actually behave (e.g., judge, reason), and a prescription of norms of valid behavior (e.g., judging soundly, reasoning correctly and rigorously)."[89] A logic of scientific method would therefore be "a set of normative standards for judging the processes used to discover or test scientific theories, or the formal structure of the theories themselves."[90]

Our concern here is to examine the different notions of philosophy and logic in their relatedness to methods in the discovery of phenomena and knowledge useful to the practice of social work, rather than to judge formal structures of theories of discovery.

SUMMARY AND ORGANIZATION OF THE BOOK

The integration of scientific scholarship, exploratory inquiry, and research with clinical social work practice provides an important avenue for theory and knowledge building for practice. The integration can also be expected to reduce strains between the practitioner and researcher. A structural scheme is presented that highlights the parallel between scientific inquiry and clinical inquiry. Philosophical and scientific thought are reviewed with reference to exploration and inquiry. The emphasis on exploration and discovery in scientific inquiry is related to controversial issues in philosophy of science on the role of discovery in science.

A broad definition of discovery is accepted for the book which is consistent with Hanson's view, but inclusive of what Laudan has identified as the "context of pursuit," which lies between the "context of discovery" as a "eureka experience" and the context of "ultimate justification."

An open-minded stance is taken that allows for orthodox inquiry and research, as well as for less conventional strategies that do not sacrifice regulative rules but have the capacity for finding meaning.

The need for practice inquiry is impelled by the proliferation of theoretical approaches in practice and the lack of a unified knowledge base in social work. The lack of unification is viewed against the background of a lack of consensus in science for standard criteria on which to evaluate theory. A hierarchical model for evaluation and consensus in a comparative model proposed by Laudan is discussed.

The book is organized into four parts. Part 1 incorporates the major thrust that embodies two interrelated threads. First, the book considers the diversity in philosophical and scientific thought and relates science and scholarship to practitioner-client clinical actions within a broad context of discovery. Discovery, therefore, incorporates: (a) creative imagination and commitment to scientific search; (b) identification of a problem domain in inquiry; (c) reflective inquiry that includes the incubation of ideas and judgment, trial-and-error reasoning, analytic analyses, and canons of logic; (d) heuristic investigations, and (e) the more formal problem-solving efforts of concept formulation, selection of propositions, or hypotheses, and model building within the realm of orthodox empiricism. A second thread considers emerging scientific thought related to an alternative paradigm, which studies dialectical and subjective processes in understanding and in building knowledge and theory. These methods can be applied concomitantly with the ongoing case process, and also as complementary to the social work research specialist in the conduct of a larger investigation.

The message of part 1 embodies a philosophy of open-minded, accountable, scientific search, because what may offer consensus in one period may be found subsequently to be in error or obsolete. In Kuhn's words, over time anomalies tend to occur that revolutionize thinking and methods. There may be mini-revolutions that occur in small steps, or a major change or shift in paradigm.[91]

Part 2 identifies science, epistemology, and research in social work, from a historical perspective with influence on current trends that integrate these dimensions in clinical practice.

Part 3 traces the influence of doctoral and post-master's education on the scientific thrust and current direction of fusion of research and practice. Current perspectives and dilemmas are discussed.

This section also addresses educational preparation for the scholar-scientist in practice, who is committed to knowledge building, as well as to the highest quality of help for clients. Coexistent with the therapeutic art of helping, the practitioner learns to question, to examine knowledge and its conceptual foundations in the arena of application, to test out new insights, and to evaluate outcomes.

Part 4 presents exemplars, i.e., clinical examples of the scholar-scientist in clinical practice.

Scientific Inquiry in Clinical Social Work Practice

This section defines the advanced social work practitioner as a scholar-scientist. At this advanced level, basic practice knowledge and helping skills should have been firmly integrated. There also exists a concomitant attitude of disciplined curiosity, a capacity to search systematically for new knowledge and theories, and the ability to test practice outcomes using different paradigms. A "cognitive-feeling" posture is embraced by the practitioner that in itself embodies imagination, questioning, empathy, logic, and a continual search for greater knowledge and efficiency in understanding and helping clients.

Differential interventive approaches already abound in social work, approaches that offer guides to working with clients. Yet uncertainties continue to exist, with reference to clients' responsiveness and to effective interventions within differing temporal, structural, and social contexts. It is hypothesized that greater clarity at this theoretical midrange can be derived from discoveries growing out of systematic, ongoing clinical work with clients who run the gamut of human problems.

Part 1 incorporates seven chapters that discuss discovery and heuristic processes philosophically and as inquiry, integrated within the clinical practitioner-client actions and contexts, with the aim of knowledge building.

CHAPTER 1

Diversity in Philosophical and Scientific Thought: Implications for Inquiry

Contemporary philosophy (from midcentury to the present) reflects linkage with many differing theoretical disciplines. It is thus important that the linkage in philosophical and scientific thought, as germane to social work, be understood in relation to scientific inquiry. Tice and Slavens have organized philosophy within at least sixteen major areas that they identify as "core" and "bridge" areas.[1] They list theory of knowledge, logic, philosophy of language, metaphysics, and philosophy of science as prominent in philosophical inquiry, but we shall be concerned here particularly with the philosophy of science.

During the first half of the twentieth century, the philosophy of science was dominated by logical positivists or empiricists who used classical empiricism and the tools of symbolic logic as their basis for analysis of science.[2] These philosophers were concerned with logical problems, particularly the logical structure of theories, and the logical relations between statements which describe observations and the laws and theories that these statements confirm or refute.[3] The major tenet of empiricism was that experience, rather than reason, constituted the source of knowledge of the world. Questions about knowledge did not start with absolute truth waiting to be contemplated or found through reason, but began with observation and the problems presented in experience. It supported induction, built on a hypothetico-deductive system, and assumed an antimetaphysical stance. Philosophers of the twentieth century reflected a particular concern with analytic issues regarding logic and language. There was, indeed, much diversity in their points of view, methods, and procedures, in their attempts to establish truths.

Philosophical problems were differentiated by analytic and synthetic truths. Carnap, in 1934, clarified and differentiated analytic and synthetic truths in the character of philosophical problems, as "analytic truths being discovered by ideas, whereas synthetic truths would be those matters of fact that if they were denied would be self-contradictory."[4] Use of the analytic method led philosophers to attempt clarification of propositions by reducing them to their basic elements through logical truth–functional analysis and to question whether empirical observation statements could be reduced in the same way.[5] It was later recognized by both philosophers and empiricists that the method could not be translated to statements, as rigorous verification or falsification was not possible.

By mid-century Quine, who was an illustrious Harvard philosopher, broke with Carnap and rejected what he termed as the two dogmas, stated as:

[1] belief in some fundamental cleavage between truths which are *analytic,* or grounded in meanings independently of matters of fact, and truth[s] which are *synthetic,* or grounded in fact. [2] The other dogma is *reductionism:* the belief that each meaningful statement is equivalent to some logical construct upon terms which refer to immediate experience.[6]

Quine believed that eliminating these dogmas would have the effect of less precise differentiation between speculative metaphysics and natural science and would support a more pragmatic approach.

With this brief introduction to interlocking themes in philosophy and science of inquiry and to the importance of scientific and empirical study for clinical social work practice, we will focus attention on empiricism from a historical perspective and the relation of differing philosophical positions with implications for inquiry.

EMPIRICISM IN HISTORICAL PERSPECTIVE

Early Empirical Thought. The notions of empiricists derived, in part, from David Hume (1711–1776), who believed that the science of man must be based on experience and observations.[7] Hume thought that perceptions of the mind were of two different kinds, impressions and ideas. For Hume, impressions were sensations, feelings, and experiences of perceptions of awareness, whereas ideas were the thoughts and memories that derive from impressions. Impressions would therefore be fundamental to ideas and basic to the perception of reality. All objects of human reason or inquiry were considered to be of two kinds, the relations of ideas and matters of fact.[8]

Hume meant, essentially that all knowledge about the world is a posteriori, "which can be confirmed or disconfirmed only by experience and observation . . . ; [whereas truths, such as] 'three times five is equal to half of thirty' is a priori—that is, its truth is 'discoverable by the mere operations of thought.' "[9]

For Hume, reasoning about the relations of ideas—such as in logic, arithmetic, and geometry—was analytic and based on principles of noncontradictions, whereas reasoning about matters of fact (empirical sciences)—such as physics, chemistry, and common factual knowledge—was a posteriori, or confirmed or refuted by experience and observations. When knowledge of matters of fact go beyond direct observation and remembered past observations, it was considered a generalization from experience inherent in the principle of cause and effect.[10]

Not only were these notions held by Hume in the eighteenth century a forerunner of those held by twentieth century empiricists, the work of many other philosophers, including Kant (1724–1804), also contributed to contemporary scientific thought. Actually, the work of different philosophers influenced each other. For example, Hume followed and repudiated George Berkeley (1685–1753), and John Locke (1632–1704) and Immanuel Kant saw a need to refute Hume.[11] A deep division in philosophies occurred, as they tended to divide into rationalists and empiricists, with a dispute forming along lines between reason and experience.[12]

We shall attempt here no more than a cursory overview of philosophy and empiricism from a historial perspective, though it is uniquely significant for viewing empiricism in social work within the context of science. For a more complete historical review, we refer the reader especially to the books *Philosophy in the Twentieth Century* and *Logical Positivism* by the eminent British philosopher, Alfred Jules Ayer, and *Research Guide to Philosophy* by Terrence N. Tice and Thomas P. Slavens, whom we have cited.

The mark of the early empiricist was that he considered sense-perception as almost entirely the legitimate source of belief about the external world, but this did not satisfy the position of the

"pure" sciences of logic and mathematics. . . . A compromise put forward by Immanuel Kant, at least with regard to mathematics, . . . [was] that its propositions owe their necessity to their stemming from an ordering of the world in space and time, which is a precondition of its being accessible to our understanding.[13]

Kant's *Critique of Pure Reason* (1781, 2d ed., 1787)[14] postulated that experience consists of a combination of form and content, with sensation providing the content of experience and mind providing the form. Knowledge may emanate from objects experienced through the senses but the experience would be located in time and space, and thus open to rational knowledge derived from experience. Concepts of the irreversibility of time, and the fact that no two objects can occupy the same space at the same time, could not be accounted for by experience alone, but were concepts of the mind.[15] Since causality was also purported to be a concept supplied to experience by the mind and thus part of the form of experience, it would be known a priori that every event has a cause, but it could not be known a priori what the particular cause of any given event might be, as this would be part of the content of experience and must be discovered by empirical research.[16] Kant was credited with laying a foundation for an empirical and scientific outlook, though his works reflected some inconsistencies. He was also an advocate of "transcendental idealism."[17]

As we shall begin to see in our exploration of the philosophy of science and twentieth-century empiricism, there was a correspondence in the procurement of facts by inquiry, impression, observation, and attention to cause and effect by the early charity workers in social work that reflected concepts inherent to the philosophy and logic of science of the period.

Not only did Hume and Kant, among others, influence nineteenth-century empiricism in philosophic thought, but there was also widespread influence of an opposite nature in the doctrine of idealism espoused by Georg Wilhelm Hegel (1770–1831). He

purported to find a place for all ideas within an all-encompassing, historical-dialectical system, offered an idealist perspective from which to criticize relatively undeveloped ideas, and enabled religious believers and non-believers, social-cultural-political conservatives and revolutionaries alike to claim a firm understanding of their destiny within the total scheme of things.[18]

The Role of Mathematics in Empirical Thought. It was in the early twentieth century that objections to the philosophy of Hume tended to concentrate in the philosophy of mathematics, particularly as mathematics was applied in science. Before the turn of the century, Gottlob Frege, a German philosopher and mathematician of the late nineteenth century, following ideas of Gottfried Wilhelm Leibniz (1646–1716), made a major contribution to mathematical logic and was credited with developing the first modern, formal system of logic.[19] In 1879, he first published *Conceptual Notations*, which contained the first formulations of quantificational logic, identity theory, and second-order logic. This work broke an impasse that logic had faced since the time of the Greeks, for it unified truth-functional and quantificational logic while simultaneously extending the latter to handle the logic of relations.[20] Frege's formal system for arithmetic and set theory was later discredited and not acclaimed until more recent years. His contribution was to the definition of numbers and reconstruction of logic. He believed that "mathematical objects were known through perception that is analogous to but distinct from ordinary perception of physical objects."[21]

Frege harshly criticized the English empiricist John Stuart Mill (1806–1873), who believed that mathematics was known inductively from experience. Mill was anxious "to refute the view that mathematics is an a priori science, which can ultimately be reduced to a series of definitions and their logical consequences."[22] He and Jeremy Bentham (1748–1833) were more utilitarian in their view. Frege and his contemporaries made major advances toward a new and comprehensive reconstruction of logic which was to lay the foundations for the later important work of Bertrand Russell and Alfred North Whitehead in *Principia Mathematica*.[23]

It was not until the early twentieth century that the central thesis of the logistic position in mathematics was formulated by Bertrand Russell in *The Principles of Mathematics*, published first in 1903, which stated:

all pure mathematics deals exclusively with concepts definable in terms of a very small number of fundamental logical concepts, and that all of its propositions are deductive from a very small number of fundamental logical principles.[24]

As background to this, Russell, who was the godson of Mill, had been interested in Mill's mathematical propositions, which were considered empirical generalizations "inductively justified by the number and variety of the observations that conform to them."[25] This conflicted, however, with Russell's view, that the "true propositions of pure mathematics are not just contingently but necessarily true."[26] Russell's solution was to postulate, within the prevailing assumption that all mathematics could be reduced to propositions about natural numbers, that these propositions could be reduced to a system of formal logic. As we have indicated, this was attempted about thirty years earlier by Frege. According to Ayer, the solution required:

first, the discovery of a method of defining the natural numbers in purely logical terms, and, secondly, the development of a system of logic which would be sufficiently rich for the propositions of arithmetic to be deducible from it.[27]

Russell's *Principles of Mathematics* satisfied the first solution. The second was satisfied in his subsequent work with his tutor, Alfred North Whitehead. They developed—in three volumes—between 1910 and 1913, a powerful new form of logic published as *Principia Mathematica*.[28] This logistic solution to the problem of mathematical truth maintained that mathematics is logic and is true in the same ways in which logic is true. A more elementary version of this monumental work was later published by Russell in 1919 as *Introduction to Mathematical Philosophy*.[29] He described as his purpose "to explain mathematical philosophy simply and untechnically, without enlarging upon those portions which are so doubtful or difficult that an elementary treatment is scarcely possible."[30]

During the late nineteenth and early twentieth century when mathematics was being defined as logic, new statistical procedures important to empirical research were also being developed. In his study of population, Francis Galton had developed simple correlational studies,[31] but it was Karl Pearson (1859–1936), the famous English mathematician of the early twentieth century, who produced the more comprehensive correlation procedures.[32]

Descriptive statistics that produced numerical descriptions of populations had been used for over two centuries; in fact, the Constitution of the Untied States in 1787 required the government to collect statistics to serve as the basis for representation in Congress. It is no wonder that descriptive statistics were used widely in early social work with the social survey emerging as a major research method in studying working conditions, causes of poverty, and population needs. The Pittsburgh survey of 1907 was an early case in point.[33]

The development of the logic of statistical theory has been essentially a twentieth-century phenomenon. Much of the basic progress in statistical theory before 1950 was credited to one individual, Roland Fisher (1890–1962). His work, *Statistical Methods and Scientific Inference*, has been published in more than a dozen editions in England and America from 1934 to 1973.[34] Actually, the development of sound sampling techniques of human populations in research has occurred almost entirely since 1935.[35] Progress in mathematics in both its logical foundations and the newer, more robust statistical measures developed in the twentieth century, has tended to coincide with the emerging pragmatism in philosophy and social theory and the developmental years of practice methodology in social work. Pragmatism, in particular, was most closely linked to the philosophy of practice in social work and to social reform in the early decades of the century, as noted in chapter 8. Major developments in logic, mathematics, and research were concomitant with developments in a new philosophy of pragmatism.

Pragmatism and Empiricism. The philosophy of pragmatism deserves special treatment, not only for its impact on philosophical thought and empiricism, but for its utilitarian stance that linked it with progress in human rights and progressive educational, social, and industrial practices. It became the dominant American philosophy in the first decade of the century and was inspiration for social reform in the progressive era. Pragmatism entertained "a more positive view of the activities of the organism, [and] looked upon the environment as something that could be manipulated."[36] It tended to turn emphasis in philosophy from "construction of finished metaphysical systems to an experimental study of the uses of knowledge."[37]

The term pragmatism was first introduced in 1878 by C. S. Peirce (a practicing physicist for the U.S. Geodetic Coastal Surveys), but its principle lay unnoticed until William James used it in an address at the University of California in 1898.[38] James thought the climate, at that time, was more receptive. Actually, the scholars most closely identified with the developments of pragmatism were James (1842–1910), Charles S. Peirce (1839–1914), John Dewey (1859–1952), and George Herbert Mead (1863–1931). (The origins of pragmatism and a critical history are elaborated by Horace S. Thayer and Alfred Jules Ayer.[39]) Peirce's interests tended toward conceptual and linguistic meanings.[40] The philosophy of James was personal in nature and showed concern for practical consequences and what James coined as "radical empiricism," whereas Dewey and Mead were more concerned with social responsibilities and change.[41]

Peirce preceded James in pragmatic thinking, but his manuscripts and papers were not published until after his death.[42] He was a friend of James, and when they were undergraduates at Harvard, he was an influence on James' thinking. The pragmatist movement was distinctly an American product of the late nineteenth and early twentieth centuries, and William James is internationally regarded by philosophers as the foremost exponent of American pragmatism.[43] It was Peirce, however, who introduced the term "pragmatism" and developed a comprehensive system of ideas.[44] Peirce's ideas were basically laid out in his collected papers, particularly in "The Fixation of Belief" and "How to Make Our Ideas Clear." He postulated that

reasoning is good if it be such as to give a true conclusion from true premises, and not otherwise. Thus, the question of validity is purely one of fact and not of thinking. A being the facts stated in the premises and B being that concluded, the question is, whether these facts are really so related that if A were B would generally be. If so, the inference is valid; if not, not.[45]

He held the validity of inference to be objective, "in the sense that a form of inference is validated by its power to convey truth from premises to conclusion, whether we recognize that it has this power or not."[46]

Peirce considered that the initiation of doubt caused a struggle to attain a state of belief or inquiry and that confidence in belief could be attained by four methods: the method of tenacity, the method of authority, the a priori method, and the method of science.[47] The latter method was favored and lauded as having made the "most wonderful triumphs in the way of settling opinion."[48] Its merit was that it set a standard for truth. For the method of science, its fundamental hypothesis is:

There are Real things, whose characters are entirely independent of our opinions about them; those Reals affect our senses according to regular laws, and, though our sensations are as different as are our relations to the objects, yet, by taking advantage of the laws of perception, we can ascertain by reasoning how things really and truly are; and any man, if he have sufficient experience and he reason enough about it, will be led to one True Conclusion. The new conception here involved is that of Reality.[49]

Peirce's statement referred to a major dispute in philosophical thought, which pertained to Realism versus Idealism.

Peirce's philosophy of science also referred to three kinds of reasoning: Deduction, Induction, and Retroduction (Retroduction or Hypothesis).[50] He held that deductive reasoning is hypothetical, and asserted on premises that a true conclusion is conditional on the truths of the premises. Induction adopts a conclusion as approximate because it results from a method of inference which most generally leads to truth over time. Retroduction was considered the provisional adoption of a hypothesis, as every possible consequence stemming from it is capable of experimental verification. Peirce suggested, as did James who followed him, that to discover principles in which a hypothesis should be consistent is to consider its consequences.

It is interesting to note the convergence of these ideas with those of William James, who thought that the pragmatic method was a means of settling metaphysical disputes, whereby one would interpret a notion by tracing its practical consequences.[51] In James' view, the pragmatist

turns away from abstraction and insufficiency, from verbal solutions, from bad *a priori* reasons, from fixed principles, closed systems, and pretended absolutes and origins. He turns towards concreteness and adequacy, towards facts, towards action and towards power. That means the empiricists temper regnant and the rationalist temper sincerely given up.[52]

James further elaborated that the pragmatic method involved bringing out of each work "its practical cash-value, set it at work within the stream of your experience."[53]

In James' view, this experiential, fact-oriented approach differed from traditional empiricism, since it embodied an instrumental view of mind that used "functions of thought to guide future actions."[54] He distinguished between philosophers as rationalists (tender-minded-going-by-principles) and as tough-minded empiricists (going-by-facts).[55] Actually, James' ideas were of a positive nature and challenged "the classic traditions of philosophy."[56] He also advocated a "radical empiricism," which he defined as distinct from pragmatism, and as his *weltanschuung* or philosophic attitude. He claimed that one could reject radical empiricism and still be a pragmatist.[57]

He saw the pragmatist theory of truth as a "step of first-rate importance in making 'radical empiricism' prevail."[58] He wrote, "radical empiricism consists (1) of a postulate, (2) next of a statement of fact, and (3) finally of a generalized conclusion."[59] Summarized, (1) the postulate, is that

the only things that shall be debatable among philosophers shall be things definable in terms drawn from experience. . . . (2) The statement of fact is that the relation between things, conjunctive as well as disjunctive, are just as much between things, matters of direct particular experience, neither more so or less so, than the things themselves, . . . (3) the generalized conclusion is that therefore the parts of experience hold together from next to next by relations that are themselves parts of experience. The directly apprehended universe needs, in short, no extraneous trans-empirical connective support, but possesses in its own right a concatenated or continuous structure.[60]

Radical empiricism provided an empirical and relational aspect to activity. Dualities such as disjunctions "between consciousness and physical nature, between thought and its object, . . . may be avoided by regarding them as differences of empirical relationship among common empirical terms."[61] In James' view, empiricism opposed rationalism, which tended to emphasize universals and to make wholes prior to parts in the order of logic and of being, whereas in the empiricist view one begins with parts and considers the whole a being of second order.[62] Radical empiricism added to empiricism the idea that "the relations that connect experiences must themselves be experienced relations, and any kind of relations experienced must be accounted as 'real' as anything else in the system."[63]

Thus, James' "radical empiricism" aligned him with the "fact oriented" empirical philosophies, which held that the foundation of reality is experience. He thought that analysis of the experience of conjunctive relations, however, could find solutions to some of the problems of metaphysics.[64]

John Dewey's social orientation in pragmatism was in juxtaposition to James' individualism. Dewey outlived James, and his faith in democracy, experimentation, education, and in action moved thinking beyond the more important debates of epistemology and metaphysics to social change. Thus, Dewey's pragmatism was remarkably in tune with the reform-minded Jane Addams, Grace and Edith Abbott, Sophonisba Breckinridge, and other leaders and scholars in social work in the progressive era of the early twentieth century. Addams, especially, was influenced by John Dewey, and leaders in social work at the University of Chicago inspired a view of social work linked to these theoretical and scientific premises.[65]

It is clear from these short excerpts on pragmatic beliefs and "radical empiricism" that, in America, philosophical issues tended to be grounded in the practical and in consequences of events or actions that could be empirically observed. Contemporaneously, the strict empiricism of logical positivism that was emerging in Europe was transplanted in America by European emigrés as they fled Europe prior to World War II. These two movements had some commonalities, though James' philosophy included him among the metaphysical adherents. His "radical empiricism," however, treated the doctrine of Monism itself as a hypothesis and did not "dogmatically affirm Monism as something with which all experience has got to square."[66]

Hocutt notes that the two movements, "which had many affinities, were often allies, [and that] Peirce, the paradigmatic pragmatist, rightly called his pragmatism a form of prepositivism. . . . [He also points out that] there is now a kind of 'humanistic' (Jamesian) pragmatism that thinks of itself as anti-positivist; but that is because it is more 'humanistic' than pragmatist."[67]

Logical Positivism and the Vienna Circle. Logical positivism emerged in philosophical thinking in the early twenties and was associated with eminent philosophers and scientists of the Vienna circle. The circle was composed of a group of scientifically trained philosophers, mathematicians, and scientists who met informally as a group in Vienna and formally in symposia conducted in Königsberg, Prague, and Paris. Founded in 1925 by Moritz Schlick, it was noted for its rejection of the metaphysical, and for empiricism that demanded strict verification of meaning.[68] It also stood for a unified science.[69]

Herbert Feigl, reflecting on the circle's origins,[70] identified the early members as Schlick, Hans Hahn (mathematician and logician), Felix Kaufman (philosopher), and Feigl himself. Otto Neurath was also an early member, as well as Hans Reichenbach and Rudolph Carnap, who were then young, outstanding scholars in mathematics, physics, logic,and epistemology. Carnap later became its leading spokesman and Reichenbach became a lecturer in philosophy at the University of Berlin, where he organized the Berlin group, which was similar to the Vienna group. There was a regular exchange of ideas between the two groups. Carl G. Hempel and Olaf Helmer were Reichenbach's students.

By 1929, the importance of the circle was such that it published a manifesto edited by Otto Neurath, Rudolph Carnap, and Hans Hahn, entitled "Wissenschaftliche Weltanffassung: Der Wiener Kreis" (The Scientific Conception of the World: The Vienna Circle). It stressed:

1. Rejection of metaphysics as nonsense.
2. Rejection of philosophy as a basic or universal science, along with or higher than fields of one empirical science.
3. Affirmation of the tautological character of the true propositions of logic and mathematics.[71]

The appendix of the manifesto listed as many as fifteen members of the group and ten sympathizers.[72] Karl Popper, who was also a contemporary scholar, was never a member of the Vienna group, nor was Ludwig Wittgenstein, both of whom interacted with the group. Feigl recounted that he and Albert Bloomberg met in 1930 in New York to work on the article "Logical Positivism: A New Movement in European Philosophy," which was published in the *Journal of Philosophy* in the spring of 1931, and which served to identify "logical positivism" and to label the Vienna group.[73]

Many of these outstanding scholars, i.e., Feigl, Carnap, Frank, Menger, Godel, Reichenbach, and Hempel, emigrated to America before World War II. They became associated with prestigious American universities, where their influence permeated intellectual interchange and empiricism in science. By 1938, the Vienna circle members had largely dispersed to other countries.[74]

The circle's logical positivist's notions were based on the tradition of Hume, as had been James and the pragmatists. The positivists, however, maintained a strict construction of empiricism, emphasizing that only the knowledge derived or founded directly on experience is genuine. They also concurred with the symbolic logic of *Principia Mathematica* and thus accepted two forms of research for deriving knowledge: (a) empirical research and (b) the logical analysis of science in philosophy.[75]

Brown asserts that:

the central doctrine of logical positivism is the *verification theory of meaning*, the thesis that a contingent proposition is meaningful if and only if it can be empirically verified, i.e., if and only if there is an empirical method for deciding if it is true or false; if no such method exists it is a meaningless pseudo-proposition.[76]

For the logical positivists, the truth-value of any meaningful proposition could be determined only by means of sensory observation or experience, and to logical or symbolic statements that correspond fundamentally to experience. For Ludwig Wittgenstein, philosophy was an activity, that of clarifying the propositions of natural science and exposing metaphysics as nonsense. Wittgenstein was a former student of Bertrand Russell, and his major publication was *Tractatus Logico-Philosophicus*,[77] a book derived from his doctoral dissertation in 1929 at Cambridge. The main thesis of the book was that the world is a set of facts (not things), which themselves exist in *Sachverhalten*, or in a state of affairs composed of single objects and "represented by elementary propositions logically independent of one another."[78] The fact that every meaningful proposition is logically reducible to elementary propositions accounts for logical inductivism. Popper, in 1934, saw that this demarcation of science was an annihilation of natural science, because scientific laws cannot be "logically reduced to elementary statements of experience."[79]

The journal *Erkenntnis* had been established by 1930 and reflected the strong views of the positivist movement. Rudolph Carnap and Hans Reichenbach were its coeditors. In its first issue, Carnap identified with specificity what he characterized as the old and new logic. The old referred to ideas or terms reducible to sense-experience as the unit of meaning. The new scientific method of philosophizing consisted of "the *logical analysis of statements and concepts of empirical science.*"[80] It meant that philosophy seeks the clarification of statements in empirical science which would require a reduction or breaking down of statements into concepts or into their more fundamental parts.[81] Logic would therefore be important to inquiry. The new logic embraced what was referred to as contemporary empiricism. Carnap differentiated between the old and the new logic, giving credit to Frege, Russell, and Whitehead for their developments in the logic of mathematics. He credited critical reexamination of the foundations of mathematics as being the most important stimulus for development of the new logic. A reconstruction of logic was necessitated as contradictions emerged in mathematics which were found to be of a logical nature. Thus, the new logic gained a special significance for the whole of science.[82] He noted the characteristics of the new logic as:

1. The symbolic method (symbols foster rigor).
2. The logic of relations (the form and range of logic changed from "the predicative form in which a predicative concept or property was attached to a subject-concept, i.e., 'Socrates is a man,' to sentence statements of relational form, i.e., 'a is greater than b' ").
3. The logical antimonies (elimination of contradictions).
4. Mathematics is a branch of logic (every mathematical concept

can be shown to derive from the basic or essential concepts of logic).

5. The tautological character of logic (the essential character of logical sentences can be understood and the distinction between fundamental and derived sentences was considered unnecessary. The validity of a sentence can be recognized from its form).

6. Unified science (the analysis of the concepts of science has shown that all concepts, whether from the natural sciences or social sciences, can be reduced to common roots which apply to the "given," or the elements of immediate experience).[83]

To quote Carnap:

We speak of "methodological" positivism or materialism because we are concerned here only with methods of deriving concepts, while completely eliminating both the metaphysical thesis of positivism about the reality of the given and the metaphysical thesis of materialism about the reality of the physical world. Consequently, the positivist and materialist constitution systems do not contradict one another. Both are correct and indispensable. The positivist system corresponds to the epistemological viewpoint because it proves the validity of knowledge by reduction to the given. The materialist system corresponds to the viewpoint of the empirical sciences, for in this system all concepts are reduced to the physical, to the only domain which exhibits the complete rule of law and makes intersubjective knowledge possible.[84]

Carnap concluded that with the aid of the new logic, logical analysis leads to a unified science (the strong position of the Vienna circle). There were, thus, not different sciences with basic differing methods or sources of knowledge, but only *one* science.

Contemporaneous with Carnap's definitive publication, Moritz Schlick, who was considered the founder of logical positivism, clarified its meaning and fundamental principles in the 1932–33 issue of *Erkenntnis*. He wrote:

If we say . . . that metaphysics is the theory of "true being" of "reality in itself" of "transcendent being" this obviously implies a (contradictory) spurious, lesser, apparent being; as has indeed been assumed by all metaphysicians since the time of Plato and the Eleatics. This apparent being is the realm of "appearances," and while the true transcendent reality is to be reached only with difficulty, by the efforts of the metaphysician, the special sciences have to do exclusively with appearances which are perfectly accessible to them. The difference between the ways in which these two "modes of being" are to be known, is then explained by the fact that the appearances are immediately present, "given" to us, while metaphysical reality must be inferred from them in some roundabout manner. And thus we seem to arrive at a fundamental concept of the positivists, for they always speak of the "given" and usually formulate their fundamental principle in the proposition that the philosopher as well as the scientist must always remain within the given, that is to go beyond it, as the metaphysician attempts, is impossible or senseless.[85]

Schlick further emphasized that the foundation of all reflection is to see that it is impossible to give meaning to any statement except by describing the fact which must exist if the statement is to be true. The meaning of a proposition consists in its expressing a definite state of affairs, and this state of affairs must be shown so as to give meaning to the proposition. Thus for Schlick, the statement of the conditions under which a proposition is true is the same as the statement of its meaning and these *conditions* must finally be discoverable in the "given." Schlick noted that he did not know whether this insight ought to be called positivism, but he liked to believe it should underlie all positivistic efforts in the history of philosophy.[86] Schlick believed that a decision regarding reality or unreality of a fact is always made in the way described.

Two outsiders who were invited to attend the symposia of the Vienna circle were A. J. Ayer from England and W. V. O. Quine from the United States. Ayer, at that time, supported the logical positivists and spread some of their ideas in his famous book *Language, Truth, and Logic*.[87] Quine accepted physicalism and was faithful to the idea of the unity of science. He, however, has become increasingly known for his ideas on ontological relativity and philosophy of logic.[88]

The Emergence of the Philosophy of Science. It is significant that Carnap's analysis of the old and new logic appeared first in 1930 and preceded by four years the philosophy of science as an organization of philosophers and scientists formed to clarify or unify the programs, methods, and results of disciplines of philosophy and of science. Philosophy of science was born in 1934 with the establishment of the journal, *Philosophy of Science*. The aim was "examination of fundamental concepts and presuppositions in the light of the positive results of science, systematic doubt of the positive results, and a thorough-going analysis and critique of logic and of language."[89]

Thirty years later, Carl G. Hempel in his book *Aspects of Scientific Explanation* identified four major topics in the philosophy of science. They were:

1. Confirmation, induction, and rational belief
2. Conception of cognitive significance
3. Structure and function of scientific concepts and theories, and
4. Scientific explanation.[90]

The sciences identified in the founding of the *Philosophy of Science* were the following: mathematics, logic, physics, chemistry, biology, psychology, and sociology.[91]

In 1984, a special tribute was paid to William M. Malisoff as the founding father, not of the journal, but of an association devoted to a specialized field of study and creating a discipline.[92] The editorial board and advisory board consisted of members who were illustrious philosophers and scientists whose work displayed the inseparability of science and philosophy.[93]

As philosophy of science has developed, some major issues for distinction have centered on the empirical character of science versus the kind of explanation science affords, and the issue of whether there are distinctions or a single pattern of explanation in science.[94] This latter issue has produced arguments as to distinction versus no distinction, in the kind of explanations to be made in the natural and in the social and behavioral sciences. These issues are of paramount concern for the social work practitioner, since human behavior and social organization are central to the tasks of social work.

Modification of Logical Positivism. By the mid-1930s, some of the logical positivists, especially Carnap, began to eliminate the strict verificationist theory of meaning and to replace it with the requirement that a meaningful proposition must be testable, by reference to observation and experiment, for confirmation of the truth or falsity of the proposition. Carnap elaborated this modification in his treatise on "Testability and Meaning" in 1937, which liberalized positivism and has been considered the founding document of what became the more liberalized "logical empiricism."[95] In the early days of the Vienna circle, a sentence was said to have empirical meaning if there was complete *verification* by observational evidence, i.e., if observational evidence would conclusively establish the truth of the sentence. Change in the conception of testability and in empirical meaning came about as it was recognized that if verification meant definitive and final establishment of truth, no sentence was verifiable. A sentence could be more and more confirmed. Carnap considered confirmation a modification of the requirement of verifiability, rather than a rejection.

He noted that the requirement of verifiability was first stated by Wittgenstein and that objections were raised to it by antiempiricist metaphysicians and by "empiricists such as Reichenbach, Popper, Lewis, Nagel, and Stace."[96] Carnap's own position was the following:

If verification is understood as a complete and definitive establishment of truth then a universal sentence, e.g., a so-called law of physics or biology, can never be verified. . . . Even if each single instance of the law were supposed to be verifiable, the number of instances to which the law refers —e.g., the space-time-points—is infinite and therefore can never be exhausted by our observations which are always finite in number. We cannot verify the law, but we can test it by testing its single instances. . . . If in the continued series of such testing experiments no negative instance is found but the number of positive instances increases then our confidence in the law will grow step by step.[97]

Thus, Carnap referred to probability and *confirmation* rather than *verification* and distinguished the testing of a sentence (method) from its confirmation.

Hempel, an early positivist, now defined cognitive and empirical significance in the principle that a statement can be deemed either true or false,

if and only if either (1) it is analytic or contradictory—in which case it is said to have purely logical meaning or significance—or else (2) it is capable, at least potentially, of test by experiential evidence—in which case it is said to have empirical meaning or significance.[98]

He considered the basic tenet of the principle as embodying the "testability-criterion of empirical meaning" and thought that the general intent of the empiricist criterion of meaning was sound.

As early as 1934, Karl R. Popper published *Logik der Forchung* (The Logic of Scientific Discovery), which both agreed and disagreed with the logical positivists. He has since been identified as a transitional theorist. Popper firmly rejected induction as a process by which scientific theories are confirmed.[99] He thought that the problem with induction was that it required a "logical justification of universal statements about reality."[100] He contended that the empirical sciences and the metaphysical should be divided or demarcated into empirical and nonempirical systems. He distinguished three requirements which an empirical theoretical system would need to satisfy:

First, it must be *synthetic*, so that it may represent a non-contradictory, a *possible* world. Secondly, it must satisfy the criterion of demarcation . . .

i.e., it must not be metaphysical, but must represent a world of possible *experience*. Thirdly, it must be a system distinguished in some way from other such systems as the one which represents *our* world of experience.[101]

Thus, Popper conceived of the system as being distinguished by the *deductive* method through submission to empirical tests. He championed the hypothetico-deductive method for deriving theoretical systems, and proposed that strict disproof of a scientific theory is impossible because experimental results can be challenged and revised.[102] In summary, he believed that "the criterion of the scientific status of a theory is its falsifiability, or refutability, or testability."[103] He viewed scientific progress as occurring when the older theories become incompatible with newer tested ones. He agreed with Reichenbach, the positivist, however, on a sharp distinction between the process of discovery (i.e., of conceiving and pursuit of a new idea) and the methods of justification. This will be further discussed in chapter 2.

Beyond the liberalization of positivism, the logical empiricists considered no presuppositions in science, as they began from the solid data of observation to confirm or to falsify propositions. They considered that observations would be theory-free. Popper seriously challenged this idea, since he considered observations and theory to be interlocked.

New criticisms and approaches to the philosophy and theory of science continued to emerge among philosophers and scientists, particularly around 1950, as there was growing criticism of strict empiricism and the role of presuppositions and observation in knowledge about the world.[104]

In 1947, Ayer in England brought out *The Foundations of Empirical Knowledge*, in which he characterized sense-data, causality, and perception; and he distinguished between appearance and reality in the construction of the material world.[105] Since empiricism rested on observations and facts in experience, these constructions were significant to use the sense-datum, of which there was much dispute. The question was whether objects in the world are directly perceived, or whether they are an object of a different kind, or "sense-datum." These latter data were said to have a "presentative function" of making one conscious of material things.[106] The dispute centered on the concern over illusions: that is, material things may present different appearances to different observers, or to the same observers under different conditions, and the character of these appearances is to some extent causally determined by the state of conditions and the observer. Ayer cited such familiar examples as the straight stick appearing crooked in water, mirror images, double vision, mirages, hallucinations, and phantom pain.[107] He wrote that if anything was established by this, it could only be that there are some cases in which the character of perceptions makes it necessary for one to say that what he is directly experiencing is not a material thing but a sense-datum, but assumed that there are some perceptions that do present material things to us as they really are. Among philosophers, there were those who used the term "sense-datum" to explain that what is immediately experienced is "always a sense-datum and never a material thing."[108]

Ayer explained that although one should be able to discern whether a perception is of a sense-datum or of a material thing, this is not always possible. He presented the example that under normal conditions, we have the experience of seeing a straight stick. We believe it is a straight stick; but when the stick appears crooked when being refracted in water, we do not believe it is crooked. This difference in beliefs which accompany our perception is not grounded in perception, but depends on past experience.[109] Therefore, all perceptions—whether veridical or delusive—are to some extent dependent upon external conditions, such as character of light, gestalt, or our own physiological and psychological states. Therefore, it was held to be characteristic of material things that their existence and their essential projectives were independent of any particular observer.[110]

The so-called "phenomenalist" had considered that a physical thing or object was a "construction out of our experiences"[111] and based on Hume's criterion of meaning, "every idea . . . is ultimately derived from sense impressions alone."[112]

In the twentieth century, however, when empiricists proposed statements or propositions rather than terms or ideas as the basic unit of meaning, the phenomenalist position, that "a physical object is a construction out of sensations" began to be interpreted as "any statement about a physical object can be paraphrased into a statement about sensations."[113] The position was challenged, however, with reference to the problem of dealing with the construct of normality in regard to observations and conditions. Phenomenalism, as a phase of post-Humean empiricism began to disappear by the 1940s.[114]

The Humean view had also induced the private language argument: that if experiences are only of one's impressions and ideas and if words derive their meaning from impressions, then the language acquired cannot be understood by any other person.[115] In transition to what is known as contemporary empiricism, Hume's doctrine that private sense impressions as objects of direct perception was replaced with the view that publicly observable physical things are the objects of perception. Observation claims about these, rather than about sense data, provide the foundations of empirical knowledge. . . . Like Hume, the contemporary empiricist holds that a priori knowledge is analytic; he holds that observation—now of publicly observable things—together with memory is the only source of empirical or a posteriori knowledge; he holds that any reasoning taking us beyond this source; i.e., any nondemonstrative (nondeductive) reasoning is basically empirical generalization from observations; and he holds that all meaningful ideas must ultimately come from experience.[116]

The contemporary empiricist now used the "as if" expression to refer to perception of objects or distortions of physical objects as in hallucinations, mirages, mental images, etc.[117] It looks "as if" the stick is crooked in the water. There was no need to use the concept of sense data to account for varying experiences.

By midcentury, there had come to be critics of the contemporary empiricism with regard to conception of the role observations play in obtaining empirical knowledge. Critics maintained that confidence in observations must take into account the background assumptions and theory, the meaning derived from this interrelatedness, and that observations cannot be considered "givens" but should be interpreted in terms of their background assumptions.[118] Some of the more recent scientists associated with these criticisms, with revisions, and advancements in science have been Rudolf Carnap,[119] Karl R. Popper,[120] Paul K. Feyerabend,[121] Thomas S. Kuhn,[122] Nelson Goodman,[123] Willard Van Ormond Quine,[124] Norwood R. Hanson,[125] Michael Polanyi,[126] Herbert Simon,[127] William Wimsatt,[128] Wesley C. Salmon,[129] Ian Mitroff,[130] and Imre Lakatos,[131] among others. The empiricist's theory of perception that pure facts are perceived in observations was countered with the argument that knowledge, beliefs, and theories already held by the observer contribute to, or color, what is perceived. The challenges to empiricism represented by critics and revisionists as identified above tended to center on perception and the role of observation, methodology, and linguistics.

Carnap sought to clarify the controversy with regard to the "nature and implications of the acceptance of a language referring to abstract entities" demonstrating that such a language can be compatible with empiricism and the rigor of scientific thinking.[132]

As indicated earlier, Quine rejected the analytic-synthetic dogma, believing that no boundary between analytic and synthetic statements has been delineated. In regard to the dogma of reductionism, Quine thought that rather than scientists comparing single individual statements with the world, a more holistic stance should be taken which assumes the interconnections of statements as elements of the total field or system. He also saw the purpose of science as pragmatic.[133]

Examples of leading scientists and critics who have especially influenced a shift from logical positivism toward the "shaping forces of historical context" have moved from "Carnap and Hempel, to Popper and Lakatos, to Kuhn, to Collingwood* and Toulmin, to Feyerabend."[134] Michael Polanyi and Norwood Hanson have also contributed to new notions of discovery and the personal dimension.

With the publication of *The Structure of Scientific Revolution* (1962, rev. 1970) Kuhn, physicist and historian of science, had a major impact. His later work, *The Essential Tension* (1977, previously cited), further clarified his philosophy. Both he and Popper rejected the notion of science progressing by accretion and saw older theories subject to test being overthrown by new incompatible ones in a revolutionary process.[135] Popper, however, conceptualized scientific method as essentially a method of trial and error (problem-solving), not empirical generalization. He wrote:

Science starts from problems, and not from observations; though observations may give rise to a problem, especially if they are *unexpected*. . . . The conscious task of the scientist is always the solution of a problem through the construction of a theory which solves the problem.[136]

Thus, by the method of conjectures and refutations he believed that experience could be used to weed out false theories. He admitted that the scientist's expectations and theoretical knowledge would precede problems for study, but thought that science begins only with problems.

Kuhn both agreed and disagreed with Popper and is well known for his elaboration of the revolutionary process. He reflected a slightly different perspective from Popper, a perspective which he termed a "gestalt switch." Both Kuhn and Popper emphasized both history and facts in data gathering, though Kuhn thought he differed from Popper in his deep commitment to tradition and in the implications of the term "falsification."[137] Kuhn wrote:

*R. G. Collingwood (1889–1943) was an English philosopher who interwove his philosophical ideas with the historicity in human experience.

there is one sort of "statement" or "hypothesis" that scientists do report only subject to systematic test . . . an individual's best guesses about the proper way to connect his own research problem with the corpus of accepted scientific knowledge . . . the next steps in his research are intended to target or test the conjecture of hypothesis. If it passes enough or stringent enough tests, the scientist has made a discovery or has at least resolved the puzzle he had been set. If not, he must either abandon the puzzle entirely or attempt to solve it with the aid of some other hypothesis. . . . Tests of this sort are a standard component of what I have elsewhere labelled "normal science" or "normal research," an enterprise which accounts for the overwhelming majority of the work done in basic science. In no usual sense, however, are such tests directed to current theory. On the contrary, when engaged with a normal research problem, the scientist must *premise* current theory as the rules of his game. His object is to solve a puzzle . . . and current theory (paradigm) is required to define that puzzle and to guarantee that . . . it can be solved.[138]

Kuhn further asserted that the test of the conjectural puzzle for solution is only the researcher's personal conjecture. If his tests fail, it is his personal test failure and not of the "corpus of science." He further postulated that such a process of normal science does—at times—produce anomalies that cannot be reconciled with current theory or paradigm and that it is from the occasional anomalies in normal science that new scientific revolutions and discoveries—necessitating a fundamental change in world view—occur.[139] He believed that Popper was particularly concerned with the procedures through which science grows, the fact that growth occurs by the "overthrow of an accepted theory and its replacement by a better one," and that Popper was thus most concerned with tests to "explore limitations of accepted theory."[140]

Kuhn did not believe that science as a whole, and the development of knowledge, should be viewed solely from the occasional revolutions they produce. He saw discovery and developments as a more ongoing process. Both of these scientists were realists and insistent "that scientists may properly aim to invent theories that explain observed phenomena and that do so in terms of real objects."[141] After 1958, Popper was credited with major concern for championing "rationality and objectivity in science"—this, against dangers he thought he saw in Thomas Kuhn, Michael Polanyi, and others.[142] He thought that their tendencies toward subjectivism and irrationalism were too great.

Imre Lakatos, a Hungarian-born student and colleague of Popper's at the London School of Economics, agreed in principle with the falsification method of Popper but also showed a historical turn. He said that:

any scientific theory has to be appraised together with its auxiliary hypothesis, initial conditions, etc., and especially together with its predecessors so that we may see what sort of change was brought about. Then, of course, what we appraise is a series of rather isolated theories.[143]

His major premise was that due to the many and varied factors in scientific change, some being idiosyncratic and uncontrollable and single experimental results being rarely decisive in themselves, the basic criterion is the formation and success of long-term research programs.

Polanyi added to a shift in emphasis from the logical-empirical by his analysis of personal knowledge[144] and tacit knowing, that begins with the fact that "we can know more than we can tell."[145] Polanyi structured tacit knowing as involving two kinds of things: we pay attention to something (proximal), while attending to something else (distal) to which there is a tacit relation. "We know the first term only by relying on our awareness of it for attending the second."[146] He used as example, experiments that presented subjects with a large number of nonsense syllables. After showing selected syllables, the researcher then administered an electric shock. Presently, the subject showed symptoms of anticipating the shock at the sight of "shock syllables." When questioned with regard to the syllables, he could not identify them. The subject knew when to expect a shock but could not tell what made him expect it. Polanyi considered that the subject had "acquired a knowledge similar to that which we have when we know a person by signs which we cannot tell."[147] Polanyi surmised that the connection was tacit because the subject's attention was directed to the shock and that he relied on his awareness of the particulars (proximal) for attending the electric shock (distal). He therefore conceptualized tacit knowing as to its "functional structure," "phenomenal structure," "semantic aspect," and "ontological aspect." He reached the conclusion that tacit knowing can be shown to account:

(1) for valid knowledge of a problem; (2) for the scientist's capacity to pursue, guided by his sense of approaching its solution; and (3) for a valid anticipation of the yet indeterminate implications of the discovery arrived at in the end.[148]

Polanyi was concerned with personal judgment and pursuit of discovery, and he rejected the notion that there can be strictly impersonal (objective) criteria of validity in discovery, such as the positivists were seeking in the philosophy of science.[149]

Stephen Toulmin has noted a shift from the formal to functional in philosophy and science but has seen this as a pendulum shift and subject to the vicissitudes of change.[150] He has taken an "instrumentalist" view in seeking the internal soundness of logical systems.

Feyerabend, another critic of positivism, conceived of the possibility of science without experience. In his work "Against Method,"[151] he raised doubts about strictures of current notions of rationality. Feyerabend's idea of a good empiricist is one who tries to proliferate theories. Starting with the development of an alternative vision to the picture embedded in some ongoing theory, the researcher will try to formulate a general view that is not directly connected to formalized observations, thus becoming a critical metaphysician. Feyerabend believed that traditional empiricism, in its desire to expel metaphysics from science and philosophy, had ignored fruitful ways in which scientists ordinarily carry on research.

For the positivists, it was theory-free observed data that guaranteed the objectivity of science. For the present-day critics and the new image, knowledge and beliefs play a central role in determining the researcher's perceptions and the scientific theories that are held also influence observations.

It is generally recognized that the challenges to empiricism that began to take place in the fifties are now taking root in the current literature of philosophers of science, natural science, social and behavioral science, and in social work.[152] Heineman observed that "although the social work literature continues generally to embrace logical empiricists' assumptions as postulated, philosophers of science have long abandoned them as universal principles."[153] It is interesting that Tice and Slavens have summarized the future prospects of philosophy of science by noting a current revolution "as significant as that of the logical empiricist one in the 1920s and 1930s."[154] They consider that the greatest impact of change is on scientific practice and on the public rise of science, particularly as the natural science models—on which social science has depended—is now considered "to be inaccurate, inadequate, or confused."[155] This is a strong statement, but as we noted earlier, there is current an argument over the distinction in kind of explanations to be made in the natural and in the social and behavioral sciences. A good general discussion of the logic and forms of scientific evaluation of explanations can be found in Peter Achinstein's *Law and Explanation*[156] and Alan Garfinkel's *Forms of Explanation.*[157]

SUMMARY AND IMPLICATIONS FOR INQUIRY

The diversity in philosophical and scientific thought has been presented with reference to the foundations of logical inquiry and empiricism that emerged prominently in the nineteenth and twentieth centuries. This historical perspective is important to the practitioner-scientist for understanding the assumptions and the differing strategies in scientific inquiry.

The historical perspective essentially began with David Hume and his notions that science of man must be based on experience and observations. Historical divisions between rationalists and empiricists were then developed with the introduction of other philosophers, such as Kant, Hegel, the early pragmatists C. S. Peirce and William James, among others. The role of mathematics as logic, developed by Russell and Whitehead, was related to scientific inquiry, and historical developments of descriptive and inferential statistics were sketched. In this chapter, the origins of empiricism as related to the Vienna circle and to a strict construction of empiricism, known as logical positivism, were developed extensively. Major figures in the movement were cited, such as Schlick, Feigl, Carnap, and Reichenbach (Berlin group). Wittgenstein and Popper were not members but substantively influenced philosophical thought of the twentieth century. Popper is considered a transitional figure in a liberalization of positivism about the 1950s and Kuhn influenced new thinking in his conceptualization of revolutionary changes that occur in science, with the appearance of anomalies in normal scientific inquiry. Currently, there are many philosophers of science and from varying disciplines who are questioning the foundations of empiricism with reference to perception, methods of inquiry, and linguistics. A historical turn is also evident in philosophy of science and concern for ontology or meaning.

From the preceding historical sketch of twentieth-century empiricism in philosophical and scientific thought, it can be seen that diverse opinions have existed with regard to scientific reasoning and empiricism. Inquiry and scientific advancement may entertain different suppositions and methodologies in the quest for knowledge. The historical materials have referred to the following questions:

Is scientific advance registered by increasing probability (Carnap), by discrete verifications (Popper), by revolutions (Kuhn), by growing consensus (Polanyi), by progressive versus degenerating research programs, con- ducted over long periods (Lakatos), or what? The debate goes on.[158]

Whatever methods characterize scientific advances, it is incumbent on the social work professional to consider the structure of theories, the range and validity of premises, and the necessary tools for build- ing and using knowledge aimed at understanding and serving clients.

This historical sketch tends to support a position that the clinical practitioner-scientist must appropriately consider varying methodol- ogies and paradigms in the "normal scientific" search for knowledge, as associated with practice.

CHAPTER 2

Discovery in Practice: Issues Related to Science

It is important for social work not only to continue the evaluation and expansion of current practice theories devoted to person/family/environmental transactions, but also, to discover what may be more efficient and fruitful in foundation and practice theories. There must be emphasis on conceptualization and evaluation of the most effective interventions with clients, under varying conditions, with varying problems and client populations. These tasks require tedious and laborious discovery and explanatory processes from observed and historical phenomena and the use of appropriate procedures in measurement, as well as planned efforts evolving from cumulative research. We believe that the practitioner-scientist must be involved in these processes—preferably in conjunction or collaboration with researchers—in order to ground new discoveries and theories in practice. Cooper has captured the essence of our concerns for discovery in practice in her statement, "Discovery and dogma do not walk comfortably together. The question is, can we face the future in our own work and for our own profession, armed with the impulse to discover, taking inspiration from these things we hold to be of value?"[1]

Exploration is germane to the professional understanding and explanation of client troubles and has been well documented in clinical research literature.[2] It is fundamental to the assessment of the client's difficulties and has traditionally aided the formulation of a psychosocial assessment.

As mutuality has emphasized mutual discovery of the client's problems in practitioner-client exploratory interactions, theorists have varied in the conceptualization of assessment as a moment-to-moment evaluation or as a formal assessment based on exploratory study.[3] Whether the accumulation of professional judgments in the assessment data is organized into a more limited, ongoing evaluation, or into a more substantive statement called "psychosocial assessment" or "family diagnosis" to guide actions, these professionals tend to vary from those of a more humanistic persuasion. The latter tend to emphasize a "subjective" ongoing process of getting into the feelings and viewpoints of the client for understanding.[4]

Whatever point of view is held, we want to emphasize in this book that, beyond mutuality in problem assessment and the professional judgments used in clinical assessment of the client's problematic functioning within a social context, professional judgments also coexist with the logic of scientific inquiry. The practitioner will draw inferences from phenomena or data, seek further evidence, and test out ideas or hypotheses through evaluative procedures. These processes may be applied at intervals in case study or simultaneously within the ongoing helping process, as portrayed in the structural framework presented in figure 1.

Our stance is that *knowledge building* must be considered an integral component of advanced practice, especially in post-master's education in social work. It is consistent with the thinking through, reasoning, planning, and evaluative tasks germane to helping or therapy; and it is herein discussed in terms of "reflection-in-the-case process" or reflective inquiry, within the naturalistic case process. Inquiry is aimed at discovery of unique phenomena and the building of valid generalizations and theory. Commitment to knowledge generation and evaluation of the effects in the therapeutic process should foster the ideal of cumulative investigations and linkage with the research specialist in the conduct of larger research projects. As we intend to relate discovery to knowledge building in the clinical case process, and we have considered scientific inquiry from a philosophical stance, it will be enlightening to review, in some detail, philosophical thought with regard to discovery and the debate it has stimulated.

DISCOVERY AS AN ISSUE IN SCIENCE

In philosophy of science, there have been differing interpretations of discovery and questions as to its logic. In 1917, F. C. S. Schiller, writing from a pragmatic tradition, introduced a distinction between the logic of *proof* and the logic of *scientific discovery*.[5] He stressed the need for a logic that was open to perceive motion and a dynamic process of knowledge growth. As we have noted earlier, the eminent philosophers and logical positivists (empiricists) Karl Popper and Hans Reichenbach denied a logic of discovery. Theories were treated "as if they arose all at once by a creative leap of the imagination of a scientist" and it was only afterward that the philosopher's logical tools were useful to evaluate the theory produced.[6]

Reichenbach, who advocated induction, explained that the inferences from observed facts (particulars) on which a theory is based are logically inductive. He saw no such regulatives for discovery and distinguished between the "context of discovery" and the "context of justification." He asserted that the act of discovery escaped logical analysis as there were no logical rules of which a "discovery machine could be constructed that would account for creative genius."[7]

Adding to the empiricist position, Karl Popper wrote in 1959:

the initial stage, the act of conceiving or inventing a theory, seems to me neither to call for logical analysis nor to be susceptible of it. The question how it happens that a new idea occurs to a man—whether it is a musical theme, a dramatic conflict, or a scientific theory—may be of great interest to empirical psychology; but it is irrelevant to the logical analysis of scientific knowledge. This latter is concerned not with *questions of fact* ... but only with questions of *justification or validity*.[8]

A logic of scientific discovery would therefore be expected to have *rules for generating new knowledge* and a logic of scientific justification to have rules for *assessing* or *evaluating* claims about the world as supported by evidence.[9]

In 1958, Norwood R. Hanson published *Patterns of Discovery*, in which he attempted to delineate a logic in the discovery processes, i.e., to articulate patterns and the anatomy of discovery.[10] Hanson considered that the approach to an area that was problematical and required in inquiry "theory-finding" thinking, analyzed science differently from that type of inquiry whose task was to rearrange "old facts and explanations into more elegant formal patterns."[11]

Referring to the hypothetico-deductive approach in science, Hanson wrote:

Physicists rarely find laws by enumerating and summarizing observables. ... [They] do not start from hypotheses; they start from data. By the time a law has been fixed into an H-D system, really original physical thinking is over. The pedestrian process of deducing observation statements from hypotheses comes only after the physicist sees that the hypothesis will at least explain the initial data requiring explanation. ... The initial suggestion of an hypothesis is very often a reasonable affair. It is not so often affected by intuition, insight, hunches, or other imponderables as biographers or scientists suggest. Disciples of the H-D account often dismiss the dawning of an hypothesis as being of psychological interest only, or else claim it to be the province solely of genius and not of logic. They are wrong. If establishing an hypothesis through its predictions has a logic, so has the conceiving of an hypothesis.[12]

Hanson affirmed the inductive view that suggested laws are obtained by inference from data, but he thought the inductive view wrongly suggested that the law is a summary of these data, from particulars to generalizations. He further asserted that "interpretation is not something a physicist works into a ready-made deductive system: it is operative in the very making of the system ... [The physicist] ... is in search rather, of an explanation of these data."[13] Hanson developed a schematic form for retroductive reasoning[14] to support a logic of discovery, but was later criticized as never clearly distinguishing between "(1) a logic of generation, by which a new hypothesis is first articulated, and (2) a logic of preliminary evaluation, in terms of which an hypothesis is assessed for its plausibility."[15]
    Laudan later offered a view of discovery within a temporal context that reflected three processes: discovery, pursuit, and ultimate justification.[16] He construed discovery narrowly, as the "eureka moment" or dawning of a new idea, and pursuit, as a "nether region" between the dawning of the idea and the ultimate justification. Laudan's conception of discovery embodied the preliminary appraisal that evaluates the idea and finds it worthy of further pursuit. He advocated such a trichotomy to prevent the "lumping together of activities and modalities of appraisal, which have frequently been confused with one another."[17] Actually, Laudan tended to agree with other philosophers that discovery belongs to the empirical sciences rather than being a concern of philosophers. Yet, he was open to the possibility of new answers, as scientists representing varying disciplines renew their

▼

interest in discovery and question the reasoning that conjecture and refutation are completely separate processes.

A symposium on the subject was held by scientists and philosophers, in Reno, Nevada, in 1978. This meeting produced the publication, *Scientific Discovery: Case Studies*, edited by Thomas Nickles. Nickles noted that logical positivists and their "behaviorist and operationalist allies were interested in concept formation, but ironically, philosophers' interest in the formative aspect of science died precisely at the time in the early 1950s when philosopher Carl G. Hempel, . . . announced the failure of the positivists' search for a criterion of cognitive significance."[18] Hempel had concluded that "concept formation and theory formation go hand in hand, neither can be carried on successfully in isolation from the other."[19] Nickles thought, based on these ideas of Hempel, that "the interest in concept formation would have matured into an interest in theory formation, but that did not happen, and the topic [discovery] is only now becoming respectable."[20] It is interesting that the Nevada symposium included historians of science, cognitive psychologists, a physicist, and several philosophers. Nickles was led to believe that there is now evidence of a " 'historical turn' in recent philosophy of science and in psychology of science as well."[21]

Some of the recent "friends of discovery" have included Kenneth Schaffner, who has postulated substantive discovery procedures in heuristic computer programming and has argued that both generation and weak evaluation are parts of discovery.[22]

Others whose papers at the symposium bore special relevance to discovery processes in clinical social work included Marx W. Wartofsky, Lindley Darden, William C. Wimsatt, Michael Ruse, and Howard Gruber. Some of their ideas will be briefly reviewed here, as they are pertinent to our development of discovery in the clinical case process.

Wartofsky considered creativity in terms of the epistemological category: *scientific judgment*, and contrasted this with the dominant epistemological category in philosophy of science, which is *scientific explanation*.[23] He proposed that the category of judgment suggests "the synthesis and bringing together of things" (ideas, concepts, etc.) in such manner that any relation among them which has not been previously perceived is recognized.[24]

The *discovery* of such a relation suggests that the relation already exists, and that the creative act consists in *recognizing* it, literally, in "uncovering," revealing it. . . . The activity of *dis*-covering these relations, however, requires the creation of new concepts, of new instruments of analysis, of new techniques of experimental intervention—in short, the introduction of new possibilities of interaction with the natural world, both theoretically and practically.[25]

Thus, the act of discovery does not invent but serves as a new way of construing the world. Therefore, for Wartofsky, scientific judgment is "essentially the category of thought as a guide to, or a suggestion of, possible action or practice." He called it "practical imagination," and saw the act of creation as "imagining new ways of relating present facts, or of imagining new facts in such a way as to realize them by some mode of action—i.e., by experimental practice, by technological innovation."[26] Scientific judgment was like judgment in law or clinical judgment in practice, with its quality lying "in the ability to interpret general maxims in their application to specific instances."[27]

We have depicted scientific judgment in a similar sense within the structural framework for the practitioner as scholar-scientist in figure 1. The thought/action processes of scientific judgment are located in the structural steps 2 and 3 of scientific inquiry.

It is interesting that caseworkers in the 1920s, who were developing the casework method of practice, used judgment in a grossly analogous context. From judgments of accumulated facts and actions, they experimented, modified, and innovated in building maxims or rules for action (see chapter 8).

Wartofsky has further explained that a theory of discovery in the terms he has described is the

doing of science . . . it focuses on the ongoing activity of scientific thought . . . it is not a discovery-generating theory, in the sense that discoveries follow from it, by the application of a rule.[28]

The relation between the theory of discovery, and discovery itself, is a heuristic one.

Scientific judgment, in the sense that has been elucidated, is explanatory of the sensibilities and creative actions in discovery that we are advocating as germane to the clinical practitioner's activity. It is also reasonable and practical for implementation.

One of the few participants at the symposium to address explicitly the problem of theory formation was Lindley Darden. She also rejected the dichotomy of discovery and justification, and traced processes of discovery and justification in their complex interrelationships in the development of theory over a span of time. One should review her schema as a pattern for reasoning in theory construction.[29] She recognized that "vague ideas about postulated explanatory factors may take on more form as new data are found and new theoretical components added," and negative results may produce only partial changes.[30] She emphasized the importance of "interfield connections" in the building of theory.

William Wimsatt considered that we are faced with problems that are so complex that we cannot solve them exactly, and to find solutions, we must use simplifying and approximate techniques such as heuristic procedures.[31]

Michael Ruse, philosopher and historian of biology, proposed that the route to discovery is important to fully understand scientific cases. He traced, as evidence, Charles Darwin's development of ideas and use of analogy in his theory of the origin of species by means of natural selection.[32] Ruse noted that Darwin had been sitting on his idea that evolution is chiefly a function of natural selection for about twenty years and explained how the *analogy* from the domestic world of artificial selection among breeders, as well as Malthus' *Principle of Population*,[33] contributed to his thinking on natural selection and eventually led him to the theory of evolution.[34] Ruse analyzed Darwin's route to discovery as being influenced by a subjective, as well as an objective, side.

Finally, Howard Gruber, a cognitive psychologist, proposed "a systemic view of the whole thinking person engaged in scientific work."[35] He suggested intensive work in case studies aimed at following the growth of a thought process over a period of time, as various facets of the study and thought are interrelated. He sketched out a conceptual frame for an *evolving systems approach* to the study of creative thinking. The conceptual scheme encompassed the creative person as an evolving system, comprised of subsystems that include: (a) organization of knowledge, (b) organization of purpose and (c) organization of affect.[36]

From this schematic review of twentieth century thought on discovery in philosophy of science, it is clear that discovery has generally been narrowly construed as the dawning of an idea and not subject to rules of logic. The current work, however, of the Nickles group, which has incorporated historical perspective, may develop logical processes that begin to respect discovery. From the philosophers' standpoint, discovery has belonged in the realm of psychology, and by affinity, social work.

The review of logic and processes of discovery is not complete, however, without some mention of current concern with heuristic research in the "discovery of meaning and essence, in significant human experience" within humanistic psychology.[37] Douglas and Moustakas describe this inquiry as using the subjective, perceptive processes of reflecting, inquiring, and sifting that clarify meaning and learning in terms of self and of self-other relations. The inquiry is not guided by rules, but by a pursuit that is stimulated by a "passionate disciplined commitment" and "search for new insights and revelations."[38] Douglas and Moustakas further state that

just as the artist must control the uses of color and shading in painting a sunset, so must the heuristic inquirer discipline the quest for knowledge, in precise and exact terms. When to probe deeper, when to shift the focus, when to pause to examine innermost layers of meaning, when to reflect, when to describe—all are considerations of timing and attunement that demand a disciplined sensitivity if the nature and essence of an experience is to be revealed.[39]

Discovery, in this sense, is obviously clinical in nature. Douglas and Moustakas' position is that in this pursuit lies the potential for obtaining truths.

It can be seen that discovery has long been a source of discussion among scientists, philosophers, and clinicians. As indicated earlier by Wartofsky, it cannot be separated from creativity and imagination. We now turn our attention to creativity—and the growth of ideas as essential ingredients for discovery in social work practice.

For our purposes, we have defined discovery within a broad context, as encompassing the dawning of an idea, as well as its pursuit of preliminary validity. It incorporates trials, case comparison, innovation, preliminary evaluation, and modification, before ultimate justification may be reached with more rigorous procedures. Our concern is not with a logic of discovery but to ask the advanced practitioner in social work to approach the helping task with a searching, creative mind-set that is open to heuristic inquiry, synthesis, and scientific judgment in the evaluation of data; refinement of acquired knowledge; and the generation of concepts in theory building.

COMMITMENT, CURIOSITY, AND CREATIVITY: ESSENTIALS IN SCIENTIFIC DISCOVERY FOR THE PRACTITIONER

Discovery in a scientific and pragmatic tradition must evolve out of commitment, curiosity, and the thirst for knowledge—a creative, imaginative search to know. The social worker, who is working with ever-changing qualities in the client-situation configuration, often imbued with pathos, must have a consistent mind-set of "wanting to know" and wanting to know with greater certainty. There must be a total commitment to knowing and to understanding the phenomena that are observed, along with the curiosity and imagination to seek and explain what they are or might be. Ideas can be expected to flash in and out of the practitioner's mind, as the clients tend to reflect varying attitudes, feelings, behavior, and relationships within contextual systems that may or may not fit within accepted theoretical constraints. The practitioner is called on to act within the realm of accumulated theoretical and empirical knowledge. How certain is he or she that understandings and the subsequent interventions will produce the desired results across different conditions? The nuances of timing and the most efficient packaging of interventions, when faced with a complexity of multifaceted, entrenched problems, may be a subject of great concern. The committed, imaginative, and creative practitioner will tend to "tinker with ideas."[40] As uncertainties in similar situations tend to repeat themselves, the practitioner may gradually delimit questions for inquiry and specify the domain of a problem for study.

A great deal of contemplative thought is expected of the practitioner. Curiosity and commitment must be grounded in personal, affective resources that embrace love of knowledge and truth, courage to risk, compassion, and the willingness to extend oneself in hard work. Curiosity is whetted by a sense of purpose and desire to help. As new and novel ideas occur, preliminary hypotheses can be tried out. These may tend to generate new questions as new ideas occur. There should be a constant interplay between what is known theoretically and believed to work in practice and new ideas, intuition, judgments, and trial actions, as the practitioner moves toward more systematic formulation and testing out of hypothetical constructs. This interplay of ideas, drawing inferences from data, testing for evidence in trial actions, in the ongoing practice process can also generate new questions and hypotheses for more rigorous study. It is foundational work in empirically based practice.[41] It is from the practical and the concrete that fruitful ideas can emerge. Kahn suggests that "if complacency and self-satisfaction can be avoided and the practitioner knows when he doesn't know, and what he doesn't know how to do, that the condition for research will be present."[42]

As we have shown, many scientists and philosophers have been concerned with "insight" and sudden new understanding in discovery. Associated with these new insights is an affective, exhilarating, emotional high. Along with these elated feelings is, also, a sense of accomplishment that can move one forward.

New insights may be frequent in scientific study and in practice, or they may be an occurrence of isolated genius. Kuhn saw new insights and ideas that have revolutionized theories as having grown out of normal scientific developments.[43] In this latter sense, the practitioner-researcher is continually testing the adequacy of accepted practice solutions as new data emerge in ongoing practice. Anomalies may occur that push the practitioner toward new solutions and new paradigms.

Creativity of the practitioner can be assumed to be interwoven with imagination, intuition, empathy, and the thought/action of scientific judgment. Imagination that brings into play empathic responsiveness in the client is essential to the therapeutic work, and basic to gaining new insights. The empathy within a positive relationship allows the imagination some flexibility. Imagination is, therefore, "a first step in generating a new idea or fresh insight" and in contemplating a desired direction within "alternative possibilities, new combinations, or altogether novel pathways."[44] Einstein referred to his rather vague play of thoughts in signs or images—rather than in words—which he could reproduce or combine, as characterizing the origin of his productive thought.[45] Not only are the play of thought, as Einstein described, and imagination inherent to creativity, but so is intuition. Actually, intuition can be basic to a judgment, without the practitioner's being conscious of it.

Intuitive leaps in the cognitive process are not wild and unconventional but are considered reasonable interchanges from unconscious or preconscious processes, or out of stored memories, that appear to illuminate and erupt into conscious perception. We shall refer subsequently to the conceptualization of "illumination"[46] within problem solving and reflective inquiry, associated with the ongoing case.

SUMMARY

Scientific discovery in practice is consistent with clinical exploration and understanding of client problems in the problem-solving or treatment process. The practitioner is reflective and committed to knowledge building, as well as to helping clients. Discovery is conceptualized within a broad context that includes the generation of an idea and its pursuit toward justification or verification. The range of pursuit includes judgments, trying-out, description, reflection, interpretation, empirical measures, etc., in the search for understanding. Discovery calls for the play of imagination, intuition, and illumination to foster creative practice insights and scientific judgments and calls for the essential qualities that we have identified as: commitment to purpose; a prepared mind-set; persistence; and openness to inquiry, learning, and change. The creative practitioner, as researcher, scholar, and scientist, must not only listen sensitively, evaluate, and act on the basis of clinical knowledge and data in serving clients, but must be attuned to anomalies that lead to questions regarding accepted knowledge and solutions.

CHAPTER 3

Problem Domain

We have defined discovery in the practice process broadly and have considered its heuristic and preliminary validational qualities. We now turn to specifics of inquiry that can offer a guide to the practitioner.

First, the domain within which inquiry is bounded is of primary consideration. It defines the circumscribed sphere of thought, influence, and actions that provide boundaries to the task of scientific exploration. Secondly, the inquiry should encompass both heuristic and validational qualities. In science, the methodology—or, rules of testing and validation of theories—is considered epistemological, whereas method in heuristics is less precise. Heuristics pose questions of how to expand or broaden theories about a particular domain and can assist in the discovery of new theories. Proponents of the epistemological tend to be concerned with truth-falsity issues and the soundness of knowledge, those of heuristics, with "scientific" progress or "growth of knowledge."[1]

These two methodologies are supportive of each other. In the clinical practice process, the heuristic fills a need for new information and innovation, whereas the validational aims to support the theories, principles, and concepts that have been discovered.

The domain of social work as a profession, defined by its purposes and objectives, has been the object of considerable discussion among professionals, as well as problematic for conceptualization. In 1977, and again in 1979, special conferences were held to discuss purposes and objectives of social work, at the request of the National Association of Social Workers Publication Committee and the editorial board of the *Journal of Social Work*. No unified decisions were reached, but the complexity of defining the purposes and objectives was recognized. The papers and summaries of the conferences were published in two special issues as *Conceptual Frameworks*.[2]

From the second conference (1979), Brieland summarized the social work domain by noting that for the special areas of practice (i.e., health and mental health, schools, justice, public welfare, family and children's services) that "except possibly family and children's services other disciplines (or at any rate, non-social workers) have a strong influence on policy determination and program operation."[3] He further noted that family and children's services are generally recognized as a domain of social work, but that in other areas, social work tends to share its "turf."[4] In the years subsequent to Brieland's remarks, there has been a major impact on family and children's services from counseling (education), and from the family therapy movement that has promoted family therapy as a discipline in its own right.[5]

Briar, at the conference in 1979, suggested that even though the profession is varied and complex with a range of specializations, there tends to be consensus for identity as based in the commonalities of "person-environment as focus" and on "values."[6] A further NASW invitational forum—held in 1979 in Denver, Colorado, and referred to in the introduction—whose aim was to arrive at a definition of clinical social work, also considered that commonality exists in the "social work process addressed to the needs of individuals and small groups, drawing on a range of knowledge as needed, and informed by the mission and values of all social work."[7] A subsequent NASW presymposium institute on clinical social work was devoted to treatment formulation and was held in Philadelphia, November 18, 1981. There was no consensus regarding treatment formulation, though the "person-in-situation" as a guiding principle was affirmed.[8]

The focus of this book on scientific inquiry within direct, clinical practice in social work is commensurate with these identified commonalities. The global domain of inquiry is thus based in theory, principles, and maxims aimed to help individuals, families, and small groups using a person-environment focus; to effect changes in problematic attitudes, feelings, behavioral transactions, destructive environmental relations or conditions; and to mobilize environmental supports for change. The complexities of this global domain for thought, influence, and action are readily apparent. But within these parameters, the practicing social worker uses the modalities of one-on-one, family, or small groups to effect change. Added to the complexity of these helping modalities are differing models of practice technology, diverse problem areas of special population groups, cultural entities, varying foundational theories, varying fields of practice, and other imponderables. Furthermore, the practitioner cannot eliminate special individuals or groups, but serves the general population in the prevention and alleviation of problematic functioning. Hence, for manageability, the practitioner must identify—within the global domain of inquiry—a circumscribed problem domain for specific inquiry.

In ongoing clinical practice, the practitioner can be expected to run into varied problem areas that require theoretical explanations for understanding, where actions are immediately necessary to bring change. Often, uncertainties exist or unpredictable responses may occur. The curious, questioning, scientifically oriented practitioner will want to study, find patterns, regularities, and new understanding of what he or she has observed or questioned and must deal with, in the face of uncertainty. Thus, the first step is the identification of the domain of the problem or specific question for inquiry within the global domain, in order to bring study and observations into manageable size.

Contemplative thought is focused so that the object of attention, or the problem, is in the foreground; the "need" for theory is generated. The practitioner-observer begins to ask questions about the content of that which has come into the problem foreground of attention and thus may begin to sort parts of what has been experienced into classes of objects or events. Other questions arise about how these parts or events are related to one another. In due course, one is able to describe the things or events in attendance and their relationship to each other.[9]

Second, an interdependent step requires knowledge of the literature regarding the problem area. Not only does the literature inform as to what is known, but also may stimulate new and different questions and problem-solving actions. The scholarship of keeping abreast of the literature in general is considered important to both the clinical and scientific tasks. It is imperative in the investigation of any designated problem area.

Science itself is a problem-solving and problem-oriented activity, seeking satisfactory solutions. The logic of thought and empirical research seek to resolve ambiguity, to find uniformities, and to bring predictability into solutions. Science, however, has not actually provided criteria for judging adequate problem solutions. On appraising theory, it is considered by some scientists to be more important to ask whether theory constitutes adequate solutions to significant problems rather than whether it is true or corroborated.[10] This view is important to the practitioner who must be concerned with the adequacy of interventions for producing relief or change. Essentially, one must ask, does the intervention into the problem situation work?

Third, the problem for study by the practitioner may be empirical or conceptual. The empirical problem asks substantive questions of the reality-experience or what is observed in the practitioner-client interaction within the given domain. The conceptual problems concern questions or characteristics of theories. Thus, empirical problems are basic, and stimulate questions about observable or experimental phenomena, whereas the conceptual problems, of higher order, pertain to the reliability and certainty of conceptual structures of theories.

Conceptual problems tend to arise in two ways:

1. When the theory demonstrates internal inconsistencies, or when its concepts or categories of analysis are not precise or clear; these are *internal conceptual problems.*
2. When the theory is in conflict with another theory or body of knowledge; these are *external conceptual problems.*[11]

An example of internal inconsistency in which a concept needs further specificity and clarity is the concept of "triangulation" in family transactional theory. Though the concept is frequently used, it lacks specificity, and evidence of generality. Calvin's recent research that developed an instrument for measuring triangulation has been a step toward greater conceptual clarification.[12] An external conceptual problem for the adherent to psychodynamic theory (ego psychology) is the conflict with basic tenets of behavioral theory. How might interventive concepts be linked to these different theories and made more compatible in the treatment process? This problem is confronted by Linda C. Flowers in chapter 12.

The conceptual problems identified in theory provide the substance for generating theoretical questions and clarifying concepts within theoretical structures. One theory, however, may tend to reinforce another theory or is compatible with it. This tends to happen across disciplines, as "the various scientific disciplines and domains are never completely independent of one another."[13] For example, social work, clinical psychology, counseling, and psychiatry have overlapping domains and theories. It is reasonable that the theories generated in these fields will be interdependent or interconnected. We refer to this interdependence and connectedness as "interfield linkage."

It is expected that all sciences and disciplines will contribute to the ongoing development of basic foundational biological, psychological, and sociocultural theories from which social work and other helping professions draw. Social work must also clearly make its own contributions, and its practice base can be a powerful fulcrum for generating researchable problems, clinical theory, and innovations. Not only is this important to clinical knowledge, but also to its relationship within organizational contexts, which can be widely applicable to other fields.[14]

The social work practitioner will, in general, begin any scientific exploration with an empirical problem that is generated in practice and is consistent with the global practice domain of helping individuals, the family, or small group of clients, resolve or alleviate their psychosocial problems. Kurt Lewin, who contributed substantially to knowledge, also began with empirical practice, "studying things through changing them and seeing the effect."[15] This action science embodied the "theme—that in order to gain insight into a process one must create a change and then observe its variable effects and new dynamics."[16] A further example is the work of Reid, with Epstein and other colleagues, who have built the widely recognized model of "task-centered practice" through experimentation and demonstration within the practice setting. The "need for problem-oriented, testable theory in clinical social work" guided their initial efforts in developing a theoretical base, which began with limited formulations, concerning the "nature, origins, and durations of psychosocial problems typically dealt with by social workers."[17] The researchers and theorists identified as a circumscribed domain the study of structured, time-limited, problem solving with clients, wherein they developed a problem classification and task-centered sequence of action, in the task-centered model of practice. The development and testing of the model have allowed for both empirical and conceptual problems to be investigated over an extended period of time with varying problems and client populations.

SUMMARY

The global domain of social work is an ill-defined complex rather than a neat, conceptual entity. There is interfield linkage with other disciplines, but a consensus exists on the commonality of person-environment as focus and on an accepted value system. The complexity of direct practice is characterized by differing modalities, practice models, foundational theories, fields of practice, problems, and population groups served. However, within the global domain of a person-environment focus and a conceptual framework of fluid biopsychosocial systems, a circumscribed problem domain can be selected for inquiry.

The practitioner-scientist must come to the helping process with knowledge of practice theory and skill in the use of practice techniques, accompanying familiarity with rational inquiry in science, and a spirit of questioning. Once the domain of a problem is identified, whether it is oriented to practice procedures or to elements of foundational knowledge within a biopsychosocial systems framework, the search is for new understanding that will draw upon some empirical or theoretical perspective.

In the following chapter, we will deal with the heuristics of discovery and knowledge development within, or associated with, ongoing practice.

CHAPTER 4

Reflective Inquiry: Orthodox Heuristic Research

Heuristic research encompasses investigation and discovery. In this context our emphasis is centered on reflective inquiry and the scientific investigative processes of research by the practitioner, processes that can lead to greater theoretical clarity and to new knowledge.[1] Investigation is therefore expected to be conducted within—or associated with—the naturalistic case process, where individual research designs or patterns for study may be: hypothetical-developmental,[2] descriptive-comparative,[3] single subject (experimental),[4] and historical-interpretive, as in case history and hermeneutics.[5]

In science, the logic of historical explanation of phenomena is considered to be little different from that of scientific explanation, as they both seek regularities, show associations among regularities, and offer causal explanations from their data.[6]

The case study has historically been a valuable methodological source for new understanding in clinical social work, though methodological disputes have occurred over reliability issues and subjective interpretation, versus the advantage of studying phenomena in their complex detail. Research designs that facilitate individual single-case study have currently emerged, and interest and impetus in this direction is increasing. The individual research designs in heuristic inquiry may not facilitate the degree of confidence for generalizations as the group designs do; however, they can suggest explanations in their application of propositions or hypotheses about association/causation to specific factual data found in the investigation of cases. According to Turk, whether the researcher may

attempt anything from the exceedingly specific and detailed explanation of a highly specific set of data to the exceedingly general and abstract explanation of a highly refined set of empirical generalizations. . . . The product should be evaluated with reference to whether the investigator did the best possible job of getting, analyzing (selectively organizing), and explaining his data.[7]

In individual research designs, both qualitative and quantitative procedures may be used in preliminary or in ongoing validation. Interestingly, the heuristic research on loneliness by Clark Moustakas was an experimental investigation of his own experience with loneliness (n = 1), in which the discovery process was distinguished from that of verification and collaboration.[8]

We do want it understood that the total research effort of the practitioner-researcher cannot be confined to the practitioner-client's interaction in interviews or to the interviews or actions with significant others in the contextual sphere. Planning for the investigation, data analysis, and computation will consume the practitioner's attention well beyond the clinical or helping sessions with clients and others. However, we want to encourage the integration of research with practice to the extent possible among practitioners, case supervisors, and academicians who teach clinical practice and theory.

The literature has for some time reflected low utilization and participation of the practitioner in research,[9] though, as noted in the introduction, in the last decade new technical literature that explicates methods for integration of research with practice has begun to emerge. A recent national survey suggested that "greater research interest and competence are needed throughout the profession to explore fully the potential of scientific research for practice.[10] It is our hope that we can contribute to this further stimulation of interest and competence.

It is assumed in this book that the cognitive aims in the science of social work practice are not limited to a search for truth and explanation, but include the aims of conceptual efficiency, predictive ability, and fruitfulness, or what works.[11] Therefore, scientific rationality is considered here from a broader stance than the logic central to the hypothetico-deductive method. Though observation-hypothesis-experiment as a paradigm is traditional in science and applicable in social work practice itself (study, assessment, intervention),[12] we shall also discuss alternatives, such as the dialectical "new paradigm,"[13] and the "new empiricists,"[14] where the cognitive aim is more likely to be that of fruitfulness.

For purposes of organization and clarity, this chapter is devoted to inquiry from the conventional scientific paradigm based on canons of scientific method. Chapter 5 is devoted to what is identified as "new paradigm research." Hermeneutic interpretation and understanding as an approach has greater affinity with the dialectics of new paradigm research, and phenomenological research is in accord with new empiricism, but is not alien to conventional logic. These philosophies and procedures will be discussed separately in chapters 6 and 7.

As we have advocated, the practitioner, as a scientist—whose therapeutic work is performed within a wider, general context of scientific inquiry—will assume a reflective and inquiring stance regarding knowledge for use in practice. This stance is essentially preparatory. Creative discovery processes are often referred to as preparation; incubation; illumination; and verification, or some variation thereof.[15] The initial preparation and incubation may include a selective trial-and-error search in areas of problem solving where the heuristics are least powerful and before the problem area is well defined.[16] The insights and later validational procedures are facilitated by research concepts and methodologies that offer guidelines to problem solving and model building. It is with these thoughts in mind that we turn to the practitioner's task of reflective inquiry and heuristic research within the conventional paradigm of science.

REFLECTION-IN-CASES PROCESS IN INQUIRY

Reflection as a thought process is an integral part of the practitioner-client interaction. It assumes varying levels, but all thought that is meaningful has an element of reflection that precedes understanding.

Reflection as a clinical intervention procedure in direct practice has often been equated with helping the client to be introspective and to achieve insights into preconscious and unconscious intrapsychic processes. The literature in the 1960s produced varied evidence that poor clients were not responsive to reflective and introspective procedures and required teaching and action for change.[17] The extent of the criticism of reflection was unfortunate, as the reflective process of the mind, to some degree, must be used by both the practitioner and client if they are to succeed, even through using teaching and action techniques, in making changes or achieving more satisfying conditions and relationships.

Hollis, during the same period, was involved in research aimed at classification of communications, within the treatment or helping interview. Her conceptualization of reflection in treatment was on a continuum, which related to quality and depth of understanding. She categorized separately the communications of sustainment, exploration-description-ventilation, and direct influence, which included teaching and advice giving. She also categorized reflective communications on a continuum that ranged from those categories directed toward problem-solving and understanding relationships in the "here-and-now," toward understanding the client's dynamic response patterns, and toward understanding influences of childhood and developmental factors on response patterns.[18] Hollis found, using a sample of clients known to family agencies, that though the percentage of communications of clients within five interviews was higher for the ventilative-descriptive category, at least a fourth of the client communications were categorized as reflective, with the exception of the first interview.[19] The percentage of practitioner communications that aimed to stimulate reflection were nearly equivalent to the percentage of communications for all of the other categories combined.[20] Her comparison of data with three other studies reflected a similar pattern of communications in interviews categorized as reflection.[21] This reflective activity was especially devoted to problem solving that considered the person-situation configuration. As reflection is reportedly a common phenomenon in practice, it is consistent with our assumption of reflection in the examination and search for practice knowledge.

Reflection, as we use it here, incorporates the creative thought and judgment processes that practitioners ordinarily use in clinical helping or problem solving with clients. Clinical reflective judgment is generally derived from a matrix of theory, practice knowledge, maxims, and creative imagination based in the perceptual and in preconscious-unconscious repository of memory. The reflective stance that we are advocating assumes a wider than clinical context. It is the reflective questioning of knowledge and theory, or the design of logic or research, that transcends the clinical, helping judgments. It considers the rightness of the interventive act, the relevance or gap in the theory, observed phenomena in variable situations, or the logic of a design for new information or evaluation. The practitioner notices "similarities and regularities," as well as differences, from one case to the next.[22] Scientific reasoning is required wherein the practitioners will formulate statements or hypotheses with regard to empirical observations of case data that may be either true or false and require further investigation to determine validity. Reflection at this level has the aim and purpose of scientific discovery, of asking new questions, finding new explanations, and new understandings.

We recognize the impossibility of designing a major group research study to be carried out within a busy practitioner's case load. Heuristic inquiry that involves individual research designs, qualitative methods, and a limited domain of inquiry would serve to delimit and make inquiry practical. It can be an especial forerunner to more robust studies. We want to stress, also, that scientific reasoning and an imaginative attitude in discovery can be brought to every helping encounter. Illumination and new insights can emerge at any time in the helping process.

We have been involved with experimentation and development of these ideas for several years.[23] We have found that doctoral students' subjective evaluation of their learning, acquired from a period of implementation of reflective, heuristic inquiry in practice increased their analytic and evaluative skills, as well as their positive attitudes and receptivity toward research of practice.[24]

Schön has also recently proposed a similar stance regarding research in practice.[25] In describing what he termed the "reflective practitioner," he said that the dilemma of rigor for practice and research relevance for practice could be dissolved if there could be developed an epistemology of practice which placed "technical problem solving within a broader context of reflective inquiry" and conjoined "the art of practice in uncertainty and uniqueness to the scientist's art of research."[26] Others in the field have emphasized single-subject experimental designs and evaluative research methods within practice, generally using behavioral science models that are conducive to developmental methods and specific measurements of behavioral change,[27] or to the problem-oriented models using measurements of task accomplishment.[28] Their conception of science is orthodox, and research underlying models is empirically grounded. Although Wodarski claims that "the traditional therapeutic methods cannot be evaluated, and that traditional research methodology cannot provide the data necessary to have these methods placed on an empirical basis,"[29] the behavioral science methods also have their shortcomings, such as being subject to operational restrictiveness and partialization of the human phenomenon.

The reflective action with which we, and others in the literature,[30] have been concerned should not only stimulate practice rigor, but should offer fertile ground for building knowledge and finding new discoveries. Scientists, in general, have tended to emphasize the more spontaneous insights of discovery, rather than to plot the heuristic and systematic activity of ongoing inquiry in practice. Though their interest in discovery has been largely with incubation and sudden illumination of a solution to a problem or an idea, their focus does have relevance to practice research.

Simon proposed that incubation and illumination, as reported by discoverers, evolved during the process of inquiry.[31] He referred to Hadamard, who claimed that a first stage of "preparation" involved conscious, prolonged investigation that does not bring success in solving, or perhaps in framing, the problem. The researcher becomes frustrated and drops the problem from his conscious attention. "Some time later, often suddenly and with little or no warning . . . or immediately upon awakening from sleep, the central idea for the solution presents itself to the conscious mind, only the details remaining to be worked out."[32] All of us have experienced such a phenomenon. Simon, however, proposed an elaborate cognitive process to explain the phenomenon and identified the time interval between "illumination" and the preceding inquiry and "preparation" as an "incubation period."

Though the cognitive processes in the incubation of ideas and leaps of insight in problem solving are important to recognize, we are particularly concerned here with the reflective judgments and systematic actions taken by the practitioner in exploration of a problem, generated from data.

It can be assumed that some kind of trial-and-error search underlies the problem solving in the early phases of building knowledge, and that there must exist a state of preparedness to observe, to formulate ideas, to define concepts, to make comparisons, to classify, or to pose propositions and hypotheses from data. Within the focused study of a specific problem, illuminating insights may occur.

THE INVESTIGATIVE PROCESS

Discussion of different ways for the practitioner to pursue investigation can best be related to general patterns or designs in scientific inquiry. As identified above, the a) hypothetical-developmental, b) descriptive-comparative, and c) single-subject (experimental) designs can be most readily adapted to the case process. The descriptive designs of case study, using qualitative methods, and the constant-comparative designs of grounded theory require extensive research activity beyond the case process, but it is important for the practitioner to consider use of these patterns in investigation. The historical-interpretive designs also require extensive study and analysis beyond the case process. The dialectical paradigm; the hermeneutic-interpretive approaches; and phenomenological research, that may include interpretive, hermeneutic qualities, are all presented subsequently in chapters 5, 6, and 7. Our intention is to foster open-mindedness in the use of different strategies and approaches in seeking knowledge, though always maintaining the discernment of scientific rigor. A quotation by Paracelsus, a German physician (1490–1541), aptly summarizes our perspective: "The striving for wisdom is the second Paradise of the world."

Hypothetical-Developmental Designs. The development of concepts, classification or typologies, and hypotheses is fundamental to scientific investigation. For the logical positivists, descriptive concepts were the first stage on the way to testing explanatory hypotheses,[33] and their importance continues within this tradition.

In our discussion of the development of logical thinking, concepts, typologies, and hypotheses, coexistent with practice, we have assumed clinical procedures within a practice frame of problem-solving and psychosocial systems, though the scientific processes may be adapted to behavioral, crisis, existential, and other practice approaches. As clients and their milieu are observed in practice, the practitioner will begin to notice and describe related factors on dimensions such as events, behaviors, affect or feelings, attitudes and thought, relational qualities in interactions, etc., that may suggest concrete descriptive patterns, concepts, and pertinent questions for study. The practitioner, as observer, will have orienting concepts at hand from the practice theory being used, but unstructured observations are important to beginning the study of a problem. They are important in the development of ideas about the problem. Structured observations, from questionnaires, scales, or other instruments, may also support the study as it progresses to a more systematized design. The unstructured data gathered in the beginning will tend to coexist with the clinically exploratory and reflective questions and interven-

tions for purposes of problem understanding or for promoting therapeutic change. The unstructured observations will generally consist
of descriptive accounts of phenomena, such as client's behavior, responses, attitudes, feelings, relationships, and conditions within the
context and milieu that pertain to the problem at hand.

As the raw data or observations are examined, the practitioner
may note a common thread or theme that pertains to a more formalized research problem. It is from this raw data of the client's report
that concepts or constructs can be defined, in order to organize the
data. "The greater the distance between one's concepts and constructs
and the empirical facts to which they are intended to refer, the greater
the possibility for their being misunderstood."[34] Therefore, concepts
must be clearly defined to give their general meaning, whether or not
they define concrete and particular things, or abstract and universal
phenomena. These concepts are referred to as nominal concepts. For
example, the practitioner's observations of an adolescent group, on
the above-cited dimensions, could lead to the definition of such abstract, nominal concepts as mutuality, oneness, or affective bond.

From these concepts, there can emerge a second step, that of classification. These concepts could then be classified conceptually as
"cohesiveness," which further defines the group. Therefore, concepts
or units are used to organize and classify the raw data, a fundamental
step for developing propositions and hypotheses from empirical data.
The concepts that the practitioner develops from observations may be
defined both nominally and operationally. The data organized and
classified in the above example as the nominal concept, "cohesiveness," may be further specified in an operational and measurable
form where it can be related to other factors or variables. That is, the
concept "cohesiveness," may be defined in terms of a scalar measurement of high-low or weak-strong cohesiveness. With the concept operationalized quantitatively, it can be measured as to its association
with other factors (variables). The practitioner may begin now to
question, from observations, whether strong cohesiveness is associated with such varying characteristics of the group as age, socioeco-
nomic status, or type of problem. Based on the evidence, a hypothesis
may be formulated in which a significant relationship is predicted
between one or more of these concepts or variables, all of which can
be quantified.

As data related to the problem under study are accumulated, the
practitioner must consider classifications or typologies that are useful
to organize the relevant data. Actually, when the practitioner is work-

ing from unstructured observations as in ongoing case data, he or she may want to proceed by posing working hypotheses that may stimulate principles for classifying the data or grouping the observations in one category or another. A helpful device is to contrast or compare events or cases wherein differences may suggest categories.[35] The typologies that are arrived at should also meet the standards of exhaustiveness and mutual exclusiveness.

In classical scientific method, the development of the hypothesis is aimed at prediction of specific relationships of association or of causal nature that can be empirically confirmed or refuted. If the hypothesis predicts relationships among variables, it is correlational; whereas, if the prediction refers to a change or conditions (independent variable) responsible for the changes in other conditions (dependent variable), it is a cause-effect relationship.[36] As we have seen there must be restrictive, specific definitions of variables in order to determine whether relationships exist, whether they are correlational or cause-effect variables.

To further explain the use of concepts, classification, and hypotheses for the purposes of science and in theory building within the logical-empiricist tradition, it is important to understand logical processes and the importance of theoretical statements to scientific knowledge. The statement is defined by a declarative sentence that purports something as true or false, or having a truth value.[37]

The issue of objective reality in scientific reasoning with regard to truth or falsity of statements has been the subject of much philosophical debate. Logical empiricism has adhered to objectivity and realism. For our consideration here, we utilize the correspondence theory of truth that requires any statement about the case data to "correspond with things as they really are."[38] The statements that the practitioner formulates will refer to concrete facts or concepts from data, as we have indicated, and may be in the form of an axiom, a proposition, or a hypothesis. The statement is, therefore, basic to scientific thinking and inquiry, and provides for the justification of the practitioner's beliefs about the observed phenomena. The statements may be constructed so that they merely state the existence of some state of affairs or objects or they may be constructed so that they express relationships between phenomena or concepts. The later relational statements of contingent or conditional relations express what "might be true and also might be false."[39] They represent propositions or hypotheses that refer to relationships that may be associational, or they may express causal relationships. It should be noted that hypotheses, as contingent, relational statements, may refer to concrete measurable concepts in the real world, or they may be theoretical statements that "USE theoretical models to make contingent claims about REAL SYSTEMS."[40]

Before the practitioner begins to formulate a hypothesis that predicts a relationship, it is necessary to state the conditions or circumstances that exist with reference to the concepts or variables under consideration. These statements are true or false and only provide for nominal classification of phenomena or variables.[41] They are, however, essential to defining the conditions or circumstances under which the relationship exists.

Before considering further the importance of these statements of conditions and their usefulness to statements of relationships in hypotheses, it is important to review schematically the logical forms in scientific reasoning that are pertinent to these processes. In logic, a conditional statement of relationship has the general form "If (antecedent), then (consequent)."[42] The condition only says that if the antecedent is true, then the consequent is true. Conditional statements, therefore, express a relationship between two statements, or between events or states of affairs. Symbolically the conditional statement for this is:

$$\text{If P, then Q} \qquad \text{P} = \text{antecedent}$$
$$\text{(P is sufficient for Q)} \quad \text{Q} = \text{consequent}$$

If the conditional relationship expressed is that the consequent Q is *necessary* for the antecedent P, then the form is:

$$\text{If P, then Q} \qquad \text{P} = \text{antecedent}$$
$$\text{(P only if Q)} \quad \text{Q} = \text{consequent}$$

In this latter form the consequent must have some requirements stipulated for it to be (of necessity) equivalent to the antecedent.

An "If, then" statement of sufficiency in relationships may be stated in the following example:

(If, then) If the father is the final authority in family decision making, then the children accept authority in family decisions.
(P) Father is the final authority in decision making.
(Q) Children accept authority in family decisions.

In this relational statement the father as the final authority is sufficient for children's acceptance of authority in family decisions.

Second, the difference in a relational statement that is true of necessity is demonstrated by:

(If, then) If the father is the final authority in family decision making, then children are required to defer to father's decisions.
P The father is the final authority in family decision-making.
Q Children are required to defer to father's decisions.

It can be observed that in the statement of necessity, there is a requirement necessary to the statement.

It can be recognized that this kind of reasoning process underlies hypothesis formulation of an associational and causal nature, and it is apparent that the formulation of "if" conditions that are sufficient for P are very different from the "only if" conditions that are necessary.

These are some of the processes of reasoning that may precede the practitioner's formulation of hypotheses for empirical testing from case observations. The formulation of the hypothesis to be tested out in practice is designed to test its truth or falsity.

Hypotheses that are designed to test for causal relationships predict that, given the initial conditions and background, the prediction will occur, i.e., if the independent variable in the hypothesis occurs, then the dependent variable will occur, as determined by it. The practitioner may want to hypothesize that the predicted relationship will occur within a designated probability level. In any case, the prediction by the hypothesis is logically deducible from it, together with the initial conditions or circumstances. The structured form in logic can be written as:

$$H \quad IC \text{ thus } P$$
$$H = \text{Hypothesis}$$
$$IC = \text{Initial Conditions}$$
$$P = \text{Prediction}$$

In hypothesis development the practitioner will use case data to formulate nominal and operational concepts that will be inherent to the subsequent formulation of associational or causal relationships in hypotheses. For example, the practitioner may desire to explore structural theory in family treatment. First, nominal concepts will be defined from case data that relate to family structure under given conditions and a relational statement or a hypothesis is devised, as in the following:

If P, then Q

Initial conditions: (1) The family is a structural organization

(2) Hierarchal relationships structure the organizational components (members)

(3) Authority is dispensed within the family structural relationships

Concepts: P = "parental denial of authority"

Q = "Shifting child authority"

If, then: If there is "parental denial of authority in the family hierarchal structure," then there is "shifting child authority in the hierarchal structure."

(Q is thus sufficient for P)

These concepts could be operationalized through scalar measurement of attitudes and behavior with reference to authority distribution in the family. The hypothesis may be stated as:

HICP: Parental denial of authority in the family structure is positively correlated with shifting child authority.

If, in the above example, shifting child authority was found to be correlated with denial of parental authority, then a further hypothesis could be tested:

HICP: Parental denial of authority in the family structure, associated with shifting child authority, produces tension and instability in the structure.

All of the above concepts ("parental denial of authority," "shifting child authority," "tension," "structural instability") could be quantified for measurement within an experimental design.

As we have indicated, elements of "parental denial" may be identified, defined, and represented in a scalar value as well as "shifting authority among child members." However, the practitioner may first design an exploratory experiment to include family interviews, where elements of "parental denial of authority" could be observed and judgments made as to evidence of whether there followed elements or patterns of "shifting distribution of authority among child members" that reflected instability in authority of the family structure. From these observations, indicators for scalar items could then be defined to identify more precisely denial, structural authority distribution, tension, structural instability, etc., that could underlie subsequent hypotheses for predicting relationships.

Using this kind of thought process and exploratory experimentation, the practitioner might examine additional families in the case load to identify whether a hypothesis relates to specific families, i.e., young, one-parent, low-income, or in varying sociocultural traditions. Thus, the exploratory hypothesis could be examined in practice even before it is experimentally tested with greater rigor in sampling and controls.

Family therapists have arrived at such conceptualizations from their clinical observations of variation and dynamics of family structure.[43] In chaotic, underorganized, out-of-control families, observations of destructive distribution of force has been clinically documented, including the parentifying of one child.[44] The testing of propositions and hypotheses under varying conditions of authority distribution and with varying populations could advance valid inference, generalization, and theory building.

In the course of development of hypotheses, the practitioner will engage in trial-and-error feedback operations. That is, exploratory experiments[45] that pose an action or an interventive method, without predicting outcome, may be set up to observe and to discover what consequences may follow. On the other hand, actions or interventions may be applied that are intended or predicted to produce changes. The practitioner then observes the outcome. From such uncontrolled experimental observations, the practitioner may be able to formulate a hypothesis for more rigorous testing under controlled conditions.

We emphasize that experiments can be of different levels. Though the practitioner may not be able to adhere in practice to rigorous experimental design, the client—as his own control—can be used where consequences and outcomes may be identified. Reliability can be checked, using interjudge agreement made by colleagues.

The practitioner may establish a demonstration or action project, setting up conditions for client(s) actions and intervening with special clinical procedures in randomly designated cases, wherein the consequences can be carefully observed. Reid notes that "the essence of experimentation is to do and to study what is done."[46] He also argues rightly that the all-too-frequent tendency to restrict experimentation to controlled experiments is unfortunate, and asserts that experimentation in practice may be well planned, systematic, and

hard to distinguish from ordinary practice, which may in itself involve innovation and monitoring of practitioners' activities and outcomes. . . . An experiment employing primitive research methodology may produce a conceptualization of a promising intervention, show how the method can be used, and provide suggestive evidence on how well it worked.[47]

That Reid,[48] Thomas,[49] and Rothman[50] have used variations in experimental design, building practice models in developmental research,
has been well explicated and will not be pursued here. We want to
foster, however, exploratory inquiry that follows canons of science,
but offers latitude in design.

To summarize, designs that develop concepts, propositions, and
hypotheses and that lead toward evaluation of outcomes, tend to be
exploratory and are feasible for the practitioner to pursue in clinical
practice.

Descriptive-Comparative Designs. Descriptive and comparative designs
that relate to qualitative and quantitative methods, to participant-
observation, and to methods of comparison are all possible for the
practitioner. Followup of cases and participation in surveys can also
be useful. We will highlight these different modes to suggest options
and their appropriateness to the problem for study and the constraints of the setting.

As we have seen, descriptions derived from observations of practitioners and information from clients can be the source of data that
facilitate typologies, explanations, and interpretation. Descriptive case
data is particularly useful for studying the person-situation in social
work where the conceptual framework embodies contextual factors.
It also allows for full longitudinal descriptions that may reflect stabil-
ity or shifts over time. Descriptions in words rather than algorithms
can add to meaning and to understanding, though quantitative procedures may also be included in the analysis of data. The qualitative
methods for analyzing descriptive data are especially useful in ascertaining meaning.[51]

The practitioner who expects to study a problem descriptively,
within the naturalistic case process, may choose direct observation
with descriptive accounts or use audiovisual devices or tapes to record observations. The electronic devices can enhance the efficiency
and reliability of the process, though the descriptive or recorded data
will tend to be voluminous.

The practitioner will begin the study with a single case and will
need to organize the data within the identified problem domain and
theoretical context of psychosocial systems, so that concepts and indicators of concepts can be identified.

Where clinical skills are used to understand the client's situation
and to enable effective solutions to problems, stress, and change, the
interview can include structured and nonstructured observations and
questions that relate to the identified problem area. Participant-ob-

servation procedures may be used in data collection, especially within the family group setting. There is not a "clear-cut progression from exploratory work to description to hypothesis testing,"[52] as the process may be interdependent, as are study, assessment, and intervention in social treatment; but the practitioner will gradually accumulate descriptive accounts of the phenomenon being studied.

The treatment relationship is actually conducive to the data gathering, and the practitioner should have in mind some relevant questions to probe the area for exploration. Some structured questions may facilitate uniformity in data gathering. Strauss and colleagues identify four kinds of questions in participant-observation that may be used with modification by the practitioner. They are: (a) questions of challenge, (b) hypothetical, (c) description of ideal situations, and (d) interpretive comments or testing propositions.[53] These different procedures can yield additional data to the exploratory-explanatory and reflective comments of both the client and practitioner in a clinical context. The object is to understand a specific problem, or what transpires after a given intervention, and for the data to be descriptive of the conditions and interventions. Audio or audiovisual tapes are crucial to preserving the detail and objectivity of the encounter. If these mechanical devices are not possible, the practitioner should record descriptive notes immediately after seeing the client or those in the client's contextual system. Depending on the problem for study, descriptive accounts may also be drawn from other case studies or records that complement the direct observations.

The task of analyzing the descriptive data through qualitative methods is laborious but also rewarding, as it can facilitate a comprehensive picture, meaning, and understanding of the data. Qualitative methods for analyzing data are described in detail in the literature,[54] and we will only highlight the major procedures that can be used. Barton and Lazarsfeld, as cited, describe qualitative methods that particularly relate to the practitioner's purposes, as practitioners begin with direct observations and proceed to systematizing and classifying the data, to finding relationships, and to a summary of general patterns.

The initial observations that constitute the unusual, that suggest problems or indicators in a study, are important. In general, the practitioner in observing phenomena is looking for meaning, and is alert to regularities, themes, patterns, configurations, and possible causal flows in the interactions.[55] The descriptive design in qualitative methods, therefore, begins with the practitioner's construction of descriptive systems and classification from the discrete observations. Categories may have been defined already, or the practitioner may develop a classification system from the data. He or she begins to categorize data on the basis of attributes in the study. For example, Lane and Russell, in studying an alternative to social control in the treatment of violent couples,[56] interviewed couples from a "neutral non-mandating stance" rather than a social control stance. From their interviews they could identify comments by the practitioner and the clients and from general contexts indicators of a "neutral non-mandated stance" and a "social control" stance. These concepts would then classify and categorize the data accordingly.

It is generally suggested that, in the beginning, the practitioner classify in a preliminary way—by summarizing or identifying themes or elements that describe the conditions, attitudes, behavior, feeling, tone, or thinking of the client and the practitioner in the helping interaction relating to the problem under study. In the above example, the theme was control/noncontrol in terms of treatment stance and of behavior.

As the data accumulate, the classification can become increasingly systematic. "The most highly developed form of descriptive system which can arise in qualitative analysis is one in which each type is explicitly derived from a logical combination of basic attributes or dimension."[57] This may be done in tabular or matrix forms. Miles and Huberman refer to it as "data display" in the flow of analysis, and note that the decisions for analysis on setting up the rows and columns are analytic and data-deductive.[58]

Quantitative methods can be used when the data are displayed in tabular form. For example, in the aforementioned study of violent couples mandated by the court to the therapeutic agency, the descriptive data from interviews with these couples were examined over the initial time period (three weeks), reflecting the engagement of the couple in the helping process. The focus and aim of interviews were to help these couples, mandated by the court to interrupt their violent behavior and seek solutions to their problems and dysfunctional relationships. Clients were seen by the practitioners from the court's mandated stance and from the agency's neutral, non-mandated stance. As the raw data from interviews were systematically analyzed, certain themes began to appear in the messages related to "control/nocontrol" issues. Such preliminary concepts as "victim/victimizer" tended to be linked to the feeling of control expressed in the mandated stance. Indicators could be identified and defined on a mandate/no-mandate dimension from practitioners' and clients' actions, questions/comments, and emotions expressed that would categorize the attitudinal data in initial sessions.

To look further at relationships on the basis of these categories, data on the incidence of interruption or continuation of violence could then be cross-tabulated with categories designating stance, i.e., mandate and no-mandate stance. A table could be constructed that would demonstrate the analysis and identify instances as frequencies of controlled behavior or continued violent behavior as related to the two categories of treatment stance (see table 4.1).

In table 4.1, X denotes instances of controlled behavior with interruption of violence, and $\overline{X}$ noncontrol with no interruption of violence. In the table, Y denotes the conditions of interruption of violence under a mandated stance and $\overline{Y}$ under a neutral, nonmandated stance. All of the incidents of controlled behavior with interruption in violence and mandated stance will be indicated in the left upper cell; all of the incidents in the lower left cell will reflect controlled behavior with interruption in violence under the conditions of no mandate.

The second column represents the instances in the upper cell of noncontrolled behavior and no interruption of violence within a mandated stance. The lower cell represents noncontrolled behavior and no interruption of violence within a nonmandated stance.

In the analytic process, the practitioner would study incidents in the left column of the table and would want to explain the frequencies observed especially in the upper and the lower cells of that column. That is, one would particularly want to understand why cases of interruption of violence occurred, with no mandate. (The aim of the

TABLE 4.1 Frequency Distribution of Controlled Behavior with Interruption of Violence versus Noncontrolled Behavior with No Interruption of Violence under Conditions of a Mandated and Nonmandated Treatment Stance

Stance	Controlled Behavior (Interruption of Violence)	Noncontrolled Behavior (No Interruption of Violence)
Mandate Y No mandate $\overline{Y}$	X	$\overline{X}$

treatment was interruption of violence.) It would give only the condition of interruption of violence with mandate or with no mandate, but it would in no way explain why this was so. It would lead to a comparison with the right side of the column, and to further exploration of the incidence and meaning of interruption of violence under the stance of a mandate or no mandate. Other variables could be suggested as well in the development of an experimental design to search out precise causal relationships.

The practitioner's general impressions had been that the "neutral–nonmandated" stance by the practitioner had a greater yield for the interruption of violence and continuation in treatment. The tabular analysis, however, can graphically identify these gross relationships and frequencies. Granted that there may be other influencing factors to support the positive findings, it provides some gross evidence grounded in practice. It was noted by Lane and Russell that within the nonmandated stance, they received such comments from clients as: a report to the judge in a couple's final court hearing that "they were returning to see the team [practitioners] because they were invited to do so."

Beyond the demonstration of the categories and relationships in the data, a final aspect of qualitative analysis is the drawing of conclusions and verification.[59] Just as the descriptive comment in the above example can be taken as evidence of client response to a neutral, nonmandated stance, this should be recognized as a tentative conclusion, and additional evidence for the position should be identified and subjected to further testing. Actually, an experimental group design with controlled conditions could be the next step to test causal relationships.

From this discussion, it is evident that both qualitative and quantitative procedures may be combined to suggest and support relationships, factors that may influence attitudes or actions, or explain associational correlations among variables. The practitioner may thus use a descriptive design in the development of discrete categories for classification of observed phenomena and for searching out relationships and meaning. Qualitative analysis can also aid the practitioner in building knowledge inductively.

There are two types of comparative descriptive designs amenable to practice process research that should be a part of the practitioner's research armament. We will thus highlight the (a) case-comparative design[60] and the (b) constant-comparative design of "grounded theory."[61] The former can lend itself to observation within the case process by the practitioner, but also requires other research colleagues in pursuit of the investigation. The practitioner can use the method of participant-observation to acquire data at one level of case observation. The constant comparative design would essentially require that case process be recorded and then analyzed, using the constant comparative method.

Case-Comparative Design. The design is descriptive of practice formulations that occur in every day ongoing practice and the method is case comparison.

This method involves comparing a new case in which what will happen is unknown with cases in which the process, dynamics, and consequences are already known. Thus, the development of action strategies in the new case can rely on what has been learned from past cases.[62]

It is a method akin to the use of precedents in the law and would fit well with discovery, in the sense that was identified earlier.

Butler, Davis, and Kukkonen have provided a detailed description of the method in the social work literature. Schematically, there are four systematic steps in the case comparison process:

1. Inquiry into preexisting formulations of practice,
2. Testing of practice formulations through comparative case observation,
3. Application of practice formulations taken from reference cases, and
4. Summary of the contributions to practice knowledge buttressed by published reference cases.[63]

The inquiry into preexisting formulations means that practitioners are asked to describe their practice interventions and their preferred theoretical concepts in some problem under study. Their conceptual understanding of the case situation and their beliefs are also extrapolated. Then, by comparing the belief systems of practitioners with their actual reported practice, there can be selected for further development categories that appear to be grounded in practice.

Therefore, the second step entails the testing of these practice formulations of the practitioner through comparative case observation. The knowledge gained from the preexisting practice formulations and categories are then compared to the incoming new observations, where they may be reworked or refined. Butler, Davis, and Kukkonen note that there are four levels of testing the observations in this case comparison method.

1. Study of archival information, such as process recordings,
2. Interviewing practitioners,
3. Direct observation of practice, including the use of audiovisual tapes, and
4. Participant-observation, in which the researcher engages in actual practice.[64]

Thus, consistent findings from all of these levels is thought to enhance the validity of the method. When the process of case comparisons is complete, then a selection of cases is made (based on judgment) to serve as the reference cases.

The third step involves the application to the new cases of the formulations from the reference cases. The new cases being compared are "always an experiment" and new observations may suggest modification of the categories that were derived from earlier grounded case knowledge. It can be seen that judgment plays a major role in this systematic operation.

Finally, it is expected that case comparison summaries can become reference cases for comparing new cases, similar to the use of cases as legal precedent in law. As can be seen, the practitioner would need full participation from colleagues as a larger group to pursue an investigation of this type, but it could capture the complexity of the case in research.

Constant-Comparative Design. This design involves a method of joint coding and analysis in the development of theory that is considered to be integrated, consistent, plausible, and also grounded in the practice data.[65] The systematic discovery of theory—grounded in data— facilitates theory that is useful to the practitioner, a fact which accords with one purpose of science that we have noted above. The method also allows the practitioner as researcher to act as a participant-observer in the collection and analysis of data.

The constant-comparative method can be described in four stages:

1. Comparing incidents applicable to each category,
2. integrating categories and their properties,
3. delimiting the theory, and
4. writing the theory.[66]

The practitioner can begin by identifying every incident in the recorded interview observations in as many categories as possible. The coding of an incident for a category, however, should be compared with the previous incidents coded in that category. This constant comparison tends to facilitate thinking about the range, conditions, and relatedness of the categories, as the practitioner codes and recodes incidents. At this point, the second basic rule is applied, which is to discontinue the coding and record a memo on the ideas categorized. At this time, the practitioner reflects on the data and the theoretical ideas that it stimulates, and may begin now to hypothesize from the data and verify through comparison of groups. To further enhance theoretical credibility and stimulation of ideas, there may be a sharing of ideas and data with colleagues. It is expected that, as the ideas and memos are recorded, theoretical ideas will be shaping into emerging theory. It is, therefore, time to return to further coding of new and incoming incidents and to continue their constant comparison, leading to the next step.

Second, the integration of the categories and their properties is undertaken. Rather than comparison of incident to incident, there is a comparison with properties of the category. Now that knowledge is accumulating on properties of the category, there may be diversity of properties and interrelationships. Glaser has asserted that "the theory develops as different categories and their properties tend to become integrated through constant comparisons which force the analyst to make some related theoretical sense of each comparison."[67]

Third, as the theory emerges, modification of categories will lessen, as the practitioner-researcher compares the new incidents of a category to its properties. It is expected that, as modifications become fewer, they will essentially be done for further clarification, relevance, or the elaboration of properties "into the major outline of interrelated categories."[68] The process tends to be characterized by increasing conformity and satiety that is delimiting for the theory.

Finally, the practitioner-researcher should report or communicate the results or theoretical findings which have emerged from the coded data and the themes expressed in the memos on each category.

It can be seen that the qualitative analysis and development of theoretical ideas will require considerable practitioner involvement well beyond the collection of data in varying interview situations. The collection of data and analysis tend to go hand-in-hand. The data are in the form of words rather than numbers, and words reveal the rich, luminous descriptions of grounded incidents. In their source book on

Qualitative Methods, Miles and Huberman have tried to capture methods for drawing valid conclusions from qualitative data with analyses "that are practical, communicable, and non-self deluding—in short, scientific in the best sense of that word."[69] They have also especially noted that qualitative inquiry is now being advanced in revised formulations by eminent methodologists, some of whom are cited here.[70]

The Survey. Though survey methods are, in general, designed for large-scale studies, it is possible for the practitioner to survey clients regarding some identified problem area through a systematic selection process. Selected structured or semistructured survey instruments may be used in concert with an interview. Use of survey instruments may be especially useful in longitudinal and followup studies of effects of services or modes of intervention with clients. Though large-scale longitudinal studies have been important in assessing the quality and effects of services[71] and followup of studies of intervention modes or on procedures,[72] the practitioner can find it practical to follow up clients who have received/not received selected interventions. Followup can be a source for analysis and understanding of differential client reactions and response to clinical help. It can also be used to ascertain attitudes and research practices by professional colleagues.

For example, the large study by Reid and Shyne of brief and extended treatment that built in a followup component made a major impact on practice and facilitated planned short-term treatment in agencies. Continued study was needed, however, to isolate those clients, circumstances, and problem entities in which brief treatment was more satisfactory. The practitioner can systematically follow up clients who have different life patterns, who receive varying interventions under different conditions. The small practitioner study will not support generalizations, but can offer new insights for more rigorous testing.

The clinical practitioner should find it especially practical to follow up clients in aftercare. Deinstitutionalization has been extremely hazardous for the mentally ill,[73] and the very nature of clinical services for aftercare patients could offer opportunity for followup studies using systematic methods of data collection. The practitioner could make a major contribution to theory and practice in this area.

The efficient use of scalar instruments for gathering data regarding attitudes, feelings, impressions, behavior, etc., has been well documented in the literature, as has the usefulness of rapid-assessment instruments for facilitating clinical evaluation and change.[74] We want to emphasize that heuristics in discovery may occur within the small-scale survey, and there are many useful instruments that are now standardized that can be appropriately used by the practitioner. There will also be the consideration of a sampling process for purposes of reliability. The practitioner may want, during a selected time period, simply to follow up all of the clients in his or her case load that fit the criteria for being screened into the study. This procedure could offer insights in an early followup survey of the results of selected interventions. When the study has become more precisely formulated, considerations for representative sampling become important. Due to practice constraints, the practitioner may wish to use a nonprobability sampling method of the accidental or purposive type, but may also be able to use a simple random-sampling procedure that could draw on a broader segment of agency clients.[75] The latter procedure could strengthen findings and would be especially useful with the experimental design.

Single-Subject Design. The single-subject design is not monolithic but encompasses varying quasi-experimental designs pertinent to the naturalistic case process. It is most useful as a design for testing the effectiveness of interventions and evaluation of the treatment process. It can be successfully used in knowledge building in the testing of interventions under varying conditions with clients of differing populations or groups.

The design has been extensively developed in the literature by methodologists in social work and in the social sciences. For this reason, the design will be only highlighted here, as the reader should consult the substantive technical literature cited and available on this subject.[76] As the design has been applied largely within a behavioral approach to treatment, Nelsen has presented an especially good analysis of the issues and methodology in single-subject research, when the approach is nonbehavioral.[77]

A good overview of single-subject or single-case design, pertinent issues, and problems in implementation is also presented by contributors to the *Handbook of Clinical Social Work.*[78] For our purposes here, we suggest that use of the single-subject design, which is operational within the case process and aimed at empirically based practice, can be used in knowledge building and discovery. It can be especially useful when it is applied broadly to nonbehavioral, as well as behavioral and task-centered, treatment approaches. Its essence is to measure outcome variables or intervention goals (targets) and to monitor the effects of intervention over time intervals. An important issue related to application of the design within nonbehavioral approaches, however, is that—in these approaches—there is predominant utilization of theory in practice decisions and in setting long term goals. Nelsen suggests that instrumental goals that are measurable and more immediate may be utilized within the context of long range treatment goals. She states:

Instrumental goals are implied by the assumptions that are inherent in the theories. For example, the assumption that people who cannot express anger openly may turn it on themselves and become depressed justifies the instrumental goal that a depressed client learn to express anger openly. . . . To treat depression, a practitioner might select the client's recognition of his or her fears about expressing anger as an instrumental goal that is likely to have to be achieved in treatment sessions before the client can learn to express anger openly in day-to-day life.[79]

By using the design to measure progress toward recognition of the fear (instrumental goal), specified objective measurable steps may be needed on the way toward achievement of this goal. Whether behavioral, task-centered, psychosocial, problem-solving, or other approaches are used, the design requires specificity and operationalized variables for measurement in a time series.

We emphasize that the single-subject design is not a singular design, but an assemblage of varying patterns or designs that relate to differential goals or needs of the case. Tripodi has presented eleven different single-subject modes of design for evaluating single case interventions that relate to four different levels of design for case study.[80] These four levels of design include:

1 Hypothetical-Developmental,
2 Quantitative-Descriptive,
3 Correlational Designs,
4 Cause-Effect Designs.

Thus, the practitioner has some range in formulating a single-case design. The designs are fundamentally grounded in the experimental and quasi-experimental designs explicated in general research texts.[81] They fall within the positivistic-empiricist assumptions in science. Therefore, objectivity, experimental manipulation for control of error and bias, independence of observations, and randomness or representativeness are fundamental. In single-subject designs, the independent variable or treatment intervention is manipulated so as to assess its effect on client change over time and with the client serving as his or her own control. Though the authors we have cited, such as Tripodi, Jayaratne and Levy, and Hersen and Barlow, describe several forms of single-subject design, the most common form in use tends to be the AB design: A = baseline, or no intervention, and B = intervention procedure. The measurement of change in target problem(s) or behavior(s) is at selected points over time and compared with the baseline. This design can be easily administered in everyday case practice and can serve the practitioner as a beginning step in the study of a selected problem. Its disadvantage is that it is tedious and when the client's problems are urgent, as in crisis, a baseline observation period is contraindicated.

The ABA and ABAB designs that go beyond the AB design are difficult to implement. The ABA design, which interrupts the intervention with a return to baseline, or no treatment, status to determine whether negative behavior resumes, is not usually in the best interest of the client being served. It may be used occasionally, however, since a return to baseline may occur under natural circumstances where treatment is interrupted. Extension of the design to ABAB, where after the withdrawal of intervention for a selected time period, intervention is resumed and progress is measured, is also difficult to implement, unless it should occur under natural conditions. In addition to the designs as described, the practitioner may choose a multiple-baseline design. In this design, different goals or targets may be measured as effects of an intervention strategy. Flowers, for example in chapter 12, used the multiple-baseline for testing the effectiveness of an intervention sequence on different aggressive, acting-out behaviors of an out-of-control school child.

These basic designs as presented offer opportunity for varying observations and measurements in before/after, longitudinal, and interrupted-time series designs.

The literature, as cited, has provided detailed, technical advice for implementation and full discussion of the assumptions, issues, and problems involved. Our focus here is to suggest that the practitioner experiment with the design as a device for measuring the success of treatment interventions under varying conditions and with varying problems, since it is particularly adaptable to the naturalistic case process. It can be most useful in measuring singularities in change, such as target problems, behaviors, or tasks. Using replication procedures, it can provide an alternative to the group design for achieving generalizations in practice.[82]

SUMMARY

This chapter has emphasized reflective inquiry and research investigation within the context of clinical practice. The empirical scientific thrust has adhered to the logical assumptions of empiricism and suggested that a design or pattern would serve to structure the clinical, heuristic investigation. The individual hypothetical-developmental, descriptive, and quasi-experimental designs were discussed as strategies in exploration, investigation, and theory development.

A creative, openminded, questioning stance is expected of the practitioner as he or she uses clinical knowledge and skill in helping clients. In the search for explanations of unexplained phenomena observed in clinical practice, or in the attempt to build conceptual structures and more effective approaches, there are some guidelines within traditional science that can aid in reflective inquiry. These guidelines offer only general directions because the practitioner will formulate a pattern or design to guide the inquiry and subsequent data collection.

1. Observation of incoming clinical data. Observe the client or client group's verbal and nonverbal communication, affective response or release, actions and interactions, decision making, etc., within varying psychosocial or ecological contexts. These observations may stimulate new ideas, novel interventions, or questioning of known theoretical concepts. They may add to uncertainties under given conditions, raise new questions about timing, about the practitioner's significance for the client or client group, or about other clinical issues. We emphasize that the practitioner should begin from his or her own empirical, clinical data to ask questions as to the adequacy of epistemology in understanding the phenomena at hand and the conditions for effecting change. The practitioner will want to raise questions within a biopsychosocial systems framework, i.e., questions that are consistent with the duality and interaction of person-environment.
2. Identification of problem with questions for study within a specified domain.
3. Consideration of concepts, theories, or what is known about the identified problem situation from literature and research.
4. Classification or categorization of specific observed phenomena,

things, or events (variables) that are the objects of the study domain.

5. Summarization of the estimated relationship between the categorized things (variables) as observed under given conditions into simple generalizations, or preliminary hypotheses, which can be experimented with in practice. These will be only general estimates, but they compose the working tools and logic from which to begin any systematic inquiry.

6. Formulation of a design for study (i.e., hypothetical-developmental, descriptive-comparative, quasi-experimental) depending on the stated objectives and rigor that can be maintained in the clinical process. If the intervention is descriptive, comparative, or evaluative of verbatim or summarized case process, steps need to be taken to insure the accumulation of data within the study domain.

7. Limitation in focus of study domain to few variable relationships, especially when quasi-experimental or experimental designs are considered, so that conditions can be manipulated under which the preliminary hypotheses or the treatment progress can be estimated as valid.

Experimental hypothesis testing can be initiated in practice to lead to more rigorous and robust methods for generalization. Furthermore, statistical procedures are being developed for testing hypotheses and change patterns in groups, when data collected over a time series contain incomplete observations.[83] This is often true in small sample studies where clients miss their appointments and interrupt the data collection series. Use of the computer in analysis and solution of statistical problems for practical application is being vastly accelerated so that it is possible for the practitioner to engage himself or herself with research colleagues in designs that investigate small and large samples with more robust analyses. It is imperative that practitioners have a good grasp of scientific logic and the basic essentials for research that is grounded to their clinical data.

CHAPTER 5

An Alternative Paradigm in Heuristic Inquiry

The conventional logic of scientific inquiry has sought bias-free objectivity and truth within a paradigm of observation-hypothesis-experiment. It is embodied within logical positivism-empiricism. That is, inductive reasoning and general laws are built upon the hypothesis deduced (particulars) about generalizations, that have been subjected to confirmation or falsification. Within this pattern, theories can be constructed and validated. Empirical research in social work and in the social sciences operate, in general, within this paradigm.

Other schools of thought in philosophy and the social sciences have also emerged, such as social phenomenology, hermeneutic interpretation, and the qualitative methodologies that tend toward more idiosyncratic, analytic, and inductive logic. Those social scientists and clinicians who have attempted to capture further the nuances of human experience and action in research have considered an alternative paradigm to that which embraces logical positivism-empiricism; this alternative is known as the "new paradigm." For a comprehensive discussion of philosophy and methodologies within the new paradigm, we suggest *Human Inquiry*, edited by Peter Reason and John Rowan.[1] The contributors to this volume represent different thinking by respected social scientists. Miles and Huberman note that it is getting harder to find any methodologists solidly encamped in one epistemology or the other. More and more "quantitative" methodologists operating from a logical positivist stance are using naturalistic and phenomenological approaches to complement tests, surveys, and structural interviews. On the other side, an increasing number of ethnographers and qualitative researchers are using predesigned conceptual frameworks and prestructured instrumentation. . . . Few logical positivists will now dispute the validity and explanatory importance of subjective data, and few phenomenologists still practice pure hermeneutics.[2]

Where the orthodox paradigm has sought "objectivity" and rigor with stringent controls for bias and error in research, the alternative or new paradigm is also systematic and rigorous in its search for truth, but is "objectively-subjective."[3] It recognizes the presence of the researcher's own perceptions, beliefs, and goals as interwoven with the contours of reality; and it incorporates an interactive dialectical paradigm, using methods that are collaborative, experiential, reflexive, and action oriented.

The new paradigm attempts to synthesize simple, intuitive inquiry with the objectivity of the more conventional paradigm. Reason and Rowan voice clear opposition to some aspects of the orthodox, or conventional, paradigm on several counts. We find some of these objections particularly relevant. They note that in the orthodox conventional paradigm, people are seen as units to be manipulated in isolation from their social contexts and stripped of what gives their action meaning. Second, they note that operational definitions, independent and dependent variables, etc., assume that people can be reduced to a set of variables which are somehow equivalent across persons and situations. Third, they consider that the reduction of persons or groups to variables does not allow for understanding in depth or knowing human phenomena as wholes. Fourth, people and processes are turned into things; and finally, a "quantophrenia," which represents too much measurement where results may be "statistically significant, but humanly insignificant."[4]

These indictments bear consideration, especially as the alternatives in research that support a new paradigm have emerged from studies of social scientists, philosophers, and clinicians across disciplines. Pieper, in social work, has identified a "heuristic approach" that is, in general, within the assumptions of new paradigm research and also has discounted some of the assumptions of orthodox empiricism as pseudo-scientific.[5] Bruyn, from a sociological perspective, has defined "new empiricist" researchers in participant observation and in phenomenological traditions that he considers "break fundamentally with those of the older schools of scientific empiricism."[6] The failure of value-free objectivity in science in the conception of the positivists should not lead us to relativism at the other extreme, an extreme that rejects objectivity and truth as only relative. The new paradigm tends to fall between these polarities. Rogers[7] and Maslow[8] in the clinical world have for many years called for new models of science that would be more relevant to human beings. Rogers, however, credits Polanyi[9] as leading the new developments in the philosophy of science and also cites as influential the new developments in physics that have changed views of the cosmos and understandings of limitations in science.[10] Openness to the unexpected has also been a factor.[11]

The new paradigm would appear to entertain special possibilities for the social work practitioner, since the person is construed within the paradigm as a holistic human system within its natural context.[12] Though clinical work associated with the paradigm has been largely identified within the realm of cognitive humanistic, existential, and "client-centered" approaches, it would appear to offer possibilities for discovery in the more traditional psychosocial and problem-solving mode in social work. Behaviorism, however, reflects the reductionist-deductive logic of positivism-empiricism and has been seen in philosophical opposition to this movement.

In view of the prevalence of a logical-empiricist view of science among researchers in social work and the current questioning of its utility in exploring social phenomena, Heineman (Pieper) has recently suggested further examination of the scientific imperatives for social work research.[13] She has stimulated a running debate in *Social Service Review* with prestigious social work academicians, such as Schuerman, Gyarfas, Geismar, Hudson, and Brekke,[14] and has made a real contribution toward the stimulation of argument related to the foundations of social work research, which she also linked to debate in philosophy of science and other social science disciplines. We concur with her rebuttal to Geismar that there is in social work "a distressing absence of critical and analytic discussion of the foundations of social work research." Though Heineman-Pieper and Brekke each feels misinterpreted by the other, it is clear that both authors essentially support critical examination of scientific assumptions in research and are attuned to concerns for alternatives in methodologies and approaches. In this vein, Goldstein also has proposed that social workers in practice "develop their reflective, theory building talents and be able to fathom the subjective world of their clients."[15] His approach coincides with the subjective aspect of the new paradigm.

Hoffman has also advocated a paradigm for systems change that incorporates circular epistemology in the study of interactional influences in treatment of the family.[16]

It is clear that the concept of questioning in science and its methods of rationality are also emerging in social work. As this questioning falls within the rubric of scientific open-mindedness, curiosity, and search that we are encouraging in this book, our presentation of the "new paradigm" will be in some detail. This is not meant to imply that we stand in opposition to orthodox empirical research, but only that other paradigms and methods should be examined and used, where appropriate, in the discovery of knowledge.

DIALECTICAL LOGIC

New paradigm research, that is subjective-objective, draws from a conception of realism and dialectical logic. Reality is not considered from a subject-object split, where reality is "all out there, objective and therefore discoverable," or else, all in the mind as subjective.[17] The position taken is that one should think dialectically, and view reality as process—neither as subject nor as object, but as both. The logic of realism purports that "theories have a characteristic content. They are to be taken as descriptions of mechanisms which might be responsible for observable patterns of events and properties of things."[18] Harré introduces two concepts, *reference* and *demonstration*, that help to clarify the position on realism.[19] He asserts that for the realists, science displays two interrelated conceptual systems. First,

an analytical scheme required to reveal, identify, partition, and classify the items which make up the field of interest . . . [and second] an explanatory scheme required to formulate theories descriptive of the mechanisms productive of the items revealed in analysis.[20]

Since the reality to be studied is subjective-objective in the alternative paradigm, it is reasonable that validity must be considered within a relational context, both of the observer and what is to be observed. The logic rejects the idea of one truth, and acknowledges there may be different ways of being right or wrong, or different interpretations.[21] (These ideas do suggest a relativism in scientific explanation.)

For the social work practitioner, this paradigm would mean taking into account dialectically what is known and experienced by the practitioner in the clinical study, as well as what is known by and reported by the client. Reflexivity in this dialectical exchange means that the practitioner has some personal involvement and is not a sterile, purposive scientist, drawing information in a mechanical manner from the client.

Reason and Rowan note that validity of data, utilizing this new paradigm, would require three assessments: (a) descriptive, (b) trying-out, and (c) meaning.[22] The descriptive assessment asks for a description of the phenomena that are being observed. Can one discriminate between what might be there and other possibilities? The second assessment, or trying-out action, is taken to make a change. The question, then, is whether the changes brought about are—in fact— results of the intentional change? This question is no different from that posed in an orthodox empirical single-subject design, where change is measured. The third assessment, for validity, questions the understanding, meaning, and interpretation of the phenomena that have been observed. Intersubjectivity of the interpretation will no doubt exist, as it will be responsive to beliefs of people who share a common cultural background. In this paradigm the concern for validity, however, is to yield what is fruitful or useful, rather than placing sole emphasis on what is truth. It can thus be seen, from this review of the logic, why the methods are identified as collaborative, experiential, reflexive, and action-oriented. Researchers using a dialectical paradigm have used it in varying research projects and in the clinical interview. We will explore ways in which the social work practitioner may find these methods fruitful, especially as the expanding analytic scheme is expected to bring new explanatory insights.

THE NEW PARADIGM: STEPS IN INQUIRY

Delineation of steps in inquiry within the new paradigm has been well elucidated by Douglas and Moustakas[23] and by Rowan;[24] and these steps are linked to our discussion of three phases in clinical inquiry that are in keeping with the premises of the paradigm.

Beginning Phase of the Inquiry. The practitioner's search for new understanding within this "new paradigm" would essentially be initiated by stimulation of ideas, concerns, questions, gaps in knowledge, etc., that emerge within the ongoing case. Spontaneous reflection on an issue by the practitioner may be further supported by consulting the literature or by talking with a colleague, to get feedback from others as to their ideas on the subject. Much contemplative action and searching into the problem are suggested, where the creative practitioner becomes immersed or consumed by it. This is the time of excitement, sharing, and readjustment of ideas in feedback from others. In addition, in this paradigm, the practitioner must reflect on his or her own frame of reference relevant to the concern. An internal search of self to know where one is coming from makes explicit the values held by the practitioner. This self-examination is not atypical in social work, as self-awareness is an essential ingredient for the professional helper. This self-search in the desire to know and understand a problem, however, promotes the experiential quality that is relevant to the paradigm. The thinking at this stage in the model is "creative intervention" and testing.[25] It is the phase of thinking that is generally equivalent to preparation and incubation in launching the process of discovery, as we have noted earlier, and a key to learning from experience.[26] It also begins the analytic process that is represented in "description" and "trying out" for validity.

Problem Investigation. The practitioner has now identified the problem domain for investigation and is ready to design a plan or formulate an active approach to collect data and, secondly, to analyze and to derive meaning from the data. This stage thus corresponds to "method, analysis, and results" in the traditional research cycle.

The practitioner has used intuition[27] and scientific judgment in sharpening impressions, formulations, or preliminary concepts that he or she is now ready to cycle as a specific research problem for investigation. In this model of inquiry, the design or action can be loosely structured and data collection can be observational, experiential, descriptive of phenomena, or experimental. Key factors of the model require it to be collaborative, experiential, and reflexive, and there is a cycling and recycling of the data collection and analytic processes to make sense and meaning out of the data. Actually, as the cycles are repeated, they move from looseness to rigor and greater specificity.

Formulation may be revised and further clarified as they are examined and reexamined in multiple research cycles. This "trying out" has validity support from the feedback of collaborators or colleagues. In addition, the client is also invited into a collaborative or coresearcher role, where the problem as experienced can be studied, with feedback in the worker-client interaction. The dialectical dimension is therefore expected to stimulate increased refinement and greater accuracy in formulations. It is also thought that the experience and self-disclosure of the practitioner will tend to stimulate understanding and disclosure by the client. Also, it is believed "when we know a thing from our experience, its meaning can be recognized in others."[28]

The dialectical in thinking and experience—in the practitioner-client and collegial collaborations—represents the "subjective-objective" of the paradigm. As we have indicated, emphasis is also placed on the fact that there must be multiple cycles of data collection, analysis, and meaning, where categories, concepts, or theories are defined, revised, redefined, differentiated, or integrated until there tends to be unity in consensus and completeness.

It is admitted that there can be threat to validity in these processes through "unaware projection and through consensus collusion."[29] Some heuristic guides, suggested by Reason and Rowan, to increase the validity are: (a) self-awareness on the part of coresearchers, (b) coresearchers' maintaining active exploration of their own inner strivings, (c) insistence that research include reaction of peers or colleagues, (d) multiple research cycles and feedback, (e) use of different forms of knowledge, such as experiential, practice, report, and logical reasoning knowledge, (f) coresearcher's explicit attempts to contradict or disprove the evidence, (g) comparison of methods or data from other sources, and (h) replication.[30]

It is clear from the foregoing description that within the new paradigm there is concern for rigor and validity in investigation. The multiple cycling of the problem being studied is especially supportive of validational procedures. In addition, phenomena can be studied more deeply and from different perspectives as the recycling of the problem under study is continued. Three ways to recycle are suggested:

1. If the practitioner is interested in a descriptive design, with descriptions of clients/case phenomena, he or she should start with simple descriptions and the construction of crude categories, which can be cycled toward increasingly subtle, logical distinctions.

2. If the practitioner is interested in finding causal factors or connections between phenomena, he or she should begin by observ-

ing relationships qualitatively within cycles and progress toward use of quantitative measures in later cycling.
3. If the practitioner's interest is in moving beyond the analytical and into the discovery of meaning, he or she can start with interpretations and move toward deeper and more critical understandings. This leads us to phase three of investigation.

Problem Resolution or Explanation. The final phase of the investigation represents the ultimate findings and interpretation. The whole of the investigation is examined for synthesis and meaning. The findings of the specific and particular are examined with regard to more general and universal meanings. This model emphasizes sensitivity, the experiential, and participatory action in the practitioner-client interchange in discovery. It is consistent with the dialectical view of truth as "becoming," for new possibilities are always emerging.[31]

The dialectical tenets of the new paradigm have been presented to explicate utilization of the collaborative, experiential, reflexive, and participatory methods. The methods require extensive thought and judgment, as well as sensitivity and experiential data. The paradigm can be used by the practitioner in the naturalistic case study.

Though many of its major proponents are "client-centered" (Rogerian) or humanistic (Goldstein) in clinical orientation, its philosophy and methods could have wider theoretical application. First, the dialectical is harmonious with systems theory in its holistic orientation, information exchange, and feedback loops. Second, it is pertinent to system exchanges with individuals and groups, and it can thus be responsive to contextual factors in the person-situation configuration. Third, it offers possibilities for investigation, formulations, and discovery in the ongoing case process, and findings could be replicated to increase validity and also fed into larger research projects, where the more traditional and robust research methods are utilized. The dialectical view and concerns regarding traditional empiricism tend increasingly to be subjects of discussion in current literature of philosophy of science.[32] There is also a need for general discussion in social work of the logic and fruitfulness of basic assumptions in science and the research relevant to problems encountered in social work.

Increased clarity is needed with regard to the phenomena of explanation. Garfinkel has argued that "there is an ethics of explanation" and the choice of "one explanatory frame over another has value presuppositions and value consequences."[33] He asserts that:

explanations can be dependent on values without thereby becoming merely relative. For insofar as we can say that the values of one explanatory frame are more appropriate to the situation, or more just, or more conducive to human welfare than another, we can argue for the superiority of the relevant explanation.[34]

This attempt to derelativize explanation has been considered from a good-bad reference point using values, rather than what is truth. In the search for valid knowledge to guide the practitioner's action and to understand psychosocial phenomena, questions of the nature of scientific predictions and explanations need to be further addressed.

SUMMARY

The orthodox paradigm that incorporates hypothesis-deduction in scientific inquiry is reviewed with reference to assumptions of objectivity and the control of bias or error. An alternative paradigm is discussed that allows for the experiential and is considered as objective-subjective. The alternative paradigm incorporates dialectical logic and uses methods that are collaborative, experiential, reflexive, and action-oriented. Three phases in inquiry are delineated as a beginning (preparatory) phase, problem investigation phase, and problem resolution or explanation phase. These phases correspond to the phases of conventional inquiry and there is also concern for validity. Importance, however, is placed on knowledge gained that is fruitful or useful rather than sole emphasis on what is truth.

The interpretive methods for finding meaning in hermeneutics draw on the dialectical process. We have chosen, however, to present the philosophies and research perspectives of hermeneutics in a separate chapter (see chapter 6). The clinical processes and actions would be the substance from which interpretations and understandings or hermeneutics would be derived, but the research interpretive-analysis would take place largely outside of the naturalistic, ongoing case process.

Hermeneutics: Philosophy and Perspectives in Inquiry

The practitioner interested in a dialectical or dialogical paradigm in knowledge building could consider the philosophy and principles of hermeneutics for understanding and interpretation. Clinical case activity as ongoing script or text can be the subject matter for interpretation and insights. The communicative relationship between subject and object is given full recognition in hermeneutic activity, with the objective of understanding. This process is referred to as "exegesis or interpretation," and known as "hermeneutics." Rules that guide successful interpretation not only promote efficiency but also safeguard the validity in interpretation.[1] In the history of hermeneutics, polarities have occurred in the development of thought between a more methodological emphasis and an experiential, ontological emphasis. Communication of subject and object, however, is fundamental to the approach.

The assumption is that people recognize and become aware of themselves as individuals through interaction and interchange with other human beings. Bleicher has asserted that access to others is possible only by indirect means, which are initially experienced as gestures, sounds, and actions, and that it is only in the process of understanding that one moves from the external signs to understanding the underlying inner life. One's own life, also, provides material for understanding the inner life of others and the establishment of a communion of the human spirit.[2] It is postulated that an object or person can only reveal himself to a kindred spirit and that understanding begins with the establishment of an "affinity," or relationship, between the subject and the object through their communication. Understanding is thus a dialogical process that is explicated on a model of human discourse. These ideas parallel the emphasis on relationship as fundamental to the helping process in clinical social work.

The communication of subject-object in hermeneutics is not generally centered on a person-to-person encounter has such, but has historically been concerned with meaning and understanding of human experience from the written texts. Hermeneutics, as a philosophical perspective, tends more toward general concern of understanding and interpretation rather than toward a method with clear criteria for the achievement of understanding.[3] It is noted by Palmer that the "task of interpretation and the meaning of understanding are different— more elusive, more historical—in relation to a work than in relation to an 'object.' "[4] He explains this as the work of words having something communicated through them, whereas an "object" can be either a work or a natural object. The interpretation of works has been generally devoted to sacred texts and to literary understanding. Contemporary hermeneutics, however, is more broadly conceived than the understanding and interpretation of texts and is applicable in the interpretation of meanings to different disciplines, including the social sciences.

With this brief description of the communal nature of understanding in hermeneutics, we will discuss aspects of the philosophy and origin of hermeneuties before moving on to discuss methodological frames and the application for achieving understandings and knowledge in clinical social work.

Philosophy and Origin. Though hermeneutics is of ancient origin, it has more recently emerged in Anglo-American thought. Hermeneutics is derived from the Greek word *hermeneutikos* (fr. *hermeneuein*), "to interpret," and is defined as the science of interpretation and explanation.[5] For many centuries, it was considered a subdiscipline of philology[6] and was used to scrutinize contending texts for authenticity and meaning. It emerged into special prominence in the sixteenth century, particularly around the Catholic-Protestant debate as to the authenticity and meaning of texts of the Bible.[7] Some of the earliest discussions of hermeneutics in an Anglo-American context were among biblical scholars and students of history of religion, who were concerned with the interpretation of sacred texts.

Hermeneutics, as it was shaped in the nineteenth century, began to take on a different complexion, especially among the intellectuals in Germany. It became more than the critique and interpretation of texts and "began to ask the difficult questions about the nature and the objectives of historical knowledge as such; indeed of knowledge in general."[8]

Friederich Schleiermacher, German philosopher and a founder of the University of Berlin (1768–1834), extended the ideas of hermeneutics to found a base for historical hermeneutics. He is credited with creating "hermeneutics as a general historical-interpretative methodology almost single handed."[9] He drew on his careful study of texts to develop his ideas. There had been no "understanding" of history apart from the continual movement from the particular or event to the total or comprehensive, and back to the particular, in widening circles, to make clear an interpretation. This was known as the "hermeneutic circle."[10] Schleiermacher, from a philosophical stance,

brought the problem of understanding and interpretation into the very center of universal human experience . . . in the practice of living. . . . [He noted that] to understand meaning, one has to literally "identify" oneself with the actor.[11]

Hermeneutics thus would involve members of one culture trying to experience that of another.

Actually, hermeneutics in the nineteenth century was developing as a reaction to what was considered the intellectual imperialism of positivism, inductivism, and scientism that required the model and standards of the natural sciences for determining any genuine knowledge.[12] The primary task was seen, especially by Wilhelm Dilthey, German philosopher and historian (1833–1911) who came after Schleiermacher, as exploring comprehensively the historical and tradition-bound nature of understanding.[13]

Dilthey set about to determine what was distinctive about humanistic and historical knowledge and to reveal its characteristic subject matter, aims, and methods, in a systematic manner that would meet and challenge the belief that only the natural sciences could provide "objective knowledge."[14] His early work tried to establish the independence of the cultural sciences (*Geisteswissenschaften*, or, human sciences) from the natural sciences.[15] Also, at the time, a historical consciousness was emerging. It was actually in the twentieth century, due primarily to the influence of the phenomenological movement identified with Edmund Husserl (1859–1938) and to Martin Heidegger's (1889–1976) publication of *Being and Time*,[16] that hermeneutics began to emerge into prominence in European continental philosophy. Actually, it flourished there well before being recognized in England and America.

Heidegger proposed that

understanding is a mode of being, rather than a mode of knowledge . . . [and] not, therefore concerned with a method which—once designed— could be learned and employed by professional hermeneuticians to resolve their conflicts of interpretation.[17]

His interest was in the ontological foundations of understanding, which people come to by the fact of their being in the world. Heidegger investigated understanding at an earlier point, beyond the "reality-founding, reality disclosing act," not as a mental process but as an ontological process. He asserted that "all understanding is temporal, intentional, historical."[18]

Some of the more contemporary contributors to hermeneutic understanding and interpretation have been Hans Georg Gadamer[19] and Jurgen Habermas[20] of Germany and Emilio Betti[21] of Italy. Of particular interest to our discussion here is Gadamer's idea of dialectical hermeneutics, which we will present in some detail. Gadamer believed that the contemporary concept of experience was too much oriented toward knowing as "a perceptual act and knowledge as a body of conceptual data."[22] In that sense, experience was considered more oriented to scientific knowledge—with its tendency to objectify —than to consideration of the historical nature of experience. He further believed that, in all experience, there is a structure of questioning, "is it thus or thus? . . . Real questioning . . . presupposes openness, i.e., the answer is unknown—and at the same time it necessarily specifies boundaries."[23] The problem of posing the right question was also recognized. When one questions the text in hermeneutic dialogue, in a deeper sense the text also poses questions to the interpreter. Gadamer suggested that in hermeneutical dialogue "the general subject in which one is immersed—both the interpreter and the text—is the tradition, the heritage."[24] The interpreter's partner in the dialogue is the text in its written form. Thus, there is need to find a way to understand, through the give and take of dialogue, between the text and the interpreter. In this question-answer encounter, the text becomes a living, present-oriented dialogue, with all of its meaning within a tradition.

According to Gadamer, to interpret a text or to understand it, was to recognize the existence of one's prejudice and tradition as well as the fact that "the past also defined the ground the interpreter himself occupies when he understands."[25] The interpreter should question and understand also what is *not* said. Going back behind what is said is, of course, customary in clinical practice, where clarification and understanding are essential elements. Therefore, the text (the historical acts or events) is approached in questioning form within the interpreter's own horizon, which is broadened in the dialectic of the dialogue and fuses with that of the acts or text in meaning. The dialectic of questions and answers works out the fusion of the horizons, as both are universal and grounded in being.[26] Gadamer considered self-understanding and self-awareness as a beginning imperative. He instructed that "a person trying to understand a text is prepared for it to tell him something."[27] The understanding of one's own "foremeanings" and awareness of prejudices must be part of the preparedness of the hermeneutic interpreter.

Some of the early philosophical writers, who stressed forestructure of understanding, or preunderstanding, saw all understanding as being prejudicial. Gadamer stressed that, for the hermeneutically trained interpreter, the important thing is awareness of personal bias so that the text may be open to the interpreter to assert its message as opposed to the interpreter's own prejudices and foremeanings. He thought that "understanding is not to be thought of so much as an action of one's subjectivity, but as the placing of oneself within a tradition, in which past and present are constantly fused."[28]

Gadamer further explained that truly scientific work involves awareness of the hermeneutic situation, which is "the situation in which we find ourselves vis-à-vis the tradition we wish to understand."[29] He also believed that human dialogue can be treated as analogous to the interpretation of a text. Just as a person seeks to reach an understanding with another in a dialogue concerning an object, so the interpreter understands the object of which the text speaks. In their dialogue, they come to some understanding and are thus bound to one another in a new community. "The central task of the interpreter is to find the question to which a text presents the answer."[30]

Gadamer identified understanding as experience of the world and noted that experiences of the world "do not consist of calculation and method. The introduction of method into the hermeneutical process leads to the objectification of the object and the subject's mastery over it."[31] He argued that the modern obsession with method had distorted and concealed the ontological character of understanding. In his view, all understanding includes interpretation and "interpretation is necessarily a historical process, continuously elaborating on the meaning grasped in an understanding and on the meaning of this understanding for itself."[32] Gadamer was criticized, however, for giving no standard for ascertaining whether an interpretation is legitimate or not.[33]

Jurgen Habermas has been considered the most "prominent living heir of the 'Frankfurt School' in German social sciences."[34] His consideration of the "model of rational agreement" demonstrated that the rationality of discourse in cultural sciences, comparable to that of empirical-analytical sciences, cannot be codified without reference to the social dimensions of the debate; that, in other words, "the epistemology of hermeneutics cannot be detached from the sociology of communications."[35] He also was not opposed to methods. He considered that the human mode can be sustained only if two interests are pursued, the technical and the practical. The first activity of interest is manifested in work; the second, in communication. In work, there is the aim to control nature, to find order, and possibilities for prediction and potential control. This he linked to the empirical-analytical sciences.

In the second activity of interest, the communication or the practical is where the interest is reflected in the cultural and "understanding" sciences.[36] Habermas parallels the technical and practical interests in search for truth or consensus, finding that each only approaches the ideal. Bauman, however, asserts that Habermas "brings the methodology of understanding sciences as close to the ideal of truth-guided criticism as the rules of experimental practice brought empirical analytic sciences."[37]

Habermas used psychoanalysis as "a model for a dialectical-hermeneutical social science."[38] He considered the objectivity of historical process in association with the motivation of the actor, wherein the actor's intentions may have been repressed and must be known for understanding. The notion has been popular that psychoanalysis is a hermeneutic discipline, since it refers to interpretation and elucidation of meanings.[39] In Eagle's review of these ideas, however, he considered that there was failure to deal adequately with issues of reliability.

As one peruses the literature on hermeneutics, it can be seen that the philosophy and methodological forms of reference have differed greatly. To summarize the meaning of hermeneutics since Dilthey in some historical order, Tice and Slavens have identified hermeneutics, along with its philosophical leaders, as coming to mean at least six different things:

(1) the basic theory of interpretation, especially of texts (attributed to Schleiermacher, though he did more than this);
(2) a particular theory of or approach to the cultural (human) sciences (Dilthey, Emilio Betti);
(3) a characteristic of philosophy that views understanding through interpretation as a basic mode of being human (Heidegger);
(4) a type of existential phenomenology, that combines motifs from Dilthy, Husserl, and Heidegger and that focuses on ontological not methodological inquiry (Hans-Georg Gadamer);
(5) a hermeneutic phenomenology, that uses numbers (1) through (4) as resources and that focuses on theory for interpreting cultural symbols, chiefly in texts (Paul Ricoeur); and
(6) an aspect of critical theory that utilizes psychoanalytic models to detect the causes of distorted understanding and communication, purveys a somewhat Marxian analysis of material conditions, and focuses on the critique of ideology (Karl-Otto Apel and Jurgen Habermas).[40]

Howard has also identified the current theories of understanding in philosophical hermeneutics in *Three Faces of Hermeneutics*, using the classification of analytic, psychosocial, and ontological.[41] A major implication is that positivism, in its search for logical precision in dealing with problems of language and meaning, has also contributed to the growth and development of hermeneutics. Howard comments: "To the degree that positivism has provoked hermeneutics into rethinking itself it is now hermeneutics' turn to provoke positivism to the investigation of its own presuppositions."[42]

IMPLICATIONS FOR CLINICAL INQUIRY

It can be clearly seen that, as hermeneutics has evolved, controversy has existed regarding the methodological versus experiential-historical characteristics of interpretation in understanding. Since the place of understanding is larger than that of interpretation in literary, theological, and philosophical disciplines, it is significant that other disciplines are also beginning to use a hermeneutic frame of reference or so-called methodology. Shoshani, in social work, has recently employed the hermeneutic frame of reference for investigating the core ideas of Gordon Hamilton.[43] From the literature of Hamilton and others, she was able to interact in hermeneutic dialogue to interpret meanings and conceptual understandings of Hamilton's ideas.

Bleicher has sought to clarify a fundamental issue of the hermeneutic perspective in his discussion of differences between Habermas and Gadamer. He thought that both theorists, in their focus on "subjectively intended meaning," accepted the "meaning of an act as defined by the actor," rather than considering "both actor and interpreter as partners within a dialogical-dialectical situation."[44] The interactive relationship that generates "fusion of horizon" justifies "understanding of subjectively intended meaning," since an interpretation will be accepted, rejected, sensed, or changed in the "dialectical process of understanding."[45]

The dialogical-dialectical dimension means that theory and concept formation will bear evidence of their historical context. The clarification of meanings with an object that can "answer back" and agree to, or refute, meanings can stimulate a theoretical framework for the explication of meaning, rather than statements for falsification or confirmation. It is a "reading," or an interpretation, of the self-interpretation of others, within a context of socially shared meaning. Interpretations are more and more clarified and judged in reference to their fruitfulness and potential for opening up new ways of understanding.

The validity and objectivity of interpretations are thus conceived of in dialogical terms. The analytic and methodological perspective, however, is apparent in the consideration of internal checks for reliability, such as patterns of relatedness of the phenomena. Therefore, the interpreter would try to formulate concepts and categories dialogically, i.e., by confronting his own concepts with those employed by the object and vice versa.

From our descriptive sketch of a hermeneutic perspective from different points of view, it is clear that it could be used in naturalistic case research within a method of participant observation or reflective clinical work.

Discovery and research within the hermeneutic dialectical model would allow for a subjectivity that brings about a fusion of the subject-object horizons in a participatory observational understanding of the client-situation in its contextual and historical reality. This would require a major emphasis on self-awareness by the practitioner to clarify himself and his biases apart from the client, a self-awareness which is fundamental to traditional clinical social work. Thus, if the practitioner becomes socialized into the particular form of life of his object while being able to widen the "horizon" of the object through offering a differing account of a given situation, new understanding and discoveries that could also suggest clinical theoretical revision may emerge in this dialogical process.

In the participatory-observation process in case activity, it is possible to test out on the spot a low-level empirical hypothesis and to corroborate some findings already observed. It would eliminate the practitioner-researcher's assuming the role of the "participant outsider" from an objectivist perspective. However, a hazard is overidentification, which can obscure objectivity and interfere with the helping process.

With some modification, participant-observation can be used successfully in work with the family as a group. In fact, the structural intervention modes have stressed the importance of the practitioner's joining the family system in balancing and unbalancing strategies.[46]

The practitioner may find the hermeneutic perspective more useful in research that is similar to the interpretation of texts of historical materials. He or she may use the transcripts of taped interviews for reflection, and the question-answer dialogue for interpretation and understanding. Whether the live interview, taped interviews, or historical materials are used, some elements for consideration by the practitioner in the hermeneutic dialogue to achieve understanding are the following:

1. attention to self-awareness;
2. attention to themes in the interchange that flow and are restricted only by the goals and aims of the interview with the client(s);
3. testing out the validity of the claim;
4. participation of the practitioner-client(s) in the dialogue is based on a common interest, in which the need for understanding and change is common to both. (Hypothetically, the client(s) want some kind of change in circumstance or relief, whereas the practitioner also wants change and relief of the client's circumstance, though he may also want to understand unique attitudes, behavior, and constraints within a social context);
5. recognition of the relationship component in the dialogue;
6. recognition that the hermeneutic experience is to understand

differently. "A question . . . posits a preliminary way of seeing; just as understanding is not placeless and empty, so questioning is not without its own horizon of expectations."[47]

In other words, the practitioners' own suppositions must be subject to change. The questioning of the person or the text allows either to answer back and question the horizon of the practitioner or interpreter. There must be an openness to what is said, and it is in this dialogue that a "fusion of horizon" tends to occur—thus, an agreement.

It is in this process that new insights may occur *and* perhaps new discoveries that may be later tested by empirical-analytical standards.

SUMMARY

Hermeneutics is discussed from a historical and methodological perspective with implications for interpretation and understanding of client systems within a dialogical or dialectical mode. The exploration of thoughts, actions, and situations can yield insights and meaning as gleaned from the dialogue of the practitioner-client/other. The hermeneutic perspective offers the opportunity for historical data to be interpreted and understood, which can also be especially useful to direct or clinical practice.

CHAPTER 7

Phenomenological Considerations in Philosophy of Science and Clinical Research

In science, phenomenology deals with the description of actual, concrete phenomena that are devoid of interpretation, explanation, or evaluation.[1] In philosophy, the word has been associated with existentialism, hermeneutics, and research. It considers the proposition that concepts, viewpoints, and methods emerge as a result of directly studying the phenomena of man.[2] Research, therefore, searches for meaning in the events and interactions of persons within given situations.

Phenomenology, as a movement in early twentieth-century philosophy, was especially associated with Edmund Husserl (1859–1938) and before the mid-1930s was largely confined to German thought.[3] Husserl was strongly influenced by his teachers, Franz Bretano (1838–1917), who emphasized descriptive psychology, and Carl Strumpf (1838–1936), founder of experimental psychology.[4] Strumpf also influenced the Lewinans and Gestalt theorists. Though Husserl's ideas shifted greatly over the years, he was especially concerned with the description and analysis of the structures of consciousness, e.g., how "constituent elements of phenomena build up from 'their essences,' " and believed that a basic perception underlies all knowledge and science, a perception which he termed "life-world."[5]

Both in Germany and France, there were many others associated with this movement, including Maurice Merleau-Ponty (1908–1961),

French philosopher and president of the Collège de France. Merleau-Ponty, a contemporary of Jean-Paul Sartre, broke with Sartre when he (Merleau-Ponty) rejected Marxism. Merleau-Ponty drew on Husserl's thought and Gestalt theory in describing structures of consciousness and spoke of a primary perceptual milieu, rather than Husserl's "life-world," as underlying all knowledge and science.[6] He believed in "the interdependence of body and mind, even in perception, and thereby assigned intentional structures to body as well as to mind."[7] For detailed references on those associated with phenomenology, both currently and historically, along with its close ally existentialism, the reader should review *Research Guide to Philosophy* by Tice and Stevens. Also a good historical introduction is Spiegelberg's *The Phenomenological Movement*.[8] For phenomenology as related to social science, see P. Filmer et al., *New Directions in Sociological Theory*.[9]

In 1970, Amedeo Giorgi brought out a volume that defined psychology as a human science based on a phenomenological approach. He identified himself with "Third Force" psychology, but approached the problems of man "as a person from a point of view that comes from within science and from an academic psychological perspective."[10] He thought that "Third Force" psychology—or humanistic psychology—had been considered the domain of clinicians or those interested in personality theory, and he wanted to challenge the perception that the movement was antiscientific or nonscientific. He insisted upon the relevance of *science* for those who want to study the humanistic aspects of man without any concern for method or rigor. His concern, as it has been that of others, is that the human sciences have accepted the natural sciences as model and method, wherein they have failed to give a complete picture of the phenomenon of man or the person.

Giorgi drew on Merleau-Ponty and used the term "structure" in his considerations of phenomenology. The ideas regarding structure are of interest and are relevant to social work and will be presented here. Three orders of structure were identified, which were considered irreducible—(a) the physical, (b) the vital, and (c) the human orders. They were then equated in the following way: (a) physical with stimulus-reflex; (b) vital with situation-instinctive reaction; and (c) human with perceived situation-work. Giorgi saw the challenge as being the latter, that of trying to establish concepts, categories, techniques, and methods that will enable one to work with the dialectic "perceived situation-work."[11]

Giorgi's characterization of psychology as a human science would even more closely relate to clinical social work in its dialogical, dynamic, situational, and holistic aspects. He begins with the phenomenological "life-world" frame of reference and asks the observer to return to the phenomenal origins of any psychological process and then move toward closure. The assumption is that psychological phenomena are dynamic and of temporal nature leading to the necessity for "a constant dialogue among the approach, the method and the phenomena (or content) in any specific research."[12]

Giorgi and others believed that psychology has tended to deal with the behavior of man at levels that are lower than his most integrated functioning, rather than at the human structural level. The more human scientific viewpoint is holistic. Within this framework there is the possibility of integrating external and internal viewpoints. Within the concept of "structure" the behavioral structures are internally related and accessible, from an internal viewpoint, but as they are not wholly private phenomena, they are visible to the external viewpoint because they are in the perceptual world.[13] In clinical research, one would seek to gain an understanding of the conceptual world of the client and to find within a dialogical exchange the meaning they construct regarding events in their lives.[14] Therefore, within a human science paradigm, it can be assumed that a reflexive method would be paramount. It is granted that the observer is connected to the world and that this can be deceptive. However, observations begin with basic phenomena, and the observer seeks the plausibility of possible relationships.

Two different features exist in phenomenological research. One is empirical-phenomenological and the other is hermeneutic activity. The difference existing between hermeneutical phenomenology and the empirical phenomenological in research is related to the origins of the data upon which the methods and the interpretations are derived. Those of empirical-phenomenological psychology begin by collecting descriptive sketches of the subjects' (clients') experience; and then, by systematically and rigorously questioning these descriptions, step by step, they arrive at the structure of the experience.[15]

In hermeneutical phenomenology, the data, as descriptive sketches or protocols, call for interpretations analogous to the interpretation of a text. The descriptions used in empirical phenomenology also meet criteria which have been identified as a text in the necessity to interpret the protocols (texts) as a whole of interconnected meanings and with a potentiality for multiple interpretations.[16] In the hermeneutical act, the interpreter's precomprehension of the phenomenon under investigation is rooted in his experience of the phenomenon. It influences the interpretative act and is considered unavoidable. Phenomenology, therefore, begins with the concrete, and progresses to the subsequent processes of conceiving, theorizing, distinguishing, comparing, and interpreting.[17]

An empirical-phenomenological approach that would be applicable to discovery for the practitioner in clinical social work would begin with a guiding theme of going back to one's own self-consciousness or how he appears to himself.[18] This means going to the everyday-life world where people are living through various experiences in actual situations. People interact and behave in variable ways, but it is assumed that interactions reflect patterns or psychosocial themes. Whatever the practitioner is expecting to study, he or she must obtain descriptive accounts that penetrate the conceptions of the client and the meaning he has constructed around events or relationships. These descriptions can be systematically examined to identify the structure and meaning of the total experience. For example, if the practitioner is studying impulsivity in overt assaultive behavior of a child, it will be necessary to ask the child (client) for detailed descriptions of triggering events, the child's feelings, perceptions, loss of controls around the behavioral impulse to assault, minute descriptions of the environmental milieu, and attitudes that enlarge the horizon of the person-situation context. Descriptions will be of both manifest and subjective content and will not be isolated from the practitioner's own self-consciousness, experience, or theoretical position. The consciousnesses of self and other are not considered to be separate.

The beginning of the phenomenological method is concrete and descriptive of things as they are perceived and experienced. It is true that all manner of bias can exist here, but it is a starting point for deciphering meaning, as illustrated by this event of the impulsive-assaultive behavior. Georgi cites four steps to be taken following the transcription of concrete units of descriptive materials. Others vary this method, which is not rigid or fixed, but—in general—the directions as elucidated by Giorgi are useful:

1. Read the entire description to get a sense of the whole statement. This is the raw, descriptive data of the events or problem of study.
2. With grasp of the whole, reread the text with the aim of discriminating "meaning units" within the perspective of psycho-social phenomena and the problem focus that are being researched.

This will tend to focus the problem, but also will break the whole into manageable units.

3. When meaning units are delineated, review all of them and express the insight contained in them more directly; that is, transform the concrete words of the client into the emphasis and language of the phenomenon being studied. Herein lies the necessity of reflection, imagination, sensitivity, judgment, and understanding. The event may be described within a theoretical perspective. Categories will emerge as the practitioner-researcher goes through the concrete expressions.

4. Synthesize all of the transformed meaning units into a coherent statement of general meaning that delineates the client's experience. This is ordinarily referred to as the structure of the experience, and it can be expressed at a number of levels.[19] The practitioner-researcher needs this final step of the analysis to integrate the insights contained in the transformed meaning units for a synthesis.

The practitioner-researcher could be expected to search for the experience of one client in the situational context for study, but insights will tend to grow if more than one subject in a comparative context is also investigated. This should pose no problem for the average practitioner whose practice may be largely devoted to an age group, problem group, or specified territory. The variable experiences of clients as synthesized may indeed provide common threads or themes that are illuminating in discovery and worthy of further investigation and verification.

The method allows for depth and meaning of the content to emerge. The meaning units in the above example for study would relate to the impulsive assaultive act of the child within a social context. These meaning units emerge as a result of the analysis, and they are the practitioner-researcher's discriminations of meaning. These meaning unit discriminations are noted directly on the descriptive accounts. Whenever the script-text is reread and the practitioner-researcher deciphers a change of meaning for the client in the psychosocial situation, it is transformed. In any event, the units must be specifically focused for manageability in delineating the theme of meaning. The concrete meaning of a word also depends on its meaning within a whole communication, paragraph, or surrounding context. It can be seen that the method allows the experience of these terms to operate spontaneously first, and later (for the practitioner-researcher) to eval-

uate the meaning of the key terms in the further analysis and transformation. The raw, spontaneous discriminations are thus transformed
into more precise psychosocial terminology of meaning. To correct
for bias, it is possible for other practice-colleagues to analyze the
script and assess or calculate for interjudge agreement. Thus, there is
opportunity for quantitative calculation. If there is significant disagreement, further examination and clarification may tend to produce a consensus. Consensus is not a requirement of the phenomenological approach, since it is more important to be open to the unusual
and to discoveries concerning a problem under study. Since the practitioner-researcher's perspective is circumscribed or limited, it is imperative that the facts or phenomena analyzed refer quite specifically
to a study problem.

"What differentiates the phenomenologically inspired method is
the fact that a disciplined spontaneity is allowed to function whereby
one first discovers the relevant meaning unit, or its category, and only
later, based upon a subsequent analysis, explicates its actual full
impact."[20] Adherents to this approach see it as the practice of science
in the "context of discovery," not the "context of verification." Their
emphasis on systematic scientific activity within the context of discovery is consistent with the aim of this book. Though we are not
proposing that this process be independent of preliminary verification
or verification over the long run, we believe that the approach offers
possibilities for discovery and clarification of insights in heuristic
research. In data collection, it is quite consistent with the "life space"
interview used in social work.[21] Any approach that can be operational
within the practitioner-client interview can also facilite clinical search
and research by the practitioner. Philosophies that expand or restate
empirical work can stimulate the imagination and the further testing
of ideas.

SUMMARY

A phenomenological approach in heuristic inquiry is discussed relative to its philosophical origins and use of concrete, basic phenomena
for deriving meaning. Phenomenology was initially influenced by
Husserl in the early twentieth century. More currently Giorgi, a leading adherent, has advocated its use for investigation in the human
sciences.

The phenomenological method is presented as beginning with concrete descriptions of phenomena as they are perceived and experienced. On-the-spot descriptions of events are favored. From this concrete beginning, relevant meaning units and categories are derived that can be analyzed for understanding and meaning. Empirical methods for achieving reliability can also be used in connection with the approach to increase the validity of interpretations.

PART II

Historical Developments in the Scientific Tradition

Social work practice in the United States had its historical roots in the early charity organization societies that emerged during the latter half of the nineteenth century. The basic principles guiding the helping activity in these societies were investigation of need, friendly visiting, registration of applicants, and the cooperation of agencies. The societies were modeled after the London Charity Organization Society founded about 1869[1] and were adopted to foster "scientific charity."[2]

This part, which is devoted to historical developments in practice in the scientific tradition, develops the thread of scientism in practice up to World War II. By that time, practice was firmly established in a variety of fields. The specific contributions of research, linked to practice development and to the fusion of the practitioner-researcher, are analyzed. Part 2 is divided into two separate chapters. The first chapter (chapter 8) presents the earliest roots of the scientific tradition and traces the thread of science in the historical development of practice method. The second chapter (chapter 9) surveys research of practice, pointing to its contributions and failures that have preceded current ideas of fusion of the practitioner-researcher. The chapters will only highlight the thread of scientism in the historical development of direct practice and the linkage of research to practice, since a large body of literature devoted to historical origins and to practice research already exists. The literature, as reviewed, was not subject to a content analysis, but was a review largely from primary sources that served to highlight the thread of scientism. The chapters in part 2 attempt to analyze the dynamic aspects of scientism, to classify the nature of practice research that has led to current concern for a closer practice-research relationship, and to demonstrate the need for cumulative research and theory building. These two chapters also reflect the many positives that pioneers of the profession have brought to the enormous task of helping people of widely heterogeneous backgrounds in a rapidly developing, industrialized nation. Their social consciousness, courage, and philosophical pragmatism have allowed them to draw on scientific thought for developing basic and practice knowledge, coexistent with the enormous burden of meeting need. It should engender respect from the present-day professional.

CHAPTER 8

Scientific Roots
in Social Work Practice

THE CHARITY ORGANIZATION SOCIETIES
AND "SCIENTIFIC CHARITY"

In the American colonial period, there were social service programs sponsored by religious and civic groups to supplement programs of public financial aid. Human need escalated, due to industrial expansion, cycles of depression, rapid urbanization, and mass immigration into the new country. It became apparent that some ordering and coordination of the many service programs were needed. Some concerned citizens thought that there could be systematic principles applied to charitable work—"a science of social therapeutics."[3] Some of these ideas were in keeping with the philosophy of philanthropy in the nineteenth century and also stemmed from what were seen as negative results from indiscriminate giving. By 1872, the Chardon Street Building was established in Boston to house offices, official boards, and major voluntary relief societies.[4] Other cities were also beginning to organize their charities. These organizations were Germantown in Philadelphia (1874), the Bureau of Charities in New York City (1874), and the Cooperative Society of Visitors in Boston (1875).[5] The London Charity Organization Society, which was seen as bringing some order out of the confusion of private charity, had already

been organized in 1869,[6] and the Rev. S. H. Gurten, an English cler-
gyman, is credited with organizing in Buffalo, New York, in 1877, the
first charity organization society in the United States.[7] He organized
the society on principles of investigation, registration, and agency
cooperation that were characteristic of the London Charity Organization Society. The society also had provision for extensive use of the
friendly visitor. The charity organization societies, as they developed
in America, were organized on specific guiding principles, which were
a hallmark of scientific charity.[8]

The agency forerunners to the charity organization society, however, were referred to as voluntary general relief societies that sought
to raise the dependent poor into independence, that acknowledged
need for investigation, and that aimed at the elimination of the impos-
ter. They differed from the new charity organization society (C.O.S.)
in that they rarely employed the friendly visitor, nor did they seek to
alleviate the conditions producing the need. They thought that "moral
nature and the social lot of the poor were large factors in the problem
of pauperism; but the efforts to extirpate it were feeble and inciden-
tal."[9]

By 1892 there had emerged ninety-two charity organizations and
affiliated societies in the United States that adhered to the new principles of scientific charity.[10] Some gave material aid, whereas others
were only investigative and referral sources.

The scientific nature of the new "scientific charity" of the C.O.S.
lay in what was described as the "intelligent," discriminating procurement of facts in the investigation of need. Decision-making was
based on the facts for the dispensation of aid, the uplifting relationships with the needy, the understanding and removal of causes of
poverty, and the cooperation and coordination of agency services so
that almsgiving would be efficient. The idea of scientific charity embraced both the institutional and structural arrangements for dis-
pensing aid, as well as the practice component of investigation
grounded in cause-effect relationships. The rudimentary practice theory required judgment and decision-making that aimed at relieving
the personal causes and promoting self-dependence. Richmond has
emphasized that not all of the charity societies sought the more positive, social rehabilitation of the poor.[11]

In the charity movement, there were clearly two divergent and
conflicting points of view among the societies that affected the investigation and the work of the friendly visitors. There were those who
supported the economic emphasis that aimed the investigation only

at the applicant's economic status and need for financial relief. The opposing emphasis was the broader inquiry aimed at the "whole person," with its purpose of social reinstatement, release of latent possibilities, regeneration of character, increasing opportunities for health, and creating opportunities for training.[12] It was this later direction that began to crystalize in the early literature of National Conferences of Charities and Correction of the 1890s and in the later in-service agency training programs for friendly visitors and paid workers. In the early years of the C.O.S., the investigations tended to be more detective-like and based on a philosophy of "deserving and non-deserving poor," with investigation to eliminate indiscriminate giving and to prevent a pauperizing effect. Actually, the original aim of the C.O.S. was not almsgiving but promoting cooperation and efficiency among relief-giving sources. They provided the friendly visitor who could investigate need scientifically and refer the needy. In doing so, the visitor was to be a friend, to give advice, and to help the needy gain self-dependence.[13] Though the C.O.S. has been criticized for its narrow view of poverty, its friendly visitors have also been credited with uncovering the many social ills of the time and promoting greater social justice, which grew out of their investigations into cause-effect relationships regarding need.[14] Certainly some of the leading representatives of the movement, whose presentations at the national conferences reflected their points of view, revealed sympathetic regard for the plight of individuals and families in need, and a restorative attitude that was associated with the principles of scientific helping.

In 1889 Mrs. Glendower Evans, who tended to represent C.O.S. thinking, defined "scientific charity" as the demand,

(1) to understand the causes of poverty, and (2) to remove poverty itself, to help the poor to be no longer poor. . . . Thus [she said] scientific charity, far from bidding us cease to give alms, only bids us not to give them when they are harmful; it bids us pause, when possible, to consider what their effect will be; and it bids us try, along with alms, to give some better gift, which may by and by put the poor beyond their need.

It must be observed, however, that the application of this theory of scientific charity is far less simple than is the statement. For in life the various classes of poverty are not clearly divided, and usually several causes have combined in varying proportion to produce any given result. So no rule laid down beforehand can be more than proximately true. Even the principle that aid is demoralizing to people whose poverty is their own fault cannot be applied in any hard and fast manner; for there are all degrees of fault, ranging from well-meaning stupidity to flagrant crime.[15]

From the papers of Evans and others,[16] presented at the National Conferences of Charities and Correction, these pioneers of practice considered scientific inquiry to be the systematic study of causation through gathering of thorough and helpful facts. Knowledge of causation was needed to help the poor and to advance general principles as laws for reducing poverty. Rosenau stated that the "cardinal principle of scientific charity is to search out causes of distress, in order that work may be begun at the foundations of the trouble."[17] He chided the seventy-eight existing societies with the fact that nothing had been funneled to the economist that was sufficient for study of the sources of poverty. At the same conference in 1890, Kellog urged societies to begin to collect statistical data systematically, suggesting that "all such statistics as will throw light upon the causes, the present condition, and the wisest treatment of poverty and pauperism: . . . statistics are the link [he said] which convert theoretical science to the practical use of life, and correct the errors of speculative generalization."[18] These statements also suggest the currents of empiricism that were reactive to speculative thought, discussed in chapter 1. It should also be remembered that C. S. Peirce at Harvard University was developing his thoughts on pragmatism during this period. Ludwig Wittgenstein, who was a student of Bertrand Russell in England, was concerned with "facts not things in empiricism."[19] By the early twentieth century empiricists had also begun to use propositions and statements, rather than terms or ideas, as the fundamental unit of meaning.

Not only was the causation of poverty and its effects considered of scientific importance by leaders in the C.O.S. movement, but the scientific method was valued in America, associated with the rise of machine technology and new developments in statistical and empirical methods. The methodological procedures devoted to the science of causation lay in the investigation of facts by interrogation and observation.

By 1890, there were charity workers, as well as the friendly visitor. Within the 78 societies that existed, reports from 37 societies indicated there were now 174 paid officers, 2,917 friendly visitors, and 1,767 officers and other workers.[20] The paid workers and those who were trained were becoming the skilled workers who could make firm, quick decisions in the investigation, using their trained sensibilities to understand the needs and aspirations of the poor. Ayers stressed that the method called "scientific" be used[21] and the differentiation of the paid and trained worker from the volunteer was beginning to evolve.

Zilpha Smith wrote in 1888 that

to talk with a poor person . . . in such a way as to gain his confidence, and to elicit at the first visit all the information necessary, is a matter requiring skill and experience. The paid agent, giving every day to the work, gains this skill, and also a general acquaintance with the conditions of life in his district, which enables him to see the bearing of trifles which would escape a less constant worker, but may prove clews [clues] to the real difficulty.[22]

She stressed learning the immediate and underlying causes of need and discovering how the causes could be removed. Though these selected excerpts reflect an individualistic approach to the science of causation, investigation makes it clear that, even before the organization of the charity societies, social factors beyond individual control were also being recognized. For example, in a highly acclaimed paper read by Dr. R. T. Davis at the National Conference of Boards of Public Charities on May 22, 1874, he described not only abuses in indiscriminate giving in New York during the panic of 1873, but also the severe hardship and need created by economic recession.[23] Some of the causative factors were identified as beyond individual control, such as irredeemable paper currency and business panics that robbed the working man of employment. The report extolled philanthropic generosity by noting

the fortunate class of the United States . . . [as] one of peculiar philanthropy and benevolence. Whenever they see misery they are only too prompt to aid it . . . . No words can ever praise too warmly—the generosity and unselfishness of motives of a large part of the New York community in their gifts of charity during the past winter [panic of 1873]. Still, it was too often a generosity without discretion.[24]

The report also went on to reveal that much indiscriminate giving had encouraged floating vagrants, street beggars, the "more respectable" seasonal farm workers from the outlying rural areas, and had a pauperizing influence on the stable wage earners who were unwilling to cut back on their wages during the business recession.[25] (This conference predated establishment of the charity organization societies by three years.)

Toward the end of the century, leaders such as Josephine Shaw Lowell, who had also originally shown concern that relief would stimulate moral deterioration and pauperism,[26] now spoke out on the evils of a repressive investigation solely for relief. She thought that "charity organization principles, though outwardly austere, had developed from a deep concern with questions of conscience and equity."[27] Edward T. Devine (in 1897) spoke of the value and dangers of investigation.[28] Devine stressed that investigation was not to be made for the purpose of labeling applicants worthy or unworthy, deserving or underserving, but solely for the purpose of ascertaining whether help could be given and in what way.[29]

It was at the National Conference of Charities and Correction, in 1897, that there was a plea for selection and training of experts for investigation that aimed not to determine worthiness but to restore or regenerate families and their abilities. Devine now identified this process as "casework" and the service as

standing by its families as their friend, to represent them in all legitimate demands, to guard them against unnecessary assistance, to reconcile them with the community, industrial, religious, and social, speaking in their behalf as the need arises.[30]

In 1901, in laying out principles of associated charities, Devine reported the positive nature of an investigation, citing it as analogous to a physician's diagnosis. He stressed the aim of organized charity as relief and restoration, with relief being prompt, efficient, and generous.[31] As the turn of the century approached, the term "scientific charity" was beginning to be replaced by the term "casework" with emphasis on understanding (diagnosis) of need and causative factors in the service of restoration. Training was required, and the first formal training, as a summer school, was founded by Robert W. de Forest (president of the C.O.S. of New York), Devine, and others, in 1898. It developed, by 1904, into the New York School of Philanthropy, with Edward T. Devine as its first director, and later became the Columbia University School of Social Work.[32] de Forest was chairman of the school's committee or board from 1898 to 1926. He had also helped to launch the periodical known as *Charities*.

In 1896, a year before Devine's plea for a more restorative approach to investigation, at the National Conference of Charities and Correction, Albert O. Wright, professor at the University of Wisconsin, described the "new philanthropy" and its close relationship with the rapid rise of the study of sociology. In his description of the "new philanthropy," he stated:

On the philosophical side it studies causes as well as individuals. On the practical side it tries to improve conditions, thus changing the environment of the defective. It tries to build up character as well as to relieve or punish, believing that the essential cause of pauperism or crime is usually some defect inside the pauper or criminal as well as bad conditions around him, and it seeks for prevention as well as cure. . . .

Philanthropy is thus raised to the rank of a science, the practical and theoretical are yoked together, and a large number of able young men and women are looking forward to making this their life work.[33]

Thus, principles that could be articulated and transmitted had begun to emerge by the last decade of the century. The philosophy of helping through organized charities, from its beginnings as early as 1888, exhorted individual worth, self-dependence, and respect; prevention and the permanent cure of need, where possible; and an impartial practice as to race, creed, and politics.[34] Help was also considered dualistic, as it was not only aimed directly at individual and family stress, but also at specific environmental influences that contributed to the stress. Costin's recent historical account considered that the environmental influence was seen as individually oriented, and its not being seen in the larger political and economic contexts was deleterious to the enhancement of scientific and theoretical development.[35]

By the turn of the century, however, "casework" was being referred to in the literature within the context of social work. Coexistent with scientific charity and the emerging caseworker, there were other roughly equivalent movements that also gave rise to casework and groupwork, such as children's agencies and schools, medical services, settlement houses, and youth organizations. The first juvenile court was established in Chicago in 1899[36] and was a response to the efforts of children's agencies, social settlements, and women's clubs that recognized the existence of social factors in delinquency.

Physicians had cooperated with charity organization societies regarding disease prevention, and they called on the caseworkers for medical social inquiry. The first medical social service department in the United States was organized at Massachusetts General Hospital, Boston, in 1905, under the leadership of Dr. Richard C. Cabot. Its aim was to improve patient care through utilizing social factors in arriving at a more accurate diagnosis and improved treatment.[37] Dr. Cabot, writing in 1920, said that from the beginning of the Medical Social Services at Massachusetts General Hospital, they had had the advice of experienced social workers from the established charities, with whom they talked over policy and details once each week. Alice Higgins Lathrop, general secretary of the Boston C.O.S., and Ida M. Cannon were instrumental in fostering the consideration of help that did not demoralize or destabilize families. They balanced the psycho-social and physical factors.[38] In this early account, the scientific emphasis was not clearly articulated, as it had been in the charity organization societies.

The settlement house and YWCA movements were also evolving in the late nineteenth century. The settlement houses developed within the philosophy of Jane Addams, who had founded the Hull House Settlement in Chicago on September 18, 1889.[39] She believed that one learned from one's neighbors, and that understanding and help could be best administered where social distance was minimized. Greenstone[40] and Franklin[41] point out that Addams' scientific thrust was pragmatic and in keeping with Dewey's ideas that experiment or actions could be observed for their effects, and that corrective or modifying actions may be taken based on these findings. (There is similarity in the current action research.) Addams' philosophy was not only to help people, but also to study their living conditions, and Franklin credits her utilization of Dewey's techniques of rational inquiry and experimentation with introducing the "concept of research and accountability into social work practice."[42]

The settlement house resident workers not only developed resources and friendly relations in neighborhoods, but coordinated charitable efforts with the friendly visitors of the C.O.S. and sought reform of degrading conditions. Mary E. M'Dowell of the University of Chicago settlement viewed the settlement and organized charity as working together—through differing and complementary methods—to help the poor and downtrodden.[43] M'Dowell stated that

the settlement resident in his or her office of neighbor has a right to help in time of need, and because of this right creates a social atmosphere which is found to be of great value to the scientific worker. The settlement is necessarily a work going on from within out, while the charity organization, with its voluntary friendly visitors and its paid agents . . . is the force from without coming into the neighborhood.[44]

She added further that

"Charity" has been undergoing a change at the hands of science. . . . It has a higher and broader meaning. . . . In the process, science is becoming more sympathetic, while philanthropy, or the sympathetic side of charity, is growing more scientific; and working together, science and sympathy, we see the professional mechanical philanthropist being transformed along with the sentimental almsgiver into the type called the Friendly Visitor.[45]

The plight and misery of the masses of new immigrants, who had not yet experienced the American Dream, were observed firsthand in the settlement neighborhoods, and social reform and advocacy became ascendant. Jane Addams became the strong leader for social reform in the progressive era, and exercised her leadership as the president of the National Conference of Charities and Correction in 1910. In her address on "Charity and Social Justice" in 1910, she spoke of charitable groups and those groups "fired by 'hatred of injustice' " uniting to demand more just social conditions. The recognition by these groups that causation of poverty and crime lay in poor industrial conditions, and that change would require an effective appeal to public opinion based on carefully collected data, was a major step.[46]

In previous conferences, there had been complaints about failures in record keeping for vital and social statistics. At the conference in 1910, new developments were reported in social statistics and its usefulness to the social workers. Research was essentially of the survey type and presented descriptive frequencies.[47] By 1916, the survey was defined and its accomplishments in community education cited.[48] The Pittsburgh Survey of 1907 had made a major impact on research and social reform. Some of the leaders for reform believed that the limitations in the individualistic focus of "scientific charity" had actually slowed the reform of social abuses. Most critics concede, however, that the friendly visitors and paid workers brought attention to the social conditions and misery from their daily contacts with people needing help and their attempts toward restoration to self-dependence. The same result also occurred from the experiences of the settlement workers, who lived among the poor and had firsthand information. By 1896, it was apparent that settlements were increasing in influence, as noted by the numbers of papers presented on settlement work at the national conferences. At these conferences, the university community was also very much in evidence as an active force.

As social work practice continued to develop within a scientific tradition during the early twentieth century, the United States was becoming the foremost industrial power of the world. With its new machine technology, continued mass immigration (8.8 million between 1900 and 1910)[49] a shift in population from rural to urban areas, migration of southern blacks to industrialized cities of the north and midwest, the rise of powerful corporate enterprises, and the struggles for recognition and fair labor practice by unions, there arose problems of adjustment and relocation. These forces combined to focus the social worker's attention on the broad social issues and reform as well as the case by case intervention.

As the thread of scientism unfolded in the early history of the profession, it tended to be characterized by attention to the logical development of factual information in the determination of causation (later, diagnosis). For casework especially, the stimulation of objectivity in reliable facts or evidence, the discovery of new insights through the use of the case conference, detailed case examination involving analytical discussion of observations, practice problems, and method were means for achieving some systematization of knowledge. Logical analysis and reason were applied to empirical data in the assessment of client conditions, causation, and effects of intervention. The insights and discoveries from case materials and discussion with participants in summer institutes in New York led Mary Richmond to her formulations in *Social Diagnosis*.[50] *Social Diagnosis* was the first major conceptualization of the casework method.[51] It was in keeping with the major tenets of classical scientific method (observation, hypothesis, experiment), yet her strong emphasis on the practical in training stimulated contemporary questions regarding her theoretical commitment.[52]

SCIENCE AND THE DEVELOPMENT OF PRACTICE METHOD

Social Diagnosis, as a conceptualization of casework within the logical process of classical scientific method was consistent with early twentieth-century empirical thinking. Scientific method was identified as a process of scientific inquiry, reasoning, and verification. The four stages recognized as inherent to scientific method consisted of:

1. observation or collection of facts relevant to the problem;
2. hypothesis or formulations to explain the facts or observations;
3. prediction, or deductions from the hypothesis or theory, and the anticipation of what will occur if certain observations are made; and
4. verification, or the observations and collection of new data to test the prediction.[53]

Similarly, these processes were identified in Richmond's emphasis on investigation, or evidence, for social diagnosis—where reliable observations and facts were to be collected with regard to the client, his environment, and his problem(s). The formulation of a social diagnosis of the nature and cause of the difficulty, based on the social evidence, became the hypotheses.

The formulation of a plan of treatment based on the diagnosis would predict modification or change. Finally, the accuracy or truth of the diagnosis that would be verified in the treatment process by the client's response to treatment lacked the conceptual development that characterized the diagnostic phase.

Richmond emphasized scientific truth in the collection of evidence that she defined as,

consisting of any and all facts as to personal or family history which taken together, indicate the nature of a given client's social difficulties and the means to their solution.[54]

The evidence for diagnosis which she developed from a legalistic perspective,

comes through the social worker's first relations (1) with his client, (2) with the client's family, and (3) with sources of insight outside the family group . . . [and] (4) of comparing the evidence gathered from these various sources (inference) and of interpreting its meaning (diagnosis).[55]

She conceptualized social diagnosis as a process in

the attempt to arrive at as exact a definition as possible of the social situation and personality of a given client. Investigation, or the gathering of evidence, begins the process, the critical examination and comparison of evidence follow, and last come its interpretation and the definitions of the social difficulty.[56]

The process had an aim or end in view, and the data collection and reasoning processes were identified by her as "social research."[57] She elaborated on rules for the careful sifting of evidence to achieve reliability through identification of multiple sources of bias or error that could contaminate decision making. Actually, hers was a forerunner of much later studies in social work of the biasing effects of the perceptual context in which clinical judgments are made, as identified by Orcutt and others in the study of anchoring effects.[58] The Anchoring Concept itself was derived from earlier experiments in psychophysics in the 1930s.[59] The minimal experimentation with clinical materials has tended to explicate aspects of Richmond's early statements on the risks of bias in making inferences. She warned against over-generalization, misapplication, mistaken analogies, and mistaken causal relations, wherein these later experiments on anchoring have documented perceptual distortion as a function of contextual stimuli and a source of bias or mistake in clinical judgments. Actually, *Social Diagnosis* itself was a major research effort, based not only on Richmond's inquiries and professional associations but on the "analysis of an extensive and widely representative collection of case records."[60] Richmond took a major step from her research analysis to the conceptualization of practice, as treatment of individuals and families as a total process,

which could be ordered, described, analyzed, and transmitted from one generation of social workers to another. . . . Selecting and applying the concepts from some of the social sciences, she gradually hammered out her own ideas of social casework as a conceptual whole within the larger whole of social work.[61]

Her definition of casework clearly stated that

its immediate aim [is] the betterment of individuals or families, one by one, as distinguished from their betterment in mass. Mass betterment and individual betterment are interdependent, however, social reform and social casework of necessity progressing together.[62]

Though Richmond classified casework in categories of direct action and indirect action, and was committed to the family as a unit of attention, she was not without her critics. At the 1918 national conference, Dr. E. E. Southard, psychiatrist, and director of the Boston Psychopathic Hospital, was critical of Miss Richmond's emphasis on the family as a unit of interest rather than on the individual.[63] Actually, he stated that he would be inclined "to replace the family as a unit of social inquiry with the individual as the unit of social inquiry."[64] Based on his own experience and the analysis of cases from which Richmond developed *Social Diagnosis*, his finding was that the maladaptive or maladjusted individual(s) rendered these families in need of help.[65] His findings further noted that poverty was generally associated with dysfunction of the person's mental state and suggested that social inquiry and case analysis be ordered or classified within five hierarchical categories of: (a) disease, (b) ignorance, (c) vices and bad habits, (d) crime and delinquency, and (e) poverty and resourcelessness.[66] Southard's paper reflected the beginning influences of psychiatry and documented the fact that the analysis of the same cases from different theoretical perspectives could stimulate different conclusions. Psychiatric social workers, such as Mary Jarrett and others, also saw client problems as generally having some facet of psychological dysfunction.[67] Porter Lee, then director of the New York School of Social Work, took issue with Dr. Southard at the very next national conference in 1919. He countered that

every family worker would cheerfully concede that the family cannot be successfully treated by any methods known to social casework without treating its individual members. Whether these critics would concede to us that the individual members of a family cannot be successfully treated without treating the family as a whole, I do not know . . . I am ready to assert that they cannot.[68]

This debate is significant in that it shows that even before 1920, when methodology was being conceptualized, the unit of attention was being debated. The issue of poverty as a factor in disease and vice versa was pursued vigorously at the national conferences by educational leaders who approached it from an environmental, legislative correctional stance, as well as direct action with the individual/family.[69]

It is also of interest in the development of scientific method that contemporaneously with Southard in 1918, Kellog of Bryn Mawr College in Pennsylvania was arguing for the use of the descriptive term "normal family" for comparative purposes in the treatment of families or individuals.[70] She attributed the rejection of a norm by caseworkers as an adherence to a "principle of individual treatment" that considered the uniqueness of the person, rather than the suggestion of uniformity. From a sociological perspective, Kellog argued that

social casework aims to be a science as well as an art, and norms, rightly conceived and utilized, are as essential to the development of a science as ideals are to the making of character.[71]

Kellog was reflecting sociology's current concern with norms, and thought this comparison allowed for a modicum of guidance in the solution of family problems. She wrote that

every caseworker would concede that one reason why she records the data gathered from her investigations, treatment, and followup work is to secure standard achievements upon which she can base more or less approximate predictabilities concerning the families and individuals with whom she will work—that is, to establish norms for a great variety of social performance, thus making for the development of a science of social economy.[72]

It is recognized that psychological understanding necessary for helping clients was emerging, but whether the individual or family was the unit of attention was less controversial at the time than whether the emphasis would be direct action with individuals and families or reform and mass betterment. During the second decade of the twentieth century, the polarization of practice and reform, as seen in some of the national conference papers, was not unlike that of the 1960s. Polarities in curriculum development by schools had already begun prior to 1915. Richmond stressed at the National Conference of 1915 that social casework is the "art of doing different things for and with different people by cooperating with them to achieve at one and the same time their own and society's betterment."[73] She deplored the attitude of the current social reformers that saw casework as "patchwork" and were ready to brush it aside altogether. She countered that

whatever else social reform eradicates, abolishes, or prevents, the two great facts of human variation and of variable human response to stimuli would seem likely to remain. . . . it will still be necessary to do different things for and with different people.[74]

The papers at national conferences tended to suggest evidence that causative and behavioral regularities from sociological and economic theories were still in vogue before 1920, but the more dynamic psychological theories of personality and illness were beginning to emerge. It should also be remembered that sociology at the time was a fledgling science enmeshed in working out its own "fundamental points of view and its concepts."[75] The evolution of mores, cultural traditions, and norms were subjects of sociological discovery. In addition, though some of the early leaders in social work were educated in economics and social economy, economics itself as a science was considered only a product of the late nineteenth century.[76]

The state of the art of psychology tended to be reflected in Jessie Taft's assertion that its focus was on mental testing and clung to the normal, or to the idea of pure science, as opposed to practical applications. Expressing her idea of normal mental life being worked out in exaggerated forms in mental illness, she saw no reason for the split between normal and abnormal psychology. "If psychology has no concern with human life beyond the testing of the intellect, it is not very much more useful than Greek to the social worker."[77]

Following the time period in which *Social Diagnosis* appeared, a new thrust for research and cooperation between social work and social science began to be noted in the literature and in papers at the national conferences. It must also be recognized that pragmatism was flourishing in American philosophy. Ellwood, in 1918, noted that

spirit and method of all true science is matter-of-fact, inductive, and pragmatic, not deductive and dogmatic. . . . Scientific social work must develop an all around program of social reconstruction based upon full knowledge of all social facts. . . . Social work cannot afford to be merely palliative.[78]

He called on social work to use modern scientific methods to accumulate bodies of social facts, to study the processes and movements in community life, and to link its efforts with the social sciences.[79]

In 1920, Arthur James Todd, Professor of Sociology and Director of the Training Course for Social and Civic Work at the University of Minnesota, brought out *The Scientific Spirit and Social Work*.[80] He acknowledged debate regarding professional status of social work, but considered that the scientific spirit was the necessary concern for social work rather than whether or not it was a profession. He thought that the "impulse to serve" must be fundamental but that science added "ordered intelligence" and the "discipline of knowledge" that expands man's sympathy and makes it effective,[81] and that " 'social work' and the 'scientific spirit' must always be linked in theory and practice."[82] He thought

social work ought to stand for organizing scientifically the forces, personal and material, of a community in such a way as to eliminate waste and friction, and to raise progressively the capacity of every member for productivity, service, and joy in life.[83]

This would be done through education, relief (alleviative and remedial work), and organized prevention.

While "scientific charity" in the earlier days had been essentially descriptive, now the dynamics and characteristics of the "scientific spirit" and a method as fundamental to practice were being articulated. Todd defined the "scientific spirit," based on the fundamental impulse to serve, as embodying:

1. Ordered intelligence and disciplined use of knowledge
2. Hope and aspirations based on facts, with a capacity to give up preconceived notions in view of contradictory facts
3. Tolerance, honesty, imagination, enthusiasm, self-control, receptivity to learning, sincerity, and openness to criticism
4. Maintenance of an open mind and critical judgment

5. Generosity, fellowship, and cooperation in the discovery and communication of findings
6. Community spirit and professional code
7. Unobtrusiveness in personality and sense of self, with recognition that the social worker represents the best thoughts of the community in giving help
8. Recognition of the strain on body and spirit of daily work with the needy and handicapped
9. Elimination of impression with a search for clarity in social problems, for the ideal of knowing the truth, and for adding to the sum of truth.[84]

It is interesting that Todd identified the role of research in fact-finding but did not identify the role of theory in knowledge development.

The literature of the first thirty years of the twentieth century continued to suggest a scientific thrust within the case method, with a rudimentary linkage of research to the case that was reflected in case record research through the decade of the 1920s. The descriptive, survey type of research was much in evidence; however, the case record was considered to be a fertile source of data. Well through the decade of the 1920s, serious discussions were held devoted to promoting the reliability and utility of the case record. Though the record was considered by some to be a "mine of social data," steps were needed in the caseworker's recording to insure its usefulness as an objective source of data. Our discussion of the use of the case record for research is cited here to highlight the case linkage to science and research.

By 1920, the C.O.S. had become the family agency, and the scope of its work with family problems was wide and varied. As other specialized agencies had also arisen to deal with specialized services, the family agency was allowed latitude in helping and the opportunity for research. It was considered a flexible adaptable organization which was open to experimentation and to varied forms of treatment and prevention. These characteristics stimulated a scientific thrust that could be identified in processes of discovery, verification, and the search for facts.

Robinson in 1921 asserted that:

like any profession which is founded on scientific method, social casework must move through three stages: (1) observation and assembling of its facts, (2) hypothetical interpretation of these facts, and (3) control of the facts for new ends.[85]

She stressed that social case treatment must be differentiated in the technical sense from the more haphazard, unscientific, kindly helping; and that its processes must be articulated in the agency case record. This would render the case record a more productive source of analysis. She classified these processes as: "(1) those processes that have to do with altering the material environment in order to meet the client's needs, and (2) those that have to do with re-education of the client's point of view or habits or attitudes or the changing of the attitudes of other people toward the client."[86] She also identified such techniques as persuasion, teaching, and use of the power of the relationship to influence the client toward change.

Though Robinson was especially concerned with the scientific in disciplined helping, she was beginning to classify a process. Critics, however, faulted family casework for its failure "to use scientifically the methods of social analysis which were available."[87] There was the claim that no identified relationship between problem and treatment was made. Phelps, of Brown University, in 1927 agreed that there was justification for much of the criticism, but suggested that there must be "solutions of other serious technical problems, namely the collection and classification of data, which must precede analysis, research, or treatment."[88] He claimed that the content of records must harmonize with methods of scientific analysis, but also must be inclusive and exhaustive of information on dissimilar social relationships.[89] He recognized the varied uses of the case record, but emphasized the need for comparability for research purposes.

Corrine Sherman, among others writing in 1925, supported the use of case records in research.[90] She emphasized that exploration in the case, and finding of relationships among facts, bore similarity to research activities by research workers in other fields. Research and scientific social work were intertwined. Phelps drew on R. E. Chaddock's *Principles and Methods of Statistics* to outline a case approach based on developing hypotheses and methods for acquiring and storing facts.[91] The scientific method should be centered on the first step of the case, or as in research, on collecting and recording data.[92] The rules of scientific method should dictate that

accurate data for the purposes of analysis or treatment consists of:

(1) careful definition of specific problems
(2) a definite method of attack . . .

(3) an outline of research (schedules, questionnaires, etc.), covering the factors involved in the problem and adaptable to the plan suggested in (2)."[93]

Burgess, a sociologist at the University of Chicago, speaking at the National Conference of Social Work in May, 1927, proposed that—to reduce bias and distortion—the recording of cases should be as nearly as possible in the language of the client.[94] He referred also to the "life history" method that was being used extensively at the time in sociological research.[95] Strong issue was taken by Robinson in social work with regard to this latter method, as it was then currently being used with the mentally disturbed. It confused relief of tension as an "operation on personality" for research purposes only.[96] Robinson countered that life histories could be useful in studying individual reactions, but they did not give "enough of the family picture for the investigator to analyze the family environment in which the reactions were taking place."[97]

It is of interest that, though Robinson was speaking relative to research in social work, her comments indicated the importance of family interactions to the casework method and added some differentials from sociology. She was really quite modern in viewing the client as vital to the core of the interaction, rather than seeing the family as a "backdrop."

Questionnaires and other measuring instruments were also used in the 1920s in the understanding of the case. Mental testing by psychologists was often part of the diagnostic understanding and practitioners were admonished to link the social, emotional, and physical aspects of the individual with this understanding.[98] Sophie Hardy, citing limitations of instruments, called on social workers to evolve tests for social work purposes and to measure their success in bringing about the client's harmonious adjustment to life.[99] She reported in 1926 on a questionnaire she had developed for measuring child-training habits of a mother and marital habits of a husband and father.[100] It was obvious that the instrument was related to Watson's behaviorism and to Thomas' translation of wishes to habits. She found that social workers were most in need of research of habit systems that related to health, recreation, work or accomplishment, budgeting and purchasing, truth, and ability to face facts without self-excuses and evasions.[101]

The scientific spirit not only incorporated attention to research, but also moved caseworkers toward varying theoretical sources. For example, in 1930, Robinson[102] referred to the twenties as the "psychological phase" and chided caseworkers for incorporating new theories indiscriminately. She cited the influence of five sources of the "new psychology: 1. the Behaviorist School; 2. Thomas' view [fundamental wishes]; 3. the Adlerian School; 4. the Freudian School; 5. the Jung School."[103] Beyond Robinson's admonition, papers published in *The Family*, which was the leading periodical, indicated concern for a disciplined development of practice theory and method. In regard to the Freudian emphasis, it has been convincingly indicated by Alexander[104] and Hellenbrand[105] that no "Freudian deluge" existed during this so-called psychological phase of the 1920s, and that Freudian theory was only emerging as a useful scientific theory.

Beyond the use of the case record as research data and the devised instruments for data collection and measurement within the case, social workers subjected their empirical observations to rigorous scrutiny and systematic study through case analysis in case conferences. Such was the study of the psychological processes in interviewing. For example, Myrick reported—in 1926—questions of "How do the emotions, behavior, attitudes, prejudices of clients and social workers, as shown in their actions, affect the processes of casework? . . . How do we become conscious of them, articulate, and control them in the interview?"[106]

She reported that a systematic study of these questions was the focus of a subcommittee on interviews which was formed from the committee on professional practice of the Chicago chapter of the American Association of Social Workers. The committee met bimonthly for six months and studied the questions theoretically and experimentally with case materials. They drew on the New York Committee of the association on interviews, the Minneapolis Group of Family Caseworkers, and the National Committee on Casework Process led by Ada Sheffield of Boston, who was studying the question for the Research Bureau on Casework in Boston.[107] Their work produced an outline for interviewing, which in some ways is very modern.

Hollis, who was a student at Smith College in the late twenties and began her practice with the Family Agency of Philadelphia in the early thirties, also has emphasized that systematic study and analysis of case materials by the professionals of the day was instrumental in building practice methods and concepts.[108] In her education at Smith College, where psychoanalytic theory was introduced, and in her practice with the Family Agency of Philadelphia, she was associated with such illustrious early leaders as Jessie Taft, Virginia Robinson,

Betsey Libby, and others. From Hollis' early recollections, corroborated by her recent review of her early practice and teaching materials, she documented that evolutionary discussions, analytical examination of case material, hypotheses from observations, and differential interventions contributed to the building of practice concepts and theory. This was an inductive reasoning process based on empirical observations and analyses. Hollis affirmed the early contributions of Freud and of the psychoanalysts, who were the agency consultants and with whom the caseworkers interacted. The psychoanalysts contributed to the understanding of personality dynamics from psychoanalytic theory, but she insisted that the social worker tended to assimilate and adapt this knowledge to his own case observations and to what made sense in terms of the evidence in examination of the practice materials. She identified the beginning of the psychosocial casework approach in those formative years. In her recent paper presented at Smith College and published in the *Smith College Journal of Social Work*, she traced the incorporation of insights from psychoanalytic theory into the early psychosocial approach through systematic review of case materials in conferences, the highlights of which are presented here.[109] (She confirmed and elaborated on this previously published material with us in personal interview.) She listed some ingredients that emerged within social work as follows:

1. Use of indirect treatment. Psychoanalytic techniques were not used in indirect treatment of the environment. The indirect actions originated historically in social work and were conceptualized as seeking to understand family relationships, their linkage to the psychology of the individual, and the identification and utilization of resources in the environment to bring about resolution of difficulties. (Multiple causation was identified in the historical roots of social work as early as 1889.)[110]
2. Use of the relationship with the client(s) by the social worker. A warm, encouraging, empathic attitude conveying respect defined the relationship as the medium for helping and was historical to social work's practice. The use of relationship in its beginning had emphasized the aim of gaining influence over the client, which had facilitated the techniques of persuasion, advice, and suggestion. As social workers studied the use of relationship, the concept of acceptance and the encouragement of self-determination emerged. Psychoanalysis later added new in-

sights to the dynamics of the relationship in the conceptualization of transference, as a phenomenon that could color the quality of the relationship and could be used in treatment.

3. Use of self-direction. This was a concept broadly used in social work and social science and referred to as self-determination. It did not originate in psychoanalysis but was consistent with the theory.

4. Use of "passivity." The concept of "passivity" came from psychoanalysis and fostered the art of listening. It influenced a change from active advice giving and persuasion. Hollis said that if the practitioner was forced to listen, advice giving was reduced, and listening fitted in with finding out what the client wanted, rather than telling the client what to do. Hollis emphasized that "passive listening" initiated the casework technique of "drawing out" the client. She reported that practitioners were amazed by the technique of "drawing out" the client, as they discovered it. They unearthed how important it was for clients to communicate how they *felt* about what had happened to them and they realized that feelings were as important as objective facts. She commented also that the psychoanalyst continued to use "free association," whereas the social worker continued to "draw out" the client. There was a distinction: in "free association," the client was to express whatever came to his mind, whereas in casework, the client was encouraged to say what he felt free to say. The acceptance and interest communicated by the practitioner stimulated the client to feel free to speak about feelings. Concepts of "listening" and "drawing the client out" became important to casework methodology.

5. Use of acceptance. The concept was evident in the training of the caseworker and historically developed in casework. Hollis noted the idea that the worker must care for people, have warm feelings, and really want to help to be of any help, all of which was notably part of Virginia Robinson's and Betsey Libby's teachings in 1928. She said, however, that the friendly visitors did not have the same concept of acceptance, as they tended to be more judgmental and teaching in attitude. Acceptance tended to relieve the strong elements of fear and guilt, on the part of the client, that could influence the relationship.

6. Use of energy release. As observed in case materials, the admixture of the concepts and techniques—described above—appeared to enable clients to reduce anxiety and guilt and to

increase self-esteem. The evidence of lessening hostility, with emergence of positive feelings, was stated in these early teaching materials and papers as "energy was released." Hollis noted that these phenomena dovetailed with transference phenomena in client-worker interactions, as observed by psychoanalysts. She further noted that the concept of "corrective relationship" was used in the social work papers as early as 1935, indicating that it was possible to effect emotional readjustment by living through a re-educational experience with the social worker.[111] Hollis noted that practitioners began to observe changes, as they helped clients through logical reasoning about their experiences and problems. They could observe that something more than from simple listening was happening within this "corrective relationship," along with "drawing the client out," and "logical reasoning."

7. Use of home visiting. The family agency especially used the home visit extensively. The worker observed family interactions, physical conditions, and came to appreciate the client's external pressures and need for change. (Well before the above documented case and teaching materials reviewed by Hollis, the observations reported in the literature had shown that parents needed help and were worked with, as well as the child, when difficulties with children emerged.)[112]

Berengarten has also identified the major contributions to a scientific base by Dr. Marion E. Kenworthy, director of the Bureau of Child Guidance in New York City in 1924 and associated with the faculty of the School of Social Work at Columbia University.[113] He referred to her incorporation of the psychoanalytically-oriented ego-libido method of assessing personalities of clients in casework. The method required the social worker to assess the client's personality strengths and the "dynamic social situation" in a purposeful, systematic approach to intervention.[114]

It can be observed from the above-cited published materials, teaching materials, case conference materials, and the personal interview with Dr. Hollis, that the knowledge base for practice—by 1930—was growing conceptually and systematically. Psychoanalytic theory supplied gaps and illuminated useful understandings of personality in human relationships, but it did not fully permeate nor teach the method of casework. How faithful these conclusions and conceptualizations were to scientific method is not precisely known. The general steps used to support the scientific process were: observing, checking and rechecking observations and findings, developing valid general conclusions, and predicting from the conclusions, depending on given general circumstances.

It is clear that the casework method was not a haphazard accumulation of knowledge, but that its different facets were constructed from a pragmatic base of observable evidence of efficacy, action experiments, systematic analysis, and logical reason. Observations and analyses were also subject to the corrective of peer review. It is clear that these advances in helping were emotionally and cognitively oriented within a social context. The deficit was in the development of a person-situation theoretical framework with linking constructs to the specifics of method, so that theoretical hypotheses could be subjected to systematic replicative tests. The analytic and inductive reasoning processes from empirical data had begun the scientific process, but a continued focus toward building theory from a cumulative stance could have facilitated the scientific development of knowledge for helping.

It has been noted that in the development of practice skills required "to draw the client out" and "to think about his problem for making change," social work was the "first discipline to develop a form of psychotherapy and social therapy that was distinct from psychoanalysis. . . . the first to devlop that middle ground"[115] of helping. The assertion tends to be further confirmed by Barlow, Hayes, and Nelson,[116] who date the birth of clinical psychology—as it is known today—to August 1949 at the psychological conference in Boulder, Colorado. Garfield, on the other hand, dates its beginning to the founding by Lightner Witmer, of the first psychological clinic in the United States at the University of Pennsylvania, in 1896.[117] Witmer's major interest was in sensory and intellectual problems, which tended to limit his scope to testing. The child guidance movement was developed much later and was devoted to social and behavioral difficulties.[118] Social casework was an integral part of this latter movement. It was as early as 1920 that "the New York School of Social Work established the first community psychiatric facility for children which was entirely administered and staffed by a school of social work; and for eleven years thereafter, participated in a program of training, research, and treatment of children with collaborative disciplines."[119]

Gordon Hamilton, a major figure in the development of casework, was also contributing to the literature as early as 1922.[120] Her articles defined the developing casework within a dualistic perspective and its value system. In 1940 she brought out *Theory and Practice of Social Case Work*, which was a substantive conceptualization of theory and practice of casework within the diagnostic tradition of Mary Richmond.[121] She had also assumed psychoanalytic theory in the science of personality development and her ideas were dualistic in focus on the person-environment. Kurt Lewin's field theory and Henry A. Murray's personology have also been credited with influencing her formulations of the dualistic of person-in-situation.[122] In her 1951 revision of the 1940 edition, she noted that she had earlier assumed psychotherapy to be identical with psychoanalysis, but she believed now, as she did earlier, that

principles of psychoanalysis can be appropriately adapted for the use of many professions, but this does not mean that casework, any more than psychology or education or other disciplines should take over a diluted sort of psychoanalysis as its own procedure. Social work always attuned to the concept of the psychosocial event, constantly finds new perspective and therapeutic opportunity for its traditional role of helping persons in their living experience.[123]

Hamilton's books and her many articles in the professional journals have been analyzed from a hermeneutic perspective by Shoshani, and the analysis has reflected Hamilton's "special skill for integration of problematic dualities in social work theory such as:

Casework as Science and Art
Casework as Method and Social Action (cause and function)
Social Values and Scientific Knowledge
Person and Environment."[124]

By the late 1930s, Hollis had published *Social Casework in Practice*,[125] which analyzed the content of practice processes in six cases. A major new development observed in this book was the shift in psychosocial understanding of the client to include ego functioning and the defensive mechanisms as articulated by Anna Freud.[126] These new psychological insights enriched the caseworkers' understanding of clients' social functioning. Review of the book indicates that treatment was directed to clients' needs in relation to the external world and to the forces within the personality. The processes involved understanding the client's problem, planning, treatment, and using techniques for reducing environmental difficulties, and inner pressures.[127]

The scientific elements seen in the development of theory and practice within the diagnostic tradition should not obscure the fact that an ideological split occurred in the mid-1930s when Jessie Taft and Virginia Robinson championed the functional approach, which was based in Rankian personality theory.[128] Development of the conflict that emerged is beyond the scope of this book. Briefly, the functional approach assumed the natural growth process of the self within its primary social relationships. It emphasized mobilization of the person's will in mastering growth obstacles, within a time-oriented, helping relationship. The psychological forces were considered of greater threat than environmental forces, since the individual cannot escape from them. A diagnosis was not required. Though the diagnostic and functional approaches stood in opposition to each other, suffice it to say that both have influenced current practice.

EARLY CONTRIBUTIONS TO THE SCIENCE OF METHOD BY DISCIPLINES OF SCIENCE AND THE UNIVERSITIES

Historically, the conferences of the state boards of charities were an integral part of the American Association of Social Science.[129] The delegates represented the different states, municipal and private charities, and those in the American Association of Social Science interested in charitable work.

The American Association of Social Science itself was only organized in 1865, and in the early 1870s its scientific sophistication was rather meager. It had been organized

to aid in the development of social science and to guide the public mind to the best practical means of promoting the amendment of laws, the advancement of education, the prevention and repression of crime, the reformation of criminals, and the progress of public morality, the adoption of sanitary regulations, and the diffusion of sound principles on the questions of economy, trade, and finance. It will give attention to pauperism and the topics related thereto; including the responsibility of the well-endowed and successful, the wise and educated, the honest and respectable, for the failures of others. It will aim to bring together the various societies and individuals now interested in these objects, for the purpose of obtaining, by discussion, the real elements of truth; by which doubts are removed, conflicting opinions harmonized, and a common ground afforded for treating wisely the great social problems of the day.[130]

Early in the life of the association, the *Journal of Social Science* was initiated, and its first issue of July 1869 contained papers presented at the General Meeting of the Association at Albany, New York, February 17–19, 1869.[131] A survey of the early issues of the journal supports its preoccupation with pauperism and its causes. The social science emphasis on developing theory and the overwhelming problems of meeting need faced by the charity workers and those of correctional and mental institutions led in 1879 to the cessation of the Conference of State Boards and Charities functioning as a section of the American Social Science Association.[132] They formed their own organization, called the National Conference of Charities and Correction, and met for the first time in 1880. They became a stronger and more active organization than they had been earlier as a section of the American Social Science Association.[133] The move was later criticized by Edith Abbott as unnecessarily limiting the development of scientific methods in social work.[134] It is not possible to conjecture what social work might have looked like if the American Social Science Association and the State Boards of Charities and Corrections could have focused their attention mutually on the linkage, or integration, of theoretical and scientific inquiry with practice application. Review of the proceedings of national conferences reflects that early leaders in the charity movement were respected community leaders, philanthropists and benefactors, directors of charity organization societies, prestigious academicians, and others of wealth and prestige who could offer support.

It can be noted from papers presented as late as the 1920s, that tensions existed between the social work professional and the academic sociologists. Even though nearly fifty years had passed, sociology's preoccupation with norms, folkways, mores, reliability of case record data, etc., were not the major concerns of practitioners. They had not come together in a mutually supportive relationship, nor recognized the strengths that each could offer the other.[135] The practitioner tended to feel a "putdown" of the practical by the sociologist, and the sociologist's abstractions that could not be immediately applied were not always credited by the practitioner.

The major strands of practice, which were casework and group work, did have publications to foster a disciplined approach and scientific thought. The charity organization societies began the publication of *Charities* before 1900, with Robert W. de Forest as editor. The publication from the perspective of the settlement movement was *The Commons*. These journals later combined, as *Charities and the Commons*, and first published in October 1906–April 1907. In this volume, it is interesting to note the accolades to Jane Addams as Chicago's most widely known and most useful citizen for her work with settlements and reform. Robert W. de Forest was also similarly acclaimed for his leadership of C.O.S. in New York since 1888, and as the first tenement commissioner of New York. In addition to articles on the expansion of settlements and conditions needing reform, a foreword by the editor of the new journal, who held both a university appointment and an administrative position with a nonsectarian agency, indicated the commitment of universities. He noted the great freedom of thought enjoyed in the "university classroom and in the executive offices of the modern nonsectarian institutions for the relief of distress and the amelioration of social conditions."[136]

Though historians note that full academic affiliation of social work education within the universities did not occur immediately and without some community pressures,[137] the proceedings of national conferences and the major journals, such as *Charities and the Commons* and *The Family*, reflect considerable interaction with the academic community. There was the university settlement and the Chicago Institute. The early field programs for friendly visitors were at some of the prestigious schools, such as Harvard, Yale, Johns Hopkins, the University of Pennsylvania, Bryn Mawr, and several state universities.[138] After the establishment in 1904 of the New York School of Philanthropy[139] with ties to Columbia University, the Social Service Center for the Practical Training in Philanthropic and Civic Work was opened at the University of Chicago Extension Center. The latter became the Independent School of Civics and Philanthropy in 1908.

Other schools, such as the schools affiliated with Simmons College, the Pennsylvania School for Social Service, the St. Louis School of Philanthropy, the Richmond School of Social Economy, and the Texas School of Civics and Philanthropy at Houston, were also opened soon after.[140] Costin has succinctly traced the early development of educational training and curricula issues regarding the scientific-theoretical and the applied practical emphasis at the University of Chicago,[141] and Berengarten's recent work has pinpointed these issues at the New York School (Columbia University).[142] The curriculum issues were brought into sharp relief in the formative social work educational programs at both the University of Chicago and Columbia University. Because our emphasis is on the thread of scientism in the development of practice, the polarities that emerged as represented in these two schools bear consideration.

At the University of Chicago, Edith Abbott, who became dean of the school in 1924 when it became fully merged within the university, championed an academic, theoretical, scientific-oriented curriculum.[143] Mary Richmond defended practical training in the academic-practice training debate. It was noted that "at one extreme, the School could have become an extension of a social science department, . . . or at the other might have focused narrowly only on the needs of the organization that established it."[144] (In this instance, the organization was the New York Charity Organization Society.) The New York School did manage to organize itself so that its educational program would possess the autonomy to develop its own educational program. The difficult issue was that the objective of university faculty members who were social scientists stressed preparing students "to analyze conditions and to design social reforms," whereas the social workers, led by Mary Richmond, proposed a curriculum in practical training which was systematic and devoted to the management of charitable organizations and direct work with families.[145]

The history of the Columbia School reflected shifts in the leadership, based on commitment regarding these issues. As we reflect on the issues of academic versus practical, it is depressing that these polarities occurred, as both elements were vitally needed in curriculum. Theory and its conceptual origins, research, and practice procedures are fundamental to the effective practitioner, who requires strong academic content along with application methods that are open to critique and to scientific examination. After a history of nearly a hundred years, the profession is still tending to polarize on the same dimension in the advanced graduate education for the doctoral degree. We continually hear educators expound that doctoral education is aimed at theory building, research, and teaching, as though a practice component would relegate the doctorate to nonscience and obscurity. Mary Richmond fought for the practice component and achieved the first "practicum" in professional education. Had the issue been depolarized so that the university would be a source of *both* in a strongly integrated curriculum, it is conceivable that the current practice-research split might not exist today. The pity is that this is still the case in doctoral education.

The clinical doctorate has emerged to further inform practice, but the orientation toward research and theory building in many schools, has tended toward incorporation with the social sciences, for a largely social science-research degree. Academicians are often lacking in strong practice-related knowledge. This dilemma has been heightened in the Ph.D.-D.S.W. degree issue. We shall refer more specifically to this situation in part 3 and suggest some remedies.

SUMMARY

This chapter has traced the essentially pragmatic development of "scientific charity" and the thread of scientism in its evolvement within casework. Groupwork evolved simultaneously from the pragmatics of organization and relationships based in the neighborhood settlement movement. Its major thrust was social reform, but its pragmatism was also said to reflect an experimental, action-oriented approach in science by some of its early leaders. Edith Abbott reported, in her 1942 edition of *Social Welfare and Professional Education*, that the professional schools were just beginning to discover "the great method of experimental research," which she believed should be as "closely knit into the work of the good school of social welfare as research has been embodied in the program of the modern medical school."[146]

The relationship of direct practice to the university, to psychiatry, and to social science disciplines has exerted some influence on scientism in the course of early practice development. Some critics, however, considered that systematic knowledge building was minimal. By 1959, Henry J. Meyer, wrote:

The knowledge base for social work [micro and macro practice] has hardly been identified, much less subjected to content analysis. The large literature on practice has not yet provided clear descriptions of the technical competence that social workers may possess.[147]

He elaborated that the character of social work knowledge reflected two characteristics: "(1) the emphasis on the primacy of experience in practice, on the one hand; and (2) almost paradoxically, the assertion of scientific knowledge as the foundation for professional competence."[148] Meyer thought that the relationship of scientific knowledge (generalization from theories to specific instances) and practice (provision of widest possible range of specific instances on which to draw) were more separate than interwoven.[149] He did credit casework with the attention to bodies of theory (psychoanalytic in particular) that "take a scientific stance." Meyer made the claim that "social work will almost surely have to support its claim to a body of fundamental knowledge by appeal to science. This will require as a first step a serious effort to analyze the actual content of what social workers know, where they obtained such knowledge, and the extent to which that knowledge has been or can be subjected to test.[150]

Meyer's criticism was harsh, considering the historical struggle for scientific method. His yardstick was doubtless classical empiricism; however, his comments reflected the growing concern of the profession with the further grounding of scientific practice. His comments were contemporaneous with the major curriculum study of 1959 directed by Werner W. Boehm, who faced the issue of science and art and considered growth of the base of scientific knowledge as necessary to the curriculum development of the future.[151]

CHAPTER 9

Research: Contributions and Foibles

The foci of major research studies devoted to direct practice knowledge development and evaluation up through the early seventies can be roughly grouped as:

1. Case study: The case record and analysis of movement
2. Prediction: Continuance/discontinuance
3. Classification of treatment or intervention
4. Evaluation of outcome and effectiveness
5. Development of practice models
6. Interpersonal dynamics and strategies
7. Survey of service
8. Clinical judgment

Though there may be some overlap among the groups we have identified as to research objective, these major foci appeared to characterize studies of prominence in the research literature. Our general review was based on reports in journals (e.g., *The Family, Social Casework, Social Work, Social Service Review, Family Process*); direct service research reported in volumes edited by Henry S. Maas;[1] family therapy research reported by William M. Pinsoff, Alan S. Gurman, and David P. Kniskern,[2] and by R.A. Wells;[3] social work encyclopedias; historical reviews, selected monographs; dissertations; and books in the social work literature. Reid, using content analysis, has classified social work research from a broader perspective into four categories, which include (a) understanding of people; (b) service characteristics and outcome; (c) studies of the profession and training; and (d) organizations, community, and social policy.[4] Our purpose here was to trace globally those developments in research that relate to direct practice methods and preceded and contributed to the call for fusion of research and practice in the decade of the seventies. We will highlight selected research studies within the groups to demonstrate development and trends. A detailed review by Briar[5] of direct service research is included in the three volumes edited by Henry S. Maas, and interesting historical reviews have been developed by MacDonald,[6] Shyne,[7] Bloom,[8] and Zimbalist,[9] among others. Briar has presented critically in the Maas volumes what has been learned through systematic study over the decades. Our review has tended to demonstrate glaring omissions in cumulative research aimed at practice knowledge development and theory building. There have been efforts in model development and classification, but other than the important and extensive model building by Reid and his colleagues with the task-centered system[10] and classification research, there has generally been little cumulative research for practice theory development. It is important at this time for universities, social agencies, and the professional associations to link their resources and manpower to assess the state of knowledge and to develop needed research that is cumulative in the building, refinement, and validation of practice theory that uniquely explains and guides action for the person-situation focus in social work. We have hardly begun to link system levels dynamically and transactionally under varying conditions, with varying populations, and with varying problems.

As we shall demonstrate, the major emphasis on evaluation and effectiveness, especially in the sixties, was actually a premature development, though it no doubt expressed the influence of social science and logical empiricism. The practice components subjected to experimental design and statistical manipulations were not always appropriately defined in the experiments, nor was there theoretical elaboration. A more fruitful course would have been to stimulate, and replicate, practice-theory-oriented and developmental research with evaluation. Clear objectives were needed for accumulating and validating practice models and theory that could link dynamics and interactions of the person/group/environment and could provide midrange theory and principles to guide the helping process depending on different conditions, individual/group response, timing, and the nature of the client and problem(s). The diverse nature of direct practice underscores the importance of theory development, evaluation, and guidelines for practice.

A sense of the historical thrust of research, and of the influence of logical positivism, on the development of quantitative methods and instrumentations in the 1930s, juxtaposed with discovery—through use of intuition and reasoned observations—can be gleaned from a paper presented by Gordon W. Allport and published in *The Family* in 1930. He wrote:

The advent of the scientific spirit in social casework has prepared a specially tempting soil for the application of the analytical tools of scientific characterology. . . . [He thought that a science of personality was entirely possible but also wanted to reserve space for intuition.] The term "intuition" is a red flag to the scientific bulls. If there were any other term to designate the process of apprehending the nature of man as a unique whole, it should certainly be used in order not to enrage them. By intuition, we need not mean direct knowledge gained in a non-empirical fashion.[11]

As Allport indicated, there was consternation at the time over the current tendencies toward segmentation of the individual through the use of varying personality tests, schedules, and scales without consideration of a "holistic" view. There was also some general concern expressed for the effect on the casework process of obtaining research data.[12] Though questions had surfaced with regard to the use of qualitative and quantitative methods in research, case study was prominent in research during the formative years of the casework method. We will, therefore, begin our discussion of research of practice from this vantage point.

CASE STUDY: THE CASE RECORD AND ANALYSIS OF MOVEMENT

Debate was prevalent during the 1920s and 1930s with regard to the validity and usefulness of the case record in case study. Critics of case study emphasized its qualitative and particularistic characteristics that would not permit generalization. Statistical methods were criticized for dealing only with an abstracted trait rather than organized wholes. Clyde R. White, who in 1930 championed case study, emphasized its potential for the study of facts, relations, and sequence.[13] He noted that its part ends with the classification of facts in the particular case; however, other cases could be studied separately and *compared* with the first case. He wrote:

Generalization is a simple statement of trend or relations which have been found, after the study of many cases, to recur with a certain regularity. ... The area to which a generalization from a statistical sample applies depends upon the simplicity of the factors involved, the regularity of their combination, and the homogeneity of the social complex within which the factors appear.[14]

The careful study of cases could be expected to throw doubt upon currently accepted generalizations which had rested upon implicit assumptions about cases. They could show the existence of cases contradictory to the older cases upon which generalizations had been made. Case studies that revealed similarities in type could also be used in classifying factors preliminary to statistical study of quantitative data.

An important example of early research using the case study method was a study conducted by the New York Bureau of Children's Guidance. The study involved a sample of 196 cases and utilized mathematical treatment of expert professional judgments.[15] Case record research of the period also explored the administrative utility of the case record and experiments on systems of recording were reported well up through the 1950s.[16]

Of different focus was the comprehensive research project launched at the Community Service Society of New York that used behavioral science methods and the case record for investigation aimed at description and evaluation of casework. The study began with instrument construction and measurement of case movement. J. McVicker Hunt, with Leonard Kogan and colleagues, developed the CSS movement scale for measuring case movement and reported, along with others, that professional judgments of case data could be used reliably.[17] Within the context of this research there were also related studies of other variables, especially the investigation of predictive factors in the initial interview, which will be discussed within the next group of studies. In 1977, Polansky said of the movement scale that "its success in achieving reliable judgments, the conduct of related followup studies with clients, and its other technical advances helped alter the climate of opinion in social work about whether the 'art of practice' could be studied with behavioral science methodology."[18] He believed, however, that the movement scale has since fallen into disuse, as it measured a mode of intervention that was not standardized. Though there was a network of related studies associated with this research, it did not make a major contribution to practice theory or to its validation.

Within the same general time frame of the development of the CSS movement scale, Geismar and Ayers developed a family functioning scale within the St. Paul Family Centered Project which aimed to measure change in functioning of the multiproblem, low-income family.[19] The St. Paul, Minnesota, family-centered project was a large demonstration project designed to study methods in service to multiproblem, low-income families known to social agencies. Differential aspects of the study also included patterns of service,[20] nature and definition of multiproblem families,[21] as well as changes in family functioning as measured by the movement scale. The demonstration project and other associated studies used descriptive records, interviews, and the schedule to study the multiproblem family as to characteristics, patterns of service, methods, and techniques of intervention and change.

The research—using case analysis—investigated important facets of practice, but continued study was needed to factor out theory and principles for practice that could serve as assessment and intervention guides within a theoretical framework of "family behavior and disorganization."[22]

The research studies, as identified, that developed instrumentation, scalar indices in movement, and patterns in helping services did lend themselves to some carry-over into later evaluative studies, though no cumulative research followed in basic or practice theory building. The CSS movement scale and the Geismar-Ayers family functioning scale were both used to measure movement in the "Chemung County Study" of effectiveness in the 1960s.[23] Practice concerns in the research were expressed by the desire to measure change in the client/situation as an index to effectiveness, and to isolate factors that could enable the practitioner to predict the client's use of, and continuance in, treatment.

PREDICTION: CONTINUANCE/DISCONTINUANCE

Studies of prediction for continuance in treatment were associated in the early 1950s with the larger research project of the Community

Service Society. Blenkner, with Hunt and Kogan, studied interrelated factors in the initial interview and developed a later study of predictive factors in the initial interview.[24] Blenkner sought to find factors in the first interview that could enable the social worker to predict the direction and quality of change. Though her study had many limitations, it was believed that further exploration along these lines could yield reliable predictive factors.

A compilation of studies related to continuance in treatment had shown that roughly 33 percent of the accepted clients in counseling agencies had not continued beyond the second or third interview.[25] Serious questions were being raised as to reasons for high dropout. Several studies emerged in the 1950s and 1960s that aimed to identify factors in continuance/discontinuance.[26] One of the most widely known was the study conducted at the University of Chicago, by Lillian Ripple, to investigate the variables of motivation, capacity, and opportunity as factors in the use of service. It was located within the Research Center, which had been established to investigate basic formulations in social work and especially in casework theory.[27] This research was expected to be a step in the direction of theory development.

The study by Ripple and her colleagues sought to investigate factors that would discriminate continuers from discontinuers in the use of casework service. They began by examining the proposition that "the client's use of casework service is determined by his motivation, his capacity, and the opportunities afforded him both by his environment and by the social agency from which he seeks help."[28] The study confirmed the possibility for structuring assessments of motivation, capacity, and opportunity for empirical study and that engagement of the client in the helping process is "dependent upon the client's motivating pressure and the extent to which service promotes the utilization of motivating pressure."[29] The hope-discomfort balance was therefore found to be of paramount importance in the early interviews, and was a major factor in client continuance. Though the findings were important, they, like the earlier research at the Community Service Society, have not stimulated a network of further comprehensive development of the theory, under differing conditions, with differing problems and clientele. Thus, the major research of the period that investigated continuance/discontinuance has not been further built upon or organized into a theoretical frame for guiding the nuances of practice. Today we are concerned, as then, with identifying factors in continuance of the family as a unit of treatment within the wider purview of the ecosystem. The discomfort-hope balance of the group entity is a further complexity that also needs to be identified and explicated in family group continuance and theoretical conceptualization.

CLASSIFICATION OF TREATMENT OR INTERVENTION

Historically, classification of treatment in casework was an "armchair," rational, intellectual endeavor. Classification was considered basic to systematic study of the parameters and dynamics of intervention. The earliest classification was referred to in chapter 8 as Richmond's simple categorization of practice as direct action and indirect action. Those who followed included Hamilton (1940),[30] Austin (1948),[31] Hollis (1949, 1964, 1972, 1981),[32] the Family Service Society (1953),[33] Community Service Society of New York (1958),[34] and Reid and Shyne (1969).[35]

Hollis was the first to develop a treatment classification based on empirical research, a classification first published in 1964. She built a typology of casework treatment based on the communications in client-practitioner interviews.[36] The typology could also classify communications with others in the client's environment. The study was begun in 1956, and it examined as separate variables the aims of treatment and method. Hollis used content analysis to delineate communications of the social worker and of the client in treatment interviews, where she identified six major categories of treatment with subcategories to identify further the means and objectives, i.e., how and why the change was to be brought about. The major categories of direct action included: (a) sustaining procedures, (b) direct influence procedures, (c) ventilation/description/exploration, (d) reflective consideration of the person-situation configuration, (e) reflective consideration of dynamic response patterns, and (f) reflection on childhood or developmental factors in response tendencies.[37]

The classification proved to be a reliable instrument for measurement. It could measure the verbal communications within interviews to reflect the work of both the practitioner and the client, or with others on his or her behalf, and the means used to support functioning or induce change. The environmental work was further classified by role. The typology has stimulated several later investigations of practice,[38] and has been recognized for its empirical contribution in measurement of psychosocial treatment.[39]

Reid and Shyne later developed a treatment classification that related more closely to the classification developed by the Community Service Society of New York (1958), which they used in the empirical study of brief and extended treatment.[40] The latter study required a classification system for the systematic study of treatment effects depending on brief or open ended conditions.

As practice has further integrated the family and group modalities and also incorporated a generic focus in the seventies, classification of treatment has received less attention in research.

EVALUATION AND EFFECTIVENESS

From the fifties to the early seventies, leaders within the profession strongly encouraged social science methodological enrichment where empirical methods and quantitative techniques were highly valued. Social scientists were often employed to conduct research studies or to serve as consultants. In the sixties, professional interests converged to develop numerous studies to evaluate practice effectiveness, studies which were consistent with use of empirical methods, including the experimental design. A few studies of effectiveness had occurred throughout the history of the profession. One of the earliest was the followup investigation in 1924, by Sophie Van Senden Theis, of the effect of foster care service on the adult social adjustment of dependent and neglected children.[41] She had found that three out of four of the adult subjects that were located could manage their own affairs and held respect in the community, though she had difficulty specifying criteria for social adjustment. The sixties produced more advanced empirical methods and many widely publicized studies, such as *Girls of Vocational High*,[42] the Chemung County Study,[43] the Community Service Society-Department of Social Services Study,[44] among others[45] that found social casework not to be significantly effective. In 1972, Geismar reported on his analysis of thirteen evaluative studies conducted during the sixties and noted that four studies found almost no significant difference between experimental and control groups; two studies found limited gains; and seven studies supported the major hypotheses or directions of objectives, though results were modest and the distributions leaned toward nonsuccess.[46]

In 1973, Fischer conducted a review of eleven controlled evaluative studies that likewise failed to demonstrate effectiveness.[47] On studying this question further, Fischer located in the literature eighty studies conducted since 1930 that proposed to examine the effectiveness of casework.[48] However, from this number, he found only seventeen studies that met his criteria for study of the effectiveness of practice.[49] Again, from the analysis of these seventeen studies, the conclusion was drawn that effective practice was not demonstrated and that there was no empirical evidence to validate the practitioners' work.[50] Though Fischer admitted that the studies varied on such probable bases as difference in casework approach, different categories of clients and different measurements, he discounted these differences, as his purpose was to review the results of the practice of social casework broadly, regardless of techniques. However, criticism had already emerged regarding such major studies as "the Chemung County Study" for failure to define precisely the casework intervention or input (independent variable) associated with the measure of outcome.[51] Others believed that probability levels of 0.10 did reflect trends and were perhaps more appropriate to the nature of the data.[52]

Though the methods of positivism may not have fully captured the true nature of the casework process in these studies, certainly the findings were cause for alarm in clinical social work. Professionals of the period were also raising questions about the value of a practice consensus which utilized psychodynamic theory.[53] The theory had historically served as theoretical underpinning for psychosocial practice. Calls were made for broadening the theoretical base. Adherents to behavioral theory believed it could provide greater specificity in the achievement of measurable results, and especially for short-term methods that did reflect increase in effectiveness and efficiency.[54] Reid and Shyne's study of brief and extended casework had revealed that, comparatively, brief term work was at least as effective as extended treatment and—on followup—the gains had been sustained.[55] Similarly, short-term family intervention was also found in some psychotherapy research to have significant effects.[56] Crisis intervention as a short-term approach was being theoretically formulated and, as will be noted later, could also be empirically examined.[57]

The shattering impact and challenges of the many research studies on effectiveness must also be considered within the context of the social climate of the decade of the sixties. The period represented a time of political upheaval and social unrest characterized by opposition to tradition, overturning established patterns, and a general questioning of what had been learned in the past. Eysenck in 1952 and Levitt in 1957 had also turned up similar research findings indicating the lack of effectiveness of psychotherapy,[58] which added grist to the findings in social work and further challenged current practice approaches. Active approaches that emphasized teaching and learning, behavior modification, and emphasis on the consultative, broker, and advocate roles were advocated.[59]

The indigent population and nonprofessionals were to become involved in new careers for the poor with career ladders opened up for advancement.[60] The literature was replete with information and research indicating that the poor would not reflect on their difficulties to achieve understanding and were weak candidates for "talking out" their problems. Psychoanalytic theory was questioned on empirical grounds. The differential in use of psychoanalytic theory for understanding personality dynamics and of psychoanalysis as a therapeutic intervention tended to be blurred among many critical professionals. Direct practice was attacked as a "bandaid." The climate as thus described, along with studies of ineffectiveness, had its negative impact on the development of practice theory, but was also associated with some positive changes that had already begun. It stimulated more timely research that focused on building practice models and it defined with greater precision the objectives, techniques, and dynamics for bringing about change; it linked services with individual and group modalities. System, communication, and structural theories were emerging and were subjected to clinical observation and selected empirical examination. An ecological frame of reference emphasized the inseparability of person-environment and the study of "relationships, patterns, and transactions."[61]

In the fifties and sixties, casework and group work were beginning to define major concepts and classify treatment techniques and goals.[62] The conceptual development was both a forerunner of, and associated in direct practice with, revision of boundaries that combined casework and the small group modalities.[63] System theory became a useful conceptual framework for organizing the person-situation focus[64] and the search for practice unity was emerging in practice.[65] Significant research developments for practice began to be aimed at model building, which offered specificity and unity in practice.

DEVELOPMENT OF PRACTICE MODELS

The Reid and Shyne study that compared the effectiveness of brief and extended casework, was a forerunner to extensive research in development of the task-centered practice model. Reid, with his colleague Epstein and others during the decade of the seventies used developmental research to create, analyze, and evaluate strategies in the short term task-centered model with varying client populations and agencies.[66] Task-centered model development was cumulative. Academicians and professionals continue to elaborate and validate its major tenets as including: problem orientation; short-term duration; specific task-centered focus; mutual contract; structural, action-oriented sequence; and being subject to empirical observation and measurement. Though the model was in the beginning developed with individuals, it has continued to be elaborated with small groups and families,[67] and its construction has served as an example of empirical model development in research.[68] The many studies that it has stimulated have been cumulative in the elaboration, refinement, and validation of the major concepts of the model, under varying conditions, problems, populations, and modalities. Developmental research is open to the use of different designs in the various sequences of its development, wherein there could be uncontrolled single group experiments followed by small-scale controlled designs.[69]

Thomas has also been a leading proponent of developmental research in direct practice, wherein he conceptualizes the phases of research as consisting of practice innovations that are analyzed, designed, monitored, and evaluated.[70]

Contemporaneous with empirical model building research, there has been a surge of clinical research in the decade of the 1970s and 1980s that has been devoted to interpersonal and group dynamics in practice with families and small groups. Research has been characterized by substantial interfield linkage, though largely by systematic clinical observation with reasoned analysis and conceptualization rather than more rigorous, controlled studies.

INTERPERSONAL DYNAMICS AND STRATEGIES

The incorporation of system theory in the fifties, along with theories of group dynamics and interpersonal transactions, escalated new developments in practice with families, dyads, and formed groups. The family treatment modality was strongly influenced by interdisciplinary practice. Its development, using empirical observations and innovation, bore some similarity to the historical development of casework and to developmental research. The new electronic devices enhanced observational procedures and analysis, and the replay could foster greater reliability of observations and confidence.

Some of the earliest leaders in development of the family modality in clinical practice were social workers at Jewish Family Service in New York, where Sanford Sherman, Frances L. Beatman, Celia Mitchell, and Arthur Leader collaborated with Nathan Ackerman.[71] On the West Coast, Virginia Satir collaborated with Gregory Bateson, Don Jackson, Jules Riskin, Jay Haley, and Paul Watzlawick, among others at the Palo Alto Medical Research Foundation (later Mental Research Institute) that pioneered developments in utilization of communication and system theories to explain and intervene in family transactional processes.[72] The early studies grew out of Gregory Bateson's "research project that attempted to classify communication in terms of levels: levels of meaning, levels of logical type and levels of learning."[73] The Bateson group that was particularly studying schizophrenia began to postulate that persons "learned to learn" within a context in which the behavior was somehow adaptive, and that if the learning context was understood, perhaps the speech and behavior of the schizophrenic could be understood.[74] Satir received a grant from the Hill Foundation of Minneapolis to study and train family therapists, and with a later large grant from the National Institute of Mental Health, the Mental Research Institute was founded at Palo Alto, California.[75] Satir became a charismatic leader and practitioner in the family therapy movement and was credited with keen accuracy in discerning the "dysfunctional family system" and in the use of therapeutic strategies to change communication sequences and patterns.[76] She used new observational insights within a treatment and training context rather than the development of new research projects to analyze, theorize, and evaluate the practice.

Simultaneous with these starts among social workers were those of the Family Service Association of America and the Committee on Family Treatment and Diagnosis in the Midwest.[77] Intervention with families as a unit was considered from the perspective of family transactional processes; the intervention was aimed at modifying dysfunctional transactions of the family unit and their environmental system. The unit of attention was the family. This form of intervention was often identified in social casework in the early fifties as *multiple client interviewing*.[78] Though differences have existed in definition of family therapy, Wells, Dilkes, and Trivelli defined it in the following statement:

A therapist engages in family therapy when he sees such natural units as parents and children, spouses, or members of the extended family together as a group over most of the duration of treatment with the goal of improving their functioning as a unit.[79]

In social work the family has been identified as the unit of attention but within an environmental, systemic context of extended intervention. Thus, "family treatment" has often been used to identify the intervention or modality, rather than "family therapy."

Early research on family treatment, under the auspices of the Family Service Association of America (FSAA), represented priority attention to marital problems and their treatment. In 1969, Couch reported on a content analysis of responses of participating professional staff of the member agencies of Family Service Association of America (FSAA) to questions regarding the use of multiple-client interviews in diagnosis and treatment of marital problems.[80] The research indicated wide use of multiple-client interviews for diagnosis and treatment. The implications for theory building were noted as:

(a) the forging of links between individual and system-level concepts, (b) the clarification of the applicability of certain specific concepts to marital treatment, (c) an improved conceptualization of the nature and life history of marital or familial relationships, and (d) an improved understanding of the treatment process itself.[81]

The research implications for theory-building from the study were not carried forward in further foundational study. We are still searching for definitive concepts that describe, link, and operationalize system-level events with evaluative measures. Reid and his colleagues have moved in this direction through developmental research with a systems-level approach to family target problems in family problem-solving within the task-centered model.[82] Reid has also emphasized the family contextual sphere.

During the early period of emerging theoretical conceptualization, Mostwin studied family treatment through demonstration and observation which uniquely emphasized the "life space" and contextual sphere in which the family functioned. The approach was multilevel, time-limited, crisis-oriented, and included a team of therapists, some of whom represented varied social agencies associated with family members.[83] The approach was complex, but represented focus on family-contextual systems in clinical social work.

More recently, Nelsen has suggested an integrative approach in family treatment that utilizes a range in theories (i.e., general systems, structural, communication, psychodynamic, ego psychological, organizational, etc.), research findings, and practice knowledge in assessment, with intervention strategies classified as knowledge-oriented or action-oriented and monitored for evaluation of outcome.[84] Nelsen's suggestion for incorporation of single-case measurement, or other evaluative procedures, makes it possible to initiate knowledge building at the case level.

In the development of family treatment, many social workers have assumed prominent roles in theoretical conceptualization—along with professionals of other disciplines—and have often been identified as "family therapists" in the interdisciplinary family therapist movement.

Parallel with social work in the interdisciplinary beginning, there were those in psychology and psychiatry, such as Bell,[85] Bowen,[86] Minuchin,[87] Framo and Boszormenyi-Nagy,[88] and Wynne[89] who were also pioneers in the family therapy movement. During the seventies, professionals engaging in family therapy—and its differential theoretical and practice approaches—vastly escalated,[90] along with considerable numbers of outcome studies.[91] In general, the family therapy field has been characterized by many theories that underlie strategies and techniques considered to be effective, but there has been a "dearth of research testing these clinical theories."[92]

The outcome studies reviewed by Gurman and Kniskern, Wells and his colleagues, among others (similar to the earlier evaluative studies of casework identified by Fischer and Geismar) have not tended to define rigorously the impact or process in relation to the outcome measures.[93] Hodgson and Lewis' survey of family research between 1969 and 1976, referred to the use of relatively unsophisticated research methodologies.[94] The extensive reviews by Gurman and Kniskern, indicated that controlled studies of nonbehavioral marital and family therapies suggested that the treatments were often effective beyond chance. Behavioral family therapies have frequently tended to show positive results.[95] However, it has been noted that the purely behavioral nature of the behavioral therapies in some studies was questionable, as treatment tended to overlap with nonbehavioral strategies.[96]

A number of limitations have been noted in much of the family therapy research that limit its reliability for the practitioner. Conte and Halpin note specifically that: (1) the outcome studies tend to treat family therapy as if it were unitary and not a wide range of procedures; (2) the research does not offer guides to clinical practice; (3)

the reviews of research tend to dichotomize behavioral and nonbehavioral; and (4) the approach to family research has tended to add in poorly controlled studies in making a statement about family therapy.[97] Therapeutic models and strategies have been largely developed from clinical observation and innovation, without an accompanying design for systematic evaluation. Social work clinicians need to take a leadership role in family research that would support practice theory building related to family dynamics, family and contextual transactions, and the evaluation of intervention strategies significant for social work.

Aponte[98] and Hoffman,[99] who collaborated with Minuchin in the evolvement and conceptualization of structural theory in family therapy have contributed to building conceptual practice knowledge in work with poor, underorganized, and dysfunctional family interactions in social work. Empirical validation needs to be further emphasized.

A relatively new development that has suggested a major epistemological shift has been elucidated by Hoffman, drawing on the work of Bateson and others of the Milan Family Therapy Associates in Italy.[100] The systemic model endemic to this group of thinkers has stimulated their rejection of homeostasis and replaced it with an evolutionary stance that conceptualizes living forms as moving "toward greater complexity and new and different states."[101] The conceptualization for family therapy has suggested, rather, that all parts of the system "are engaged in whatever ordering of constancy or change is in question, in an equal and coordinate fashion."[102]

These epistemological changes have moved thinking from causation, the independent/dependent variable, to the circular concept of "fit," which posits that whatever behaviors, symptoms, or other occurrences in the family that appear, emerge as a form in a complementary fit and as distinguished from causation.[103] In this shift from a homeostatic to an evolutional paradigm, predictable changes in the family system would be difficult to anticipate. The "ecosystem" epistemology, as further alluded to by Keeney, would suggest that the therapist could never be an outside agent to the family but would always be a part of the ecosystem in the therapeutic work.[104]

These shifts in perspective tend to coincide with theorists who promote an ecological perspective[105] in practice and those who have sought an alternative to classical empiricism in research, as indicated in chapter 5. Further research is needed to develop and validate the concepts that define the fluidity of object-space or person-environment in an ecological perspective, with explicating transactions and patterns that promote or negate adaptive fit considering varying circularity in conditions.

As family therapy has escalated, a plethora of interdisciplinary therapists who promote differing and overlapping approaches both in the United States and abroad, have tended to develop their ideas largely from clinical experimentation and demonstration. It is not our purpose here to develop this broad field of therapies, but to address the scientific stance and research of the modality in clinical social work. From this brief overview of research and theoretical conceptualizations of family treatment, it is clear that necessity and wide opportunity exist for comprehensive research development of this modality in social work.

Research with regard to unrelated small groups, such as family group treatment, has enjoyed interdisciplinary contributions—especially from the social science disciplines. Research has been especially related to the areas of cooperation-competition and interpersonal attraction. The group processes of attraction, problem solving, conformity, social influence, reinforcement effects, and cooperation-competition, and the structural characteristics of communication, power, leadership, and membership have been the focus of research attention.[106] Silverman in 1966 surveyed articles devoted to group work in social work journals, papers, and books from 1956–1964 and identified only four articles related to "research and surveys."[107] As doctoral programs were beginning to escalate in the sixties, research related to small groups increased and began to contribute knowledge with reference to group integration, balance, and composition.[108]

As in casework, group work has been concerned with linking the processes of change with outcome, and to better understand their relationship. A major study of this nature was the Chicago Youth Development Project.[109] Feldman has more recently surveyed group work research, comparing it with Silverman's survey of 1966, and concluded that there has been an increase in systematic research from the time period of 1956–1964 to that of 1975–1983, but the "quantity and the quality of the extant research are inadequate for a profession that wishes its practice principles to be grounded in scientific study."[110] The application of meta-analysis within developmental research would appear to hold promise for small group research in direct practice, where the treatment interventions can be studied within a cumulative scheme.[111]

SURVEY OF SERVICE

Research in social work emerged historically under the aegis of social agencies and as surveys. The surveys gathered broad social facts and identified needs of diverse populations of communities. Rather than building theory, the survey tended to identify and support need for resources, reform, or legislation. As casework became more clearly formulated and systematized, the case record emerged as a recognized source of data. The survey related to direct practice accelerated with the Great Depression of the 1930s as the energies of social workers were being consumed with this crisis. Of the more than thirty studies reported in *The Family* during this decade, nearly one half dealt directly with the impact of the Depression.[112] They surveyed problems such as the effect of unemployment and dependency on family life, relief in the private agency, characteristics of families on relief, emergency training of staff, nonresident unemployment, and other similar problems.

Beyond major concern with broad social issues and economic problems in the Depression years, there continued to be selected studies more directly oriented toward processes of practice and the evaluation of intervention. The separation of the function of the family agency from the public relief-giving agency stimulated research devoted to family adjustment problems that were beyond the need for relief.[113]

After World War II, research studies that related to casework practice accelerated, especially as there was also reinforcement of the idea of scientific research as a basis for professional practice.[114] Many surveys of varying scope and purpose emerged. Some addressed the use of research by practitioners and the number of articles available for research consumption in the social work journals. For example, Rosenblatt, in 1968, found underutilization of research by practitioners.[115] Simpson also found for the years 1962, 1966, 1970, and 1974 that in the journal *Social Work* under two-thirds of the articles published did not refer to empirical research.[116]

Other large surveys identified patterns of service with evaluative components. For example, at the beginning of the 1960s, the Family Service Association of America conducted a survey of member agencies which aimed to describe service patterns.[117] Ten years later, it was followed by a second survey to identify any changes in patterns.[118] The research report published in 1962 drew the criticism that it had demonstrated disengagement from the poor by the private family agency,[119] which was rebutted by Beck from analysis of additional data.[120] The followup study reported in 1973 that "young families with an above-average number of children continued in 1970 as in 1960 to be the major users of family service."[121] A "downward shift in socio-economic characteristics" of clients was also identified among other significant variable relationships.[122]

Among other large-scale studies that have had an impact on practice was the five-year longitudinal study, directed by Fanshel, that assessed children in foster care over three time periods.[123] It made a major impact on service programs in linking the relationship of care to the probability of continuation of children in foster care. The research encompassed three separate, but integrated, studies that assessed the children moving in and out of care, the agency system, and the parental response.[124] The empirical research used varying data-gathering measures, including standardized instruments as well as interviews. A striking finding was that 36.4 percent of the children in the study sample remained in foster care at the end of five years, and 57 percent of the children in care for five years had not been visited by their parents.[125] "Permanency planning" and "continuity of relationship" for children have emerged as major child-welfare concepts that bear relationship to this research.

CLINICAL JUDGMENT

Research of clinical judgment process emerged in conjunction with the use of clinical judgments as data in research and the finding of its reliability as a source of data. Hunt had stressed, however, the need for more empirical research on the clinical judgment process itself, as there could be sources of error in the judging process.[126] A good summary of the literature related to the reliability of judgment process and decision making has been developed by Tripodi and Miller.[127]

In the 1960s, Bieri and his colleagues at the Columbia University Research Center pursued fundamental, empirical, behavioral, science-oriented research that investigated the process of judgment, which included the basic processing of information, distortions in judgment dependent on anchoring contexts in which judgments were made, and the role of social class variables.[128] These studies in clinical judgment reflected a shift from the more pragmatic practice-oriented research toward theoretical and foundational knowledge. A large body of dissertation research and subsequent journal articles was reported, but without further cumulative efforts, the contribution to a comprehensive theory of clinical judgment has been limited. The research began foundational work for knowledge building in an important area. My own leadership with Arangio in replicative research on anchoring distortions in clinical judgment again demonstrated, using a large sample of professional social workers, that clinical judgments were significantly distorted within the context of anchoring or extremes of behavior.[129] The professional social worker also tended to use the more pathological end of the scale. In psychophysics, there had been early efforts to find a general law of anchoring distortion, whereas studies of anchoring in clinical judgments have been found to exist, but replication has been insufficient to generalize the phenomena.

Franklin has recently extended earlier studies by Briar, Fischer, and Brieland in the investigation of the influence of race and social class on the clinical judgment process, where she has demonstrated that changes in the label of race and social class were associated with differential judgments apart from factors related to the client's behavior.[130]

RAPPROCHEMENT OF RESEARCH AND SCIENTIFIC CLINICAL PRACTICE

By the end of the 1970s, there had emerged strong impetus for the rapprochement and fusion of research with social work practice. There was professional concern that research and clinical practice tended to be split off from each other and were even antagonistic,[131] though the research literature has been of wide scope. There was concern about accountability and scientifically based practice.[132]

In the mid-1970s, along with the rapid escalation of doctoral programs in social work, a new emphasis began to emerge that supported increased linkage of research and practice. Papers presented at the annual program meetings of the Council on Social Work Education,[133] National Conference of Social Work,[134] at the meetings of the Group for Advancement of Doctoral Education,[135] and publications of social workers in journals[136] and books[137]—all reflected a new emphasis on narrowing the gulf between the researcher and practitioner through innovative training approaches. The stimulation of developmental research, new methodological procedures, and the integration of research into the practice process could support case evaluation and the role of clinical scientist. Hudson, especially, clarified the situation with his comments on the nature of research education.[138] He noted that students concentrating in macro practice needed research methodologies to deal with large populations, agencies, and institutions, whereas those concentrating in micro practice needed methodologies to deal with individuals, families, and small groups. Yet the research, as generally taught in the schools of social work, referred mainly to macro needs. By the early 1980s, the literature reflected increasing attention to methodology for micro practice in education and the integration of research in practice (see chapter 11).

The review of approximately twenty-five studies of effectiveness from 1972 to 1981 by Reid and Hanrahan, revealed a reversal of the earlier negative findings of ineffectiveness reported by Fischer and by Geismar.[139] Reid has noted that when these later studies were compared to the experiments of the 1960s, the interventions tended to be structured, with limited and specific goals, with improved designs, and used more observational and objective measures.[140] The positive results of the more recent studies appear to be in part a function of the increased use of modified procedures that are more applicable to the experimental design and the measurement of specific objectives in micro practice.

SUMMARY

In this chapter, we have identified in a historical perspective, foci of research with regard to direct practice within eight groups, and have selectively referred to examples of research. We have by no means identified the large body of research studies of practice that exist, but those identified in the eight groups tend to demonstrate areas of major research efforts. Though many studies were comprehensive, they have not generated cumulative efforts for foundational or for comprehensive practice knowledge and theory. Practitioners and researchers alike should begin to assess what is known, what is validated or fruitful, what is needed to further understand and explain phenomena appropriate to social work practice, and search for ways to build on, extend, and standardize new and existent knowledge. There needs to be some consistency in the integration of a network or web of theories offering fruitful guides for practice.

Though the long-term goal of the profession may be comprehensive unified theory of the person-situation configuration in social work, it is of fundamental importance in the short term to build on and evaluate concepts at the midrange of theories that can be explanatory and operational for practice. Practitioners too often tend to extrapolate from emerging charismatic theories without sufficient evaluation or linkage to what is known. Especially when an eclectic view of practice is taken, it is of fundamental importance to understand theories of opposing and of complementary stance and their basic assumptions. As indicated in the introduction, practitioners must know how theoretical assumptions differ, how these differences effect explanations of phenomena, how theories can be linked, where the gaps are, how efficient a theory is in terms of the aims and purposes of social work, and if there is validation of the major concepts. The practice scientist as the imaginative-reflective practitioner who has the tools of logic and science for heuristic investigation and evaluation of change in the practice process—as depicted in figure 1—can contribute substantively to the science of practice and to a comprehensive network of research.

The current literature reflects some advancement in the integration into practice of research technology in the support of scientific method. Advancement has been largely with regard to the technologies for measuring change and the effectiveness of the practice process within the single-case design. Zimbalist suggests that this integration may help the profession finally realize the early scientific goals of "scientific charity."[141] Levy also notes that the attention to design methodologies of the single-subject or time series will provide the tools for answering such questions as:

What is the outcome of this case? How is the client progressing through the course of treatment? Am I (or is my agency) providing service that can be demonstrated to be effective? What techniques work with what kinds of clients? Is treatment X better than treatment Y? Is the intervention producing the change I see in the client?[142]

These are important questions, though they do not fully capture the scope of practice knowledge or theory that underlies explanations of phenomena or practice theory. The single-subject design has been particularly useful in the evaluation of techniques aimed at behavior modification. However, greater applicability to nonbehavioral approaches must also be devised, as they represent the tradition, the environmental systems, and the major practice of clinicians. Other approaches that move beyond the assumptions of logical empiricism must also be scientifically examined and subjected to evaluation procedures. The advanced practitioner must try out alternatives in inquiry within the clinical action, to analyze, to compare, and to follow up, in fostering discovery and knowledge building. There must be a synthesis of what is known with the search for new directions, new meanings, and propositions for testing in the building of new knowledge and theory. The practitioner-scientist must seek coordination with the research specialist in specifying, testing, and validation of theory. Hopefully, more research that is theory-related and cumulative can be stimulated than was characteristic of the overview we have presented in this chapter. The goals for the practitioner-scientist are consistent with the view of Scott Briar as reported by Kirk and Rosenblatt:

Clinical scientists are practitioners who do much more than use the techniques of research in practice. . . . They continuously and rigorously evaluate their practice. . . . The clinical scientist participates in the discovery, testing, and reporting of more effective ways of helping clients.[143]

The goals and spirit of inquiry that we have advocated also tend to be inherent in Witkin's recent suggestion for an "open" model of science that includes methodological flexibility in inquiry.[144]

PART III

Education for Scholarship and Scientific Development

This section traces the development of doctoral education in social work and the influence on research of practice and conceptual development. It addresses the general need for integrative educational content that supports the theoretical-philosophical in science, research methodology, and practice modes. Practice is not categorized simply as technology, but as thoroughly integrative of theory, scientific inquiry, assessment, and practice interventions. Suggestions are developed for achieving a curriculum in advanced education which supports scholarly scientific inquiry in social work practice.

CHAPTER 10

Doctoral Education: Influence for Research and Scientific Development

Historically, social work education began at the graduate level.[1] As social work programs developed, they were either affiliated with universities and colleges or fully incorporated into the university system. The master's degree became the hallmark of beginning professional competence.

Doctoral education in social work was begun as early as 1920, only three years after publication of *Social Diagnosis*, with the establishment of the doctoral program leading to the Ph.D. degree in social research at Bryn Mawr College in Pennsylvania.

The program emphasized, beyond research, the social and behavioral sciences of psychology and social economy. It also provided opportunity for the student to include a practice component by a choice of course work in casework, in psychiatry, and in the dissertation research.[2]

From 1920 to 1950, there emerged four additional doctoral programs. These were:

University of Chicago, Ph.D. (Social Administration) 1934
Catholic University, Ph.D. 1937 (later D.S.W.)
Ohio State University, Ph.D. 1941
University of Pittsburgh, D.S.A. (Social Administration)
    1949, Ph.D. 1963[3]

The doctoral programs were organized as components of university graduate schools and their standards and research orientation were consistent with the parent universities. This university association not only strengthened the scientific attitude of inquiry, but also led to research. However, the early educational programs generally focused on research and theoretical issues germane to social policy and administration of services, rather than on direct practice. These early doctorates were also largely staffed by research faculty and faculty from the social and behavioral sciences. The University of Chicago School of Social Service Administration was the legacy of Edith Abbott and Sophonisba Breckinridge who, along with Grace Abbott, were giants in early social work education, social reform, and legislation for humane policies.[4] Edith Abbott received her Ph.D. in political economy at the University of Chicago in 1905, later studied at the London School of Economics and Political Science, and has been credited as a major architect of current social work curriculum.[5]

The School of Social Work at the University of Pittsburgh began its program by offering the doctorate in social administration. It was clear that the emphasis was on education of the social worker for research, policy analysis, social planning, and administration of social programs. Three of the five earliest degree programs were not even identified by the term "social work."

After 1950, doctoral programs began to increase, and there emerged in the profession a strong impetus for the doctoral degree to reflect the identity of social work. Schools founded after this date began to offer the Doctor of Social Work (D.S.W.) degree, and advanced education was seen as a major source of preparation for leadership, for development of faculties to transmit knowledge, and for strengthening of professional knowledge and competence in research.[6]

Between 1950 and 1968, there emerged twelve new doctoral programs in the United States and one in Canada. These included:

Columbia University, D.S.W. 1951
University of Pennsylvania, D.S.W. 1951
University of Minnesota, Ph.D. 1961
Case Western Reserve University, D.S.W. 1951; Ph.D. 1970
Washington University, St. Louis, D.S.W. 1955; Ph.D. 1971
University of Southern California, D.S.W. 1955; Ph.D. 1982
University of Toronto, D.S.W. 1958
Brandeis University, Ph.D./D.S.W. 1961 (later Ph.D.)
University of Michigan, Ph.D. 1961

University of California-Berkeley, D.S.W. 1964
Smith College, D.S.W. 1965; Ph.D. 1981
Tulane University, Ph.D. 1965 (later D.S.W.)
University of Wisconsin-Madison, Ph.D. 1968[7]

All eighteen of these programs established between 1920 and 1968 awarded 618 degrees, with slightly more than half of these degrees conferred by four schools: University of Chicago, Columbia University, University of Pennsylvania, and Catholic University.[8] As we now look back over the last twenty-five to thirty years, it is clear that educational leadership today is derived, to a great extent, from these graduates, a fact which suggests the impact of doctoral education on the profession.

The Committee on Advanced Curriculum in Social Work was formed, and under its sponsorship a series of monographs was published by the Council on Social Work Education and funded by the National Institute of Mental Health.[9] The committee was composed of an illustrious group that represented the original doctoral programs, as identified, and newly emerging programs. The committee included:

Eveline Burns (chair)	Columbia University
Eleanor Cockerill	University of Pittsburgh
Grace Coyle	Western Reserve University
Florence Day	Smith College
William Gordon	Washington University [St. Louis]
Gordon Hamilton	Columbia University
Marion Hathway	Bryn Mawr College
Arlien Johnson	University of Southern California
John Kidneigh	University of Minnesota
Very Rev. Msgr. J. J. McClafferty	Catholic University
Charlotte Towle	University of Chicago
William Turner	University of Pennsylvania
Helen Wright	University of Chicago
Milton Wittman	National Institute of Mental Health (ex officio)[10]

Advanced education, which was the perspective of the group, included both third-year and doctoral programs. The group enunciated standards and principles as guides to schools in providing advanced education of high quality. It also articulated the aims and characteristics of advanced education, the progress in its development, and the nature and purpose for social work practice emphasized in the third year.

Eveline Burns, chairman of the Committee on Advanced Curriculum, identified the objectives of doctoral education as follows:

1. To increase the flow of research and an attitude of scientific inquiry. (Research was construed as an essential focus of the doctoral program and the scientific underpinning of practice.)
2. To improve faculty and practitioners grounding in the social sciences that underpin practice.
3. To facilitate fruitful collaboration with other disciplines in the solution of problems that transcend any one professional field.[11]

The doctoral programs were expected to produce researchers, teachers, and leaders for the profession.

The polarities of theoretical and scientific inquiry versus education for advanced practice were clearly established by these doctoral objectives and by the emphasis of the practice component in the "third year" programs. The Committee on Advanced Curriculum differentiated the two programs by the following resolution: "Whereas the third year program would place emphasis on practice, the doctoral program would emphasize teaching and research."[12] It was expected that the doctoral student with a further year and dissertation would be equipped to contribute to advancement in knowledge and to strengthen the scientific base of practice. The realities were that the third-year preparation was used by students to increase their practice competence, but they also became teachers. Actually, at Columbia University the third year program had been established four years before the doctorate, and the "already existing advanced casework seminars became a part of the technical concentration which might be elected for the doctoral degree,"[13] though there was emphasis on the social sciences and research, as consistent with the academic standards of the larger university and the principles enunciated by the Committee on Advanced Curriculum in Social Work. The third year programs began to disappear in the 1960s, as students tended to prefer entry into the doctoral degree program and as third year students often transferred into it.

The Committee on Advanced Curriculum in Social Work ceased to exist after publication of its final monograph in 1955. In 1961, the Council on Social Work Education appointed the Advisory Committee on Advanced Education, again funded by the National Institute of Mental Health, which had as its major aim "to strengthen social work education at the advanced level, particularly in the areas of research and the social sciences."[14] This committee emphasized the study of curriculum and found that there tended to be the following core areas of curriculum among doctoral programs:

1. practice, as broadly defined
2. research, inclusive of dissertation
3. related disciplines and professions
4. social welfare as an institution[15]

The issue of specialization in a direct service method had been regularly addressed but was still unresolved. There were also variables in the extent and nature of social and behavioral science content among doctoral programs.[16]

However, the University of Michigan had already established its program of study to advance the social worker–social scientist model, noting that the "social worker's mastery of knowledge of a social science discipline is considered just as central as the mastery of knowledge developed in the profession."[17]

William E. Gordon of the committee envisioned the social work scientist, and noted that "a major objective of the program [George Warren Brown School of Social Work] is to equip the graduates with the fundamental ideas and procedures, the strategy and the tools of knowledge building, science making, or basic research, and a sense of mission to develop the social work perspective as a dependable science among sciences. The program attempts to produce 'doctors of social work' rather than doctors of an area or aspect of social work."[18] Gordon stressed that the doctoral program should be grounded in both social work and science in a generic sense.[19] This point of view would suggest foundation work in the logic and philosophy of science and the related basics of research. It would further the science of social work and produce the social-work scientist. Though Gordon was referring to a research specialist, his basic ideas of curriculum are important to the practitioner as scholar-scientist that we envision. The tools of science can be employed with regard to observational data and inquiry in practice that also can lead to knowledge building.

Doctoral programs continued to expand in the 1960s and beyond. Following the development of twelve new programs in the United States between 1950 and 1968, there was unprecedented growth. After 1968, thirty new programs were established with a total of forty-seven doctoral programs existing at the time of our survey in 1984. These new programs included:

Adelphi University, D.S.W.
Atlanta University, Ph.D.
Arizona State University, D.S.W.
Barry University, Ph.D.
Boston College, D.S.W.
Boston University, Ph.D.
Florida State University, Ph.D.
Fordham University, D.S.W.
Howard University, Ph.D.
Hunter College, D.S.W.
Michigan State University, D.S.W.
New York University, D.S.W. (Ph.D. 1987)
Rutgers University, Ph.D.
Simmons College, D.S.W.
St. Louis University, Ph.D.
State University of New York-Albany, Ph.D.
University of Alabama, D.S.W.
University of California, Los Angeles, D.S.W.
University of Denver, D.S.W., Ph.D. 1979
University of Illinois-Champaign, D.S.W., Ph.D. 1981
University of Illinois-Chicago Circle, D.S.W., Ph.D. 1981
University of Kansas, Ph.D.
University of Maryland, D.S.W., Ph.D. 1981
University of Tennessee, Ph.D.
University of Texas-Arlington, Ph.D.
University of Texas-Austin, Ph.D.
University of Utah, D.S.W.
University of Washington, Ph.D.
Virginia Commonwealth University, Ph.D.
Yeshiva University, D.S.W.

By the end of 1987, one additional doctoral program had been established at Loyola University of Chicago, a D.S.W. program. Two of the earlier programs established at Brandeis University and Boston University were no longer considered social work programs and were eliminated. Therefore, there are currently forty-six doctoral programs in social work.

When doctoral programs first began to proliferate after 1950, leaders of these programs were often social scientists and from the social policy planning area of the profession.[20] In the 1960s with the "war on poverty," and community action programs, there was an increased emphasis on macro practice. Men were largely attracted to this component of social work and were also moving into doctoral programs. Baldi noted that between 1960 and 1968 men earned 65.5 percent of all social work doctorates.[21] Those who achieved doctorates tended to become academicians.

It was clear from the resolution of the 1948 Committee on Advanced Curriculum that a discipline model of doctoral programs was envisioned. Though the research emphasis had been clearly affirmed by the Advanced Curriculum Committee as needed to permeate the entire doctoral curriculum, the need for advanced knowledge relevant to social work and other fields was also recognized.[22] However, by 1977, Shore observed that because doctoral programs had developed largely along the lines of a "discipline," they did not tend to focus on direct practice, neither its specialization nor its research, and she asserted that a great need existed for the study of practice and related research.[23] There had developed an attitude that research, the social sciences, and social policies and theories were to be emphasized, whereas education—other than theoretical, for clinical practice— was considered terminated at the master's degree level.

In 1974, the *Report of the Task Force on Structure and Quality in Social Work Education*, edited by Lillian Ripple,[24] called for upgrading the master's degree content to a doctoral degree in practice. This recommendation was rejected and further study of the issue suggested. Thus, the dilemma for advanced practice education was well described at the time by Siporin. He wrote in 1973 that "a de facto policy [exists] within the social work profession and in the schools of social work that gives low priority to, and in effect discourages, needed doctoral education for the individualized services."[25] Siporin pleaded for corrective action to better prepare practitioners for "comprehensive multifunctional direct service."[26] He thought that the stance then current encouraged "training of practitioners for subordinate positions in the practice field, and for disadvantaged competitive status relative to other helping professions."[27] Not only was there disadvantage in the practice world, as Siporin noted, but there was also a major disadvantage in the failure by universities to prepare faculties adequately for teaching and for scholarly clinical social work. Speaking in another context, Thurz has emphasized that "clinical practice and social strategy are both valid and legitimate practice models within the profession. . . . [However,] all social workers cannot be expert in skills or commitment to both ends of the continuum."[28]

These issues have been debated often at annual meetings of the Group for Advancement of Doctoral Education (GADE). The group, representing doctoral programs, first met in 1975 as a forum to discuss the Ripple report. It has subsequently become the formal organization of representatives of doctoral programs,[29] and the advisory relationship with committees associated with the Council on Social Work Education, as observed earlier, no longer exists.

Selected doctoral programs have subsequently begun to respond to the growing demand of clinical social workers for further expansion of their competencies and have offered the clinical doctorate. The Smith College program, which began in the early 1960s, was the first.

Among the schools that later began to offer these programs were Adelphi University, New York University, Barry University, and Simmons College. Rothman and Kaplan, at the 1978 GADE meeting, indicated that the trend corresponded

with the expansion of social work doctoral education in the 60's and 70's in the social policy and planning concentrations. Not only have these specializations benefitted from the accrual of formalized research and knowledge, but graduates attaining a degree in these areas have had access to expanded opportunities for career advancement. The time seems to have come for the clinically oriented in the profession to strive for similar gains.[30]

Rothman and Kaplan's presentation graphically portrayed the point of view that we hold in this book. They stated:

The interrelationship among theory, practice and research is a logical one for a profession whose major function is to provide services toward the prevention and remediation of societal or individual dysfunctions. An advanced clinical study program which emphasizes theory and research detached from the practice world of the professional fails to offer a sufficient educational experience for the scholar-practitioner.[31]

At this same GADE conference, I presented a model of doctoral education aimed at bridging the academic and the professional requirements. It would not only incorporate the course content and dissertation that emphasize practice theory, the social-behavioral sciences, and research, but in addition would include a seminar/practicum structured as a clinical/research laboratory. The laboratory would offer an opportunity to integrate the study of theoretical conceptual notions, the logic of scientific inquiry, a research strategy, and practice.[32] The model was aimed at enabling the doctoral student to conceptualize and scientifically inquire within a limited "hands on" practice domain. It was expected that this added educational experience in the laboratory would integrate knowledge, support inquiry, and promote the scholar-scientist ideal.[33]

Though the discipline model in doctoral education has been characteristic of its development, relevant practice-oriented research has not escalated nor has research been widely utilized among practitioners.[34] It has not accelerated the practice-scholar-scientist component needed for clinical social work in either education or practice. Recently, special projects for research-practice integration in master's programs have produced some encouraging results, which we will discuss in chapter 11. However, it may be inferred that the research component in doctoral education has added to the general research competence of faculties. Reid found that from 1980 through 1982 nearly 80 percent of the articles published in *Social Work Research and Abstracts* were authored by academicians.[35]

In the 1970s, advocates of the integration of research with practice emerged prominently in the literature and at GADE and other professional meetings.[36] The procedures and methods of measurement in empirically based practice were widely advocated and disseminated, as we have also noted in the introduction.[37] The scholar-scientist that we envision in this book clearly represents the science of discovery, knowledge building, and research methods integrated with—or associated with—highly competent practice. We consider this as important to the clinical educator as to the practitioner.

Bloom has identified the scientific practitioner as committed to the understanding/knowledge-building aspect of science and the understanding/knowledge-using aspect of practice. . . . The ultimate goal of the scientific practitioner is effective, efficient, and humane practice through the application of the scientific method in the ongoing evaluation of intervention.[38]

We support this definition, but with the broader aim that the post-master's practitioner or practice educator will move beyond use of scientific method in ongoing evaluation of practice to examine, reflect, discover, build, and contribute to practice research and theory. This aim challenges master's and doctoral programs and post-master's educational programs to stimulate attitudes of philosophical and scientific questioning, the debate of assumptions in science, of methodological issues for research of practice, of theoretical explanations, and the formulation of alternatives in research strategies that can facilitate practice discoveries. This does not mean that the practice researcher abandons regulative methodological principles,[39] but may use alternative and less doctrinaire rules in scientific inquiry within the practice process. Actually, from this perspective, there is no need in doctoral education to dichotomize a theory/research model and a model of clinical doctorate. Doctoral education, especially in this view, would prepare the graduate with some competence in the logic and philosophy of science; theory development and analysis; social science; research; and advanced practice as it relates to theory, research, and application. An integrative component that would include "hands on" practice would be tailored to student needs. It might be more limited as in the laboratory, or more extended as in an internship. The dissertation would continue as basic to the curriculum and would be theoretically grounded, but open to differential designs and to systematic qualitative and quantitative methods. Within the above framework, as suggested, the relevance of theory and research to practice is assured as well, as the scientific stimulus and potential for knowledge building.

There is no intention here to reject preparation of the career research specialist. The specialist would acquire advanced levels of scientific research theory and statistical methods, along with an integrative experience within the controlled environment of an internship or laboratory. Many schools already have this pattern in place.

Not only has social work wrestled with the dilemma of providing clinical or direct service content versus theory/research content in its doctoral programs, but, also according to Barlow, Hayes, and Nelson, clinical psychology has faced a similar dilemma.[40] They have pointed to a similar disillusionment by clinical psychologists, who find that the scientific research methodology has not always been applicable to the concrete problems of practice.

As we considered the seminar/practicum to be an appropriate integrative medium, we surveyed the existing thirty-four doctoral programs in social work in 1977 with reference to whether they included a practicum within the doctoral curriculum. The findings reflected that the practicum was on the rise in doctoral programs and was associated with all areas of curriculum, e.g., clinical, research, education, social planning, and administration (see table 10.1). Many re-

TABLE 10.1 Comparison of the Number of Doctoral Programs in Social Work Offering a Practicum in 1977 and 1984

Practicum	1977[a]	1984[b]
	Number	
Practicum Offered	19	28
Practicum Not Offered	11	9
No Report	4	10
Total number of doctoral programs	34	47

[a]Orcutt and Mills, "A Model of Doctoral Education," p. 103.
[b]Orcutt, Survey of doctoral programs in social work in the United States, 1984.

spondents, however, viewed a direct practice practicum as inappropriate to a "research" degree or a "research oriented program."[41] Their comments reflected a split among doctoral educators, with reference to the aim of a clinical practicum at the doctoral level. The integration of the science of knowledge building and research with achievement of advanced practice knowledge and expertise appeared incompatible to some. However, the split seems to have narrowed subsequently, with the new emphasis on empirical practice and the clinician-researcher. Yet the split has continued in the structural arrangements of many doctoral programs, where the emphasis tends to favor research, social science, and social policy for a research-oriented degree.

I again surveyed the forty-seven doctoral programs existing in the spring of 1984 and found that inclusion of a practicum had increased proportionately with the increase in programs. About two-thirds of the reporting programs offered some type of practicum, and they represented a pattern similar to the practica in 1977. As can be observed in table 10.2, the research practicum led all other types of practicum. This appeared to be consistent with the idea of a research/theory curriculum. Table 10.2 also demonstrates that many schools offering the practicum, tended also to offer practica in a range of content areas in which the school purported to educate for competence, as well as in research. In the seven-year interval, there was a

TABLE 10.2 Comparison of the Different Content Areas of Practica Offered by Doctoral Programs in Social Work in 1977 and 1984

Type of Practicum	1977[a]	1984[b]
	Number	
Teaching	5	9
Research[c]	17	19
Social Planning	8	8
Clinical/Direct Intervention	10	13
Administration	8	10
Other		1

[a] Orcutt and Mills, "A Model of Doctoral Education," p. 104.
[b] Orcutt, Survey of doctoral programs in social work in the United States, 1984.
[c] One school offered the research practicum in a policy area such as health, aging, etc.

small increase in practica offered for teaching, for clinical or direct service, and for administration. Schools that offered the practicum tended to offer either the internship or the laboratory, or both. Five offered only the laboratory and eight indicated other structures, such as required professional practice or field study. Some schools that admitted the non-M.S.W. graduate required a field work practicum.

Whether or not the doctoral programs in the survey made a concerted effort to educate for broad objectives, they ranged widely in the number of credits required for the doctoral degree and with regard to requirements for research and statistics courses in their curricula. The required number of course credits ranged from 10 to 155* credits, with a mean of 49 credits. However, approximately one-half, or fifteen of the thirty-four respondents, required 36 to 45 course credits beyond the master's degree. Schools with lower credit requirements indicated that students took more credits than those required in order to prepare themselves sufficiently for examinations and for dissertation research. Three schools did not require a course credit minimum, as students' programs varied, or they required a full two year residence.

The minimum research requirement was 3 credits in two schools and the maximum was 50 credits in a program that aimed solely to train the specialist researcher. The latter school also required 72 credits for the degree and offered both a research internship and laboratory. However, the mean credits required by doctoral programs in research, as indicated by the thirty-seven respondents, were 12.8 credits with both a median and mode of 12. Schools that required fewer than 12 credits, indicated that students might structure their program for more credits, according to their interests and needs. Many schools also granted additional credit hours for the dissertation, hours which tended to vary up to 24 credits.

From our own experience in the administration of a doctoral program, the 12-hour research and statistics requirement appears to be a minimum and generally insufficient for the scholar-scientist preparation that we envision. The modal student does not enter with strong research credentials. The same also tends to be true of the practice competence of many clinical students, who have advanced rapidly to administrative and teaching positions and have often not been directly involved in ongoing practice for a period of time. We also found it of particular interest in our 1984 survey that fourteen of the thirty-

---

*The school reporting 155 credits was on a quarter system, which tended to inflate the report.

seven respondent schools required more than 45 course credit hours for the doctoral degree. This finding tends to lend support to the feasibility of the organization of doctoral programs along lines that can substantially deepen knowledge in the sciences, research, and practice. Hopefully, we can infer from this finding that there is a shift away from the state of affairs that Patchner reported in his study of doctoral graduates from the decade of the 1970s, where more than one-half considered that they did not receive thorough knowledge in any curriculum area.[42] A concern reported by many of the graduates in Patchner's study, who later taught or engaged in direct practice, was that they did not find direct practice content in their curriculum. Equally serious was the report that graduates "also studied in related disciplines while content for specialized fields within the social work profession was often limited or unavailable."[43]

The Patchner findings, as reported above, were serious indictments. It is imperative that doctoral education prepare the practice educator and practice leadership with substance in direct practice, or in other practice areas, and be structured so that graduates achieve the competence necessary for advancing the science, art, and practice of the profession for the ultimate benefit of clients. Though doctoral education has produced many research-oriented professional leaders, there is still a major task ahead for the profession to truly integrate science into practice.

SUMMARY

Doctoral education in social work developed historically along the lines of a discipline model and has neglected the full integration of science, research, and practice. Selected doctoral programs have offered the clinical doctorate in response to the growing need for the expansion of direct practice competencies. Suggestions are supported in the chapter for further integration of science, research, and practice in doctoral education. It is expected that with greater attention to the practice component, as integrated with science and research in the triology, the competencies of social work educators and practitioners can be enhanced as practitioner-scientists.

CHAPTER 11

Educational Preparation for the Scholar-Scientist in Social Work Practice

Educational preparation for the scholar-scientist in social work practice is addressed in the specialized curriculum of graduate education and in foundation coursework at the bachelor's level. At the master's level, curriculum is based on the standards and curriculum requirements prescribed by the Council on Social Work Education, universities, and colleges for the master's degree. The clinical practitioner, who holds the M.S.W. degree, can be assumed to have mastered the basic fundamentals of scientific inquiry and research methodology required at this educational level. Many schools and faculties have organized the master's curriculum or special projects so as to integrate and fuse research with practice methods courses and field work, where special emphasis has been on evaluation of practice.[1] Richey, Blythe, and Berlin note that little data has existed on the carry-over into practice of this training, but cite two studies (Welch and Gingerich) as well as their own report on their integrated educational unit, a curriculum model, all of which suggest under-utilization.[2] However, though there were varying percentage levels of carry-over, a major advantage was the positive attitudes reported toward the educational training.[3] These attitudes can not only stimulate carry-over in practice but can lay a foundation for further enrichment in post-master's educational programs. Our experience with the integration of theoretical-research-practice content in a seminar/practicum for doctoral students was also reported by these students as stimulating more positive attitudes toward research and knowledge building for practice, and was believed to be integrative of their total doctoral learning.[4]

It is expected that the clinical practitioner or clinical educator will use the path of post-master's education to further integrate scientific scholarship, research competence, and practice knowledge. Doctoral education is currently the major avenue, with its formal structure, for furthering the education of the scholar-scientist in practice.

The polarities that have tended to divide orientation in doctoral education into social theory/research aimed at preparing teachers and researchers versus practice should be reordered to accommodate more of an amalgam in program structure. This admixture should include essentials from philosophy of science, generic elements of scientific reasoning, exploration of basic scientific assumptions, issues in generation of knowledge for practice, alternative paradigms and research methodologies, varying theoretical conceptualizations and interventions in practice, essentials of social policy and interactional organization theories, selected socio-behavioral science theories, and the opportunity for theoretical and practice exploration from observational or other data within a "hands on" practice component.

The path of continuing education has not been characterized by regularly packaged, attractive offerings to fill this larger need for competence. We hope that continuing education, provided by different universities and practice institutes, can become a greater stimulus and source for further scholarly and scientific advancement of the practitioner.

In 1982, Lieberman factored out sets of abilities or skills that clinical practitioners should own as graduates of postgraduate training programs.[5] She based her criteria on a definition of practice as "improvement of the relationship between individuals and their social environment" and categorized the abilities separately according to "differential diagnosis and treatment of the person-problem-situation gestalt."[6]

Though Lieberman's categorization stressed abilities for competence in the diagnostic assessment and treatment process, she also identified competence in systematic evaluation of treatment and contribution to the behavioral sciences, which accords with integration of science.[7] From the point of view of a scientific perspective and an amalgam in the structural arrangements of doctoral programs, we have conceptualized the following abilities and competencies that the post-master's clinical scholar-scientist should own. These competencies include ability:

1. To assess with a high degree of accuracy the person-family-situation gestalt in understanding the client(s) problem(s) for appropriate planning and intervention.
2. To exert skill in arriving at differential diagnostic assessments and in the selection of appropriate theoretical frame and concepts for problem understanding and use of different modalities in intervention.
3. To demonstrate capacity for precision in the identification of goals and objectives of intervention.
4. To demonstrate a high level of competence in the implementation of the intervention plan, in the exercise of self-awareness, and in the use of skilled techniques in the ongoing intervention process.
5. To demonstrate appropriate evaluation of intervention strategies and the achievement of goals and objectives, which may include instrument development, use/modification of standardized instruments, and differential research design.
6. To engage in ongoing analysis of scientific perspectives, designs, and methods for their applicability to the practice objectives in social work.
7. To keep abreast of scientific thought and new developments in knowledge for social work practice.
8. To contribute to interfield linkages from a scientific perspective, to foundational knowledge in social/behavioral sciences, and to practice knowledge.
9. To contribute to larger, group research projects, when applicable or feasible.
10. To disseminate new practice findings and understandings as a contribution to knowledge in the profession.
11. To transmit theoretical and practice knowledge effectively.

It is clear that these competencies require advanced post-master's education. However, persons with these competencies will contribute to practice knowledge, theory, and research. They will become the necessary leaders for advancement of direct, clinical education and practice for the ultimate benefit of clients known to social work.

Doctoral programs currently constitute a substantive base for the scientific and research thrust of the practice professional. The clinical doctoral programs have tended to tie research offerings closely to clinical practice problems. The relationship of the research to practice has provided a new impetus for fusion of research and theory building, even though programs vary as to the magnitude of research requirements.

The oldest among the programs offering the "clinical doctorate" is Smith College, whose research requirements are strong, and it also integrates a clinical internship. Miller refers to the clinical focus in doctoral study as being accommodated within doctoral education; and central to the program is a conception of knowledge building opportunities that become accessible within advanced clinical competence.[8] Though the school provides for didactic and experiential study of practice, having a thirty-seven-month practicum, it also requires study of research and behavioral sciences, as well as the dissertation.

We believe that it is both possible and practical in doctoral education to provide appropriate foundational theory generic to logic and science; selected sociobehavioral science theory; specialized practice theory; research and statistics; and an advanced integrative seminar/practicum, conceptualized along the lines suggested in this book, that will further the competencies of the practice educator and practitioner. Some general suggestions for curriculum in doctoral education that can bridge these areas are:

1. Content concerning logic and philosophy of science, issues related to objectivity-subjectivity, theory construction, explanation, prediction, etc.
2. Advanced content related to statistics and research with linkage to science, theory development, and evaluation in practice.
3. Advanced general content in social policy and theories of organization.
4. Advanced specialized content in social and behavioral sciences.
5. Advanced specialized content related to clinical practice (theories, methods, modalities, etc.).
6. A seminar/practicum that integrates with practice scientific inquiry and research, theoretical explanations, gaps in knowledge, and selected areas of social/behavioral science. The seminar provides for the didactic development of focused content regarding scientific inquiry and theoretical foundations and the "hands on" experience provides opportunity for experimentation and practice enrichment. For example, a particular student might study a selected aspect of object relations theory for explaining

family or couple dynamics and offering guides to intervention. The didactic and experiential should be a microcosm of the total curriculum in action. The questioning, searching practitioner-student may also serendipitously find ideas or hypotheses for pursuit in dissertation research. The length of the practicum should be tailored to student interest and to practice/research needs. A weekly seminar, along with the individual conference and one full day of practice a week has been found to be minimal for a laboratory experience. The time span of an internship would, of course, add substantively to the learning experience.

7. Dissertation research.
8. A minor area in another department of the university and/or one or two languages may be additionally required by the university. The minor area offers a unique opportunity to increase the student's knowledge content in areas such as the social and behavioral sciences, research and computer sciences, business management sciences, family practice and medical sciences, etc. The minor can offer further development in an area of student theoretical or research needs.

The general curriculum content areas as indicated above should equip either the clinical practice educator, the practitioner, supervisor, or consultant with added knowledge and skill to advance practice research, theory, transmission of knowledge, and effectiveness in helping. The practitioner as scholar-scientist is needed, not only for leadership and as a role model, but to debate issues in scientific practice related to research and to build a substantive science of social work that speaks to the complexities of practice. From the finding in our survey of 1984 that a total of 49 credit hours was average for doctoral programs (see chapter 10), the number of credit hours needed for the curriculum, as proposed, would not appear to be an insurmountable obstacle.

It appears that advancement has already begun in the 1970s and 1980s with regard to research applicability to practice and practice effectiveness. General optimism has been expressed by Reid and Hanrahan from their more recent studies of practice effectiveness. They found that methods of clinical social work yielded evidence of effectiveness in all but two of the twenty-two studies of effectiveness published from 1973 to 1979 that met their criteria for assessment of outcome.[9] Furthermore, Reid and Hanrahan's important observations that "the researcher as evaluator is giving way to the researcher as developer of models," is another important facet.

The new look in methodology is characterized by experiments in which developers of practice methods devise and implement experiments to test them. . . . Researchers now hope to improve the range and strength of treatment variables through a sequence of experiments. . . . What appears to be emerging is a strategy of incremental experimentation.[10]

The depressing finding in 1980 by Glisson that there was inadequate research content in doctoral programs[11] hopefully is being reversed. In our survey of 1984, we found that twenty-three of the thirty-seven reporting doctoral programs required at least a minimum of 12 hours of research and statistics, along with the additional dissertation requirement.

It was also significant in our survey that of the thirty-seven reporting doctoral programs, seventeen considered that their programs emphasized all practice areas of social work, which included clinical or direct service, and social policy, planning and administration (see table 11.1). All programs emphasized research, though five programs considered it their major focus. Other programs emphasized research along with selected practice areas or combinations with education for social work as shown in table 11.1.

Though there were only two of the reporting programs (N-37) that considered their offerings as research and direct service only, over one third combined micro and macro practice content with the research offerings (see table 11.1). Among these latter programs that offered a broad emphasis, twice as many (twelve) offered the Ph.D. degree. Five of the schools whose program focus was chiefly research conferred the Ph.D. degree. The two programs whose educational focus was clinical social work combined with research both currently

TABLE 11.1. Content Emphasis of Doctoral Programs

Content Emphasis	Number of Doctoral Programs
Research	5
Research/Clinical, Direct Service/Social Policy, Planning, Administration	17
Research/Clinical, Direct Service	2
Research/Social Policy, Planning, Administration	7
Research/Education for Social Work	0
Other Combinations (Research/Education/ Administration/Clinical Theory	6
N-37	37

offer the Ph.D. degree. It is significant that in 1984, there were thirty schools in the United States that conferred the Ph.D. degree and seventeen schools that conferred the D.S.W. These statistics shifted only slightly by 1987, as there are currently twenty-eight schools that offer the Ph.D. and eighteen schools that confer the D.S.W.

It may be conjectured that a strong research and scientific emphasis is associated with the emerging change in doctoral degrees conferred by the schools. The newer programs have tended to offer the Ph.D. degree and many of the older schools have converted their degree programs to the Ph.D. degree. A research thrust is endemic to Ph.D. programs. The early stress in the 1950s on professional identity in offering the professional degree has appeared to subside. The D.S.W. programs have also tended to uphold strong research standards, nor have schools offering strong clinical content attempted to lower standards of research to emphasize practice.

Social and political changes have also emerged that have had their influence on the offering of the Ph.D. degree. Third-party payments have been more open to the holders of the Ph.D. degree, and undergraduate faculties have found the Ph.D. better understood by colleagues. The doctoral programs themselves have considered the D.S.W. and Ph.D. degrees to be of equivalent standards.

Over the past decade, a plethora of interventive techniques related to differing theories and modalities have emerged among helping disciplines. The *Handbook of Clinical Social Work* presents a wide assortment of perspectives and practice models in social work.[12] Meyer has dealt with the complexity by suggesting an ecosystemic epistemology as a theoretical perspective for assessing and utilizing differential practice models in intervention, which draw on a range of personal, developmental, interactional, and social theories.[13] The assumptions of ecosystemic epistemology that pose a network of fluid, ever changing, circular interactions, which have functional utility for the system, open up vistas for discovery of adaptive patterns in interactions and conceptual linkages among systems for adaptive "fit."

In the literature, there has also been noticeable advocacy of a behavioral approach for use in practice, as it lends itself to specificity and measurement.[14] The task-centered approach developed by Reid and his associates in social work has also facilitated objective evaluation, quantification, and model building.[15] These latter approaches have especially stimulated emphasis on empirically based practice and the fusion of research with practice. They have tended to utilize single case design, time series measurements, and instrumentation that measures target problem objectives. Empirical models for measurement of different goals in nonbehavioral approaches have also been advanced,[16] as well as differing descriptive, survey, and case study designs.

Considering the profusion and complexities of differing intervention strategies and research options, master's and doctoral social work education and continuing education for the practitioner must facilitate the sorting out, critical examination, and validation of theoretical explanations and interventions appropriate to the values and parameters of social work's focus on person-in-situation in preparation of its educators and advanced practitioners. Clinical practice has been criticized as laying too much emphasis—in the past—on diagnosis, with insufficient attention to intervention.[17] The situation may now be tilting too far in the opposite direction. We need to examine, as do the philosophers of science and other theoreticians, the theoretical assumptions, approaches to systematized knowledge-building, and alternatives in scientific methods, and to search for the most appropriate and efficient ways to examine, evaluate, integrate, and build knowledge for social work. The advanced practitioner must have the basic scholarly tools to engage in appropriate research tasks and an attitude of scientific inquiry, interwoven with competent helping skills.

The thrust of this book has been toward stimulation of the creative, reflective, inquiring, scientifically oriented practitioner, who as educator, consultant, supervisor, or clinician can support new conceptualizations, discoveries, and evaluation of outcome. The practitioner can contribute not only to larger research projects, but to the solution of "basic problems confronting social work research at practical as well as epistemological levels."[18]

SUMMARY

Components of educational preparation for the practitioner-scientist in social work have been delineated. Education at the level of the master's degree is expected to lay the basic foundations for integration of scholarship and research in practice, whereas doctoral education will further develop and strengthen competencies. It is expected that doctoral education, as a major educational structure, will emphasize scientific philosophies, generic elements of scientific reasoning, knowledge building, alternative paradigms, and research methodologies. Coexistent with the scientific thrust as delineated, emphasis is also laid on selected areas of the sociobehavioral sciences, social policy, and direct practice theories. Strengthened integration of the curriculum elements, as cited, is recommended within a "hands-on" practice component. Either the laboratory or internship, depending on the needs of the student, is recommended. The integrative medium, as a practicum, offers the student experience in the full integration of science, research, and practice. It is also recommended that continuing education for social work practice foster offerings that can add substance to the practitioner's knowledge of science and heuristic inquiry.

The goal of practitioner-scientist-researcher is not only important to the profession of social work but to the quality of help offered to clients.

PART IV

Exemplars

The following two chapters—as exemplars—aim to illustrate ideas presented in this book and to demonstrate scientific inquiry in practice. Flowers, in chapter 12, presents an example of empirical research in the case process using the single-case design with evaluation of outcome, whereas Seinfeld, in chapter 13, presents an example of theoretical investigation in the clinical process that evolved into dissertation research. The latter presentation represents an effort to advance foundational theory.

An Example of Clinical Inquiry in Practice: The Direct Influence Treatment Model

Linda C. Flowers

This chapter is an example of how ideas for a treatment model surfaced and were developed and tested in a practice setting. The major issues of the study will be outlined in the following six areas: (a) how the research question surfaced; (b) the assumptions underlying the study; (c) the development of the treatment model; (d) the linkage of elements of opposing theories; (e) the method of research; and (f) the findings. The study will then be summarized.

SURFACING OF THE PROBLEM

The researcher, as a practitioner in a mental health center, became aware of a particular area of concern when a number of children were referred to her with the problem of being unable to perform or achieve in a normal classroom setting, even though they possessed average or above-average intelligence. In addition, the children were experiencing difficulties in their interpersonal relationships. The major areas of

Linda Cox Flowers is Field Coordinator and Supervisor of the Alcohol and Drug Program of the Cumberland River Comprehensive Care Center and Field Supervisor at the University of Kentucky in Corbin.

concern were failure in academic performance, aggressive acting-out behavior, and interpersonal conflicts at school.

The mental health center served a rural area, and it was often difficult to engage the family system on a continuing basis in treatment of a child's problems. In addition, children could generally be seen only during the school day. These constraints in practice led to some initial experimentation with selected practice procedures that would emphasize direct work with the child, aimed at directly influencing his or her functioning. Play therapy has traditionally been a treatment of choice, along with the involvement of one or both parents. Under the circumstances, the practitioner decided to search for some effective direct procedures that could be used successfully with the maladapted child, within the limitations of time and the constraints of the familial and school systems. The practitioner sought to strengthen ego controls through influences that aided suppression, impulse control, social learning, and healthy identification in the nonpsychotic, aggressively acting-out child. Intervention in the school and familial systems, when that could be sustained, would be aimed at reduction of stress and support.

The initial experimentation in practice led to a belief that selected procedures of direct influence could be useful. The practitioner's subsequent involvement in doctoral study that included the seminar/practicum, a laboratory experience, allowed for further theoretical study and firming up of a sequence of procedures for direct influence that could also include a single-case design for evaluating effectiveness.

The early work on the task-centered model by Reid and Epstein was drawn on as a helpful guide.[1] The practitioner drew on a range of theories and practices, similar to the task-centered model as it was developed, and designed a series or sequence of interventive procedures.[2] These procedures could be assumed to directly influence the child's behavioral functioning, could be subject to modification, and began initially with a systemic psychosocial assessment of the problem for client selection. The aim was to help the child cope with the immediate demands of the school system and home. Persistent study, along with some experimentation, led to the formulation of a sequence of interventive measures—or a treatment model—for testing.

ASSUMPTIONS UNDERLYING THE STUDY OF DIRECT INFLUENCE IN TREATMENT

A number of assumptions were made in the development of the direct influence treatment mode.

1. Maladjusted, aggressively acting-out school children were assumed to be experiencing some internal conflict and anxiety because they were unable to perform in accordance with their known intellectual capacities.
2. Associated with continual internal conflict, the child's identifications and sense of self were assumed to be weak.
3. Repeated failures in daily school tasks were assumed to heighten apprehension and anxiety, along with sanctions from parents and teachers.
4. Sanctions were assumed to result in conflicts with authority figures, which in turn fostered poor identification and weak internal control.
5. Anxiety, self-concept, and internal control were assumed to cluster as major factors in school maladjustment and interpersonal conflict.
6. It was assumed that normal growth and development would aid a treatment process carried on within a caring, accepting, empathic relationship that aimed to directly influence new learning, controls in behavior, and interpersonal relationships.

The above assumptions played a major role in the development of the direct influence treatment model.

DEVELOPMENT OF THE TREATMENT MODEL

If the assumptions of the study were correct, then a direct treatment model that would foster changes in self-concept, reduce tension and anxiety, promote internal control, and foster identification in a caring, positive relationship and a growth-accelerating external environment, would lead to changes in academic performance and level of interpersonal conflict. A treatment model was needed that would break down the clustered elements into approachable, changeable units of behavior, foster internal control, and that could be applicable within the constraints of the school and familial systems. It was recognized that the disruptive, maladaptive behavior could be reactive and reciprocal to internal and external stress and conflict. Hence support and/or changes from teachers and parents were important elements. It was also postulated that a model of direct external influence could include elements of a behavioral orientation where there might be residual support of deeper emotional needs. The external environmental system (parents, teachers, etc.) as reciprocally interactive was penetrated for the initial psychosocial assessment and for supporting the intervention and change. The focus for research purposes, however, had to be limited and was therefore centered on the child, subject to a series of sequential steps of direct therapeutic intervention or treatment.

The first step in the direct influence treatment model necessitated exploring the interactive relationships of the child, along with an assessment of the problem areas in behavior and interpersonal relationships. Severely disturbed children were not considered for this treatment. After the problem areas were identified, the child's dysfunctional behaviors needed to be reframed in order to be approached and ameliorated. Reframing specific disruptive behaviors into positive tasks that could be substituted for the disruptive behaviors would hopefully result in a change in behavior, provided the other elements in the clustering could also be addressed. The change in behavior could be expected to lead to improvements in academic performance and decreases in interpersonal conflict. The reframing of the behavior into substitute behavioral tasks became the second step in the direct influence treatment model. Since the symptomatic behavior was to be a direct target for change, it was possible to use the single-case design as it would be particularly suitable to the evaluation. The practitioner was also desirous of gaining experience with this evaluative procedure in research.

Anxiety was considered to be associated with the disruptive behavior. Merely reframing the problem and substituting alternative positive behavior would not specifically address the issue of anxiety. Therefore, the direct influence treatment model needed to contain an element focused on the issue of anxiety. As behavioral change was a direct target for the experiment, elements of behavioral and learning theories were drawn on rather than a psychodynamically oriented theory of anxiety. Therefore, anxiety was hypothesized as embodying two different components. One component was conceptualized as relating to "anticipated aversive consequences" and the other component comprised conditioned stimuli. The practitioner hypothesized that anxiety could occur in both manners. Therefore, it was necessary to deal with both learning and conditioning. As it was known that anxiety could not be physiologically maintained concurrently with a state of muscle relaxation, it was also believed that relaxation could be used to break the pairing. Thus, muscle relaxation became the third step in the direct influence treatment model.

It was further hypothesized by the practitioner that if the child could practice the substitute behavioral tasks while in a state of muscle relaxation, the anxiety level would be decreased. The question then arose as to how the child could actually practice the substitute behavioral tasks while in a state of muscle relaxation? The answer was visual imagery rehearsal. Visual imagery rehearsal became the fourth step in the direct influence sequence.

While in a state of muscular relaxation, the child using visual imagery rehearsal as directed by the research practitioner would visualize acting out the appropriate substitute behavioral tasks instead of the usual disruptive pattern that had created difficulties in the classroom. The positive emotions and feelings that were related to the substitute behavioral tasks would be labeled. Suggestions would be given by the practitioner that these feelings could and would occur when the behavioral tasks were implemented in the classroom. Therefore, the fifth step in the direct influence model included labeling of positive feelings, suggestions to the child that he or she would be able to perform these positive substitute behavioral tasks, and pairing the positive feelings with the appropriate substitute behavioral tasks.

After the completion of a period of muscle relaxation and visualizing substitute tasks that could be implemented in the environment, the child's cooperative behavior would be rewarded by verbal praise and an edible treat. The verbal praise and concrete reward comprised the sixth step of the treatment model.

The edible treat was thought to impact the child in several ways. It would give the child a concrete reason to be involved in treatment. From a behavioral orientation, it would reward and reinforce the child's positive behavior in treatment. From a psychodynamic orientation, it would serve the dependency needs of the child in being cared for and fed by a caring, positively related object. Finally, it would impact the child's internal control and cognitive development as the child would be given by the practitioner the choice of one treat from three different articles of food.

The direct influence treatment model, as described above, had six specific elements: assessment, task formulation, muscle relaxation, visual imagery in rehearsal of specified tasks, positive suggestions as to feelings and performance of tasks, and verbal and concrete rewards. The implementation of the treatment model was within an accepting, empathic relationship. It was hypothesized that the sequence could be carried out with a school-maladapted, impulsive child and could bring about changes in academic performance, conflictual interaction, anxiety, internal control, and improved self-image. Dynamically and residually, the process could also improve psychic identifications that would also increase internal control and a sense of self. As indicated earlier, for research purposes, the influences from the environment were limited to information and support for change.

LINKAGE OF ELEMENTS OF OPPOSING THEORIES

This study attempted to combine practice procedures that derived from different theoretical perspectives into a workable model. The overall person-environment relatedness and interchange could be viewed globally within a theoretical biopsychosocial system framework. Psychodynamic theory was used as a basic orientation for understanding the developmental and adaptive needs and tasks of children and of parents. It was basic to the assessment of problem areas that were interactive in the child-environmental system.

The configuration of direct influence, as a category of directive procedures for social work intervention, was articulated by Hollis in her treatment classification.[3] Based on a psychosocial frame of reference, Hollis categorized directive procedures as consisting of processes that reflected differing degrees of directiveness.[4] In this experiment, the practitioner mainly used suggestion in direct influence, along with task formulation, relaxation, images of adaptive actions, feelings, and rewards. The problem assessment of the person-situation configuration was derived from theories of psychosocial systems in social work practice. Internal and external stresses in functioning could be identified and were used to prevent selection of severely disturbed children in the study.[5]

The contracted behavioral change component in problem assessment and task formulation drew on the work of Reid and his associates in the development of the task-centered approach in social work.[6] The direct influence treatment model required that the child be able to visualize alternatives in behavior and agree to new tasks formulated to address the problem areas. In addition, the behavioral component was also considered to include the element of anxiety. In behavior and learning theory, according to Bandura, anxiety could occur as a result of "anticipated aversive consequences."[7] This meant that information could be discriminative, signalling the occasion for reinforcement or punishment with the individual learning to anticipate aversive consequences. When the "anticipated aversive consequences" were no longer present due to successful task completion, anxiety could be expected to decrease.

Another explanation from these theories has linked anxiety with conditioned stimuli.

Anxiety is taken as a response to some immediately preceding stimulus and is maintained by reinforcing consequences (proximal stimuli). Proximal stimuli can be external (such as an upcoming examination or expressions of rejection or approval by an important other) or internal (such as self-statements about worthlessness or imagined stimuli and consequences). The important consideration, according to learning and behavioral theories, is that anxiety and avoidance behavior are responses elicited and maintained by specifiable proximal stimuli.[8]

The learning and behavioral theories thus differ from the psychodynamic theory of anxiety, as the latter considers it distal stimuli (underlying intrapsychic conflict), whereas the former considers it a response to proximal or immediate stimuli maintained by reinforcing consequences.[9] For purposes of this experiment, the research practitioner drew on theory that considered proximal stimuli.

In this treatment, the unconditional stimulus that was considered to reflexively elicit a response was disruptive behavior. The conditional stimulus was anxiety. After repeated pairing of disruptive behavior with anxiety, anxiety would naturally occur any time a form of disruptive behavior occurred and/or the environment acted as a discriminative stimulus for disruptive behavior.

Since research had demonstrated that "subjects can acquire emotional responses when both the CS [conditioned stimuli] and UCS [unconditioned stimuli] are symbolic,"[10] the practitioner decided to use suggestions, with visual images, and self-statements of the child as a way to elicit reduction in fear and anxiety in order to effect changes in behavior. In addition, relaxation procedures that could add a physiological component could be expected to aid in tension reduction, as had been noted in Jacobson's work.[11]

The component of internal control could be conceptualized as an ego function within psychodynamic theory,[12] or from theories of behavior and learning. Since the practitioner had referred to behavioral and learning theories with regard to anxiety and behavioral change in the experiment, she continued to draw on these proximal theories, which were consistent with a scalar instrument that could be used in measurement of "locus of control."[13]

Beyond the six steps in the treatment sequence, the research practitioner was also interested in evaluating the self-concept of the child, since anxiety was considered to be interwoven with those mechanisms of personality which maintain a negative or positive self-concept. It was also possible to obtain scalar measures of self-concept which could add further meaning to the study.[14] The above theoretical perspectives and references indicate the attempt by the research practitioner to combine some elements from different theories in guiding the development of a treatment sequence that could be grossly evaluated in practice.

It was a beginning research evaluation, and the questions of fit in theoretical explanation as referred to in the introduction should be explored in further study and in replication of these ideas for practice. For example, the explanations of anxiety from psychodynamic and from behavioral and learning theories are opposed. In this experiment, they were not joined but used for different purposes in the treatment process.

METHOD OF RESEARCH

An across-problems, multiple baseline, single-subject design[15] was selected by the research practitioner for determining whether a specified set of procedures identified under the rubric of direct influence would bring about change in a child's aggressive, maladaptive behavior, level of anxiety, ability to control impulses, and self-concept. The model specified procedures of assessment, tasks for behavioral change, relaxation, guided visual imagery rehearsal, suggestions, and verbal and concrete rewards within the therapeutic interview. It was expected that the evaluation would be gross. However, if it reflected measurable change, it could be replicated many times in practice, and various elements in the sequence could be specifically measured in order to enhance reliability and to determine the effectiveness of each procedure in the cluster. In addition, the effect of the penetration into the familial and school systems was not subject to specific measurement in the experiment and the effect of the limited involvement was not known.

Study Design. This study used the single-subject across-problems, multiple baseline design to test the efficacy of a therapeutic intervention with different problems of the same client system. Therefore, multiple baselines were taken on three targeted problems, and the interventions that incorporated the direct influence treatment sequence were staggered across the problems.

This type of design revolved around the ability to pinpoint the time of treatment in a time series of occurrences. Observation data were collected in baseline, treatment, and followup phases. This type of data collection allowed the research practitioner to continuously plot —in graphic form—changes in the behavioral problems. The graphic plotting of the data allowed visual inspection of behavioral change or lack of change prior to, throughout, and after treatment was initiated and completed.

In addition, the research practitioner used the distinct phases of baseline, treatment, and followup in data collection, which was used in the construction of celeration lines and Shewart charts, as presented by Bloom and Fischer,[16] to provide a means of statistical investigation of the data.

From the above methods, it followed that if A (the treatment) preceded B (the behavioral change) in a controlled series of at least three baseline periods, one could be reasonably assured that A was the causal factor in the change of B, and not C (a third, alternative, unknown variable).

The original design was to have been completed after eleven weeks. However, change did not begin to occur and was not observed in the statistical data until the seventh week of the study. Because the research was secondary to the human problems of the child and changes in the behavior were just beginning to occur, the research practitioner made the decision to replicate the design insofar as time would permit, given the termination of school for the summer recess. The original design was identified as Phase I and the replication as Phase II.

Sample. The child selected for the study attended a public, city school in southeastern Kentucky. She was ten years of age. This age was selected because behavioral patterns at that age are not generally as rigid as in the preteenage child, yet there was sufficient chronological maturity so that the child could act on suggestions and could control her small and large muscles as necessary in the relaxation process. She was also old enough to distinguish between make-believe and reality in visual imagery rehearsal.

The child was defined as school-maladjusted by her teacher and by the school principal. She was described as unable to function due to personal qualities or skill deficiencies that rendered her unable to cope with the educational or behavioral demands that the school environment placed upon her.

Prior history, described in her cumulative school record, reflected repeated behavioral difficulties. The child's record also indicated that she was unable to follow school routine from the time of her attendance in Head Start through the first four grades in elementary school. Her record included her recent failure and retention in the fourth grade. At the time of the research project, she had failed the first semester of her second year in the fourth grade and had failed the first six weeks of the second semester.

The problem behaviors centered around the characteristics of hostile disobedience (the child refused to comply with almost every request or demand placed upon her by the teacher), quarrelsomeness, physical and verbal aggressiveness, temper outbursts, hostile teasing of other children (particularly teasing of a child who had less academic ability than she), chronic anxiety as demonstrated by the child's fingernails being bitten into the quick on every finger and thumb, excessive and unrealistic fears of being kidnapped, and the inability to form close, meaningful personal relationships.

The child's intellectual ability was reported to be in the normal range (90–110) as measured by a group intelligence test that had been administered by the school system. Because of school regulations, the exact score could not be provided to the research practitioner.

The psychosocial assessment reflected a tense, action-oriented, defensive mother who denied interpersonal problems at home, but did reveal a prior traumatic, life-threatening accident in which the child was involved. The assessment suggested from a psychodynamic perspective that play therapy and consistent work with the mother/family could deal with the problems of fear, guilt, self-esteem, and interpersonal relationships. Since more extensive therapeutic involvement in the familial system was not possible, the child was screened into the experiment.

Treatment Process. The child was seen twice each week in one-hour sessions for a total of twenty-four sessions. In the initial phase of treatment, the child was seen for eleven weeks. The first week of the research project was observation. During the observation period, the research practitioner did not see the child. The second and third weeks of the research were used for pretesting, using the Nowicki-Stickland "A Locus of Control Scale for Children"[17] and the Piers-Harris "Children's Self-Concept Scale,"[18] the introduction of biofeedback equipment, and problem-task assessment. Beginning with the fourth week, treatment was begun and continued through the ninth week. Followup occurred in the tenth and eleventh weeks. When the design was partially replicated over an additional five-week period, there was one additional week of observation without intervention and then four additional weeks of treatment.

During the treatment hour, the child's problem behaviors were assessed and defined in precise terms. Contracts for behavioral change were based on the assessment and on what the child wanted to change in her behavior. As the child could not acknowledge negative behavior, the task usually centered on ways of behaving that allowed the child to do something she wished to do, such as going out for recess.

After the task formulation, the muscle relaxation process was begun. The child was taught to relax the different muscle groups that composed her body, beginning with the eyelids and moving in a downward direction toward—and including—the feet and toes. In the tensing and relaxing of muscle groups, the child produced physiological signals of which she was unaware. A biofeedback machine was used to give the child immediate feedback as to her progress in relaxation. The aim was to help the child develop awareness of these signals in order to develop control over her body. With this type of body control, positive changes in locus of control and self-concept were hypothesized to occur. In addition, the EMG (electromyographic) biofeedback machine furnished the research practitioner with specific numerical data as to the level of anxiety the child was experiencing.

After the child reached a stage of deep muscle relaxation, she was asked to watch herself in her mind's eye successfully perform the agreed-upon behavioral task. The research practitioner repeated and described in minute detail the behaviors the child was to perform in the completion of her agreed-upon task. The research practitioner continually checked with the child to learn whether she was able to visualize the descriptions of the appropriate behaviors and maintain an appropriate level of relaxation. The child was asked to assume the feelings that accompanied successful vicarious task completion. The rehearsal of these positive emotions was considered to be a vital element in this model. It was assumed that if one rehearsed positive emotions and enjoyed the feelings vicariously experienced, an attempt would be made to replicate the experiences in the real world.

After rehearsal of the appropriate positive emotions, the child was given positive suggestions that she would be able to replicate her vicarious experiences in her real world. Between sessions, the child's task was to implement the agreed-upon rehearsed behaviors. Through the repetition of this process, it was hypothesized that she would successfully change the disruptive behaviors, and decreases in anxiety level would occur.

At the beginning of the sessions, task progress was reviewed. At times, this was an exciting and rewarding period in the treatment process. At this stage of treatment, the child and the research practitioner reviewed the implementation process the child had undertaken. If the child successfully completed the task, her pleasure with herself and her accomplishment was rewarded verbally by the research practitioner. Through her successes, she was encouraged and motivated to attempt more difficult tasks that could eventually lead to the successful accomplishment of her long-range goal.

When difficulties were encountered and the child was unable to complete the task, the obstacles surrounding the task failure were explored. It was critical that the research practitioner understand the feelings the child was experiencing as a result of her failure. Without this assessment and exploration of feelings, the research practitioner believed that she would not have been able to be supportive and to instill hope that the child would be able to complete the newly reformulated task. Without support and facilitation of hope, it is believed that the child would not have attempted the reformulated task.

At the end of each treatment session, the child was allowed to choose one physical reward from an array of fruit, crackers, and cakes. The reward was for her active involvement during the treatment session. The forced choice was used to set limits and to aid the child in developing internal control. The reward of food was also expected to have a deeper emotional meaning for the child.

Instrumentation of Measurement Variables. The variables in the study were addressed by the development of three hypotheses for investigation.

HYPOTHESIS 1: The application of the direct influence treatment model which included relaxation, contracted behavioral change, visual imagery rehearsal, suggestions, and verbal and concrete rewards will significantly decrease the level of anxiety and targeted disruptive behaviors in the aggressive, acting-out child in the classroom setting.

To measure changes in anxiety (dependent variable) during the treatment process, the child was attached to an EMG biofeedback machine. Readings were taken at the beginning, middle, and ending of the relaxation phase in each of the treatment sessions. Readings were hypothesized to be highest at the beginning of the relaxation phase and to decrease after the relaxation phase had been completed. Further, it was hypothesized that the level of anxiety that the child was experiencing would gradually decrease over the treatment sessions.

To measure changes in disruptive behavior (dependent variable), baseline data using number of frequencies of the disruptive behaviors under investigation were tallied by two independent observers prior to, throughout, and during the followup phase of the treatment. The same process was followed in the replication phase of treatment.

The data collected on disruptive behaviors were plotted graphically and analyzed statistically using celeration lines and Shewart Charts as presented by Bloom and Fischer.[19]

HYPOTHESIS 2: The application of the direct influence treatment model which includes relaxation, contracted behavioral change, visual imagery rehearsal, suggestions, and verbal and concrete rewards will demonstrate a significant increase in internal locus of control in the aggressive acting-out child.

To measure changes in the child's locus of control, the research practitioner administered the scale, "A Locus of Control Scale for Children," as referred to above. The scale was administered on four separate occasions: at the beginning of the study, in the middle of Phase I, at the conclusion of Phase I, and at the conclusion of Phase II. The scale scores were compared and analyzed.

HYPOTHESIS 3: The application of the direct influence treatment model which includes relaxation, contracted behavioral change, suggestions, and verbal and concrete rewards will demonstrate a significant increase in the self-concept of the aggressive, acting-out child.

To measure changes in the child's self-concept, the research practitioner administered the Piers-Harris "Children's Self-Concept Scale," as referred to above, on four separate occasions. The scale was administered at the beginning of the study, in the middle of Phase I, at the conclusion of Phase I, and at the conclusion of Phase II. The scale scores were compared and analyzed.

Measurement of the Independent Variable. The independent variable in this practice research was the proposed treatment model that expanded the holistic term of direct influence to include a sequential clustering of contracted behavioral change, relaxation, visual imagery rehearsal, suggestions, and verbal and concrete rewards. In order to determine that the proposed model was being utilized in treatment, line-by-line content analysis of what transpired during the treatment sessions was conducted.

To allow the judges to analyze the content, the treatment sessions were tape recorded. A third of the transcribed recordings was randomly selected for review by two judges. The research practitioner trained two judges to recognize nine specific categories of communication. The categories were (a) background information; (b) problem identification; (c) contracted behavioral change; (d) relaxation; (e) guided visual imagery; (f) suggestions; (g) rewards; (h) technical comments; and (i) other.

The two judges analyzed the content, line-by-line, in eight of the randomly selected transcribed sessions. In this manner, the type of communication between the child and the research practitioner was coded.

Lines of Analysis. The variation of the single-case design known as the across-problems or multiple baseline design relied on interrupted time-series analysis for the evaluation of data generated by the research. Using celeration lines and Shewart charts constructed from the observation data collected by the classroom observers, the research practitioner statistically measured the effects of treatment on the three targeted behaviors.

The interrelated dependent variables—consisting of targeted behaviors, anxiety, locus of control, and self-concept—were measured by independent observers, mechanical means, and validated scales. The observers tallied the frequencies of the targeted behaviors throughout the study. Anxiety was measured with an EMG biofeedback machine at the beginning, middle, and ending of the relaxation phase in each treatment session. Locus of control was measured by the Nowicki-Strickland Locus of Control Scale for Children at the pre, mid, and post phases of the first intervention phase. It was administered again at the conclusion of the replication phase. Self-concept was measured by the Piers-Harris Self-Concept Scale for Children at the pre, mid, and post phases of the first intervention phase and again at the conclusion of the replication phase.

The independent variable, the direct influence model, was measured by two independent judges through line-by-line content analysis of eight of the randomly selected transcribed sessions.

THE FINDINGS

The direct influence treatment model was conceptualized in the research as a treatment sequence to be tested with one aggressive, acting-out child. It was, therefore, the independent variable used in hypothesis testing. Evaluation of the independent variable was based on study of the reliability of interjudge agreement in coding categories in a line-by-line analysis of the transcribed tape interview sessions that implemented the direct influence treatment model. The statistical analysis of data in this study required an 0.05 level for acceptance of significance.

Eight of the total twenty-four interviews that used the direct influence treatment model were randomly selected for line-by-line content analysis. The eight interviews were transcribed verbatim from the tape recordings of the sessions. The lines of the transcript were numbered consecutively. The content of the lines were coded using the nine categories identified for coding the communications of the child and the research practitioner within the interview. The specified direct influence procedures followed the exploration of problem and task development, and the nine categories captured this holistic process of intervention. The categories were as follows: (a) background information; (b) problem identification; (c) contracted behavioral change; (d) relaxation; (e) guided visual imagery rehearsal; (f) suggestions; (g) rewards; (h) technical comments; and (i) other.

All eight interviews were then coded by two judges trained in the use of the categories of the direct influence treatment mode.

The reliability of the coding was studied through comparisons of how the line content was distributed into the nine direct influence categories. All nine categories were used in all eight of the randomly selected interviews. The number of lines in the interviews ranged from a low of 274 in the twelfth interview to a high of 632 in the sixth interview. The mean number of lines for the eight sessions transcribed was 447.25.

To determine the degree of reliability between the two judges, a measure of association, the Spearman Rank Correlation Coefficients, R_s, as presented by Siegel,[20] was used to study the strength of the relationship or interjudge agreement. The judgments were considered to be reliable if the resulting statistic achieved was significant at the 0.05 level.

The analysis proceeded by tallying the number of times the communication of the research practitioner and the child was judged to occur in each of the nine categories in each of the eight sessions. In this manner, a numerical score for the research practitioner and the child in each of the nine categories for each of the eight transcribed sessions was achieved. The differences between the two judgments in each category in each of the eight sessions were computed and ranked. Therefore, the scores in each category in each session were ranked from the lowest to the highest. The Spearman Rank Correlation Coefficient was then computed on each category to ascertain the level of agreement between the two judges.

The results of the computations demonstrated that of the total nine categories of judgments by the two judges measured by the Spearman Rank Correlation Coefficient, five categories were found to be statistically significant (p.<0.01), two categories were found to be statistically significant at an 0.05 level, and only the D category of relaxation that coded the communication of the child was found not to be statistically significant at an 0.05 level. This could be a result of the limited use of this particular category by the child in all of the eight transcribed interviews. The nature of the procedure would logically suggest a small number of communications for the child in this category.

The level of interjudge agreement supported the finding that, indeed, the direct influence treatment model—or the independent variable—was being utilized with the child in the treatment interviews.

Evaluation of Hypothesis 1. Observational data for Hypothesis 1 were collected daily from the beginning of the research and throughout its entirety by two independent classroom observers. The observational data were subjected to mathematical computations to remove the auto-correlation. The data were then subjected to time-series analysis that employed celeration lines and Shewart charts as we use statistical computations based on the cumulative binomial probability distribution.

Hypothesis 1 stated that treatment using the proposed model of direct influence would decrease the anxiety level and the frequency of aggressive acting-out behavior in three targeted problem behaviors. The problem behaviors were identified as: (a) talking-out behavior, (b) interfering with other student's study, and (c) demanding the teacher's attention.

Behavior A: Talking-Out. The celeration line constructed for Behavior A that computed the frequencies of the daily fifteen-minute time periods of observation showed a definite acceleration of the acting-out behavior during the first baseline, intervention, and follow-up phase. The statistical analysis, using the binomial probability distribution, required that 24 behavioral points should occur below the acceleration line to occur beyond chance and to be significant at less than a 0.05 level. In the study data, only 21 behavioral points occurred below the acceleration line. Therefore, change beyond chance was not achieved. However, a positive decrease in problem behavior was developing.

A second celeration line was constructed on Behavior A for the second baseline period, intervention, and follow-up in the replication phase, using the fifteen-minute time periods of observation. The celeration line was descending in direction. The binomial probability distibution required that 22 behavioral points should occur below the deceleration line to achieve a 0.05 level of significance. Only 20 behavioral points occurred below the deceleration line. Therefore, significance was not achieved. However, a positive decrease in problem behavior was developing.

Behavior B: Interrupting Other Student's Study. The celeration line constructed for Behavior B using four fifteen-minute time periods demonstrated a definite decline in the acting-out behavior during the first baseline, intervention, and follow-up phase. The statistical analysis using the binomial probability distribution indicated that 21 behavioral points or events of acting-out should occur below the deceleration line to achieve significance at the 0.05 level. There were 15 behavioral points below the deceleration line, which did not demonstrate significance.

A second celeration line was constructed to demonstrate change in Behavior B for the second baseline and intervention phase of the replication, using the fifteen-minute time periods. A follow-up phase was not included as the research was terminated because of the closing of school for the summer recess. The celeration line demonstrated a decelerating slope in the desired direction. The statistical analysis using the binomial probability distribution required that 37 behavioral points should occur below the deceleration line in order to achieve statistical significance. Thirty-two behavioral points occurred below the deceleration line, and significance was not demonstrated at the 0.05 level.

Behavior C: Demanding the Teacher's Attention. The celeration line constructed for Behavior C using four fifteen-minute time periods showed a definite decline in the acting-out behavior during the baseline, intervention, and follow-up phase. The statistical analysis of the data at the 0.05 level required that 25 behavioral points should occur below the deceleration line. Only 20 behavioral points occurred. Therefore, significance was not achieved.

A second celeration line was not constructed on Behavior C for the second phase of treatment, as the research was terminated prior to the beginning of the second phase because of summer recess.

Analysis of Data by Shewart Charts. To further analyze the data, Shewart charts were constructed on all of the three problem behaviors using the observation data to compute two standard deviation levels above and below the mean. The data had been subjected to second difference transformations to remove the autocorrelation and consisted of frequency of occurrence of the behavioral events in the fifteen-minute time periods.

The Shewart charts constructed for Behaviors A, B, and C using fifteen-minute time periods did not, during the first intervention phase, demonstrate two consecutive observations outside of the two standard deviation bands. Therefore, any change was no more than chance and statistical significance was not achieved.

Shewart charts were also constructed on Behaviors A and B using fifteen-minute time periods for the second baseline, intervention, and follow-up in the replication phase. The Shewart charts again did not demonstrate two consecutive observations two standard deviations below the mean in the desired direction during the intervention phase. Therefore, statistical significance was not achieved.

As school was recessed for the summer months prior to the second intervention phase for Behavior C, data could not be collected for the replication of the design. Hence, observations for Behavior C included only Phase I.

For more detailed information on the above analysis of data with analytic charts and scales, see Flowers, *A Social Work Paradigm for Treatment of One Aggressive, Acting-Out Child.*[21]

Summary of Findings on Hypothesis 1. Hypothesis 1 stated that a statistically significant decrease would occur in all three targeted behaviors as a result of the application of the direct influence treatment model. This part of the hypothesis was rejected. The analysis indicated some changes in the desired direction in all three targeted behaviors, but not at a significant level.

The hypothesis also stated that treatment with the direct influence treatment model would significantly decrease anxiety in the aggressive, acting-out child. The biofeedback data clearly demonstrated reduction in anxiety level. However, the high initial readings of 30 and 20 microvolts could possibly be the result of anxiety generated by the beginning of treatment and the introduction of a strange mechanical device. The continued gradual reduction in motor unit firings, as measured in microvolts, did demonstrate that the child was able to learn how to successfully control her body and decrease her level of tension. Therefore, this part of Hypothesis 1 which stated that a significant decrease in anxiety level in the aggressive acting-out child would occur with application of the direct influence treatment model was accepted.

Changes Reflected in Substitute Behaviors as Demonstrated by Using Other Measures. Even though statistical differences were not demonstrated in the three specified areas for behavioral change, the substitute behaviors of paying attention in class and completing homework assignments, reflected change in the form of completed homework assignments submitted to the teacher and by grades earned. The change in the level of completing homework assignments was demonstrated by the decrease in the number of zeros received by the child. In the first six weeks of the second semester, the child received a total of thirty-seven zeros in her subjects. The third six weeks of the second semester, the child received a total of two zeros in her subjects. As there could have been a number of undetermined variables that could have accounted for this change, it cannot be said the direct influence treatment model was the sole determining factor in this remarkable change.

Additionally, in the area of grades earned, the child's grade point average for the first six weeks of the second semester was 0.57. The child's grade point average for the third six weeks of the second semester was 1.86. Again, as there could have been a number of undetermined variables that could have accounted for this change, it cannot be said the direct influence treatment model was the sole determining factor in this remarkable change in grade level.

Summary of Findings on Hypothesis 2. Hypothesis 2 stated that treatment with the proposed model would increase the internal locus of control in the aggressive, acting-out child.

The concept was operationally measured by "A Locus of Control Scale for Children," as previously indicated. The scale was administered to the child on four separate occasions and the scores are presented in table 12.1.

The scalar scores indicated a marked increase in external locus of control. Therefore, the hypothesis was rejected. However, the scoring pattern on the scale is quite consistent with the findings in the treatment sessions. Originally, the child was unable to acknowledge any negative behavior. Toward the end of treatment, the child was developing a much more realistic picture of herself and of her relationships with others. Therefore, she was less defensive and coming under the control of significant others in her life. As a result, the locus of control was shifting in an external direction. This was a more socially acceptable outcome. In essence, the change demonstrated more appropriate interaction of the child with her world.

Summary of Findings on Hypothesis 3. Hypothesis 3 stated that treatment with the proposed direct influence treatment model would increase the self-concept of the aggressive, acting-out child.

The concept was operationally defined by Piers in the scale entitled

TABLE 12.1 Scores Attained by the Subject on the Nowicki-Strickland Locus of Control Scale by Periods of Administration

	Administration Periods			
	1st *1/18/83*	*2d* *2/10/83*	*3d* *4/21/83*	*4th* *5/17/83*
Scores on Locus of Control Scale	13	13	10	22

the "Piers-Harris Children's Self-Concept Scale," as referred to above. It was administered to the child at four separate intervals. The data from the self-concept scales are presented in table 12.2. The child's scores on the self-concept scale were compared and demonstrated a decrease in self-concept as measured by the scale. Therefore, the hypothesis was rejected.

The child's first three scale scores of 71, 78, and 67 indicated a high level of self-concept. The last score of 56, however, indicated a much lower self-concept level. In the Piers-Harris School Age Norms, the child's first score of 71 occurred at the 94th percentile range and was in the 8th stanine. The child's second score of 78 occurred above the 99th percentile range and was above the 9th stanine. The child's third score of 67 occurred in the 87th percentile range and was in the 7th stanine. The child's final score of 56 occurred at the 57th percentile range and was in the 5th stanine.

These comparative scores indicated that the child's scores varied from 4 to 5 stanines from the time of the first administration of the scale to the last administration of the scale. The last administration of the scale occurred at the time of termination. This could have affected the score. However, if the findings are viewed in relation to the research practitioner's other findings, the scoring pattern on the scale was quite consistent with the findings during the treatment sessions and on the locus of control scale. Originally, the child was unable to acknowledge any of her negative behavior. Toward the end of treatment, she was developing a much more realistic picture of herself and of her relationship to others. Therefore, her former unrealistic self-concept scores were shifting in a more realistic direction.

Hypothesis 3, which stated that a significant increase in self-concept in the aggressive, acting-out child should occur, was rejected. Instead, a marked change occurred with decrease in the self-concept

TABLE 12.2 Scores Attained by the Subject on the Piers-Harris
Self-Concept Scale

| | Administration Periods | | | |
	1/18/83	2/10/83	4/21/83	4/17/83
Scores on Self-Concept Scale	71	78	67	56

score as measured by the Piers-Harris scale. In essence, change in the opposite direction demonstrated the ability of the child to ask for and to receive help when needed, which reflected reduction in defensiveness, improved sense of self, and a socially more acceptable behavior.

SUMMARY

The research practitioner evaluated, in the single-system, across-problems, multiple baseline design, a direct influence treatment model with one aggressive, acting-out child. The nonprobability selection of one child naturally limited any generalization but allowed the research practitioner to evaluate in a single-case design a treatment sequence of direct influence on behavioral problems that represented extremes in disruptive school behavior. The application of the model during the treatment sessions specified procedures for implementation. The procedures were: (a) problem assessment, (b) contracted behavioral change through substitute tasks, (c) relaxation, (d) guided visual imagery rehearsal, (e) suggestions, and (f) verbal and concrete rewards.

Three problem areas of aggressive, disruptive behavior in the classroom were identified for change. The three problems were: (a) talking out, (b) interfering with other student's study, and (c) demanding the teacher's attention. None of the three targeted behaviors demonstrated statistically significant changes. However, the behaviors did demonstrate change trends in a positive direction.

In addition to changes in disruptive behaviors, Hypothesis 1 also stated that with the treatment of the direct influence model, a significant decrease in anxiety level would occur. This component of the hypothesis required use of an EMG biofeedback machine to measure the level of anxiety. The readings of the machine demonstrated marked change, indicating that the child's anxiety level had indeed decreased.

The model required that the child imagine substitute behaviors of paying attention in class, handing in homework assignments, reading to the class, etc. The behavior of handing in homework assignments was reflected in grades earned, which indicated a marked positive change.

Hypothesis 2 stated that with the model of treatment a significant increase in internal locus of control would occur. Changes were measured by "The Locus of Control Scale for Children," which reached statistically significant levels but in the opposite direction from what was hypothesized. Instead of change occurring in internal control, a change toward accepting external control took place. However, for this aggressive, acting-out child who was too vulnerable to accept limitations and controls, the direction of change was appropriate.

Hypothesis 3 stated that—with the model of treatment—a significant increase in self-concept would occur. Change was measured by the Piers-Harris Children's Self-Concept Scale which demonstrated statistically significant levels of change. However, the change was in a descending direction, or lowering of self-concept. However, for this aggressive, acting-out child, whose pretest measures were abnormally high, reflecting the child's marked defensiveness, fantasy, and inability to acknowledge her disruptive behavior, the direction of change was more realistic and represented change in the appropriate direction.

It is recognized that the sequence of direct influence was subject to uncontrolled biasing influences. The specific influences of the worker-client relationship and sustaining work with the mother and the school system were not specifically measured. In no way can it be said that the model is superior to the more traditional model of play therapy, where psychodynamic explanations underlie the treatment process. However, as the model has drawn on differing theories and practices, it may be further replicated and refined. Each element of the sequence should be tested and evidence acquired for incorporating it within a treatment program under selected conditions, or discarded.

The study reflects an example of empirical research in practice that derived from a practitioner's concern about a genuine practice problem. It was a beginning attempt to find a fruitful way to deal with the problem and be helpful to clients. It is of interest that follow-up of the child in the experiment did indicate that she was making an adequate school adjustment in the subsequent school year (fifth grade).

CHAPTER 13

A Historical Study of Object Relations and the Borderline Patient

Jeffrey Seinfeld

This chapter will describe how a theoretical/clinical study evolved as a dissertation for graduate work. In the introduction to this book, Orcutt has stressed that social workers should not only apply theory but also make advances in theory and practice knowledge. This study was an effort in that direction.

The study concerns object relations theory and the borderline patient. No attempt was made to apply object relations theory to practice or to develop principles of practice, based on object relations theory for borderline patients. Rather, the study viewed both the existing theoretical literature and the clinical data of the practitioner's own patients as objects of study. The literature was not only used to inform his clinical-research observations and interventions, but it was also studied on the basis of his clinical observations.

The study of the borderline patient from an object relations perspective could encompass a vast range of theoretical and clinical issues including descriptive, structural, and developmental assessment and diagnosis, and implications for psychotherapeutic technique in intensive and supportive treatments. The practitioner focused his study on one particular issue: the rejection of empathy by

Jeffrey Seinfeld is Assistant Professor in the School of Social Work at New York University and Consultant for the Jewish Board of Family and Children's Services in New York City.

the borderline patient. In discussing the borderline patient's psychic structure, primitive defenses, transference evolution in treatment, and intervention strategies, the practitioner remained focused on studying how these phenomena relate to the borderline patient's rejection of empathy.

The study, therefore, focused on a specific question: how and why does the borderline patient reject empathy? Process recordings of the practitioner's long-term intensive work with borderline patients were used as data. The patient's transference to the practitioner was the context in which the patient's rejection of empathy was studied. At the same time, the practitioner also reviewed the theoretical view on object relations concerning this issue. Since the issue was limited in scope to the investigation of a practitioner-patient dynamic, other elements of the person-situation context were not the direct focus of study.

The review of object relations literature included ego psychology, especially the work of Mahler and colleagues in *The Psychological Birth of the Human Infant*.[1] Other important literature included American object relations theory as developed by Kernberg[2] and Masterson,[3] the British school of object relations associated with Fairbairn,[4] and self psychology.[5] The practitioner identified the contradictions and problems among these different schools and then attempted to evaluate them from the perspective of what was being learned from his own clinical experience, while he also utilized these theories to inform his own clinical observation. He was especially interested in making sense—from his own experience—of some of the contradictions and problems that were identified in the literature.

To study the borderline patient's rejection of the empathy of the practitioner, it was tracked how the patient related to his own internal image of the practitioner. Toward this end, the patient was worked with on tracking what he did or did not do with his image of the practitioner at intervals between sessions. It was of special interest to study whether a relationship existed between those patients who angrily rejected an empathic image of the practitioner and those patients who indifferently forgot his existence. Constructs of the British school of object relations were integrated with American ego psychology to arrive at certain conclusions about the psychodynamics of the borderline patient's rejection of the empathic image of the practitioner and contributed specific new theoretical ideas concerning the borderline patient's impairment in self and object constancy. Toward this end, the borderline patient's present rejection of the empathic image of his clinical worker was studied as it related to the patient's developmental experiences with early external objects.

For instance, the child's object constancy becomes impeded, not only because of a deficit in external good object or parenting experience, but also because of an identification with the parental rejection of the child's need for a good object. In this regard, the patient rejects his own need for the good parental object. For instance, in the treatment setting, the borderline child will sometimes repeatedly draw pictures but then throw them away as worthless. With this behavior, the child rejects his own need to exhibit his individualist achievements to the practitioner as the good, admiring external object. In throwing away the drawing, the child is identified with the rejecting object and projectively identifying the rejected self-representation into the drawing.

The internalized object situation results in the child closing himself off and not taking in the accepting object. In this case example, the child's need for mirroring or acceptance was severely rejected by the parent. Therefore, the child did not internalize a good mirroring object that would eventually result in object constancy, but instead internalized rejection of the good object. This rejection remained an active process in terms of the child's continued rejection of his needs for the good parental object. Instead, the child internalized the rejecting parental object and remained loyal and in relationship with it by continuing to reject his own need for a good object. In the treatment setting, the child continued to enact the rejection of the need for a good object by rejecting his own productions and the need for the other's acceptance. In this way, the impairment of object constancy not only results from the lack of good object experience, but also from the continuation of an active rejection of the taking in of an external good object.

The practitioner's interest in this study had developed out of the clinical experience of trying to understand why some patients rejected efforts at empathy and the desire to arrive at some techniques that would help them to accept empathy.

As Orcutt points out in earlier chapters, Kuhn has shown how scientific observers do not approach their field of study from the vantage point of pure empiricism but are influenced in their perception and understanding by past ideas, concepts, and theories, which they reorganize into a novel synthesis. Kuhn's views are consistent with a dialectical perspective in philosophy. In the dialectical view, Engels has stated: "Further, we find that upon closer investigation

the two poles of anti-thesis, like positive and negative, are as inseparable as they are opposed, and despite all their opposition, they inter-
penetrate."[6] The practitioner approached this study from the dialectical perspective of juxtaposing autonomy and dependence as the two
poles of Mahler's conceptualization of the rapprochement subphase
in human development that are both opposed but inevitably inseparable. In this regard, as the rapprochement youngster discovers his
autonomy, he will inevitably experience a heightening of vulnerability and dependency needs. Therefore, in the clinical experience, a
similar paradox is often seen in which the patient's greater intrapsychic autonomy is manifested by intensified interpersonal dependency.

In this study, the American and British object relations theories of
borderline pathology were approached from a dialectical viewpoint.
The American school emphasizes that borderline pathology results
from the parental object's rejection of the child's autonomy strivings
and rewarding of dependency needs. The British school, on the other
hand, focuses on the parental object's rejection of dependency and
rewarding of pseudo-autonomy. The contradiction between these
models was illustrated. Then, a resolution was attempted by suggesting that the parental object of the borderline patient rejected both
autonomy and dependency during rapprochement. Furthermore, the
inseparable, interpenetrable aspect of these two poles during rapprochement subphase and in borderline pathology was emphasized.
In developing the study, no attempt was made to arrive at a new
general theory of borderline pathology but focus was limited to the
specific issue of how and why the borderline patient rejects the practitioner's empathy, and the relationship of this issue to the impairment of object constancy. A brief clinical vignette will serve to illustrate this phenomenon.

Marsha, a young adult, came for treatment because of oversensitiv-
ity to rejection and criticism in interpersonal relationships. She would
talk on the telephone with friends and never end the conversations
herself. However, when the friends finally said goodbye, she'd feel
rejected. She would want to be with her boyfriend constantly so that
whenever he had to leave her or do something on his own, she'd feel
rejected. Through such repeated occurrences, the practitioner demonstrated that she maintained a rejecting image of the other and a
rejected image of the self, and constantly projected this all-negative
internal self object relations unit into her interpersonal relationships.
When Marsha became convinced that the rejecting self and object
relations unit dominated her relationships, the practitioner wondered

aloud why she needed to maintain a rejected image of the self and rejecting image of the other.

Marsha now began to manifest evidence of the activation of the all-negative object relations unit in the transference. For instance, once she went out of state for a few days and asked the practitioner if she could call if a problem arose. When she called, she left the wrong telephone number on his answering machine and then felt rejected and disappointed that the practitioner never returned her call. She then came for her treatment appointment at the wrong time but imagined that the practitioner forgot about her and stood her up. She then dreamt that she expressed anger at him and called to make sure he was not angry at her. In the dream, he had told her that he was sick of her craziness and terminated the treatment.

The practitioner interpreted that Marsha had him reject her in the dream, illustrating that she needed to maintain a rejecting image of him. He recommended that they track her image of him between sessions to further understand the dynamic. Marsha followed the recommendation and, after a time, noticed that whenever she experienced positive feelings for the practitioner as accepting, empathic, or caring, she automatically thought of a reason to be angry with him and his image then became a rejecting one. She then rejected the image of the practitioner as a "good parent" in the relationship and thereby impeded the development of the object constancy in the transference. The study also investigated the development problems that resulted in the patient's rejecting of an empathic image of the object and what difficulties arose once she began to maintain the empathic object image.

It is very important for anyone attempting theoretical/clinical research to select one specific idea and to study and describe all theoretical and clinical phenomena, no matter how wide ranging, from this specific viewpoint. The limitation of the domain in developing this study guided the practitioner with the idea of sticking to the issue. Much of the study also centered on developing interventions and practice principles that could deal with the borderline patient's stormy behavior and the borderline patient as related to the rejection of empathy. It was questioned whether there is any relationship between one patient's angry and overt rejection of the practitioner's empathy and another patient's indifferently forgetting his existence, appointment hours, etc.? What do patients do with the empathic image of their clinical helper at intervals between sessions? What treatment interventions might help the patient internalize the practitioner's empathy? To answer these questions, the clinical researcher looked at a broad range of borderline phenomena but always with these questions in mind.

In conclusion, this chapter discusses the process of developing a theoretical/clinical dissertation in social work, which is apropos to the clinical research orientation suggested in the book. The author, as a clinical practitioner, focused on a specific issue, the borderline patient's rejection of empathy in the transference relationship. The existing object relations literature informed clinical observation and practice, but clinical experience also raised questions about contradictions and problems in the literature.

The theoretical views that were advanced in this study stated that the borderline patient identified with the parental object's rejection of his autonomy and dependency during the rapprochement subphase. Fairbairn, in his endopsychic structural theory, said that the patient develops an antilibidinal self-representation that identifies with the external object's rejection of his dependency needs.[7] Fairbairn says that the patient antilibidinally grows up to reject his own infantile dependency needs and an external good object. Fairbairn's views were advanced further in this study by stating that not only does the patient reject an external relationship to a good object but also the internalization of that relationship, as was illustrated in the above clinical vignette. Furthermore, the study suggested that the patient rejects the internalization of the good object with the same attitudes and behavior through which the external object originally rejected the patient's need to take in a good object.

For instance, if the patient's parental objects angrily rejected his vulnerability and need for a good object, the patient will now angrily attack his helper or practitioner's image. If the parental object rejected the child with indifference, the patient will reject the practitioner's image by indifference. For instance, the adult male patient continually stood up the practitioner by not coming for sessions and not calling to cancel. When the practitioner would explore the failed sessions, the patient said that he forgot. In the course of the treatment, it was learned that during the patient's early childhood, his mother would often promise to be home by a certain hour but not return, saying that she forgot. The patient thereby experienced rejection of his need for a good dependable parent in the form of being stood up and forgotten. In the treatment, he was identified with the object who stood him up in that he now rejected his own need for a good object by standing up and forgetting the practitioner. Therefore, in early childhood, his object constancy was impaired by the parental figure's inability to remember him. He now impaired his own object constancy in the same manner, by not remembering the good object.

Fairbairn's views were also synthesized with ego psychology by suggesting that the patient not only rejects dependency needs but also autonomy strivings. Toward this view, the dialectical inseparability of these two opposing poles may be examined. Further details of the examination of these theoretical positions and their dialectical insep…arability may be found in Seinfeld, "An Object Relations Theoretical Contribution to the Understanding of the Psychopathology and Intensive Psychotherapy of the Borderline Personality Organization" and *The Bad Object: Handling the Negative Therapeutic Reaction.*[8]

Notes

INTRODUCTION

1. The concept, "person-in-situation," has been used historically as a focus in social casework; however, we have also used "person/family-in-environment" to highlight orientation to the family system, as noted in our earlier writings. We believe the family system is of such importance to the individual system that it should be highlighted in orientation, though we use the two concepts interchangeably; Ben A. Orcutt, "Casework Intervention in the Problems of the Poor," p. 89; Gordon Hamilton, "Basic Concepts Upon Which Case-work Practice is Formulated," pp. 138–149; Gordon Hamilton, *Theory and Practice of Social Casework*, pp. 3–4; Florence Hollis, *Social Casework in Practice*, p. 279; Florence Hollis, *Casework*, p. 10.

2. Gordon Hearn, "General Systems Theory and Social Work," pp. 333–339; William Gordon, "Basic Constructs for an Integrative and Generative Conception of Social Work," pp. 8–10; James G. Miller, "Living Systems," pp. 51–133.

3. Ludwig von Bertalanffy, "General Systems Theory and Psychiatry," pp. 33–46.

4. Helen Northen, *Clinical Social Work*, p. 1; Hollis and Woods, *Casework*, pp. 25–55; Phyllis Caroff, ed., *Treatment Formulations and Clinical Social Work*, pp. 1–10.

5. Carol H. Meyer, ed., *Clinical Social Work in the Eco-Systems Perspective*; Carol Meyer, "Trends and Issues in Direct Social Work Practice," pp. 225–236. The ecological perspective advocated by Carol B. Germain and Alex Gitterman, in *The Life Model of Social Work Practice*, also focuses on person-environment and reciprocal adaptational processes. Some differences in perspective with ecosystems is

highlighted by Geoffrey L. Greif, "The Eco-Systems Perspective, 'Meet the Press,' " pp. 225–226.

6. Alan Garfinkel, *Forms of Explanation*, p. 1.

7. Oscar C. M'Culloch, "The Organization of Charities," pp. 10–35.

8. Charles D. Kellog, "Statistics," pp. 31–32.

9. Scott Briar, "Incorporating Research Into Education for Clinical Practice in Social Work," pp. 132–140; Scott Briar, "Toward the Integration of Practice and Research," pp. 31–37.

10. Martin Bloom, "Empirically Based Clinical Research," pp. 560–582.

11. William J. Reid and Audrey D. Smith, *Research in Social Work*, pp. 16–63.

12. William J. Reid, "Developing Intervention Methods Through Experimental Designs," pp. 650–675; William Reid, *Family Problem Solving;* William Reid, *The Task-Centered System;* William J. Reid and Laura Epstein, *Task-Centered Casework.*

13. Edwin J. Thomas, "Mousetraps, Developmental Research and Social Work Education," pp. 468–483; Edwin Thomas, "Beyond Knowledge Utilization in General Human Service Technology," pp. 91–103; Edwin Thomas, *Designing Interventions for the Helping Professions.*

14. Jack Rothman, *Research and Development in the Human Services.*

15. Edward J. Mullen, "Personal Practice Models," pp. 623–649.

16. Aaron Rosenblatt, "The Practitioner's Use and Evaluation of Research," pp. 53–59; Stuart A. Kirk and Aaron Rosenblatt, "New Applications of Research in Clinical Practice," pp. 549–559; Briar, "Toward the Integration of Practice and Research," pp. 31–37.

17. Some significant publications include: Srinika Jayaratne and Rona L. Levy, *Empirical Clinical Practice;* Tony Tripodi, *Evaluative Research for Social Workers;* Tony Tripodi and Irwin Epstein, *Research Techniques for Clinical Social Workers;* Reid and Smith, *Research in Social Work;* John S. Wodarski, *The Role of Research in Clinical Practice;* Martin Bloom and Joel Fischer, *Evaluating Practice: Guidelines for the Accountable Professional;* Walter W. Hudson, *The Clinical Measurement Package.*

18. Rino J. Patti, "The Prospects for Social R & D," p. 38.

19. William Gordon, "Does Social Work Research Have a Future?" p. 4.

20. Betty J. Blythe and Scott Briar, "Developing Empirically Based Models of Practice," p. 487.

21. Max Siporin, "Current Social Work Perspectives on Clinical Practice," p. 206.

22. Ibid.

23. Martha B. Heineman, "The Obsolete Scientific Imperative in Social Work Research," pp. 371–397; Martha Heineman Pieper, "The Future of Social Work Research," pp. 3–11; John S. Brekke, "Scientific Imperative in Social Work Research," pp. 538–554; Edward J. Mullen, "Methodological Dilemmas in Social Work Research," pp. 12–20; Vernon R. Wiehe, "Scientific Technology and the Human Condition," pp. 88–97.

24. Robert Dubin, *Theory Building*, pp. 17–18.

25. Reid, *Task-Centered System*, p. 12.

26. Lindley Darden and Nancy Maull, "Interfield Theories," pp. 43–64; Stephen Toulmin, "From Form to Function," p. 158.

27. Henry S. Maas, *People and Contexts.*

28. Toulmin, "From Form to Function," pp. 143–162.

29. Discussion of the liberalization of logical positivism as logical empiricism is found in chapter 1.

30. Hans Reichenbach, *The Rise of Scientific Philosophy*.

31. Karl R. Popper, *The Logic of Scientific Discovery;* Karl Popper, *Conjectures and Refutations*.

32. Toulmin, "From Form to Function," p. 156.

33. Ibid.

34. Mary Hesse, *Revolutions and Reconstruction in the Philosophy of Science*.

35. Terrence W. Tice and Thomas P. Slavens, *Research Guide to Philosophy*, p. 422.

36. For example, in the last twenty years, the psychology department of Duquesne University, Pittsburgh, Pennsylvania, has been engaged in a project of reformulating the science of psychology as a human science. Amedeo Giorgi, Richard Knowles, and David L. Smith, eds., *Duquesne Studies in Phenomenological Psychology*, p. ix; Rom Harré, "The Positivist-Empiricist Approach and its Alternative," pp. 3–17. Rom Harré, *An Introduction to Logic of The Sciences;* Rom Harré, *The Philosophy of Science;* Richard J. Bernstein, *Praxis and Action*, Severyn T. Bruyn, "The New Empiricists," pp. 283–287.

37. Richard P. Bagozzi, "Theoretical Concepts, Measurements, and Meaning," pp. 24–38.

38. Marx W. Wartofsky, *Conceptual Foundations of Scientific Thought*, p. 4.

39. Reid and Smith, *Research in Social Work*.

40. Carol B. Germain, "Casework and Science," p. 7; Aaron Rosenblatt, "The Utilization of Research in Social Work Practice," pp. 548–559; Kirk and Rosenblatt, "New Applications of Research in Clinical Practice," pp. 549–559.

41. Eda G. Goldstein, "Issues in Developing Systematic Research and Theory," pp. 5–25.

42. Francis J. Turner, ed., *Social Work Treatment*.

43. Harriette C. Johnson, "Emerging Concerns in Family Therapy," pp. 225–236.

44. Lynn Hoffman, *Foundations of Family Therapy*.

45. Scott Briar, "Practice Trends," p. 106.

46. Turner, ed., *Social Work Treatment*, p. xv.

47. Patricia Ewalt, ed., *Toward a Definition of Social Work*.

48. Carol H. Meyer, "Selecting Appropriate Practice Models," pp. 731–749.

49. Henry S. Maas, "Research in Social Work," p. 1192.

50. Ibid.

51. Batya Schneider Shoshani, "Gordon Hamilton," pp. 389–390.

52. Harold Lewis, *The Intellectual Base of Social Work Practice*, pp. 54–59.

53. Larry Laudan, *Science and Values*, pp. 1–3.

54. Ibid., pp. 5–6.

55. Ibid., p. 5.

56. Ibid., p. 6.

57. Ibid., p. 15.

58. Thomas S. Kuhn, *The Essential Tension*, pp. 320–339. Kuhn ranked the standard criteria as to applicability, beginning with (a) accuracy, (b) fruitfulness, (c) scope, (d) consistency, and (e) simplicity. He considered consistency and simplicity to be very problematic and to need the collective judgment of scientists.

59. Thomas S. Kuhn, *The Structure of Scientific Revolutions*, p. 44.

60. Ibid., pp. 48–49.

61. Heineman, "The Obsolete Scientific Imperative in Social Work Research," pp. 371–397; John R. Scheurman, "The Obsolete Scientific Imperative in Social

Work Research," pp. 144–146; Martha Brunswick Heineman, "Author's Reply," pp. 146–148; Walter W. Hudson, "Scientific Imperatives in Social Work Research and Practice," pp. 246–258; Ludwig L. Geismar, "Comments on 'The Obsolete Scientific Imperative in Social Work Research,' " pp. 311–312; Martha Heineman Piper [Pieper] "Author's Reply," p. 312; Mary Gorman Gyarfas, "The Scientific Imperative Again," pp. 149–150; John S. Brekke, "Scientific Imperatives in Social Work Research," pp. 538–554; Martha Heineman Pieper, "Comments on 'Scientific Imperatives in Social Work Research,' " pp. 368–370; John S. Brekke, "Author's Reply," pp. 370–373.

62. Martha Heineman Pieper, "The Future of Social Work Research," pp. 3–11.

63. Shirley Cooper, "Concepts and Practice Issues in Clinical Social Work," p. 257.

64. Laudan, *Science and Values*, pp. 23–41. Laudan credits for their contributions Popper and Richenbach (already cited) and Carl E. Hempel, *Aspects of Scientific Explanation and Other Essays in the Philosophy of Science.*

65. Laudan, *Science and Values*, p. 26.

66. Ibid., pp. 27–28.

67. Stephen J. Gould. *The Mismeasure of Man*, p. 22.

68. Stephen L. Schensul, "Science, Theory, and Application in Anthropology," pp. 164–185.

69. Ibid.

70. Kurt Lewin, "Group Decision and Social Change," pp. 459–473.

71. Nevitt Sanford, "A Model for Action Research," p. 174.

72. Loren R. Graham, "Concerns about Science and Attempts to Regulate Inquiry," p. 15.

73. Ibid., pp. 1–21.

74. Robert L. Sinsheimer, "The Presumptions of Science," pp. 23–35.

75. Ibid., p. 33.

76. Mary Richmond, *Social Diagnosis*, p. 25.

77. Ibid., p. 365.

78. Donna L. Franklin, "Mary Richmond and Jane Addams," p. 519.

79. Ibid., p. 520.

80. Max Siporin, *Introduction to Social Work Practice*, pp. 61–90.

81. *NASW Policy Statement I: Code of Ethics.*

82. Laudan, *Science and Values*, pp. xi–xiv.

83. Lydia Rapoport, "Creativity in Social Work."

84. Chester Barnard, *The Function of the Executive*, pp. 290–291.

85. Karl Popper, *The Logic of Scientific Discovery;* Hans Reichenbach, *Experience and Prediction;* Hans Reichenbach, *The Rise of Scientific Philosophy.*

86. Norwood R. Hanson, *Patterns of Discovery;* Carl G. Hempel, *Philosophy of Natural Science.*

87. Ernan McMullin, "Panel Discussion of Explanation of Historical Discoveries," p. 29.

88. Larry Laudan, *Science and Hypothesis*, pp. 1–5.

89. Herbert A. Simon, "Does Scientific Discovery Have A Logic?," p. 473.

90. Ibid.

91. Thomas S. Kuhn, *The Essential Tension.*

1. DIVERSITY IN PHILOSOPHICAL AND SCIENTIFIC THOUGHT: IMPLICATIONS FOR INQUIRY

1. Terrence N. Tice and Thomas P. Slavens, *Research Guide to Philosophy*, pp. 306–307.
2. Harold I. Brown, *Perception, Theory, and Commitment*, p. 9.
3. Ibid.
4. Rudolf Carnap, "On the Character of Philosophic Problems," p. 12. Carnap offered the following examples: " 'It is raining here' as synthetic [a matter of fact that is neither analytical or contradictory]; 'It is raining or it is not raining' is analytic [a matter of thought or an internal relation of ideas]; 'It is raining and it is not raining' is contradictory. An analytic proposition is true in every possible case and therefore does not state which case is on hand. A contradictory proposition on the contrary says too much, it is not true in any possible case. A synthetic proposition is true only in certain cases, and states therefore that one of these cases is being considered—all (true or false) statements of fact are synthetic."
5. Tice and Slavens, *Research Guide to Philosophy*, pp. 150–151.
6. Willard Van Orman Quine, "Two Dogmas of Empiricism," p. 20.
7. Harold Morick, ed., *Challenges to Empiricism*, p. 2. Morick's development of the ideas of Hume are drawn from Hume's *A Treatise on Human Nature* and *An Inquiry Concerning Human Understanding and Concerning the Principles of Morals*. Also see Norman Kemp Smith, *The Philosophy of David Hume: A Critical Study of its Origins and Central Doctrines*.
8. Morick, *Challenges to Empiricism*, pp. 3–4.
9. Ibid.
10. Ibid., p. 3.
11. Alfred Jules Ayer, *Philosophy in the Twentieth Century*, p. 2.
12. Ibid., p. 3.
13. Ibid., pp. 3–4.
14. Norman Kemp Smith, *A Commentary to Kant's "Critique of Pure Reason."*
15. Alfred E. Taylor, *Elements of Metaphysics*.
16. Brown, *Perception, Theory and Commitment*, p. 102.
17. Tice and Slavens, *Research Guide to Philosophy*, pp. 114–115.
18. Ibid., pp. 135–136.
19. Michael Resnik, *Frege and the Philosophy of Mathematics*.
20. Ibid., p. 13.
21. Ibid., p. 16.
22. Ibid., p. 138.
23. Alfred North Whitehead and Bertrand Russell, *Principia Mathematica*.
24. Bertrand Russell, *Principles of Mathematics*, p. xv.
25. Ayer, *Philosophy in the Twentieth Century*, p. 22.
26. Ibid.
27. Ibid., p. 23.
28. Whitehead and Russell, *Principia Mathematica*.
29. Bertrand Russell, *Introduction to Mathematical Philosophy*.
30. Ibid., p. 2.
31. Karl Pearson, *The Life, Letters and Labors of Francis Galton*.

32. Karl Pearson, *The Grammar of Science;* Karl Pearson, ed., *Tables for Statisticians and Biometricians.*

33. Clark A. Chambers, *Paul U. Kellog and the Survey.*

34. Roland A. Fisher, *Statistical Methods and Scientific Inference.*

35. W. Allen Wallis and Harry V. Roberts, *Statistics,* p. 15.

36. Richard Hofstadter, *Social Darwinism in American Thought,* p. 124.

37. Ibid.

38. William James, *Pragmatism,* p. 47.

39. Horace S. Thayer, *Meaning and Action;* Alfred Jules Ayer, *The Origins of Pragmatism.*

40. Tice and Slavens, *Research Guide to Philosophy,* p. 232.

41. Ayer, *The Origins of Pragmatism.*

42. Charles Sanders Peirce, *Collected Papers of Charles Sanders Peirce.*

43. Ayer, *Philosophy in the Twentieth Century,* p. 70.

44. Ayer, *The Origins of Pragmatism,* p. 3.

45. Peirce, *Collected Papers,* 5:226–227.

46. Ayer, *The Origin of Pragmatism,* p. 8.

47. Peirce, *Collected Papers,* 5:235–247.

48. Ibid., 5:243–244.

49. Ibid., 5:243.

50. Ibid., 1:28–29.

51. James, *Pragmatism,* p. 51.

52. Ibid.

53. Ibid., p. 53.

54. Patrick Kiaran Dooley, *Pragmatism as Humanism,* p. 121.

55. Ayer, *The Origins of Pragmatism,* p. 182.

56. Horace M. Kallen, *The Philosophy of William James,* p. 8.

57. James, *Pragmatism,* p. ix.

58. William James, *The Meaning of Truth,* p. xii.

59. Ibid., pp. xi–xii.

60. Ibid.

61. Ibid., p. xi.

62. William James, *Essays in Radical Empiricism,* pp. 41–42.

63. Ibid., p. 42.

64. Dooley, *Pragmatism as Humanism,* p. 134.

65. Donna F. Franklin, "Mary Richmond and Jane Addams, pp. 504–525.

66. William James, *The Will to Believe,* pp. vii–ix.

67. Max O. Hocutt, "Comments on Pragmatism."

68. Ayer, *Philosophy in the Twentieth Century,* p. 121.

69. Otto Neurath, Rudolf Carnap, and Charles Morris, eds., *International Encyclopedia of Unified Science,* p. 69.

70. Robert S. Cohen, *Herbert Feigl,* pp. 57–94.

71. Ayer, *Philosophy in the Twentieth Century,* pp. 127–129.

72. Ibid., p. 129. The Vienna circle members included: M. Schlick, R. Carnap, O. Neurath, G. Bergmann, H. Feigl, V. Kraft, M. Natkin, T. Radakovic, F. Waismann, K. Godel, H. Hahn, K. Menger, O. Hahn, and P. Frank. Hans Reichenbach was listed as a sympathizer.

73. Herbert Feigl and Albert E. Blumberg, "Logical Positivism: A New Movement in European Philosophy," pp. 281–296; Cohen, *Herbert Feigl,* p. 70.

74. Ayer, *Philosophy in the Twentieth Century*, p. 139.
75. Brown, *Perception, Theory and Commitment*, p. 21.
76. Ibid.
77. Ludwig Wittgenstein, *Tractatus Logico-Philosophicus*.
78. Ayer, *Philosophy in the Twentieth Century*, pp. 111–112.
79. Karl R. Popper, *The Logic of Scientific Discovery*, p. 36.
80. Rudolf Carnap, "The Old and New Logic," p. 133.
81. Ibid.
82. Ibid., pp. 135–136.
83. Ibid., pp. 136–144.
84. Ibid., p. 144.
85. Moritz Schlick, "Positivism and Realism," p. 83.
86. Ibid., pp. 86–87.
87. Alfred Jules Ayer, *Language, Truth, and Logic*. In the preface of the second edition, he holds that the testability criterion is a definition, which is not entirely arbitrary.
88. Willard Van Orman Quine, *Ontological Relativity and Other Essays*.
89. William Marias Malisoff, "What is Science?," p. 1.
90. Carl G. Hempel, *Aspects of Scientific Explanation and Other Essays in the Philosophy of Science*, p. vii.
91. William Marias Malisoff, *Meet the Sciences*.
92. Robert E. Butts, "Philosophy of Science, 1934–1984," p. 1.
93. Ibid., pp. 1–2.
94. Karel Lambert and Gordon G. Brittange, *An Introduction to the Philosophy of Science*, p. 2; Baruch Brody, *Readings in the Philosophy of Science;* Michael Scriven, "A Possible Distinction Between Traditional Scientific Disciplines and the Study of Human Behavior," pp. 330–339.
95. Rudolf Carnap, "Testability and Meaning," 3:420–471; 4:2–40.
96. Ibid., p. 422.
97. Ibid., p. 425.
98. Hempel, *Aspects of Scientific Explanation*, p. 101.
99. Brown, *Perceptions, Theory and Commitment*, p. 67.
100. Karl R. Popper, *The Logic of Scientific Discovery*, p. 37.
101. Ibid., p. 39.
102. Ibid., pp. 39–48.
103. Karl R. Popper, *Conjectures and Refutations*, p. 37.
104. Morick, ed., *Challenges to Empiricism*, p. 1.
105. Alfred Jules Ayer, *The Foundations of Empirical Knowledge*.
106. Ibid., p. 2.
107. Ibid., pp. 3–5.
108. Ibid., p. 5.
109. Ibid., p. 7.
110. Ibid., pp. 9–10.
111. Morick, ed., *Challenges to Empiricism*, p. 7.
112. Ibid., pp. 8–9.
113. Ibid., p. 9.
114. Ibid.
115. Ibid., p. 13.
116. Ibid.

117. Ibid., p. 11.
118. Ibid., pp. 16–17.
119. Rudolf Carnap, *Meaning and Necessity;* Rudolf Carnap, *The Logical Foundations of Probability;* Rudolf Carnap, "Empiricism, Semantics, and Ontology," pp. 28–46; Rudolf Carnap, "The Methodological Character of Theoretical Concepts," pp. 38–76.
120. Popper, *The Logic of Scientific Discovery.*
121. Paul K. Feyerabend, "Problems of Empiricism," pp. 114–260; Paul Feyerabend, "Against Method," pp. 17–130; Paul Feyerabend, "How to be a Good Empiricist," pp. 164–193; Paul Feyerabend, *Philosophical Papers,* vols. 1 and 2.
122. Thomas S. Kuhn, *The Structure of Scientific Revolutions;* Thomas Kuhn, *The Essential Tension.*
123. Nelson Goodman, *Fact, Fiction, and Forecast;* Nelson Goodman, *The Structure of Appearance.*
124. Willard Van Orman Quine, *From a Logical Point of View;* Willard Van Orman Quine, *Methods of Logic;* Willard Van Orman Quine, *Theories and Things.*
125. Norwood Russell Hanson, *Patterns of Discovery;* Norwood Russell Hanson, *Observational Explanation.*
126. Michael Polyani, *Science, Faith, and Society;* Michael Polyani, *Personal Knowledge;* Michael Polyani, *The Tacit Dimension.*
127. Herbert Simon, *Models of Discovery;* Herbert Simon, "Thinking by Computers," pp. 3–21; Herbert Simon, "Scientific Discovery and Psychology of Problem Solving," pp. 22–40.
128. William Wimsatt, "Reductionistic Research Strategies and Their Biases in the Units of Selection Controversy," pp. 213–259.
129. Wesley C. Salmon, "The Foundations of Scientific Inference," pp. 135–275.
130. Ian I. Mitroff and Richard O. Mason, *Creating a Dialectical Social Science.*
131. Imre Lakatos and A. Musgrove, *Criticism and the Growth of Knowledge;* Imre Lakatos, *Mathematics, Science and Epistemology.*
132. Carnap, "Empiricism, Semantics, and Ontology," pp. 28–46.
133. Quine, "Two Dogmas of Empiricism," pp. 20–43.
134. Tice and Slavens, *Research Guide to Philosophy,* p. 411.
135. Kuhn, *The Essential Tension,* p. 267.
136. Popper, *Conjectures and Refutations,* p. 222.
137. Kuhn, *The Essential Tension,* pp. 267–269.
138. Ibid., pp. 270–271.
139. Ibid., 293–319. Kuhn clarifies his use of the word "paradigm" in *The Essential Tension:* it is equivalent to the theory or world view held by a "scientific community" or by members of a specific discipline.
140. Ibid., p. 271.
141. Ibid., p. 267.
142. Tice and Slavens, *Research Guide to Philosophy,* p. 201.
143. Imre Lakatos, *The Methodology of Scientific Research Programmes,* p. 33.
144. Michael Polyani, *Personal Knowledge: Toward a Post-Critical Philosophy.*
145. Polyani, *The Tacit Dimension,* p. 4.
146. Ibid., p. 10.
147. Ibid., p. 7–8.
148. Ibid., p. 24.

149. Ibid., p. 25.

150. Stephen Toulmin, "From Form to Function," pp. 143–162.

151. Feyerabend, "Against Method."

152. Martha Brunswick Heineman, "The Obsolete Scientific Imperative in Social Work Research," pp. 371–397.

153. Ibid., p. 377.

154. Tice and Slavens, *Research Guide to Philosophy*, p. 422.

155. Ibid.

156. Peter A. Achinstein, *Law and Explanation*. The logic is developed within conditions for considering sufficiency in explanation such as, relevance, correctness, depth, completeness, unification, and manner of presentation.

157. Alan Garfinkel, *Forms of Explanation*.

158. Tice and Slavens, *Research Guide to Philosophy*, p. 418.

2. DISCOVERY IN PRACTICE: ISSUES RELATED TO SCIENCE

1. Shirley Cooper, "Concepts and Practice Issues in Clinical Social Work," p. 261.

2. Florence Hollis, *Casework: A Psychosocial Therapy*, 1st and 2d ed.; Florence Hollis and Mary Woods, *Casework: A Psychosocial Therapy*, 3rd ed.; Hollis, *A Typology of Casework Treatment*; William J. Reid, "Characteristics of Casework Intervention," pp. 11–19; Anne E. Fortune, "Communication Processes in Social Work Practice," pp. 93–128; Edward J. Mullen, "Casework Communication," pp. 546–551; Ben A. Orcutt, "Process Analysis of the First Phase of Treatment," pp. 147–164.

3. See the following for selected examples of variation in assessment: William J. Reid, *The Task-Centered System*, pp. 88–96; Carol B. Germain and Alex Gitterman, *The Life Model of Social Work Practice*, pp. 18–20; Hollis and Wood, *Casework: A Psychosocial Therapy*, pp. 378–404; Gordon Hamilton, *Theory and Practice of Social Casework*, pp. 213–236; Florence Hollis, "Personality Diagnosis in Casework," pp. 83–96; Carol H. Meyer, "The Search for Coherence," pp. 5–34; Helen Harris Perlman, *Social Casework: A Problem-Solving Process*, pp. 164–182; Francis J. Turner, *Differential Diagnosis and Treatment in Social Work*; Helen Northen, *Clinical Social Work*, pp. 60–95; Ann Hartman and Joan Laird, *Family-Centered Social Work Practice*, pp. 157–304; Herbert S. Strean, *Clinical Social Work*, pp. 77–132; Max Siporin, *Introduction to Social Work Practice*, pp. 219–250; Beulah R. Compton and Burt Galaway, *Social Work Processes*.

4. Howard Goldstein, Harvey H. Hilbert, and Judith Hilbert, *Creative Change*.

5. F. C. S. Schiller, "Scientific Discovery and Logical Proof," pp. 235–289.

6. Lindley Darden, "Theory Construction in Genetics," p. 151.

7. Hans Reichenbach, *The Rise of Scientific Philosophy*, p. 231.

8. Karl R. Popper, *The Logic of Scientific Discovery*, p. 31.

9. Kenneth F. Schaffner, "Discovery in the Biomedical Sciences," p. 171.

10. Norwood Russell Hanson, *Patterns of Discovery*; Norwood Russell Hanson, "Is There a Logic of Scientific Discovery?", pp. 20–35; Norwood Russell Hanson, "An Anatomy of Discovery," pp. 321–352.

11. Hanson, *Patterns of Discovery*, pp. 2–3.

12. Ibid., pp. 70–71.

13. Ibid., p. 72.

14. Hanson, "Is There a Logic of Scientific Discovery?" p. 33.

15. Schaffner, "Discovery in the Biomedical Sciences," p. 179.

16. Larry Laudan, *Science and Hypotheses*, pp. 181–182.

17. Ibid., p. 182.

18. Thomas Nickles, ed., *Scientific Discovery: Case Studies*, p. xxi.

19. Carl G. Hempel, *Aspects of Scientific Explanation*, p. 113.

20. Nickles, ed., *Scientific Discovery: Case Studies*, p. xxi.

21. Ibid., p. xiii.

22. Schaffner, "Discovery in the Biomedical Sciences," pp. 171–205.

23. Marx W. Wartofsky, "Scientific Judgment," p. 1.

24. Ibid., p. 13.

25. Ibid.

26. Ibid., p. 14.

27. Ibid. He explains that "a logic of suggestion is in effect a logic of maxims," which suggest rules—such as what might be better or more effective. These rules of judgment or practical wisdom may be stated as maxims. However, he noted that what "follows from them *deductively alone* has very little force, and is too unspecified in its reference."

28. Ibid.

29. See Lindley Darden, "Theory Construction in Genetics," pp. 151–170.

30. Ibid., p. 151.

31. William C. Wimsatt, "Reductionist Research Strategies and Their Biases," pp. 213–259.

32. Charles Darwin, *On The Origin of Species by Natural Selection*.

33. Thomas Robert Malthus, *An Essay on the Principle of Population*.

34. Michael Ruse, "Ought Philosophers Consider Scientific Discovery?," pp. 131–149.

35. Howard E. Gruber, "The Evolving Systems Approach to Creative Scientific Work," pp. 113–130.

36. Ibid., p. 115.

37. Bruce Douglas and Clark Moustakas, "Heuristic Inquiry," pp. 39–55.

38. Ibid., pp. 41–42.

39. Ibid., p. 42.

40. Wartofsky, "Scientific Judgment," p. 12.

41. William J. Reid and Audrey D. Smith, *Research in Social Work*, p. 16.

42. Alfred J. Kahn, "Research Planning," p. 331.

43. Thomas S. Kuhn, *The Structure of Scientific Revolutions*.

44. Lydia Rapoport, "Creativity in Social Work," pp. 152–153.

45. A letter written by Albert Einstein to M. Hadamard on the subject of creative thinking is reproduced in Brewster Ghiselin, *The Creative Process*, pp. 32–33.

46. Herbert A. Simon, *Models of Discovery*, pp. 292–294.

3. PROBLEM DOMAIN

1. Larry Laudan, *Science and Hypothesis*, pp. 3–4.

2. *Conceptual Frameworks*, p. 22; *Conceptual Frameworks II*, p. 26.

3. Donald Brieland, "Definition, Specialization, and Domain in Social Work," p. 83.

4. Ibid.

5. Carlfred B. Broderick and Sandra S. Schrader, "The History of Professional Marriage and Family Therapy," pp. 5–35.

6. Scott Briar, "Needed: A Simple Definition of Social work," p. 83.

7. Patricia L. Ewalt, "Social Work Process as an Organizing Concept."

8. Phyllis Caroff, ed., *Treatment Formulations and Clinical Social Work*, pp. ix–x.

9. Robert Dubin, *Theory Building*, pp. 12–13.

10. Larry Laudan, *Progress and Its Problems*, p. 4.

11. Ibid., pp. 48–49.

12. Richie Calvin, "The Measurement of Triangulation."

13. Laudan, *Progress and Its Problems*, p. 53.

14. Nancy Feyl Chavkin, "The Practice-Research Relationship," pp. 241–250.

15. Nevitt Sanford, "A Model for Action Research," p. 174.

16. Ibid.

17. William J. Reid, *The Task-Centered System*, pp. 17–18; William J. Reid and Laura Epstein, *Task-Centered Casework*.

4. REFLECTIVE INQUIRY: ORTHODOX HEURISTIC RESEARCH

1. We use heuristic research in its generic sense in science, i.e., in discovery and the stimulation of investigation. For a recent discussion of methodological implications in heuristic research for social work, see Edward J. Mullen, "Methodological Dilemmas in Social Work Research," pp. 12–20.

2. Tony Tripodi, *Evaluative Research*, pp. 6–7.

3. In this category of design, we have included the qualitative-descriptive, case-comparative, and the constant comparative of grounded theory. See Harry Butler, Inger Davis, and Ruth Kukkonen, "The Logic of Case Comparison," pp. 3–11; Barney G. Glaser, "The Constant Comparative Method of Qualitative Analysis," pp. 436–445; also in George J. McCall and J. L. Simmons, ed., *Issues in Participant Observation*, pp. 216–228; Barney G. Glaser and Anselm Strauss, *The Discovery of Grounded Theory;* Barney G. Glaser, *Theoretical Sensitivity;* William J. Filstead, ed., *Qualitative Methodology;* David Silverman, *Qualitative Methodology and Sociology;* Patricia Yancey Martin and Barry K. Turner, "Grounded Theory and Organizational Research," pp. 141–157; Robert C. Bogdan and Sari Knopp Biklen, *Qualitative Research for Education*.

4. See Martin Bloom and Joel Fischer, *Evaluating Practice;* Michel Hersen and David H. Barlow, *Single-Case Experimental Designs;* Srinika Jayaratne and Rona L. Levy, *Empirical Clinical Practice;* Tripodi, *Evaluative Research*.

5. Joseph Bleicher, *Contemporary Hermeneutics;* Zigmunt Bauman, *Hermeneutics and Social Science*.

6. Ernest Nagel, *The Structure of Science*, pp. 548–575.

7. Austin T. Turk, "The Sociological Relevance of History," p. 289.

8. Clark Moustakas, "Heuristic Research," pp. 101–107.

9. Aaron Rosenblatt, "The Practitioner's Use and Evaluation of Research," pp. 53–59; Aaron Rosenblatt, "The Utilization of Research in Social Work Practice," pp. 548–559; Scott Briar, Harold Weissman, and Allen Rubin, *Research Utilization in Social Work Education;* David Fanshel, "The Future of Social Work Research," pp. 3–18.

10. Catherine A. Faver, Mary Frank Fox, Mary Ski Hunter, and Coleen Shannon, "Research and Practice," p. 282.

11. For a discussion of cognitive aims and their relatedness to philosophical notions, such as those of realists, instrumentalists, pragmatists, conventionalists, etc., see Larry Laudan, *Science and Values*, pp. 42–66.

12. Scott Briar and Henry Miller, *Problems and Issues in Social Casework*, p. 81.

13. Peter Reason and John Rowan, eds., *Human Inquiry*.

14. Severyn T. Bruyn, "The New Empiricists," pp. 283–287.

15. Herbert Simon, *Models of Discovery*, pp. 290–303.

16. Ibid., p. 290.

17. Frank Riessman, Jerome Cohen, and Arthur Pearl, eds., *Mental Health of the Poor*.

18. Florence Hollis, *Casework*, 1st, 2d ed.; Florence Hollis and Mary E. Woods, *Casework*, 3d ed.

19. Hollis and Woods, *Casework*, p. 349.

20. Ibid.

21. Ibid., p. 353.

22. Elizabeth M. Timberlake and Lewis Carr, "Research and the Social Work Practitioner," p. 26.

23. Ben A. Orcutt and Paul R. Mills, Jr., "The Doctoral Practice Laboratory," pp. 633–643; Ben A. Orcutt and Paul R. Mills, Jr., "A Model of Doctoral Education," pp. 100–108; Ben A. Orcutt and Paul R. Mills, Jr., "Education for Doctoral Social Work Clinical Practice in the 1980s," p. 38–49.

24. Orcutt and Mills, "Education for Doctoral Social Work Clinical Practice in the 1980s," p. 46.

25. Donald Schön, *The Reflective Practitioner*.

26. Ibid., p. 69.

27. John Wodarski, *The Role of Research in Clinical Practice*; Edwin J. Thomas, *Designing Interventions for the Helping Person*; Edwin J. Thomas, "Mousetraps, Developmental Research, and Social Work Education," pp. 468–483; Joel Fischer, "New and Emerging Methods of Direct Practice," pp. 525–547; Jayaratne and Levy, *Empirical Clinical Practice*; Eileen D. Gambrill, *Behavior Modification*.

28. Anne E. Fortune, *Task-Centered Practice with Families and Groups*; William J. Reid, *The Task-Centered System*; William J. Reid, "Developing Intervention Methods Through Experimental Design," pp. 650–672.

29. Wodarski, *The Role of Research in Clinical Practice*, p. 2.

30. W. David Harrison, "Reflective Practice in Social Care," pp. 393–404.

31. Simon, *Models of Discovery*, p. 294.

32. Ibid.

33. Silverman, *Qualitative Methodology and Sociology*, p. 95.

34. Claire Selltiz, Marie Jahoda, Morton Deutsch, and Stuart Cook, *Research Methods in Social Relations*, p. 41.

35. Ibid.

36. Tripodi, *Evaluative Research*, p. 7.

37. Max O. Hocutt, *The Elements of Logical Analysis and Inference*, p. 3.

38. Ronald N. Giere, *Understanding Scientific Reasoning*, p. 18. Other useful philosophical texts on logic and reasoning include: Irving M. Copi, *An Introduction to Logic*; Wesley C. Salmon, *Logic*; Michael Scriven, *The Logic of Evaluation*; Hocutt, *The Elements of Logical Analysis and Inference*.

39. Giere, *Understanding Scientific Reasoning*, p. 23.

40. Ibid., p. 81.

41. Paul D. Reynolds, *Primer in Theory Construction*, pp. 67–68.

42. For our discussion of conditional statements and the form used in logic, we have drawn from the formulations of Giere, *Understanding Scientific Reasoning*, pp. 51–107; Hocutt, *The Elements of Logical Analysis and Inference*, p. 117.

43. Salvador Minuchin, *Families and Family Therapy*, pp. 51–56.

44. Harry J. Aponte, "Under Organization in the Poor Family," pp. 432–448.

45. Schön, *The Reflective Practitioner*, pp. 145–147.

46. Reid, "Developing Intervention Methods Through Experimental Design," pp. 650–651.

47. Ibid., p. 651.

48. William J. Reid, "Research Strategies for Improving Individualized Services," pp. 38–52; William J. Reid, *Family Problem Solving*, pp. 285–308.

49. Thomas, "Mousetraps, Developmental Research, and Social Work Education."

50. Jack Rothman, *Research and Development in the Human Services;* Jack Rothman, "Harnessing Research to Enhance Practice."

51. Robert Bogdan and Steven J. Taylor, *Introduction to Qualitative Research Methods.*

52. George J. McCall and J. L. Simmons, eds., *Issues in Participant Observation*, p. 61.

53. Ibid., pp. 71–72.

54. Allen H. Barton and Paul F. Lazarsfeld, "Some Functions of Qualitative Analysis in Social Research," pp. 163–196; Filstead, ed., *Qualitative Methodology;* Mathew B. Miles and A. Michael Huberman, *Qualitative Data Analysis;* Bogdan and Biklen, *Qualitative Research for Education.*

55. Miles and Huberman, *Qualitative Analysis*, p. 22.

56. Gerry Lane and Tom Russell, "Systemic Therapy: An Alternative to Social Control for Violent Couples."

57. Barton and Lazarsfeld, "Some Functions of Qualitative Analysis," p. 177.

58. Miles and Huberman, *Qualitative Data Analysis*, p. 21.

59. Ibid., p. 22.

60. Butler, Davis, and Kukkonen, "The Logic of Case Comparison," pp. 3–11; Timberlake and Carr, "Research and the Social Work Practitioner," p. 29; Harry Butler and Samuel A. Richmond, "Concrete Comparison, Generalization, and Validation in Social Research and Practice," pp. 82–105.

61. Barney G. Glaser, "The Constant Comparative Method of Qualitative Analysis," pp. 216–228; Glaser and Strauss, *The Discovery of Grounded Theory.*

62. Butler, Davis, Kukkonen, "The Logic of Case Comparisons," p. 3.

63. Ibid., pp. 4–5.

64. Ibid., p. 5.

65. Glaser, "The Constant Comparative Method of Qualitative Analysis," pp. 216–228.

66. Ibid., p. 220.

67. Ibid., p. 222.

68. Ibid.

69. Miles and Huberman, *Qualitative Data Analysis*, p. 15.

70. Lee J. Cronbach, "Beyond the Two Disciplines of Scientific Psychology,"

pp. 116–127; Donald T. Campbell, "Degrees of Freedom and the Case Study," pp. 178–193; Thomas D. Cook and Donald T. Campbell, *Quasi-experimentations;* Richard E. Snow, "Representative and Quasi-representative Designs for Research in Teaching," pp. 265–292.

71. For example, David Fanshel and Eugene B. Shinn, *Children in Foster Care;* Lynn Videka-Sherman, "Research on the Effect of Parental Bereavement: Implications for Social Work Intervention," pp. 102–116; Lynn Videka-Sherman and Morton Lieberman, "The Effects of Self-Help and Psychotherapy Intervention on Child Loss," pp. 70–82; Dorothy Fahs Beck and Mary Ann Jones, *Progress on Family Problems.*

72. For example, William J. Reid and Ann W. Shyne, *Brief and Extended Treatment;* Richard O'Connor, "Clients' Reactions to Brief Treatment"; Richard O'Connor and William J. Reid, "Dissatisfaction with Brief Treatment," pp. 526–537; Cheryl A. Richey, Betty J. Blythe, and Sharon B. Berlin, "Do Social Workers Evaluate Their Practice?," pp. 14–20.

73. Jody D. Iodice and John S. Wodarski, "Aftercare Treatment for Schizophrenics Living at Home," pp. 122–128.

74. John L. Levitt and William J. Reid, "Rapid-Assessment Instruments for Practice," pp. 13–19.

75. For a discussion of sample procedures, see Tony Tripodi and Irwin Epstein, *Research Techniques for Clinical Social Workers*, pp. 165–186.

76. See, for example, Martin Bloom and Joel Fischer, *Evaluating Practice;* David Barlow and Steven C. Hayes, "Alternating Treatment Design," pp. 199–210; David Barlow and Michel Hersen, "Single-Case Experimental Designs," pp. 319–325; Michel Hersen and David Barlow, *Single-Case Experimental Designs;* Walter W. Hudson, "Elementary Techniques for Assessing Single Client/Single Worker Interventions," pp. 311–326; Walter W. Hudson, *The Clinical Measurement Package: A Field Manual;* Srinika Jayaratne, "Analytic Procedures for Single-Subject Designs," pp. 30–40; Srinika Jayaratne and William Daniels, "Measurement Cross-Validation Using Replication Procedures Within Single-Case Designs," pp. 4–10; Jayaratne and Levy, *Empirical Clinical Practice;* Thomas R. Kratochwill, ed., *Single Subject Research;* William J. Reid and Audrey Smith, *Research in Social Work;* Edwin J. Thomas, "Research and Service in Single-Case Experimentation," pp. 20–31; Tripodi, *Evaluative Research for Social Workers;* Tripodi and Epstein, *Research Techniques for Clinical Social Workers.*

77. Judith C. Nelsen, "Issues in Single-Subject Research for Nonbehaviorists," pp. 31–37.

78. Rosenblatt and Waldfogel, eds., *Handbook of Clinical Social Work*, pp. 549–720.

79. Nelsen, "Issues in Single-Subject Research for Nonbehaviorists," pp. 33–34.

80. Tripodi, *Evaluative Research for Social Workers*, pp. 100–120.

81. See, for example, Donald T. Campbell and Julian C. Stanley, *Experimental and Quasi-experimental Designs and Research;* Charles R. Atherton and David L. Klemmack, *Research Methods in Social Work*, pp. 37–58; Reid and Smith, *Research in Social Work;* Frederick N. Kerlinger, *Foundations of Behavioral Research.*

82. Jayaratne and Daniels, "Measurement Cross-Validation Using Replication Procedures Within Single-Case Designs"; Srinika Jayaratne, "Single-Subject and Group Designs in Treatment Evaluation," pp. 35–43.

83. Hang-Ling Chang, "Comparisons of Hypothesis Testing Procedures for the

Two-Group Growth Curve Problems in Incomplete-Data and Small-Sample Situations"; Nan M. Laird and James H. Ware, "Random Effects Models for Longitudinal Data," pp. 963–974; David G. Kleinbaum, "A Generalization of the Growth Curve Model Which Allows Missing Data," pp. 117–124.

5. AN ALTERNATIVE PARADIGM IN HEURISTIC INQUIRY

1. Peter Reason and John Rowan, eds., *Human Inquiry.*
2. Mathew B. Miles and A. Michael Huberman, *Qualitative Data Analysis*, p. 20.
3. Reason and Rowan, eds., *Human Inquiry*, pp. xiii–xx.
4. Ibid., p. xiv.
5. Martha Heineman Pieper, "The Future of Social Work Research," pp. 3–11.
6. Severyn T. Bruyn, "The New Empiricists," pp. 283–287.
7. Carl Rogers, "Toward a More Human Science of the Person," pp. 7–24; Carl Rogers, "A Theory of Therapy, Personality, and Interpersonal Relationships as Developed in the Client-Centered Framework," pp. 184–256. (It is of interest that Carl Rogers and associates have recently complained of discrimination in academic psychology against humanistically oriented programs of graduate study. Rogers, in 1985 ["Toward a More Human Science of the Person"], could find none that led to a doctorate in psychology. It was proposed that this results from a narrow definition of science that is rooted in logical positivism, and Rogers called for new models in science. Rejection of the naturalistic methods of observations by most publishers of scholarly books or journals was noted.)
8. Abraham Maslow, *The Psychology of Science.*
9. Michael Polanyi, *Personal Knowledge.*
10. Rogers, "Toward a More Human Science of the Person," p. 10.
11. Kenneth J. Gergen, *Toward Transformation in Social Knowledge.*
12. Paul Deising, *Patterns of Discovery in the Social Sciences.*
13. Martha B. Heineman [Pieper], "The Obsolete Scientific Imperative in Social Work Research," pp. 371–397.
14. See John R. Schuerman, "The Obsolete Scientific Imperative in Social Work Research," pp. 144–146; Martha Heineman [Pieper] "Author's Reply," pp. 146–148; Ludwig L. Geismar, "Comments on the Obsolete Scientific Imperative in Social Work Research," pp. 311–312; Martha [Heineman] Piper [Pieper], "Author's Reply," p. 312; Walter W. Hudson, "Scientific Imperatives in Social Work Research and Practice," pp. 246–258; Mary G. Gyarfas, "The Scientific Imperative Again" pp. 149–150; John S. Brekke, "Scientific Imperatives in Social Work Research," pp. 538–554; Martha Heineman Pieper, "Comments on 'Scientific Imperatives in Social Work Research,' " pp. 368–370; John S. Brekke, "Author's Reply," pp. 370–373.
15. Howard Goldstein, "Toward the Integration of Theory and Practice," p. 356.
16. Lynn Hoffman, *Foundations of Family Therapy*, pp. 339–349.
17. Peter Reason and John Rowan, "Issues of Validity in New Paradigm Research," p. 241.
18. Rom Harré, "The Positivist-Empiricist Approach and its Alternative," p. 3.
19. See Rom Harré, *The Philosophies of Science*, pp. 90–91. An explanation of the two concepts used to clarify realism begins with *reference*, which can be illustrated by a person's proper name. The name refers to him, whether he is present

or not; thus, words can be understood in isolation from the entities they represent. *Demonstration* (and indication) are usually acts in which an entity is pointed out. Harré indicates that, in a theory, there are theoretical terms, and they can be used to make verbal reference to hypothetical entities, whether or not they can be observed in experience. If, in addition to verbal reference, an act of demonstration can be performed by which a hypothetical entity is pointed out or indicated, then that entity must be said to exist. He then lays out—schematically—the realist position in the principles, as listed:

1. Some theoretical terms can be used to make reference (verbal) to hypothetical entities.
2. Some hypothetical entities are candidates for existence (i.e., some could be real things, qualities, and processes in the world).
3. Some candidates for existence, for reality, are demonstrable, i.e., can be indicated by some sort of gesture of pointing in the appropriate conditions.

20. Harré, "The Positivist-Empiricist Approach and Its Alternative," p. 5.
21. Reason and Rowan, "Issues of Validity in New Paradigm Research," p. 242.
22. Ibid., pp. 242–243.
23. Bruce E. Douglas and Clark Moustakas, "Heuristic Inquiry," pp. 39–55.
24. John Rowan, "A Dialectical Paradigm for Research," pp. 93–112.
25. Ibid., p. 98.
26. Evelyn M. Boyd and Ann W. Fales, "Reflective Learning," pp. 99–117.
27. Michael Polanyi, *The Tacit Dimension.*
28. Douglas and Moustakas, "Heuristic Inquiry," p. 51.
29. Reason and Rowan, "Issues of Validity in New Paradigm Research," p. 244.
30. Ibid., pp. 245–250.
31. Ibid., p. 243.
32. Harold I. Brown, *Perception, Theory, and Commitment;* Harold Morick, ed., *Challenges to Empiricism.*
33. Alan Garfinkel, *Forms of Explanation,* p. 156.
34. Ibid., p. 157.

6. HERMENEUTICS: PHILOSOPHY AND PERSPECTIVES IN INQUIRY

1. Joseph Bleicher, *Contemporary Hermeneutics,* pp. 9–10.
2. Ibid., p. 9.
3. Gary Shapiro and Alan Sicada, eds., *Hermeneutics.*
4. Richard E. Palmer, *Hermeneutics: Interpretation Theory,* p. 7.
5. *Webster's Collegiate Dictionary.*
6. Zygmunt Bauman, *Hermeneutics and Social Science,* p. 7. Also see Bauman for a lucid and detailed discussion of the origin and rise of hermeneutics and its relations to social science.
7. Ibid.
8. Ibid., p. 8.
9. Terrence N. Tice and Thomas P. Slavens, *Research Guide to Philosophy,* pp. 293–294.
10. David Couzens Hoy, *The Critical Circle,* pp. vii–viii. Hoy investigates the hermeneutic circle as it relates to historical inquiry and to criticism of literary

works. He notes that it is formulated differently in different theories of hermeneutics, but basically is descriptive of how "in the process of understanding and interpretation, part and whole are related in a circular way: in order to understand the whole, it is necessary to understand the parts, which to understand the parts it is necessary to have some comprehension of the whole." Hoy points out that in earlier hermeneutics, the circle was used in understanding texts, but later (Martin Heidegger and Hans-Georg Gadamer) the circle has become "a fundamental principle of man's understanding of his own nature and situation."

11. Bauman, *Hermeneutics and Social Science*, p. 29.

12. Richard J. Bernstein, *Beyond Objectivism and Relativism*, p. 112.

13. Wilhelm Dilthey, *Der Aufbau der Geschichtlichen Welt in den Geisteswissenschaften.*

14. Bernstein, *Beyond Objectivism and Relativism*, p. 112.

15. Tice and Slavens, *Research Guide to Philosophy*, p. 296.

16. Martin Heidegger, *Being and Time.*

17. Bauman, *Hermeneutics and Social Science*, p. 148.

18. Palmer, *Hermeneutics: Interpretation Theory*, p. 140.

19. Hans-Georg Gadamer, *Truth and Method;* Hans-Georg Gadamer, *Philosophical Hermeneutics.*

20. Jurgen Habermas, *Theory and Practice;* Jurgen Habermas, "The Hermeneutic Claim to Universality."

21. Emilio Betti, "Die Hermenetic als Allgemeine Metodik der Geisteswissenschaften."

22. Palmer, *Hermeneutics: Interpretation Theory*, p. 194.

23. Ibid., pp. 198–199.

24. Ibid., p. 199.

25. Gadamer, *Philosophical Hermeneutics*, p. xv.

26. Ibid., p. xix.

27. Joseph Bleicher, *The Hermeneutic Imagination*, p. 70.

28. Ibid., p. 72.

29. Ibid., p. 75.

30. Ibid.

31. Ibid., p. 86.

32. Hoy, *The Critical Circle*, pp. 51–52.

33. Roy J. Howard, *Three Faces of Hermeneutics*, p. 168.

34. Bauman, *Hermeneutics and Social Science*, p. 239.

35. Ibid., p. 244.

36. Ibid., p. 240.

37. Ibid., pp. 243–244.

38. Bleicher, *Contemporary Hermeneutics*, p. 152.

39. Morris N. Eagle, *Recent Developments in Psychoanalysis*, pp. 164–171. Eagle cites the following authors who hold this position: Gerald Radnitzky, *Contemporary Schools of Metascience;* Paul Ricoeur, *Freud and Philosophy;* Roy Schafer, *Language and Insight;* Roy Schafer and R. S. Steele, "Psychoanalysis and Hermeneutics," pp. 389–411.

40. Tice and Slavens, *Research Guide to Philosophy*, p. 297.

41. Howard, *Three Faces of Hermeneutics*, pp. 35–160.

42. Ibid., p. 174.

43. Batya Schneider Shoshani, "Gordon Hamilton."

44. Bleicher, *Contemporary Hermeneutics*, p. 153.
45. Ibid.
46. Salvador Minuchin, *Families and Family Therapy.*
47. Palmer, *Hermeneutics: Interpretation Theory*, p. 233.

7. PHENOMENOLOGICAL CONSIDERATIONS IN PHILOSOPHY OF SCIENCE AND CLINICAL RESEARCH

1. *Webster's Collegiate Dictionary.*
2. Amedeo Giorgi, *Psychology as a Human Science;* Amedeo Giorgi, *Phenomenology and the Human Sciences.*
3. Terrence N. Tice and Thomas P. Slavens, *Research Guide to Philosophy*, p. 285; Edmund Husserl, *Ideas;* Edmund Husserl, *The Crisis of European Sciences and Transcendental Phenomenology.*
4. Tice and Slavens, *Research Guide to Philosophy*, p. 288.
5. Ibid., pp. 288–292.
6. Ibid., p. 292.
7. Ibid.
8. Herbert Spiegelberg, *The Phenomenological Movement.*
9. Paul Filmer, et al., *New Directions in Sociological Theory.*
10. Giorgi, *Psychology as a Human Science*, p. xi. For a good discussion of the humanistic linkage with existentialism in social work, see Donald F. Krill, "Existential Social Work," pp. 147–175.
11. Giorgi, *Psychology as a Human Science*, pp. 180–181.
12. Ibid., p. 178.
13. Ibid., p. 198.
14. Robert C. Bogdan and Sari Knopp Biklen, *Qualitative Research for Education*, p. 31.
15. Amadeo Giorgi, Richard Knowles, and David L. Smith, eds., *Duquesne Studies in Phenomenological Psychology*, 3:179.
16. Ibid., 3:180.
17. Ibid., 3:3.
18. Husserl, *The Crisis of European Sciences and Transcendental Phenomenology*, pp. 252–253.
19. Amadeo Giorgi, *Phenomenology and Psychological Research*, pp. 10–19.
20. Ibid., p. 14.
21. Fritz Redl, "Strategy and Technique in the Life Space Interview," pp. 1–18; Anthony Maluccio, "Promoting Competence Through Life Experiences," pp. 293–295.

8. SCIENTIFIC ROOTS IN SOCIAL WORK PRACTICE

1. Kathleen Woodroofe, *From Charity to Social Work in England and the United States*, pp. 25–55.
2. Oscar C. M'Culloch, "The Organization of Charities," pp. 11–12.
3. Robert H. Bremner, "Scientific Philanthropy: 1873–93," pp. 168–173; Bremner also cites D. O. Kellog, "The Principle and Advantage of Association in Charities," p. 86, and Amos G. Warner, *American Charities*, pp. 399–402.

4. Charles D. Kellog, "Report of the Committee on History of Charity Organizations," p. 54.

5. Ibid.

6. Bremner, "Scientific Philanthropy: 1873–93," p. 169.

7. Nathan E. Cohen, *Social Work in the American Tradition*, p. 66.

8. M'Culloch, "The Organization of Charities," pp. 11–12. The guiding principles of the Charity Organizations of America were:

1. Cooperation of the existing charitable organizations, relief societies, and benevolent individuals in any city or town.

2. Registration of all dependent classes, of all relief given or asked, whether public or private; exchange of such information among all relief agencies.

3. Investigation of all cases applying for relief, for the purpose of ascertaining the existence of real need, and to discriminate between those who are honest and those who are imposters.

4. Prompt and adequate relief through affiliated agencies of all needy and deserving cases, and the prompt exposure of all imposters.

5. The substitution of work for physical relief or alms, where ever it can be done, and the establishing of provident schemes and educational methods.

6. The encouragement of personal friendly relations between the well-to-do and the unfortunate. (The role of the upper-class friendly visitor was to uplift the less fortunate.)

7. Frequent conferences for the report of abuses in existing laws, the securing of justice, and the modification of conditions which make for poverty and crime.

From these principles, M'Culloch extrapolated that "scientific charity is but love working in association, intelligently, by natural methods, to large ends."

9. Kellog, "Report of Committee on History of Charity Organization," p. 53.

10. Ibid., p. 61.

11. Mary E. Richmond, *Social Diagnosis*, p. 33.

12. Ibid., p. 29.

13. The following selected references will provide the reader with a good historical overview of the nature of poverty in America and the response to meeting need: Robert H. Bremner, *From the Depths*; Bremner, "Scientific Philanthropy: 1873–93," pp. 168–173; Beulah R. Compton, *Introduction to Social Welfare and Social Work*; Daniel Coit Gilman, *The Organization of Charities*; Paul E. Pumphrey and Muriel W. Pumphrey, *The Heritage of American Social Work*; Walter I. Trattner, *From Poor Law to Welfare State*; Amos G. Warner, *American Charities*.

14. Bremner, "Scientific Philanthropy: 1873–93," pp. 172–173.

15. Glendower Evans, "Scientific Charity," pp. 25–33.

16. Zilpha Smith, "Report of the Committee on the Organization of Charity," pp. 128–130; Nathaniel S. Rosenau, "Report of the Committee on Charity Organization," pp. 25–31.

17. Ibid., p. 30.

18. Charles D. Kellog, "Statistics," pp. 32–33.

19. Alfred Jules Ayer, *Philosophy in the Twentieth Century*, pp. 111–112.

20. Rosenau, "Report of the Committee on Charity Organization," pp. 25–26.

21. P. W. Ayers, "Report of the Committee on Charity Organizations," pp. 236–237.

22. Smith, "Report of the Committee on the Organization of Charity," p. 127.

23. Robert T. Davis, "Pauperism in the City of New York," p. 74.

24. Ibid., pp. 74–75.

25. Ibid., pp. 75–77.

26. Trattner, *From Poor Law to Welfare State*, pp. 82–83.

27. Dorothy G. Becker, "Exit Lady Bountiful," p. 61.

28. Edward T. Devine, "The Value and Dangers of Investigation," pp. 198–199.

29. Ibid., p. 195.

30. Ibid., p. 196.

31. Edward T. Devine, "The Principles of the Associated Charities," pp. 321–324.

32. Elizabeth G. Meier, *A History of the New York School of Social Work*, pp. 8–9; Sidney Berengarten, ed., *The Columbia University School of Social Work*, pp. 1–2.

33. Albert O. Wright, "The New Philanthropy," pp. 4–5.

34. Smith, "Report of the Committee on the Organization of Charity," p. 124.

35. Lela B. Costin, "Edith Abbott and the Chicago Influence on Social Work Education," pp. 94–111.

36. Richmond, *Social Diagnosis*, p. 33.

37. Richard C. Cabot, "Colleague of the Medical Social Workers," pp. 9–11.

38. Ibid.

39. Mary L. Gottesfeld and Mary E. Pharis, *Profiles in Social Work*, p. 32.

40. David Greenstone, "Dorothea Dix and Jane Addams," pp. 527–559.

41. Donna L. Franklin, "Mary Richmond and Jane Addams," pp. 504–525.

42. Ibid., p. 520.

43. Mary E. M'Dowell, "The Settlement and Organized Charity," pp. 123–127.

44. Ibid., p. 124.

45. Ibid., p. 123.

46. Jane Addams, "Charity and Social Justice," pp. 1–18.

47. Kate Holladay Claghorn, "Some New Developments in Social Statistics," pp. 597–615.

48. Shelby M. Harrison, "Community Action Through Surveys," pp. 52–62.

49. Cohen, *Social Work*, p. 83.

50. Florence Hollis, "How it Really Was," p. 4.

51. Richmond, *Social Diagnosis*.

52. Costin, "Edith Abbott and the Chicago Influence," p. 96; Berengarten, ed., *The Columbia University School of Social Work*, pp. 1–4.

53. W. Allen Wallis and Harry V. Roberts, *Statistics*, pp. 5–6. The analogous casework process with scientific method has likewise been referred to by others in the literature, e.g., Scott Briar and Henry Miller, *Problems and Issues in Social Casework*, pp. 81–82; Mary E. MacDonald, "Social Work Research," p. 10.

54. Richmond, *Social Diagnosis*, p. 43.

55. Ibid., p. 38.

56. Ibid., p. 51.

57. Ibid., p. 52.

58. Ben A. Orcutt, "A Study of Anchoring Effects in Clinical Judgment," pp. 408–417; Anthony J. Arangio, "A Study of the Effects of Eight Sequential Phases of Alternated Anchors on the Clinical Judgments of Social Caseworkers;" James Bieri et al., *Clinical and Social Judgment;* Donald J. Campbell, William A. Hunt, and Nan A. Lewis, "The Effects of Assimilation and Contrast in Judgments of Clinical Materials," pp. 347–360; Donald J. Campbell, William A. Hunt, and Nan A. Lewis,

"Context Effects with Judgmental Language that is Absolute, Extensive, and Ex-tra-Experimentally Anchored," pp. 220–228.

59. John Volkmann, "The Anchoring of Absolute Scales," pp. 743–744; William A. Hunt and John Volkman, "Anchoring Effects in Judgments," pp. 395–403; Leo Postman and G. A. Miller, "Anchoring of Temporal Judgments," pp. 43–53.

60. Mary E. MacDonald, "Social Work Research."

61. Woodroofe, *From Charity to Social Work*, p. 105.

62. Richmond, *Social Diagnosis*, p. 25.

63. E. E. Southard, "The Kingdom of Evil," pp. 334–340.

64. Ibid., p. 337.

65. Ibid., p. 335.

66. Ibid., p. 336.

67. Mary E. Jarrett, "The Psychiatric Thread Running Through all Social Case-work," pp. 587–593; Jessie Taft, "Qualifications of the Psychiatric Social Worker," p. 595.

68. Porter R. Lee, "The Fabric of the Family," pp. 324–325.

69. C. E. A. Winslow, "Poverty as a Factor in Disease," pp. 153–156; Karl de Schweinitz, "Sickness as a Factor in Poverty," pp. 156–164; Edward T. Devine, "The Outlook for the Future on Poverty and Disease," pp. 173–177.

70. Angie L. Kellog, "What Educational Psychology Can Contribute to Case-work with the Normal Family," pp. 329–334.

71. Ibid., p. 330.

72. Ibid.

73. Mary Richmond, "The Social Caseworker in a Changing World," p. 43.

74. Ibid., p. 45.

75. Ernest W. Burgess, "The Contribution of Sociology to Family Social Work," p. 191.

76. H. Scott Gordon, "Alfred Marshall and the Development of Economics as a Science," p. 234.

77. Jessie Taft, "Qualifications of the Psychiatric Social Worker," p. 595.

78. Charles A. Ellwood, "Social Facts and Scientific Social Work," p. 687.

79. Ibid., pp. 686–693.

80. Arthur James Todd, *The Scientific Spirit and Social Work*.

81. Ibid., pp. 66–70.

82. Ibid., p. 65.

83. Ibid.

84. Ibid., pp. 66–85.

85. Virginia P. Robinson, "Analysis of Processes in the Records of Family Case-working Agencies," p. 101.

86. Ibid., p. 102.

87. Harold A. Phelps, "The Case Record and Scientific Method," p. 103.

88. Ibid.

89. Ibid.

90. Corrine A. Sherman, "The Caseworker and Social Research," pp. 100–102.

91. Phelps, "The Case Record," pp. 104–105.

92. Ibid., p. 104.

93. Ibid., p. 105.

94. Burgess, "The Contribution of Sociology to Family Social Work," pp. 191–193.

95. Ibid., p. 192.

96. Virginia P. Robinson, "Case Studies of the Family for Research Purposes," pp. 298–300.

97. Ibid., p. 298. Robinson pointed out that:

formerly, the family appeared [as] a legitimate subject of study for theoretical sociology, which traced its origin, history, and evolution as a social institution; or as a field of research for applied sociology, where it was investigated as a social problem, in its economic or biological aspects. Today, the interest focused on the individual and personality by the newer developments in psychology and psychiatry has drawn attention to the family as the environment in which personality is conditioned and built up. A study of the family as a "unit of interacting personalities" . . . takes us into a new brand of science, social psychology, and into a new realm of facts . . . an analysis of the family group itself in the constant interplay of its members forces us into a new field of more subtle psychological and social facts, attitudes and interests, loves and hatreds, attachments an antagonisms.

98. Jeanette Regensberg, "Social Implications of Mental Testing," pp. 295–300.

99. Sophie Hardy, "What Measures Have We for Growth in Personality," pp. 254–258.

100. Ibid., pp. 256–257.

101. Ibid.

102. Virginia Robinson, *A Changing Psychology in Social Casework*, p. 183.

103. Ibid.

104. Leslie B. Alexander, "Social Work's Freudian Deluge," pp. 517–538.

105. Shirley Hellenbrand, "Main Currents in Social Casework, 1918–1936."

106. Helen L. Myrick, "Psychological Processes in Interviewing," p. 25.

107. Ibid., pp. 25–29.

108. Personal discussion with Dr. Florence Hollis, September 22, 1985.

109. Hollis, "How It Really Was," pp. 3–7.

110. Evans, "Scientific Charity," pp. 30–33.

111. The concepts "corrective relationships," "reliving," "expressive techniques," "re-education," "self-awareness," and "adaptation to reality" were all defined by Gordon Hamilton in 1947. See Gordon Hamilton, *Psychotherapy in Child Guidance*, pp. 123–155.

112. Jessie Taft, "The Effect of an Unsatisfactory Mother-Daughter Relationship Upon the Development of Personality," pp. 10–17.

113. Berengarten, ed., *The Columbia University School of Social Work*, pp. 8–10.

114. Ibid., pp. 9–10.

115. Hollis, "How It Really Was," p. 7.

116. David Barlow, Steven C. Hayes, and Rosemary O. Nelson, *The Scientist-Practitioner*, p. 5.

117. Sol L. Garfield, *Clinical Psychology*, p. 2–3.

118. Ibid., p. 3.

119. Berengarten, ed., *The Columbia University School of Social Work*, p. 6.

120. Gordon Hamilton, "The Bad Penny," p. 95.

121. Gordon Hamilton, *Theory and Practice of Social Casework*.

122. Sheila B. Kammerman, Ralph Dolgoff, George Getzel, and Judith Nelsen, "Knowledge for Practice," p. 103.

123. Hamilton, *Theory and Practice of Social Casework*, 2d ed., p. v.

124. Batya Schneider Shoshani, "Gordon Hamilton," p. 6.

125. Florence Hollis, *Social Casework in Practice.*

126. Anna Freud, *The Ego and Mechanisms of Defense.*

127. Hollis, *Social Casework in Practice*, pp. 295–296.

128. Jessie L. Taft, "A Conception of the Growth Process Underlying Social Casework Practice," pp. 311–318; also in Cora Kasius, ed., *Principles and Techniques of Social Casework*, pp. 247–259; Jessie L. Taft, "The Relation of Function to Process in Social Casework," pp. 23–31; Jessie L. Taft, "Function as the Basis of Development in Social Work Processes"; Virginia P. Robinson, *The Dynamics of Supervision Under Functional Controls;* Otto Rank, *The Trauma of Birth;* Otto Rank, *Will Therapy and Truth and Reality;* Ruth E. Smalley, *Theory for Social Work Practice;* Ruth E. Smalley, "Social Casework," pp. 1195–1206.

129. Proceedings: Conference of Boards of Public Charities, pp. 60–99.

130. F. B. Sanborn, "The Work of Social Science, Past and Present," p. 25.

131. Ibid., p. 30.

132. F. B. Sanborn, ed., *Proceedings of the Sixth Annual Conference of Charities, Chicago, June 1879;* Frank J. Bruno, *Trends in Social Work 1874–1956*, pp. 133–134.

133. Bruno, *Trends in Social Work 1874–1956*, p. 8.

134. Edith Abbott, *Social Welfare and Professional Education*, rev. ed., pp. 131–173; Lela B. Costin, "Edith Abbott and the Chicago Influence on Social Work Education," pp. 98–99.

135. Burgess, "The Contribution of Sociology to Family Social Work," pp. 191–193.

136. "Social Forces," p. 1.

137. David M. Austin, "The Flexner Myth and the History of Social Work," pp. 357–377.

138. Jeffrey R. Brackett, "The Worker," pp. 1–12.

139. Berengarten, ed., *The Columbia University School of Social Work*, p. 2.

140. Brackett, "The Worker," pp. 1–12; Costin, "Edith Abbott and the Chicago Influence on Social Work Education," pp. 93–96.

141. Costin, "Edith Abbott and the Chicago Influence on Social Work Education," pp. 93–96. The commitment of Edith Abbott to the academic curriculum, to field work, and to social research are poignantly expressed in her own volume, Abbott, *Social Welfare and Professional Education.*

142. Berengarten, ed., *The Columbia University School of Social Work*, pp. 1–117.

143. Costin, "Edith Abbott and the Chicago Influence," pp. 94–111; Costin, *Two Sisters of Social Justice*, pp. 184–187.

144. Berengarten, ed., *The Columbia University School of Social Work*, p. 1.

145. Ibid., pp. 1–2.

146. Abbott, *Social Welfare and Professional Education*, p. 15.

147. Henry J. Meyer, "Professionalization and Social Work," p. 326. Meyer drew, among others, from the following sources in his discussion: Harold L. Wilensky and Charles N. Lebeaux, *Industrial Society and Social Welfare;* Grace L. Coyle, *Social Science in Professional Education;* and Herman D. Stein, "Social Science in Social Work Practice and Education," pp. 147–155.

148. Meyer, "Professionalization and Social Work," p. 326.

149. Ibid., p. 327.

150. Ibid., p. 329.

151. Ludwig L. Geismar, "Strengthening the Scientific Base of Social Work."

9. RESEARCH: CONTRIBUTIONS AND FOIBLES

1. Henry S. Maas, ed., *Five Fields of Social Service;* Henry S. Maas, ed., *Research for the Social Services;* Henry S. Maas, ed., *Social Service Research.*

2. William M. Pinsoff, "Family Therapy Process Research," pp. 699–741; Alan S. Gurman and David P. Kniskern, "Family Therapy Outcome Research," pp. 742–775.

3. Richard A. Wells, "The Empirical Base of Family Therapy," pp. 248–305.

4. William J. Reid, "Research Developments," p. 129.

5. Scott Briar, "Family Services," pp. 9–50; Scott Briar, "Family Services Casework," pp. 108–129; Scott Briar and Jon R. Conte, "Families," pp. 9–38.

6. Mary E. MacDonald, "Social Work Research," pp. 1–23.

7. Ann W. Shyne, "Casework Research," pp. 467–473.

8. Martin Bloom, "Empirically Based Clinical Research," pp. 560–582.

9. Sidney E. Zimbalist, *Historic Themes and Landmarks in Social Welfare Research.*

10. William J. Reid, *The Task-Centered System.*

11. Gordon W. Allport, "Some Guiding Principles in Understanding Personality," p. 127.

12. Clifton Kirkpatrick, "Community of Interest and the Measurements of Marriage Adjustment," pp. 133–137.

13. R. Clyde White, "The Relative Value of Case Study and Statistics," pp. 259–265.

14. Ibid., p. 261.

15. Ibid., p. 262.

16. Leonard S. Kogan and Benjamin H. Brown, "Two Year Study of Casework Uses," pp. 252–257; John Frings, "Experimental Systems of Recording," pp. 55–63; John Frings, Ruth Kratofil, and Bernice Polemis, *An Assessment of Social Case Recording.*

17. J. McVicker Hunt and Leonard S. Kogan, *Measuring Results in Social Casework;* Ann W. Shyne and Leonard S. Kogan, "A Study of Components of Movement," pp. 333–342; J. McVicker Hunt, "Measuring Movement in Casework," pp. 343–351; Leonard S. Kogan, J. McVicker Hunt, and Phyllis F. Bartelme, *A Follow-up Study of the Results of Social Casework;* J. McVicker Hunt, Margaret Blenkner, and Leonard S. Kogan, *Testing Results in Social Casework.* Nathaniel Goodman, "The Use of the Movement Scale in Brief Recording," pp. 282–285; Helen Northen, "Evaluating Movement of Individuals in Social Group Work," pp. 28–37; Ann W. Shyne, ed., *Use of Judgments as Data in Social Work Research.*

18. Norman A. Polansky, "Research in Social Work," p. 1210.

19. Ludwig L. Geismar and Beverly Ayres, *Patterns of Change in Problem Families;* Ludwig L. Geismar and Beverly Ayres, *Measuring Family Functioning;* Ludwig Geismar, *Family and Community Functioning.*

20. Katherine H. Tinker, *Patterns of Family-Centered Treatment.*

21. Alice Overton and Katherine H. Tinker, *Casework Notebook;* Ludwig L. Geismar, *Report on Check List Survey.*

22. Scott Briar, "Family Services," p. 39; also see citations and detailed discussion of research directed toward the multiproblem family, pp. 30–39.

23. Gordon E. Brown, ed., *The Multiproblem Dilemma.*

24. Margaret Blenkner, "Predictive Factors in the Initial Interview in Family Casework," pp. 65–73; Margaret Blenkner, J. McVicker Hunt, and Leonard S. Kogan, "A Study of Interrelated Factors in the Initial Interview with New Clients," pp. 23–30.

25. Irving A. Fowler, "Family Agency Characteristics and Client Continuance," p. 271; George Levinger, "Continuance in Casework and Other Helping Relationships," pp. 40–51.

26. Merton S. Krause, "Predicting Client Discontinuance at Intake," pp. 308–312; David Fanshel, "A Study of Caseworkers' Perception of Their Clients," pp. 543–551; Edgar F. Borgatta, David Fanshel, and Henry J. Meyer, *Social Workers' Perceptions of Clients;* Lillian Ripple, with Ernestine Alexander and Bernice W. Polemis, *Motivation, Capacity, and Opportunity;* Aaron Rosenblatt and James Mayer, "Client Disengagement and Alternative Treatment Resources," pp. 515–519; Norman Polansky and Jacob Kounin, "Clients' Reactions to Initial Interviews," pp. 237–264; Florence Hollis, "Continuance and Discontinuance in Marital Counseling and Some Observations on Joint Interviews," pp. 167–174.

27. Lillian Ripple, "Factors Associated with Continuance in Casework Service," p. 87.

28. Ibid.

29. Ripple, with Alexander and Polemis, *Motivation, Capacity, and Opportunity,* pp. 205–206.

30. Gordon Hamilton, *Theory and Practice of Social Casework.*

31. Lucille Austin, "Trends in Differential Treatment in Social Casework," pp. 203–211; also in Cora Kasius, ed., *Principles and Techniques of Social Casework,* pp. 324–338.

32. Florence Hollis, "The Techniques of Casework," pp. 235–244; also in Kasius, ed., *Principles and Techniques in Social Casework,* pp. 412–426; Florence Hollis and Mary E. Woods, *Casework.*

33. *Scope and Methods of the Family Service Agency.*

34. *Methods and Process in Social Casework.*

35. William J. Reid and Ann W. Shyne, *Brief and Extended Casework.* pp. 70–71.

36. Hollis and Woods, *Casework.*

37. Ibid., 3d ed., pp. 104–105.

38. Louise Boatman, "Caseworkers' Judgments of Clients' Hope"; Edna Chamberlain, "Testing with a Treatment Typology," pp. 3–8; Shirley Ehrenkranz, "Study of the Techniques and Procedures Used in Joint Interviewing in the Treatment of Marital Problems"; Shirley Ehrenkranz, "A Study of Joint Interviewing in the Treatment of Marital Problems," pp. 498–502, 570–574; Edward J. Mullen, "Casework Treatment Procedures as a Function of Client Diagnostic Variables"; Edward J. Mullen, "Casework Communication," pp. 546–551; Edward J. Mullen, "The Relation Between Diagnosis and Treatment in Casework," pp. 210–226; Edward J. Mullen, "Differences in Worker Style in Casework," pp. 345–353; Ben A. Orcutt, "Process Analysis in The First Phase of Treatment," pp. 147–164; Helen Pinkus, "Casework Techniques Related to Selected Characteristics of Clients and Workers"; Francis J. Turner, "Social Work Treatment and Value Differences"; Francis J. Turner, "A Comparison of Procedures in the Treatment of Clients with Two Different Value Orientations," pp. 273–277; Francis J. Turner, "Ethnic Difference and Client Performance," pp. 1–10.

39. Richard D. Woodrow, "Casework," p. 100.

40. Reid and Shyne, *Brief and Extended Treatment*, pp. 69–72.
41. Sophie Van Senden Theis, *How Foster Children Turn Out*.
42. Henry J. Meyer, Edgar F. Borgotta, and Wyatt C. Jones, *Girls of Vocational High*.
43. Brown, ed., *The Multiproblem Dilemma;* David Wallace, "The Chemung County Evaluation of Casework Service to Dependent Multiproblem Families," pp. 379–389.
44. Edward J. Mullen, Robert M. Chazin, and David M. Feldstein, *Preventing Chronic Dependency*.
45. Identification and critiques of evaluative studies of the period can be found in: Edward J. Mullen and James R. Dumpson and Associates, *Evaluation of Social Intervention;* Joel Fischer, *The Effectiveness of Social Casework*.
46. Ludwig Geismar, "Thirteen Evaluative Studies," p. 37.
47. Fischer, *The Effectiveness of Social Casework*, p. 8.
48. Ibid., p. 14.
49. Ibid., p. 16.
50. Ibid., pp. 137–139.
51. Helen H. Perlman, "Casework and the Case of Chemung County," pp. 47–50.
52. Florence Hollis, "Evaluation," pp. 205–222.
53. Louise S. Bandler, *Education for Clinical Social Work Practice*, p. 4.
54. Joel Fischer, "New and Emerging Methods of Direct Practice," pp. 525–547; Briar, "Family Services Casework," p. 125.
55. Reid and Shyne, *Brief and Extended Casework*.
56. Bruce V. Parsons and James F. Alexander, "Short-Term Family Intervention," pp. 195–201.
57. Lydia Rapoport, "Crisis Intervention as a Mode of Brief Treatment," pp. 265–311.
58. Hans Jurgen Eysenck, "The Effects of Psychotherapy: An Evaluation," pp. 319–324; Hans Jurgen Eysenck, *The Effects of Psychotherapy;* Eugene E. Levitt, "The Results of Psychotherapy with Children," pp. 189–196.
59. Elizabeth McBroom, "Socialization and Social Casework," pp. 316–351; Lynne Riehman, "Beginning Where the Client Is," pp. 73–107; Edwin J. Thomas, "Behavioral Modification and Casework;" pp. 181–218; Francine Sobey, ed., *Changing Roles in Social Work Practice;* Gerald Caplan, *Support Systems and Community Mental Health*.
60. Arthur Pearl and Frank Riessman, *New Careers for the Poor;* Francine Sobey, *The Nonprofessional Revolution in Mental Health*.
61. Carel B. Germain, "Casework and Science: A Historical Encounter," p. 29.
62. Hollis, *Casework;* Howard J. Parad, ed., *Ego Psychology and Dynamic Casework;* Howard J. Parad and Roger Miller, eds., *Ego-Oriented Casework;* Helen H. Perlman, *Casework;* Robert W. Roberts and Robert H. Nee, eds., *Theories of Social Casework;* Robert W. Roberts and Helen Northen, *Theories of Social Work with Groups;* Isabel L. Stamm, "Ego Psychology in Casework," pp. 80–109.
63. Helen H. Perlman, "Social Work Method: A Review of the Past Decade," pp. 166–178; Helen H. Perlman, "Social Work Method: A Review of the Decade 1955–65," pp. 99–124; Carol H. Meyer, *Social Work Practice;* Carol H. Meyer, "Purposes and Boundaries," pp. 268–275; Carol H. Meyer, "Direct Services in New and Old Contexts," pp. 26–54.

64. Gordon Hearn, ed., *The General Systems Approach;* Ben A. Orcutt, "Poverty on the American Scene," pp. 1–38; Ben A. Orcutt, "Casework Intervention and the Problems of the Poor," pp. 85–95; Sister Mary Paul Janchill, "Systems Concepts in Casework Theory and Practice," pp. 74–82; Ann Hartman, "To Think About the Unthinkable," pp. 467–474; William E. Gordon, "Basic Constructs for Integrative and Generative Conception of Social Work"; Gordon Hearn, "General Systems Theory and Social Work," pp. 333–359; Carel B. Germain, "General Systems Theory and Ego Psychology," pp. 535–550.

65. Howard Goldstein, *Social Work Practice;* Max Siporin, *Introduction to Social Work Practice;* Helen Northen, *Clinical Social Work;* Allen Pincus and Anne Minahan, eds., *Social Work Practice.*

66. William J. Reid and Laura Epstein, *Task-Centered Casework;* William J. Reid, *The Task-Centered System.*

67. See, for example, William J. Reid, *Family Problem Solving;* Ann E. Fortune, *Task-Centered Practice with Families and Groups;* Charles Garvin, "Task Centered Group Work," pp. 494–507; Charles Garvin, "Developmental Research for Task Centered Group Work with Chronic Mental Patients," pp. 31–42.

68. William J. Reid, "The Model Development Dissertation," pp. 215–225.

69. William J. Reid, "Developing Intervention Methods Through Experimental Designs," p. 668.

70. Edwin J. Thomas, *Designing Interventions for the Helping Professions;* Edwin J. Thomas, "Mousetraps, Developmental Research, and Social Work Education," pp. 468–483.

71. Nathan W. Ackerman, Frances L. Beatman, and Sanford N. Sherman, eds., *Exploring the Base for Family Therapy;* Nathan W. Ackerman, Frances L. Beatman, and Sanford Sherman, eds., *Expanding Theory and Practice in Family Therapy;* Arthur L. Leader, "The Role of Intervention in Family Group Treatment," pp. 327–332.

72. Virginia Satir, *Conjoint Family Therapy;* Virginia Satir, James Stachowiak, and Harvey A. Taschman, *Helping Families to Change.*

73. Lynn Hoffman, *Foundations of Family Therapy,* p. 17.

74. Ibid., p. 18.

75. Arthur M. Bodin, "The Interactional View," p. 268.

76. Hoffman, *Foundations of Family Therapy,* pp. 220–221.

77. Curtis Janzen and Oliver Harris, *Family Treatment in Social Work Practice,* p. 4.

78. Ibid.

79. Richard A. Wells, Thomas C. Dilkes, and Nina Trivelli, "The Results of Family Therapy," p. 191.

80. Elsbeth H. Couch, *Joint and Family Interviews in the Treatment of Marital Problems.*

81. Ibid., pp. 292–293.

82. Reid, *Family Problem Solving,* pp. 1–66.

83. Danuta Mostwin, *Social Dimensions of Family Treatment,* p. 54.

84. Judith C. Nelsen, *Family Treatment: An Integrative Approach,* pp. 28–54.

85. John E. Bell, *Family Group Therapy.*

86. Murray Bowen, "Theory in the Practice of Psychotherapy," pp. 42–90.

87. Salvador Minuchin, *Families and Family Therapy.*

88. Ivan Boszormenyi-Nagy and James L. Framo, *Intensive Family Therapy;* James L. Framo, ed., *Family Interaction.*

89. Lyman Wynne, "Communication Disorders and the Quest for Relatedness in Families of Schizophrenics."

90. It is not our purpose in this chapter to trace the historical details of the development of the varied practice approaches and the different family therapists associated with them. The reader should review the following references that highlight coverage of these developments: Guerin, ed., *Family Therapy;* Tolson and Reid, eds., *Models of Family Treatment;* Gurman and Kniskern, eds., *Handbook of Family Therapy;* J. Haley, ed., *Changing Families;* Janzen and Harris, eds., *Family Treatment in Social Work Practice;* Hoffman, *Foundations of Family Therapy;* Gerald Erickson and Terrence P. Hogan, *Family Therapy;* Peggy Papp, *The Process of Change.*

91. Alan S. Gurman and David P. Kniskern, "Research on Marital and Family Therapy," pp. 817–901; Wells, Dilkes, and Trivelli, "The Results of Family Therapy," pp. 189–207; Richard A. Wells and Alan E. Dezen, "The Results of Family Therapy Revisited," pp. 251–274; Paul F. Dell, "Researching Family Theories of Schizophrenia," pp. 321–335; Richard A. Wells, "The Empirical Base of Family Therapy," pp. 248–305.

92. Pinsoff, "Family Therapy Process Research," p. 699.

93. Ibid.

94. James W. Hodgson and Robert A. Lewis, "Pilgrim's Progress III," pp. 163–173.

95. Alan S. Gurman and David P. Kniskern, "Family Therapy Outcome Research," p. 745; M. Duncan Stanton and Thomas C. Todd, "A Critique of the Wells and Dezen Review of the Results of Non-Behavioral Family Therapy," pp. 169–178.

96. Pinsoff, "Family Therapy Process Research," p. 699.

97. Jon R. Conte and Terese M. Halpin, "New Services for Families," pp. 1125–1126.

98. Harry Aponte and Lynn Hoffman, "The Open Door," pp. 1–44; Harry Aponte, "Under-Organization in the Poor Family," pp. 432–448; Harry Aponte, "The Family-School Interview," pp. 303–311.

99. Hoffman, *Foundations of Family Therapy.*

100. Ibid., pp. 339–349; Gregory Bateson, *Mind and Nature.*

101. Hoffman, *Foundations of Family Therapy,* p. 340.

102. Ibid., p. 343.

103. Paul F. Dell, "Beyond Homeostasis," pp. 21–41.

104. Bradford P. Keeney, "Ecosystemic Epistemology," pp. 117–129.

105. Carel B. Germain, *Social Work Practice;* Carel B. Germain and Alex Gitterman, *The Life Model of Social Work Practice.*

106. William Schwartz, "Neighborhood Centers and Group Work," p. 154.

107. Marvin Silverman, "Knowledge in Social Group Work," p. 58.

108. Ronald A. Feldman, "Three Types of Group Integration"; William Shalinsky, "The Effect of Group Composition on Aspects of Group Functioning"; Baruch Levine, "Factors Related to Interpersonal Balance in Social Work Treatment Groups."

109. Nathan Caplan, "Treatment Intervention and Reciprocal Interaction Effects," pp. 63–88.

110. Ronald A. Feldman, "Group Work Knowledge and Research," p. 13.

111. Steven H. Tallant, "Meta-Analysis," pp. 43–53.

112. Esther S. Swerdloff, "The Effect of the Depression on Family Life," pp.

310–334; Cherry Reed, "Family Dependency Roles," pp. 64–70; Ralph G. Hurtin, "Relief in Private Family Agencies in the Post Depression Period," pp. 121–124; Helen M. Walker, "Some Data Regarding 162 Families Affected by Unemployment Known to the Cleveland Associated Charities," pp. 131–135; Dorothy R. Bucklin, "Studies of Breakdowns in Family Incomes," pp. 3–13; Catherine Small Haman and David Haman, "Studies of Breakdowns in Family Income," pp. 127–130; Rosemary Reynolds, "They Have Neither Money Nor Work," pp. 35–39; Lillian L. Otis, "Unemployment and Its Treatment in Non-Resident Families," pp. 136–143.

113. Florence Hollis, "Casework as a Supplemental Service," pp. 186–191; Florence Hollis, "The Function of a Family Society," pp. 280–283.

114. Donald S. Schön, *The Reflective Practitioner*, pp. 37–38.

115. Aaron Rosenblatt, "The Practitioner's Use and Evaluation of Research," pp. 53–59.

116. Richard Simpson, "Is Research Utilization for Social workers?", pp. 142–157.

117. Dorothy Fahs Beck, *Patterns in Use of Family Agency Service.*

118. Dorothy Fahs Beck and Mary Ann Jones, *Progress on Family Problems.*

119. Richard A. Cloward and Irwin Epstein, "Private Social Welfare's Disengagement from the Poor," pp. 623–643.

120. Nancy Robinson, "Current Issues for Social Casework in the Provision of Services to Lower Socio-economic Groups," pp. 44–46.

121. Beck and Jones, *Progress on Family Problems*, p. 3.

122. Ibid.

123. David Fanshel and Eugene B. Shinn, *Children in Foster Care.*

124. Deborah Shapiro, *Agencies and Foster Children;* Shirley Jenkins and Elaine Norman, *Filial Deprivation and Foster Care.*

125. Fanshel and Shinn, *Children in Foster Care*, p. 476.

126. J. McVicker Hunt, "On the Judgment of Social Workers as a Source of Information in Social Work Research," pp. 38–52.

127. Tony Tripodi and Henry Miller, "The Clinical Judgment Process," pp. 63–69.

128. James Bieri, Alvin Atkins, Scott Briar, Robin Leamon, Henry Miller, and Tony Tripodi, *Clinical and Social Judgment: The Discrimination of Behavioral Information;* Ben A. Orcutt, "A Study of Anchoring Effects in Clinical Judgment," pp. 408–417; Tony Tripodi and James Bieri, "Information Transmissions in Clinical Judgments as a Function of Stimulus Dimensionality and Cognitive Complexity," pp. 119–137; Henry Miller and James Bieri, "An Informational Analysis of Clinical Judgment," pp. 317–325; Scott Briar, "Use of Theory in Studying Effects of Client Social Class on Students' Judgments," pp. 91–97.

129. Anthony J. Arangio, "A Study of the Effects of Eight Sequential Phases of Alternated Anchors on Clinical Judgments of Social Case Workers."

130. Donna L. Franklin, "Differential Clinical Assessments," pp. 44–61.

131. Aaron Rosenblatt, "The Practitioners' Use and Evaluation of Research," p. 55; David Fanshel, "The Future of Social Work Research," pp. 3–18; Stuart A. Kirk and Aaron Rosenblatt, "New Applications of Research in Clinical Practice," pp. 550–551.

132. William J. Reid, "Research Developments," p. 128.

133. Harry Butler and Samuel A. Richmond, "Education for the Integration of Research and Practice."

134. Barbara Shore, "The Future of Doctoral Education in Social Work."

135. Scott Briar, "Major Trends and Issues in the Future of Doctoral Training in Social Work"; William J. Reid, "Practice Research."

136. For example, Michael W. Howe, "Casework Self-Evaluation," pp. 10–15; Walter W. Hudson, "Research Training in Professional Social Work Education," pp. 116–121; Martin Bloom and Stephen R. Block, "Evaluating One's Own Effectiveness and Efficiency," pp. 130–136; Ben A. Orcutt and Paul R. Mills, Jr., "The Doctoral Practice Laboratory," pp. 633–643.

137. Martin Bloom and Joel Fischer, *Evaluating Practice;* Martin Bloom, *The Paradox of Helping;* Srinika Jayaratne and Rona L. Levy, *Empirical Clinical Practice;* William J. Reid and Audrey Smith, *Research in Social Work;* Scott Briar, "Incorporating Research into Education for Clinical Practice in Social Work," pp. 132–140.

138. Hudson, "Research Training in Professional Social Work Education," pp. 116–121.

139. William J. Reid and Patricia Hanrahan, "Recent Evaluations of Social Work," pp. 328–340.

140. Reid, "Research Developments," p. 130.

141. Sidney E. Zimbalist, "The Single Case Clinical Research Design in Developmental Perspective," pp. 61–66.

142. Rona L. Levy, "Overview of Single-Case Experiments," p. 583.

143. Kirk and Rosenblatt, "New Applications of Research in Clinical Practice," p. 554.

144. Stanley L. Witkin, "Toward a Scientific Social Work," pp. 83–98.

10. DOCTORAL EDUCATION: INFLUENCE FOR RESEARCH AND SCIENTIFIC DEVELOPMENT

1. The New York School of Philanthropy established in 1904 was a one-year graduate program. Sidney Berengarten, ed., *The Columbia University School of Social Work,* p. 2.

2. Mary L. Gottesfeld and Mary E. Pharis, *Profiles in Social Work,* p. 138.

3. John J. Baldi, "Doctorates in Social Work, 1920–1968," p. 14.

4. Lela B. Costin, *Two Sisters of Social Justice.*

5. Lela B. Costin, "Edith Abbott and the Chicago Influence in Social Work Education," p. 94.

6. *Social Work Education in the Post-Master's Program: Guiding Principles,* pp. 9–11; Maurice B. Hamovitch, "The Ph.D. versus the D.S.W. in Social Work."

7. Data Bank, Doctoral Programs in Social Work, Case Western Reserve University, Cleveland, 1984; Baldi, "Doctorates in Social Work, 1920–1968," p. 14; Leila Calhoun Deasy, ed., *Doctoral Students Look at Social Work Education,* pp. 112–113.

8. Baldi, "Doctorates in Social Work, 1920–1968," pp. 11–14.

9. *Social Work Education in the Post-Master's Program: Guiding Principles; Social Work Education in the Post-Master's Program: Approaches to Curriculum Content; Social Work Education in the Post-Master's Program: Field Work and Related Issues.*

10. *Social Work Education in Post-Master's Programs: Guiding Principles,* Foreword.

11. Ibid., pp. 63–64.

12. Ibid., p. 20. In the early fifties, there were six third-year programs. The relationship between the third-year and the doctoral programs generally consisted of the specialized practice emphasis, including field work, in the third year, along with the more generic social work content in the doctoral curriculum. Thus, many students entering the third year to advance their practice competence moved into the formal doctoral program applying those credits to the degree. The Committee on Advanced Curriculum in Social Work had held lengthy discussions on the place of field work in doctoral and third-year education. Helen R. Wright reported that the committee had considered field work as legitimate for a doctoral program, but there were still questions as to whether it should be required and as to its nature as an offering. *Social Work Education in the Post-Master's Program: Field Work and Related Issues*, pp. 47–49.

13. Lucille N. Austin, "The Content of the Advanced Casework Seminars," p. 35.

14. Jeanette Regensberg, ed., *Some Educational Patterns in Doctoral Programs in Schools of Social Work*, p. 13.

15. Ibid., p. 14.

16. Ibid., pp. 23–27.

17. Henry J. Meyer, "Social Worker-Social Scientist," p. 87.

18. William E. Gordon, "Social Work Scientist," p. 78.

19. Ibid.

20. Gottesfeld and Pharis, *Profiles in Social Work*, p. 135.

21. Baldi, "Doctorates in Social Work, 1920–1968," p. 12.

22. William E. Gordon, "Scientific Training in the Social Work Doctorate," pp. 7–21.

23. Barbara Shore, "The Future of Doctoral Education in Social Work."

24. Lillian Ripple, *Report of the Task Force on Structure and Quality in Social Work Education*.

25. Max Siporin, "Doctoral Education for Direct Service Practice in Social Work," p. 78.

26. Ibid., p. 86.

27. Ibid.

28. Daniel Thurz, "Professional Education for Expected Political Action by Social Workers," p. 88.

29. Aaron Rosen and John J. Stretch, eds., *Doctoral Education in Social Work*, p. 3.

30. Beulah Rothman and Bert Kaplan, "The Practice Internship in Clinical Doctoral Education," p. 82.

31. Ibid., p. 83.

32. Ben A. Orcutt and Paul R. Mills, Jr., "A Model of Doctoral Education," pp. 100–108; Ben A. Orcutt and Paul R. Mills, Jr., "The Doctoral Practice Laboratory," pp. 533–543.

33. At that time, we identified the scholar-scientist as theoretician-researcher-practitioner.

34. David Fanshel, "The Future of Social Work Research," pp. 3–18; Aaron Rosenblatt, "The Utilization of Research in Social Work Practice," pp. 548–559.

35. William J. Reid, "Research Developments."

36. Scott Briar, "Toward the Integration of Practice and Research," pp. 31–37;

Scott Briar, "Major Trends and Issues in the Future of Doctoral Training in Social Work"; William J. Reid, "Research Strategies for Improving Individualized Services," pp. 38–52; Orcutt and Mills, "A Model of Doctoral Education," pp. 100–108.

37. Walter W. Hudson, "Elementary Techniques for Assessing Single-Client/ Single-Worker Interventions," pp. 311–326; Michael W. Howe, "Casework Self-Evaluation," pp. 10–15; Srinika Jayaratne and Rona L. Levy, *Empirical Clinical Practice;* Martin Bloom and Stephen R. Block, "Evaluating One's Own Effectiveness and Efficiency," pp. 130–136; Martin Bloom and Joel Fischer, *Evaluating Practice;* Edwin J. Thomas, "Uses of Research Methods in Interpersonal Practice"; Eileen Gambrill, *Behavior Modification;* Srinika Jayaratne, "Single Subject and Group Designs in Treatment Evaluation," pp. 35–42; Michel Hersen and David H. Barlow, *Single Case Experimental Designs.*

38. Martin Bloom, "Empirically Based Clinical Research," p. 561.

39. Edward J. Mullen, "Methodological Dilemmas in Social Work Research," p. 18.

40. David H. Barlow, Stephen C. Hayes, and Rosemary A. Nelson, eds., *The Scientist-Practitioner,* pp. 1–37.

41. Orcutt and Mills, "A Model of Doctoral Education," p. 104.

42. Michael A. Patchner, "A Decade of Social Work Doctoral Graduates," p. 40.

43. Ibid.

11. EDUCATIONAL PREPARATION FOR THE SCHOLAR-SCIENTIST IN SOCIAL WORK PRACTICE

1. Cheryl A. Richey, Betty J. Blythe, and Sharon B. Berlin, "Do Social Workers Evaluate Their Practice?" pp. 14–20; Robert W. Weinbach and Allen Rubin, eds., *Teaching Social Work Research;* Claire Rabin, "Matching the Research Seminar to Meet Practice Needs, pp. 5–12; Deborah H. Siegal, "Effective Teaching of Empirically Based Practice," pp. 40–47.

2. Richey, Blythe, and Berlin, "Do Social Workers Evaluate Their Practice?" p. 14; Gary John Welch, "Will Graduates use Single-Subject Designs to Evaluate Their Case Work Practice?," pp. 42–47; Wallace J. Gingerich, "Generalizing Single Case Evaluation from Classroom to Practice," pp. 74–82.

3. Richey, Blythe, and Berlin, "Do Social Workers Evaluate Their Practice?," p. 18.

4. Ben A. Orcutt and Paul R. Mills, Jr., "Education for Doctoral Social Work Clinical Practice in the 1980's," pp. 46–47.

5. Florence Lieberman, *Social Workers as Psychotherapists.*

6. Ibid., pp. 40–41.

7. Ibid., p. 41; Lieberman categorized the abilities as follows:

1. To establish a differential biopsychosocial diagnostic assessment based on a specialized body of knowledge.
2. To establish a basic treatment plan derived from the psychosocial diagnostic assessment.
3. To establish progress through specific steps, leading to completion of the treatment plan.

4. To select from and carry out alternative treatment strategies (including variations in modality and duration).
5. To engage in continuous, objective, and systematic evaluation of treatment.

Treatment category:

1. To demonstrate an independent and high level of competence in carrying out one's practice skills.
2. To communicate one's rationale for a particular course of intervention to others, using commonly understood and utilized theoretical behavioral science and practice knowledge.
3. To make contributions to behavioral science and practice knowledge that are relevant to the field of clinical social work.
4. To utilize self-awareness in an integrative manner in relation to one's practice.

8. Roger Miller, "Observations on a Clinical Doctorate," p. 78.
9. William J. Reid and Patricia Hanrahan, "Recent Evaluations of Social Work," pp. 328–340.
10. Ibid., pp. 338–339.
11. Charles A. Glisson, "Are Social Work Doctoral Program Graduates Quantitative Illiterates?," pp. 66–69.
12. Aaron Rosenblatt and Diana Waldfogel, eds., *Handbook of Clinical Social Work*.
13. Carol H. Meyer, ed., *Clinical Social Work in an Eco-Systemic Perspective*, pp. 238–256.
14. Scott Briar, "Practice Trends," pp. 107–108.
15. William J. Reid, *The Task-Centered System*.
16. Judith C. Nelsen, "Issues in Single-Subject Research for Nonbehaviorists," pp. 31–37.
17. Joel Fischer, "New and Emerging Methods of Direct Practice," p. 535.
18. Mary Gorman Gyarfas, "The Scientific Imperative Again," p. 150.

12. AN EXAMPLE OF CLINICAL INQUIRY IN PRACTICE: THE DIRECT INFLUENCE TREATMENT MODEL

1. William J. Reid and Laura Epstein, *Task-Centered Casework*, pp. 1–40.
2. Ann E. Fortune, *Task-Centered Practice with Families and Groups*, p. 7–26.
3. Florence Hollis and Mary Woods, *Casework*.
4. Ibid., pp. 116–122.
5. The screening assessment was consistent with an ecosystems perspective in social work. See Carol H. Meyer, ed., *Clinical Social Work in the Eco-Systems Perspective*.
6. William J. Reid, "Characteristics of Casework Intervention," pp. 11–19; William J. Reid, "Target Problems, Time Limits, Task Structure," pp. 58–68; William J. Reid, "A Test of a Task-Centered Approach," pp. 3–9; Reid and Epstein, *Task Centered Casework*; William J. Reid and Laura Epstein, eds., *Task-Centered Practice*, pp. 1–18; William J. Reid, *The Task-Centered System*; William J. Reid, "Task-Centered Treatment," pp. 479–494.
7. Albert Bandura, "Self-Efficacy," p. 209.
8. Richard R. Bootzin and David Max, "Learning and Behavioral Theories," p. 37.

9. Ibid.

10. Ibid., p. 44.

11. Edmund Jacobson, *You Must Relax;* Edmund Jacobson, *Anxiety and Tension Control;* Edmund Jacobson, *Teaching and Learning New Methods for Old Arts.*

12. Leopold Bellack, Marvin Hurvich, and Helen K. Gediman, *Ego Functions in Schizophrenics, Neurotics, and Normals.*

13. Stephen Nowicki, Jr., and Bonnie R. Strickland, "A Locus of Control Scale for Children," pp. 148–154.

14. Ellen V. Piers, *Manual for the Piers-Harris Children's Self-Concept Scale.*

15. Tony Tripodi, *Evaluative Research for Social Workers,* pp. 118–120.

16. Martin Bloom and Joel Fischer, *Evaluating Practice,* pp. 329–345, 443–462.

17. Nowicki and Strickland, "A Locus of Control Scale for Children," pp. 150–151.

18. Piers, *Manual for the Piers-Harris Children's Self-Concept Scale.*

19. Bloom and Fischer, *Evaluating Practice,* pp. 443–462.

20. Sidney Siegel, *Nonparametric Statistics for the Behavioral Sciences,* pp. 202–212.

21. Linda Cox Flowers, "A Social Work Paradigm for Treatment of One Aggressive, Acting-Out Child."

13. A THEORETICAL STUDY OF OBJECT RELATIONS AND THE BORDERLINE PATIENT

1. Margaret S. Mahler, Fred Pine, and Anni Bergman, *The Psychological Birth of the Human Infant.*

2. Otto Kernberg, *Borderline Conditions and Pathological Narcissism.*

3. James F. Masterson, *Psychotherapy of the Borderline Adult.*

4. William Ronald Dodds Fairbairn, "Endopsychic Structure Considered in Terms of Object-Relationships," pp. 82–136.

5. Heinz Kohut, *The Restoration of the Self.*

6. Frederick Engels, *Socialism: Utopian and Scientific,* p. 66.

7. Fairbairn, "Endopsychic Structure Considered in Terms of Object-Relationships," p. 135.

8. Jeffrey Seinfeld, "An Object Relations Theoretical Contribution to the Understanding of the Psychopathology and Intensive Psychotherapy of the Borderline Personality Organization"; Jeffrey Seinfeld, *The Bad Object.*

Bibliography

Abbott, Edith. *Social Welfare and Professional Education*. Chicago: University of Chicago Press, 1931; rev. ed. 1942.

Achinstein, Peter A. *Law and Explanation*. Oxford: Clarendon Press, 1971.

Ackerman, Nathan W., Frances L. Beatman, and Sanford N. Sherman, eds. *Expanding Theory and Practice in Family Therapy*. New York: Family Service Association of America, 1967.

Ackerman, Nathan W., Frances L. Beatman, and Sanford N. Sherman, eds. *Exploring the Base for Family Therapy*. New York: Family Service Association of America, 1961.

Addams, Jane, "Charity and Social Justice." In *Proceedings-National Conference of Charities and Correction, St. Louis, May 19–26, 1910*, pp. 1–18. Fort Wayne: Archer, 1910.

Alexander, Leslie B. "Social Work's Freudian Deluge: Myth or Reality." *Social Service Review* (December 1972), 46:517–538.

Allport, Gordon W. "Some Guiding Principles in Understanding Personality." *The Family* (June 1930), 11:124–128.

Aponte, Harry J. "The Family-School Interview: An Eco-Structural Approach." *Family Process* (September 1976), 15:303–311.

Aponte, Harry J. "Under Organization in the Poor Family." In Philip J. Guerin, Jr., ed., *Family Therapy*, pp. 432–448. New York: Gardner Press, 1976.

Aponte, Harry J., and Lynn Hoffman. "The Open Door: A Structural Approach to a Family with an Anorectic Child." *Family Process* (March 1973), 12:1–44.

Arangio, Anthony J. "A Study of the Effects of Eight Sequential Phases of Alternated Anchors on Clinical Judgments of Social Case Workers." M.S.W. thesis, Louisiana State University, 1964.

Armer, Michael, and Allen D. Grimshaw, eds. *Comparative Social Research: Methodological Problems and Strategies*. New York: Wiley, 1973.

Atherton, Charles R., and David L. Klemmack. *Research Methods in Social Work*. Lexington, Mass.: Heath, 1982.

Austin, David M. "The Flexner Myth and the History of Social Work." *Social Service Review* (September 1983), 57:357–377.

Austin, Lucille N. "The Content of the Advanced Casework Seminars." In *Social Work Education in the Post-Master's Program: Approaches to Curriculum Content*, monograph no. 2, pp. 35–46. New York: Council on Social Work Education, April 1954.

Austin, Lucille. "Trends in Differential Treatment in Social Casework." *Journal of Social Casework* (June 1948), 29:203–211. In Cora Kasius, ed., *Principles and Techniques in Social Casework*, pp. 324–338. New York: Family Service Association of America, 1950.

Ayer, Alfred Jules. *The Foundations of Empirical Knowledge*. London: Macmillan, 1940; repr. 1947.

Ayer, Alfred Jules. *Language, Truth, and Logic*. London: Gollancz, 1936, 2d ed. 1946; repr. New York: Dover, 1952.

Ayer, Alfred Jules. *The Origins of Pragmatism*. 2d ed. San Francisco: Freeman, Cooper, 1968.

Ayer, Alfred Jules. *Philosophy in the Twentieth Century*. London: Weidenfeld and Nicolson, 1982.

Ayer, Alfred Jules, ed. *Logical Positivism*. New York: Free Press, 1959.

Ayers, P. W. "Report of the Committee on Charity Organization." In *Proceedings-National Conference of Charities and Correction, Grand Rapids, Michigan, June 4–10, 1896*, pp. 235–242. Boston: Ellis, 1896.

Bagozzi, Richard P. "Theoretical Concepts, Measurements, and Meaning." In Claes Fornell, ed., *A Second Generation of Multivariate Analysis*, vol. 2, pp. 24–38. New York: Praeger Press, 1982.

Baldi, John J. "Doctorates in Social Work, 1920–1968." *Journal of Education for Social Work* (Winter 1971), 7:11–22.

Bandler, Louise S. *Education for Clinical Social Work Practice: Continuity and Change*. New York: Pergamon Press, 1983.

Bandura, Albert. "Self-Efficacy: Toward a Unifying Theory of Behavioral Change." *Psychological Review* (March 1977), 84:191–215.

Barlow, David H., and Steven C. Hayes. "Alternating Treatment Design: One Strategy for Comparing the Effects of Two Treatments in a Single Subject." *Journal of Applied Behavior Analysis* (Summer 1979), 12:199–210.

Barlow, David H., Steven C. Hayes, and Rosemary O. Nelson. *The Scientist-Practitioner: Research and Accountability in Clinical and Educational Settings*. New York: Pergamon Press, 1984.

Barlow, David H., and Michel Hersen. "Single-Case Experimental Designs: Uses in Applied Clinical Research." *Archives of General Psychiatry* (September 1973), 29:319–325.

Barnard, Chester. *The Function of the Executive*. Cambridge, Mass.: Harvard University Press, 1938.

Barton, Allen H., and Paul F. Lazarsfeld. "Some Functions of Qualitative Analysis in Social Research." In George J. McCall and J. S. Simmons, eds., *Issues in Participant Observation*, pp. 163–196. Reading, Mass.: Addison-Wesley, 1969.

Bateson, Gregory. *Mind and Nature: A Necessary Unity*. New York: Dutton, 1979.

Bauman, Zygmunt. *Hermeneutics and Social Science*. New York: Columbia University Press, 1978.

Beck, Dorothy Fahs. *Patterns in Use of Family Agency Service*. New York: Family Service Association of America, 1962.

Beck, Dorothy Fahs and Mary Ann Jones. *Progress on Family Problems*. New York: Family Service Association of America, 1973.

Becker, Dorothy G. "Exit Lady Bountiful: The Volunteer and the Professional Social Worker." *Social Service Review* (March 1964), 38:57–72.

Bell, John E. *Family Group Therapy*. Public Health Monograph No. 64, U.S. Department of Health, Education and Welfare. Washington, D.C.: U.S. Government Printing Office, 1961.

Bellack, Leopold, Marvin Hurvich, and Helen K. Gediman. *Ego Functions in Schizophrenics, Neurotics, and Normals: A Systematic Study of Conceptual, Diagnostic, and Therapeutic Aspects*. New York: John Wiley, 1973.

Berengarten, Sidney, ed. *The Columbia University School of Social Work: A History of Social Pioneering*. New York: Columbia University Press, 1987.

Bernstein, Richard J. *Beyond Objectivism and Relativism: Science, Hermeneutics and Praxis*. Philadelphia: University of Pennsylvania Press, 1983.

Bernstein, Richard J. *Praxis and Action: Contemporary Philosophies of Human Activity*. Philadelphia: University of Pennsylvania Press, 1971.

Bertalanffy, Ludwig von. "General Systems Theory and Psychiatry: An Overview." In William J. Gray et al., eds., *General Systems Theory in Psychiatry*, pp. 33–46. Boston: Little, Brown, 1969.

Betti, Emilio. "Die Hermenetic als Allgemeine Metodik der Geisteswissenschaften." *Philophie und Geschichte Series*, Nos. 78–79. Tubingen: Mohr, 1962.

Bieri, James, Alvin Atkins, Scott Briar, Robin Leamon, Henry Miller, and Tony Tripodi. *Clinical and Social Judgment: The Discrimination of Behavioral Information*. New York: Wiley, 1966.

Bleicher, Joseph, ed. *Contemporary Hermeneutics: Hermeneutics as Method, Philosophy and Critique*. London: Routledge and Kegan Paul, 1980.

Bleicher, Joseph. *The Hermeneutic Imagination*. London: Routledge and Kegan Paul, 1982.

Blenkner, Margaret. "Predictive Factors in the Initial Interview in Family Casework." *Social Service Review* (March 1954), 28:65–73.

Blenkner, Margaret, J. McVicker Hunt, and Leonard S. Kogan. "A Study of Interrelated Factors in the Initial Interview with New Clients." *Social Casework* (January 1951), 32:23–30.

Bloom, Martin, "Empirically Based Clinical Research." In Aaron Rosenblatt and Diana Waldfogel, eds., *Handbook of Clinical Social Work*, pp. 560–582. San Francisco: Jossey-Bass, 1983.

Bloom, Martin. *The Paradox of Helping: Introduction to the Philosophy of Scientific Practice*. New York: Wiley, 1975.

Bloom, Martin, and Stephen R. Block. "Evaluating One's Own Effectiveness and Efficiency." *Social Work* (March 1977), 22:130–136.

Bloom, Martin, and Joel Fischer. *Evaluating Practice: Guidelines for the Accountable Professional*. Englewood Cliffs, N.J.: Prentice-Hall, 1982.

Blythe, Betty J., and Scott Briar. "Developing Empirically Based Models of Practice." *Social Work* (November–December 1985), 30:483–488.

Boatman, Louise. "Caseworkers' Judgments of Clients' Hope: Some Correlates Among Client-Situation Characteristics and Among Workers' Communication Patterns." D.S.W. dissertation, Columbia University, 1974.

Bodin, Arthur M. "The Interactional View: Family Therapy Approaches of the Mental Research Institute." In Alan S. Gurman and David P. Kniskern, eds., *Handbook of Family Therapy*, pp. 267–309. New York: Brunner/Mazel, 1981.

Bogdan, Robert C., and Sari Knopp Biklen. *Qualitative Research for Education: An Introduction to Theory and Methods.* Boston: Allyn and Bacon, 1982.

Bogdan, Robert C., and Steven J. Taylor. *Introduction to Qualitative Research Methods: The Search for Meanings.* 2d ed. New York: Wiley, 1984.

Bootzin, Richard R. and David Max. "Learning and Behavioral Theories." In Irving Kutash and Louis B. Schlesinger et al., *Handbook on Stress and Anxiety*, pp. 36–47. San Francisco: Jossey-Bass, 1980.

Borgatta, Edgar F., David Fanshel, and Henry J. Meyer. *Social Workers' Perceptions of Clients.* New York: Russell Sage Foundation, 1960.

Boszormenyi-Nagy, Ivan, and James L. Framo, eds. *Intensive Family Therapy.* New York: Harper and Row, 1965.

Bowen, Murray. "Theory in the Practice of Psychotherapy." In Phillip J. Guerin, Jr., ed., *Family Therapy*, pp. 42–90. New York: Gardner Press, 1976.

Boyd, Evelyn M., and Ann W. Fales. "Reflecting Learning: Key to Learning From Experience," *Journal of Humanistic Psychology* (Spring 1983), 23:99–117.

Brackett, Jeffrey R. "The Worker: Purpose and Preparation." In *Proceedings-National Conference of Charities and Correction, Portland, Maine, June 15–22, 1904*, pp. 1–12. Fred J. Heer, 1904.

Brekke, John S. "Author's Reply." *Social Service Review* (June 1987), 61:370–373.

Brekke, John S. "Scientific Imperatives in Social Work Research: Pluralism is Not Skepticism." *Social Service Review* (December 1986), 60:538–554.

Bremner, Robert H. *From the Depths: Discovery of Poverty in the United States.* New York: New York University Press, 1956; 4th repr. 1967.

Bremner, Robert H. "Scientific Philanthropy: 1873–93." *Social Service Review* (June 1956), 30:168–173.

Briar, Scott. "Family Services." In Henry S. Maas, ed., *Five Fields of Social Service: Reviews of Research*, pp. 9–50. New York: National Association of Social Workers, 1966.

Briar, Scott. "Family Services Casework." In Henry S. Maas, ed., *Research in the Social Services: A Five Year Review*, pp. 108–129. New York: National Association of Social Workers, 1971.

Briar, Scott. "Incorporating Research into Education for Clinical Practice in Social Work: Toward a Clinical Science in Social Work." In Allen Rubin and Aaron Rosenblatt, eds., *Sourcebook on Research Utilization*, pp. 132–140. New York: Council on Social Work Education, 1979.

Briar, Scott. "Major Trends and Issues in the Future of Doctoral Training in Social Work." Paper presented at the Conference on Issues in Social Work Doctoral Education, University of Michigan, Ann Arbor, October 26–27, 1976.

Briar, Scott. "Needed: A Simple Definition of Social Work." *Social Work* (January 1981), 26:83–84.

Briar, Scott. "Practice Trends." In *1983–1984 Supplement to the Encyclopedia of Social Work*, 17th ed., pp. 106–111. Silver Spring, Md.: National Association of Social Workers, 1983.

Briar, Scott. "Toward the Integration of Practice and Research." In David Fanshel, ed., *Future of Social Work Research*, pp. 31–37. Washington, D.C.: National Association of Social Workers, 1980.

Briar, Scott. "Use of Theory in Studying Effects of Client Social Class on Students' Judgments." *Social Work* (July 1961), 6:91–97.

Briar, Scott, and Jon R. Conte. "Families." In Henry S. Maas, ed., *Social Service Research: Reviews of Studies*, pp. 9–38. New York: National Association of Social Workers, 1978.

Briar, Scott, and Henry Miller. *Problems and Issues in Social Casework*. New York: Columbia University Press, 1971.

Briar, Scott, Harold Weissman, and Allen Rubin. *Research Utilization in Social Work Education*. New York: Council on Social Work Education, 1981.

Brieland, Donald. "Definition, Specialization, and Domain in Social Work." *Social Work* (January 1981), 26:79–83.

Broderick, Carlfred B., and Sandra S. Schrader, "The History of Professional Marriage and Family Therapy." In Alan S. Gurman and David F. Kniskern, eds., *Handbook of Family Therapy*, pp. 5–35. New York: Brunner/Mazel, 1981.

Brody, Baruch. *Readings in the Philosophy of Science*. Englewood Cliffs, N.J.: Prentice Hall, 1970.

Brown, Gordon E., ed. *The Multiproblem Dilemma*. Metuchen, N.J.: The Scarecrow Press, 1968.

Brown, Harold I. *Perception, Theory and Commitment: The New Philosophy of Science*. Chicago: Precedent, 1977; Chicago: University of Chicago Press, 1979.

Bruno, Frank J. *Trends in Social Work 1874–1956: A History Based on the Proceedings of the National Conference of Social Work*. New York: Columbia University Press, 1957.

Bruyn, Severyn T. "The New Empiricists: The Participant Observer and Phenomenologist." In William J. Filstead, ed., *Qualitative Methodology: First Hand Involvement with the Social World*, pp. 283–287. Chicago: Markham, 1970.

Bucklin, Dorothy R. "Studies of Breakdowns in Family Incomes: Broken Homes." *The Family* (March 1930), 11:3–13.

Bugental, James F. T., ed. *Challenges of Humanistic Psychology*. New York: McGraw-Hill, 1967.

Burgess, Ernest W. "The Contribution of Sociology to Family Social Work." *The Family* (October 1927), 8:191–193.

Butler, Harry, Inger Davis, and Ruth Kukkonen. "The Logic of Case Comparison." *Social Work Research and Abstracts* (Fall 1979), 15:3–11.

Butler, Harry, and Samuel A. Richmond. "Concrete Comparison, Generalization, and Validation in Social Research and Practice." *Philosophy in Context* (1977), 6:82–105.

Butler, Harry, and Samuel A. Richmond. "Education for the Integration of Research and Practice." Paper presented at the annual program meeting of the Council on Social Work Education, Phoenix, Ariz., February 18, 1977.

Butts, Robert E. "Philosophy of Science, 1934–1984." *Philosophy of Science* (March 1984), 51:1–2.

Cabot, Richard C. "Colleague of the Medical Social Workers." *The Family* (December 1920), 1:9–11.

Calvin, Richie. "The Measurement of Triangulation: The Development of a Questionnaire for Adolescent Respondents." D.S.W. dissertation, University of Alabama, 1986.

Campbell, Donald J., William H. Hunt, and Nan A. Lewis. "Context Effects with

Judgmental Language That is Absolute, Extensive, and Extra-Experimentally Anchored." *Journal of Experimental Psychology* (March 1958), 55:220–228.

Campbell, Donald J., William H. Hunt, and Nan A. Lewis. "The Effects of Assimilation and Contrast in Judgments of Clinical Materials." *American Journal of Psychology* (September 1957), 70:347–360.

Campbell, Donald T. "Degrees of Freedom and the Case Study." *Comparative Political Studies* (July 1975), 8:178–193.

Campbell, Donald T., and Julian C. Stanley. *Experimental and Quasi-experimental Designs and Research.* Chicago: Rand McNally, 1963.

Caplan, Gerald. *Support Systems and Community Mental Health.* New York: Behavioral Publications, 1974.

Caplan, Nathan. "Treatment Intervention and Reciprocal Interaction Effects." *Journal of Social Issues* (January 1968), 24:63–88.

Carnap, Rudolf. "Empiricism, Semantics, and Ontology." In Harold Morick, ed., *Challenges to Empiricism*, pp. 28–46. Indianapolis, Ind.: Hackett, 1980.

Carnap, Rudolf. *Logical Foundations of Probability.* Chicago: University of Chicago Press, 1950; repr. 1962.

Carnap, Rudolf. *Meaning and Necessity.* Chicago: University of Chicago Press, 1947; 2d ed., 1956.

Carnap, Rudolf. "The Methodological Character of Theoretical Concepts." In Herbert Feigl and Michael Scriven, eds., *Minnesota Studies in the Philosophy of Science*, vol. 1, pp. 38–76. Minneapolis: University of Minnesota Press, 1958.

Carnap, Rudolf. "The Old and New Logic." Isaac Levi, trans. In Alfred Jules Ayer, ed., *Logical Positivism*, pp. 133–146. New York: Free Press, 1959.

Carnap, Rudolf. "On the Character of Philosophic Problems." *Philosophy of Science* (January 1934), 1:5–19.

Carnap, Rudolf. "Testability and Meaning." *Philosophy of Science* (October 1936), 3:420–471; (January 1937), 4:1–40.

Caroff, Phyllis, ed. *Treatment Formulations and Clinical Social Work.* Silver Spring, Md.: National Association of Social Workers, 1982.

Chamberlain, Edna. "Testing with a Treatment Typology." *Australian Journal of Social Work* (December 1969), 22:3–8.

Chambers, Clark A. *Paul U. Kellog and the Survey.* Minneapolis, Minn.: University of Minnesota Press, 1971.

Chang, Hang-Ling. "Comparisons of Hypothesis Testing Procedures for the Two-Group Growth Curve Problems in Incomplete-Data and Small-Sample Situations." Ph.D. dissertation, University of Alabama, 1986.

Chavkin, Nancy Feyl. "The Practice-Research Relationship: An Organizational Link." *Social Service Review* (June 1986), 60:241–250.

Claghorn, Kate Holladay. "Some New Developments in Social Statistics." In *Proceedings-National Conference of Charities and Correction, St. Louis, Mo., May 19–26, 1910*, pp. 597–615. Fort Wayne: Archer, 1910.

Cloward, Richard A., and Irwin Epstein. "Private Social Welfare's Disengagement from the Poor: The Case of Family Adjustment Agencies." In Mayer N. Zald, ed., *Social Welfare Institutions: A Sociological Reader*, pp. 623–643. New York: Wiley, 1965.

Cohen, Nathan E. *Social Work in the American Tradition.* New York: Dryden Press, 1958.

Cohen, Pauline, and Merton Krause, eds., *Casework with Wives of Alcoholics.* New York: Family Service Association of America, 1971.

Cohen, Robert S. *Herbert Feigl: Inquiries and Provocations, Selected Writings, 1929–1974*. Dordrecht, Holland, and Boston: Reidel, 1981.

Colodny, Robert G., ed. *Beyond the Edge of Certainty: Essays in Contemporary Science and Philosophy*. Englewood Cliffs, N.J.: Prentice Hall, 1965.

Colodny, Robert G., ed. *Mind and Cosmos*. Pittsburgh: University of Pittsburgh Press, 1966.

Compton, Beulah R. *Introduction to Social Welfare and Social Work*. Homewood, Ill.: Dorsey Press, 1980.

Compton, Beulah R., and Burt Galaway. *Social Work Processes*. 3d ed. Homewood, Ill.: Dorsey Press, 1984.

Conceptial Frameworks, Social Work (September 1977), Special Issue, vol. 22; *Conceptual Frameworks II, Social Work* (January 1981), Special Issue, vol. 26.

Conference of Boards of Public Charities, New York, May 20–22, 1874, *Journal of Social Science Proceedings* (July 1874), 6:60–99.

Conte, Jon R., and Terese M. Halpin. "New Services for Families." In Aaron Rosenblatt and Diana Waldfogel, eds. *Handbook for Clinical Social Work*, pp. 1120–1142. San Francisco: Jossey-Bass, 1983.

Cook, Thomas D., and Donald T. Campbell. *Quasi-experimentations: Design and Analysis Issues for Field Settings*. Chicago: Rand McNally, 1979.

Cooper, Shirley. "Concepts and Practice Issues in Clinical Social Work." In Carel B. Germain, ed., *Advances in Clinical Social Work Practice*, pp. 252–263. Silver Spring, Md.: National Association of Social Workers, 1985.

Copi, Irving M. *An Introduction to Logic*. 7th ed. New York: Macmillan, 1986.

Costin, Lela B. "Edith Abbott and the Chicago Influence on Social Work Education." *Social Service Review* (March 1983), 57:94–111.

Costin, Lela B. *Two Sisters For Social Justice*. Urbana and Chicago: University of Illinois Press, 1983.

Couch, Elsbeth H. *Joint and Family Interviews in the Treatment of Marital Problems*. New York: Family Service Association of America, 1969.

Coyle, Grace L. *Social Science in Professional Education*. New York: Council on Social Work Education, 1958.

Cronbach, Lee J. "Beyond the Two Disciplines of Scientific Psychology." *American Psychologist* (February 1975), 30:116–127.

Darden, Lindley. "Theory Construction in Genetics." In Thomas Nickles, ed., *Scientific Discovery: Case Studies*, pp. 151–170. Dordrecht, Holland: Reidel, 1980.

Darden, Lindley, and Nancy Maull. "Interfield Theories." *Philosophy of Science* (March 1977), 44:43–64.

Darwin, Charles. *On the Origin of Species by Natural Selection*. London: Murray, 1859.

Davis, Robert T. "Pauperism in the City of New York." Report from the Department of Social Economy, Conference of Boards of Public Charities, New York, May 22, 1874. *Journal of Social Science* (July 1874), 6:74–83.

Deasy, Leila Calhoun, ed. *Doctoral Students Look at Social Work Education*. New York: Council on Social Work Education, 1971.

Deising, Paul. *Patterns of Discovery in the Social Sciences*. Chicago: Aldine-Atherton, 1971.

Dell, Paul F. "Beyond Homeostasis: Toward a Concept of Coherence." *Family Process* (March 1982), 21:21–41.

Dell, Paul F. "Researching Family Theories of Schizophrenia: An Exercise in Epistemological Confusion." *Family Process* (December 1980), 19:321–335.

Devine, Edward T. "The Outlook for the Future on Poverty and Disease." In *Proceedings-National Conference of Social Work, Atlantic City, N.J., June 1–8, 1919*, pp. 173–177. Chicago: Rogers and Hall, 1919.

Devine, Edward T. "The Principles of the Associated Charities." In *Proceedings-National Conference of Charities and Correction, Washington, D.C., May 9–15, 1901*, pp. 321–324. Boston: Ellis, 1901.

Devine, Edward T. "The Value and Dangers of Investigation." In *Proceedings-National Conference of Charities and Correction, Toronto, July 7–14, 1897*, pp. 193–199. Boston: Ellis, 1897.

Dilthey, Wilhelm. *Der Aufbau der Geschichtlichen Welt in den Geisteswissenschaften.* In *Gesammelte Schriften*, vol. 7. Leipzig and Berlin: Teubner, 1927.

Dinerman, Miriam, ed. *Social Work Futures.* New Brunswick, N.J.: Rutgers University Press, 1983.

Dinerman, Miriam, and Ludwig L. Geismar eds. *A Quarter-Century of Social Work Education.* New York: National Association of Social Workers, ABC-CLIO, and Council on Social Work Education, 1984.

Dooley, Patrick Kiaran. *Pragmatism as Humanism: The Philosophy of William James.* Chicago: Nelson-Hall, 1974.

Douglas, Bruce E., and Clark Moustakas. "Heuristic Inquiry: The Internal Search to Know." *Journal of Humanistic Psychology* (Summer 1985), 25:39–55.

Dubin, Robert. *Theory Building*, rev. ed. New York: Free Press, 1978.

Eagle, Morris N. *Recent Developments in Psychoanalysis.* New York: McGraw-Hill, 1984.

Ehrenkranz, Shirley. "A Study of the Techniques and Procedures Used in Joint Interviewing in the Treatment of Marital Problems." D.S.W. dissertation, Columbia University, 1967.

Ehrenkranz, Shirley. "A Study of Joint Interviewing in the Treatment of Martial Problems." *Social Casework* (October and November 1967), 48:498–502, 570–574.

Ellwood, Charles A. "Social Facts and Scientific Social Work." In *Proceedings-National Conference of Social Work, May 15–22, 1918*, pp. 686–692. Chicago: Rogers and Hall, 1919.

Engels, Frederick. *Socialism: Utopian and Scientific.* 1st ed. Peking: Foreign Language Press, 1975.

Erickson, Gerald, and Terrence P. Hogan. *Family Therapy.* Monterey, Cal.: Brooks/Cole, 1972; 2d ed., 1981.

Evans, Glendower. "Scientific Charity." In *Proceedings-National Conference of Charities and Correction, San Francisco, Cal., September 11–18, 1889*, pp. 24–35. Boston: Ellis, 1889.

Ewalt, Patricia L. "Social Work Process as an Organizing Concept." In Patricia L. Ewalt, ed., *Toward a Definition of Clinical Social Work*, pp. 87–91. Washington, D.C.: National Association of Social Workers, 1980.

Ewalt, Patricia L., ed. *Toward a Definition of Clinical Social Work.* Washington, D.C.: National Association of Social Workers, 1980.

Eysenck, Hans Jurgen. *The Effects of Psychotherapy.* New York: International Science Press, 1966.

Eysenck, Hans Jurgen. "The Effects of Psychotherapy: An Evaluation." *Journal of Consulting Psychology* (October 1952), 16:319–324.

Fairbairn, William Ronald Dodds. "Endopsychic Structure Considered in Terms of

Object-Relationships." In *Psychoanalytic Studies of the Personality*, pp. 82–136. London: Routledge and Kegan Paul, 1981.

Fanshel, David. "The Future of Social Work Research: Strategies for the Coming Years." In David Fanshel, ed., *Future of Social Work Research*, pp. 3–18. Washington, D.C.: National Association of Social Workers, 1980.

Fanshel, David. "A Study of Caseworkers' Perception of Their Clients." *Social Casework* (December 1958), 39:543–551.

Fanshel, David, ed. *Future of Social Work Research*. Washington, D.C.: National Association of Social Workers, 1980.

Fanshel, David, and Eugene B. Shinn. *Children in Foster Care: A Longitudinal Investigation*. New York: Columbia University Press, 1978.

Faver, Catherine A., Mary Frank Fox, Mary Ski Hunter, and Coleen Shannon. "Research and Practice: Orientations of Social Work Educators." *Social Work* (July–August 1986), 31:282–293.

Feigl, Herbert, and Albert E. Blumberg. "Logical Positivism: A New Movement in European Philosophy." *Journal of Philosophy* (May 1931), 28: 281–296.

Feigl, Herbert, and Grover Maxwell, eds. *Current Issues in the Philosophy of Science*. New York: Holt, Rinehart and Winston, 1961.

Feigl, Herbert, and Michael Scriven, eds. *Minnesota Studies in the Philosophy of Science*. Minneapolis: University of Minnesota Press, 1958.

Feldman, Ronald A. "Group Work Knowledge and Research: A Two Decade Comparison." In Sheldon D. Rose and Ronald A. Feldman, eds., *Research in Social Group Work*, pp. 7–14. New York: Haworth, Press, 1986.

Feldman, Ronald A. "Three Types of Group Integration: Their Relationships to Power, Leadership, and Conformity Behavior." Ph.D. dissertation, University of Michigan, 1966.

Feyerabend, Paul K. "Against Method: Outline of an Anarchistic Theory of Knowledge." In *Minnesota Studies in the Philosophy of Science*, vol. 4, pp. 17–130. Minneapolis: University of Minnesota Press, 1970.

Feyerabend, Paul K. "How To Be a Good Empiricist—A Plea for Tolerance in Matters Epistemological." In Harold Morick, ed., *Challenges to Empiricism*, pp. 164–193. Indianapolis: Hackett, 1980.

Feyerabend, Paul K. "Problems of Empiricism." In Robert G. Colodny, ed., *Beyond the Edge of Certainty: Essays in Contemporary Science and Philosophy*, University of Pittsburgh Series in the Philosophy of Science, vol. 2, pp. 114–260. Englewood Cliffs, N.J.: Prentice-Hall, 1965.

Feyerabend, Paul K. *Philosophical Papers*. Vol. 1: *Realism, Rationalism, and Scientific Method*; vol. 2: *Problems of Empiricism*. Cambridge: Cambridge University Press, 1981.

Filmer, Paul, et al. *New Directions in Sociological Theory*. Cambridge, Mass.: Massachusetts Institute of Technology Press, 1973.

Filstead, William J., ed. *Qualitative Methodology: First Hand Involvement with the Social World*. Chicago: Markham, 1970.

Fischer, Joel. *The Effectiveness of Social Casework*. Springfield, Ill.: Charles C. Thomas, 1976.

Fischer, Joel. "New and Emerging Methods of Direct Practice: The Revolution in Social Work." In Neil Gilbert and Harry Specht, eds., *Handbook of the Social Services*, pp. 525–547. Englewood Cliffs, N.J.: Prentice-Hall, 1981.

Fisher, Roland A. *Statistical Methods and Scientific Inference*. Edinburgh, Scotland: Oliver and Boyd, 1959; New York: Hafner, 1973.

Flowers, Linda Cox. "A Social Work Paradigm for Treatment of One Aggressive, Acting-Out Child." D.S.W. dissertation, University of Alabama, 1984.

Fornell, Claes, ed. *A Second Generation of Multivariate Analysis*. New York: Praeger Press, 1982.

Fortune, Anne E. "Communication Processes in Social Work Practice." *Social Service Review* (March 1981), 55:93–128.

Fortune, Anne E. *Task-Centered Practice with Families and Groups*. New York: Springer, 1985.

Fowler, Irving A. "Family Agency Characteristics and Client Continuance." *Social Casework* (May 1967), 48:271–277.

Framo, James L., ed. *Family Interaction: A Dialogue Between Family Researchers and Family Therapists*. New York: Springer, 1972.

Franklin, Donna L. "Differential Clinical Assessments: The Influence of Class and Race." *Social Service Review* (March 1985), 59:44–61.

Franklin, Donna L. "Mary Richmond and Jane Addams: From Moral Certainty to Rational Inquiry in Social Work Practice." *Social Service Review* (December 1986), 60:504–525.

Freud, Anna. *The Ego and Mechanisms of Defense*. London: Hogarth Press, 1937.

Frings, John. "Experimental Systems of Recording," *Social Casework* (February 1957), 38:55–63.

Frings, John, Ruth Kratofil, and Bernice Polemis. *An Assessment of Social Case Recording*. New York: Family Service Association of America, 1958.

Gadamer, Hans-Georg. *Philosophical Hermeneutics*. David E. Linge, ed. and trans. Berkeley: University of California Press, 1976.

Gadamer, Hans-Georg. *Truth and Method*. Garrett Barden and John Cumming, trans. New York: Seabury Press, 1975.

Gambrill, Eileen D. *Behavior Modification: Handbook of Assessment, Intervention, and Evaluation*. San Francisco: Jossey-Bass, 1977.

Garfield, Sol L. *Clinical Psychology*, 2d ed. N.Y.: Aldine, 1983.

Garfield, Sol L., and Allen E. Bugin, eds. *Handbook of Psychotherapy and Behavior Change: An Empirical Analysis*, 2d ed. New York: Wiley, 1978.

Garfinkel, Alan. *Forms of Explanation*. New Haven: Yale University Press, 1981.

Garvin, Charles. "Developmental Research for Task Centered Group Work with Chronic Mental Patients." In Sheldon D. Rose and Ronald A. Feldman, eds., *Research in Social Group Work*, pp. 31–42. New York: Haworth Press, 1986.

Garvin, Charles. "Task Centered Group Work." *Social Service Review* (December 1974), 48:494–507.

Geismar, Ludwig L. "Comments on the Obsolete Scientific Imperative in Social Work Research." *Social Service Review* (June 1982), 56:311–312.

Geismar, Ludwig L. *Family and Community Functioning: A Manual of Measurement for Social Work Practice and Policy*. Metuchen, N.J.: Scarecrow Press, 1971.

Geismar, Ludwig L. *Report on Checklist Survey*. St. Paul, Minn.: Greater St. Paul United Fund and Council, 1960.

Geismar, Ludwig L. "Strengthening the Scientific Base of Social Work." In Miriam Dinerman and Ludwig L. Geismar, eds., *A Quarter-Century of Social Work Education*, pp. 133–155. New York: National Association of Social Workers, ABC-CLIO, and Council on Social Work Education, 1984.

Geismar, Ludwig L. "Thirteen Evaluative Studies." In Edward J. Mullen, James R.

Dumpson et al., eds., *Evaluation of Social Intervention*, pp. 15–38. San Francisco: Jossey-Bass, 1972.

Geismar, Ludwig L., and Beverly Ayres. *Measuring Family Functioning*. St. Paul: Minnesota Family-Centered Project, Greater St. Paul Community Chest and Council, 1960.

Geismar, Ludwig L., and Beverly Ayres. *Patterns of Change in Problem Families*. St. Paul: Greater St. Paul United Fund and Council, 1959.

Gergen, Kenneth J. *Toward Transformation in Social Knowledge*. New York: Springer-Verlag, 1982.

Germain, Carel B. "Casework and Science: A Historical Encounter." In Robert W. Roberts and Robert H. Nee, eds., *Theories of Social Casework*, pp. 5–32. Chicago: University of Chicago Press, 1970.

Germain, Carel B. "General-Systems Theory and Ego Psychology: An Ecological Perspective." *Social Service Review* (December 1978), 52:535–550.

Germain, Carel B., ed. *Advances in Clinical Social Work Practice*. Silver Spring, Md.: National Association of Social Workers, 1985.

Germain, Carel B., ed. *Social Work Practice: People and Environments*. New York: Columbia University Press, 1979.

Germain, Carel B., and Alex Gitterman. *The Life Model of Social Work Practice*. New York: Columbia University Press, 1980.

Ghiselin, Brewster. *The Creative Process*. Berkeley and Los Angeles: University of California Press, 1952.

Giere, Ronald N. *Understanding Scientific Reasoning*, 2d ed. New York: Holt, Rinehart and Winston, 1984.

Giere, Ronald N., and Richard S. Westfall, eds. *Foundations of Scientific Method: The Nineteenth Century*. Bloomington: Indiana University Press, 1973.

Gilbert, Neil, and Harry Specht, eds. *Handbook of the Social Services*. Englewood Cliffs, N.J.: Prentice-Hall, 1981.

Gilman, Daniel Coit. *The Organization of Charities*. Baltimore: Johns Hopkins Press, 1894.

Gingerich, Wallace J. "Generalizing Single Case Evaluation from Classroom to Practice." *Journal of Education for Social Work* (Winter 1984), 20:74–82.

Giorgi, Amadeo. *Phenomenology and the Human Services*. Norman, Okla.: University of Oklahoma Printing Services, 1983.

Giorgi, Amadeo. *Phenomenology and Psychological Research*. Pittsburgh, Pa.: Duquesne University Press, 1985.

Giorgi, Amadeo. *Psychology as a Human Science*. New York: Harper and Row, 1970.

Giorgi, Amadeo, Richard Knowles, and David L. Smith, eds. *Duquesne Studies in Phenomenological Psychology*, vol. 3. Pittsburgh, Pa.: Duquesne University Press, 1979.

Glaser, Barney G. "The Constant Comparative Method of Qualitative Analysis." *Social Problems* (Spring 1965), 12:436–445. Also in George J. McCall and J. L. Simmons, eds., *Issues in Participant Observation*, pp. 216–228. Reading, Mass.: Addison-Wesley, 1969.

Glaser, Barney G. *Theoretical Sensitivity: Advances in the Methodology of Grounded Theory*. Mill Valley, Cal.: Sociology Press, 1978.

Glaser, Barney G., and Anselm Strauss. *The Discovery of Grounded Theory*. Chicago: Aldine Press, 1967.

Glisson, Charles A. "Are Social Work Doctoral Program Graduates Quantitative

Illiterates?" In Aaron Rosen and John J. Stretch, eds., *Doctoral Education in Social Work*, pp. 66–69. St. Louis, Mo.: Group for the Advancement of Doctoral Education in Social Work, 1982.

Goldstein, Eda G. "Issues in Developing Systematic Research and Theory." In Aaron Rosenblatt and Diana Waldfogel, eds., *Handbook of Clinical Social Work*, pp. 5–25. San Francisco: Jossey-Bass, 1983.

Goldstein, Howard. *Social Work Practice: A Unitary Approach*. Columbia, S.C.: University of South Carolina Press, 1973.

Goldstein, Howard. "Toward the Integration of Theory and Practice: A Humanistic Approach." *Social Work* (September–October 1986), 31:352–357.

Goldstein, Howard, Harvey H. Hilbert, and Judith Hilbert. *Creative Change: A Cognitive Humanistic Approach to Social Work Practice*. New York: Tavistock, 1984.

Goodman, Nathaniel. "The Use of the Movement Scale in Brief Recording." *Social Casework* (May 1958), 39:282–285.

Goodman, Nelson. *Fact, Fiction, and Forecast*. Indianapolis: Bobbs-Merrill, 1965.

Goodman, Nelson. *The Structure of Appearance*. Indianapolis: Bobbs-Merrill, 1966.

Gordon, H. Scott. "Alfred Marshall and the Development of Economics as a Science." In Ronald N. Giere and Richard S. Westfall, eds., *Foundations of Scientific Method: The Nineteenth Century*, pp. 234–258. Bloomington: Indiana University Press, 1973.

Gordon, William E. "Basic Constructs for an Integrative and Generative Conception of Social Work." In Gordon Hearn, ed., *The General Systems Approach: Contributions Toward a Holistic Conception of Social Work*, pp. 5–11. New York: Council on Social Work Education, 1969.

Gordon, William E. "Does Social Work Research Have a Future? A Book Review." *Social Work Research and Abstracts* (Summer 1980), 16:3–4.

Gordon, William E. "Scientific Training in the Social Work Doctorate." In *Social Work Education in the Post-master's Program: Approaches to Curriculum Content*, monograph no. 2, pp. 7–21. New York: Council on Social Work Education, 1954.

Gordon, William E. "Social Work Scientist." In Jeanette Regensburg, ed., *Some Educational Patterns in Doctoral Programs in Schools of Social Work*, pp. 78–86. New York: Council on Social Work Education, 1966.

Gottesfeld, Mary L., and Mary E. Pharis. *Profiles in Social Work*. New York: Human Sciences Press, 1977.

Gould, Stephen J. *The Mismeasure of Man*. New York: Norton, 1981.

Graham, Loren R. "Concerns about Science and Attempts to Regulate Inquiry." *Daedalus* (Spring 1978), 107:1–21.

Gray, William J., et al., eds. *General Systems Theory and Psychiatry*. Boston: Little, Brown, 1969.

Greenstone, David. "Dorothea Dix and Jane Addams: From Transcendentalism to Pragmatism in American Social Reform." *Social Service Review* (December 1979), 53:527–559.

Greif, Geoffrey L. "The Eco-Systems Perspective, 'Meet the Press.' " *Social Work* (May–June 1986), 31:225–226.

Grinnell, Richard M., Jr., ed. *Social Work Research and Evaluation*, 2d ed. Itasca, Ill.: Peacock, 1985.

Gruber, Howard E. "The Evolving Systems Approach to Creative Scientific Work: Charles Darwin's Early Thoughts." In Thomas Nickles, ed., *Scientific Discovery: Case Studies*, pp. 113–130. Dordrecht, Reidel, 1980.

Guerin, Phillip J., Jr., ed. *Family Therapy*. New York: Gardner Press, 1976.

Gurman, Alan S., and David P. Kniskern. "Family Therapy Outcome Research: Knowns and Unknowns." In Alan S. Gurman and David P. Kniskern, eds., *Handbook of Family Therapy*, pp. 742–775. New York: Brunner/Mazel, 1981.

Gurman, Alan S., and David P. Kniskern. "Research on Marital and Family Therapy: Progress, Perspective and Prospect." In Sol L. Garfield and Allen E. Bergin, eds., *Handbook of Psychotherapy and Behavior Change: An Empirical Analysis*, 2d ed., pp. 817–901. New York: Wiley, 1978.

Gurman, Alan S., and David P. Kniskern, eds. *Handbook of Family Therapy*. New York: Brunner/Mazel, 1981.

Gyarfas, Mary Gorman "The Scientific Imperative Again." *Social Service Review* (March 1983), 57:149–150.

Habermas, Jurgen. "The Hermeneutic Claim to Universality." In Joseph Bleicher, ed., *Contemporary Hermeneutics: Hermeneutics as Method, Philosophy and Critique*. London: Routledge and Kegan Paul, 1980.

Habermas, Jurgen. *Knowledge and Human Interests*. Jeremy J. Shapiro, trans. Boston: Beacon Press, 1971.

Habermas, Jurgen. *Theory and Practice*. John Viertel, trans. Boston: Beacon Press, 1973.

Haley, Jay, ed. *Changing Families: A Family Therapy Reader*. New York: Grune and Stratton, 1971.

Haman, Catherine Small, and David Haman. "Studies of Breakdowns in Family Income: Pregnancy in Dependent Families—Detroit Department of Public Welfare." *The Family* (June 1931), 13:127–130.

Hamilton, Gordon. "The Bad Penny." *The Family* (1922), 3:95.

Hamilton, Gordon. "Basic Concepts Upon Which Case-work Practice is Formulated." In *Proceedings of the National Conference of Social Work, Indianapolis, Ind., May 23–29, 1937*, pp. 138–149. Chicago: University of Chicago Press, 1937.

Hamilton, Gordon. *Psychotherapy in Child Guidance*. New York: Columbia University Press, 1947.

Hamilton, Gordon. *Theory and Practice of Social Casework*. New York: Columbia University Press, 1940, 2d ed., 1951.

Hamovitch, Maurice B. "The Ph.D. versus the D.S.W. in Social Work." Paper presented at the annual conference of the Group for the Advancement of Doctoral Education. Philadelphia, Pa., October 11, 1982.

Hanson, Norwood Russell. "An Anatomy of Discovery." *Journal of Philosophy* (1967), 64:321–352.

Hanson, Norwood Russell. "Is There a Logic of Scientific Discovery?" In Herbert Feigl and Grover Maxwell, eds., *Current Issues in the Philosophy of Science*, pp. 20–35. New York: Holt, Rinehart and Winston, 1961.

Hanson, Norwood Russell. *Observational Explanation*. New York: Harper & Row, 1971.

Hanson, Norwood Russell. *Patterns of Discovery*. Cambridge: Cambridge University Press, 1958.

Hardy, Sophie. "What Measures Have We for Growth in Personality." *The Family* (December 1926), 7:254–258.

Harré, Rom. *An Introduction to Logic of the Sciences*. 2d ed. London: Macmillan Co., 1983.

Harré, Rom. *The Philosophies of Science*. 2d ed. New York: Oxford University Press, 1984.

Harré, Rom. "The Positivist-Empiricist Approach and Its Alternative." In Peter Reason and John Rowan, eds, *Human Inquiry*, pp. 3–17. New York: Wiley, 1981.

Harrison, Shelby M. "Community Action Through Surveys." In *Proceedings-National Conference of Charities and Correction, Indianapolis, May 10–17, 1916*, pp. 52–62. Chicago: Hildmann, 1916.

Harrison, W. David. "Reflective Practice in Social Care." *Social Service Review* (September 1987), 61:393–404.

Hartman Ann. "To Think About the Unthinkable." *Social Casework* (October 1970), 51:467–474.

Hartman, Ann, and Joan Laird. *Family-Centered Social Work Practice*. New York: Free Press, 1982.

Hearn, Gordon, ed. *The General Systems Approach: Contributions Toward a Holistic Conception of Social Work*. New York: Council on Social Work Education, 1969.

Hearn, Gordon. "General Systems Theory and Social Work." In Francis J. Turner, ed., *Social Work Treatment: Interlocking Theoretical Approaches*, 2d ed., pp. 333–359. New York: Free Press, 1979.

Heidegger, Martin. *Being and Time*. John Macquarrie and Edward Robinson, trans. New York: Harper and Row, 1962.

Heineman, Martha Brunswick. "The Obsolete Scientific Imperative in Social Work Research." *Social Service Review* (September 1981), 55:371–397.

Hellenbrand, Shirley. "Main Currents in Social Casework, 1918–1936." D.S.W. dissertation, Columbia University, 1965.

Hempel, Carl G. *Aspects of Scientific Explanation and Other Essays in the Philosophy of Science*. New York: Free Press, 1965.

Hempel, Carl G. *Philosophy of Natural Science*. Englewood Cliffs, N.J.: Prentice-Hall, 1966.

Heron, John. "Dimensions of Facilitator Style." Human Potential Research Project, University of Surrey, England, 1977.

Hersen, Michel, and David H. Barlow. *Single-Case Experimental Designs: Strategies for Studying Behavior Change*. New York: Pergamon Press, 1976.

Hesse, Mary. *Revolutions and Reconstruction in the Philosophy of Science*. Bloomington: Indiana University Press, 1980.

Hocutt, Max O. "Comments on Pragmatism." Unpublished memorandum, University of Alabama, May 15, 1987.

Hocutt, Max O. *The Elements of Logical Analysis and Inference*. Cambridge, Mass.: Winthrop, 1979.

Hodgson, James W., and Robert A. Lewis. "Pilgrim's Progress III: A Trend Analysis of Family Theory and Methodology." *Family Process* (June 1979), 18:163–173.

Hoffman, Lynn. *Foundations of Family Therapy*. New York: Basic Books, 1981.

Hofstadter, Richard. *Social Darwinism in American Thought*. Boston: Beacon Press, 1944.

Hollis, Florence. *Casework: A Psychosocial Therapy*. New York: Random House, 1964; 2d ed., 1972; with Mary E. Woods, 3rd ed., 1981.

Hollis, Florence. "Casework as a Supplemental Service." *The Family* (October 1931), 12:186–191.

Hollis, Florence. "Continuance and Discontinuance in Marital Counseling and Some Observations on Joint Interviews." *Social Casework* (March 1968), 59:167–174.

Hollis, Florence. "Evaluation: Clinical Results and Research Methodology." *Clinical Social Work* (1976), 4(3):205–222.

Hollis, Florence. "The Function of a Family Society." *The Family* (December 1932), 13:280–283.

Hollis, Florence. "How It Really Was." *Smith College Journal* (Fall 1983), 10:3–9.

Hollis, Florence. "Personality Diagnosis in Casework." In Howard J. Parad, ed., *Ego Psychology and Dynamic Casework*, pp. 83–96. New York: Family Service Association of America, 1958.

Hollis, Florence. *Social Casework in Practice*. New York: Family Service Association of America, 1939.

Hollis, Florence. "The Techniques of Casework." *Social Casework* (June 1949), 30:235–244. In Cora Kasius, ed., *Principles and Techniques in Social Casework*, pp. 412–426. New York: Family Service Association of America, 1950.

Hollis, Florence. *A Typology of Casework Treatment*. New York: Family Service Association of America, 1968.

Howe, Michael W. "Casework Self-Evaluation: A Single-Subject Approach." *Social Service Review* (March 1974), 48:10–15.

Howard, Roy J. *Three Faces of Hermeneutics*. Berkeley: University of California Press, 1982.

Hoy, David Couzens. *The Critical Circle*. Berkeley: University of California Press, 1978.

Hudson, Walter W. *The Clinical Measurement Package: A Field Manual*. Homewood, Ill.: Dorsey, Press, 1982.

Hudson, Walter W. "Elementary Techniques for Assessing Single-Client/Single-Worker Interventions." *Social Service Review* (June 1977), 51:311–326.

Hudson, Walter W., "Indexes and Scales." In Richard M. Grinnell, Jr., ed., *Social Work Research and Evaluation*, 2d ed., pp. 185–205. Itasca, Ill.: Peacock, 1985.

Hudson, Walter W. "Research Training in Professional Social Work Education." *Social Service Review* (March 1978), 52:116–121.

Hudson, Walter W. "Scientific Imperatives in Social Work Research and Practice." *Social Service Review* (June 1982), 56:246–258.

Hume, David. *An Inquiry Concerning Human Understanding and Concerning the Principles of Morals*, 2d ed. L. A. Selby-Bigge, ed. Oxford: Clarendon Press, 1902.

Hume, David. *A Treatise of Human Nature*. L. A. Selby-Bigge, ed. Oxford: Clarendon Press, 1888.

Hunt, J. McVicker. "Measuring Movement in Casework." *Social Casework* (November 1948), 29:343–351.

Hunter, J. McVicker. "On the Judgment of Social Workers as a Source of Information in Social Work Research." In Ann W. Shyne, ed., *Use of Judgments as Data in Social Work Research*, pp. 38–54. New York: National Association of Social Workers, 1959.

Hunt, J. McVicker, Margaret Blenkner, and Leonard S. Kogan. *Testing Results in Social Casework: A Field Test of the Movement Scale*. New York: Family Service Association of America, 1950.

Hunt, J. McVicker, and Leonard S. Kogan. *Measuring Results in Social Casework: A Manual on Judging Movement*, rev. ed. New York: Family Service Association of America, 1952.

Hunt, William A. and John Volkman. "Anchoring Effects in Judgment." *American Journal of Psychology* (July 1941), 54:395–403.

Hurtin, Ralph G. "Relief in Private Family Agencies in the Post Depression Period." *The Family* (June 1937), 18:121–124.

Husserl, Edmund. *Crisis of European Sciences and Transcendental Phenomenology: An Introduction to Phenomenological Philosophy.* David Carr, trans. Evanston, Ill.: Northwestern University Press, 1970.

Husserl, Edmund. *Ideas: General Introduction to Pure Phenomenology.* W. R. Boyce Gibson, trans. New York: Macmillan; London: Allen and Unwin, 1931.

Iodice, Jody D., and John S. Wodarski. "Aftercare Treatment for Schizophrenics Living at Home." *Social Work* (March–April 1987), 32:122–128.

Jacobson, Edmund. *Anxiety and Tension Control: A Physiologic Approach.* Philadelphia: Lippincott, 1964.

Jacobson, Edmund. *Teaching and Learning New Methods for Old Arts.* Chicago: National Foundation for Progressive Relaxation, 1973.

Jacobson, Edmund. *You Must Relax: A Practical Method of Reducing the Strains of Modern Living,* 4th ed., rev. New York: McGraw-Hill, 1957.

James, William. *Essays in Radical Empiricism.* Ralph Barton Perry, ed. London: Longmans, Green, 1912.

James, William. *The Meaning of Truth.* London: Longmans, Green, 1909.

James, William. *Pragmatism.* London: Longmans, Green, 1907.

James, William. *The Will to Believe.* London: Longmans, Green, 1897.

Janchill, Sister Mary Paul. "Systems Concepts in Casework Theory and Practice." *Social Casework* (February 1969), 15:74–82.

Janzen, Curtis, and Oliver Harris. *Family Treatment in Social Work Practice.* Itasca, Ill.: Peacock, 1980.

Jarrett, Mary E. "The Psychiatric Thread Running Through all Social Casework." In *Proceedings-National Conference of Social Work, Atlantic City, N.J., June 1–8, 1919,* pp. 587–593. Chicago: Rogers and Hall, 1919.

Jayaratne, Srinika. "Analytic Procedures for Single-Subject Designs." *Social Work Research and Abstracts* (Fall 1978), 14:30–40.

Jayaratne, Srinika. "Single-Subject and Group Designs in Treatment Evaluation." *Social Work Research and Abstracts* (Fall 1977), 13:35–42.

Jayaratne, Srinika, and William Daniels. "Measurement Cross-validation Using Replication Procedures Within Single-Case Designs." *Social Work Research and Abstracts* (Fall 1981), 17:4–10.

Jayaratne, Srinika, and Rona L. Levy. *Empirical Clinical Practice.* New York: Columbia University Press, 1979.

Jenkins, Shirley, and Elaine Norman. *Filial Deprivation and Foster Care.* New York: Columbia University Press, 1972.

Johnson, Harriette C. "Emerging Concerns in Family Therapy." *Social Work* (July–August 1986), 31:225–236.

Kahn, Alfred J. "Research Planning: Facilitating Social Work Research." *Social Service Review* (September 1956), 30:331–345.

Kahn, Alfred J., ed. *Issues in American Social Work.* New York: Columbia University Press, 1959.

Kahn, Alfred J., ed. *Shaping the New Social Work.* New York: Columbia University Press, 1973.

Kallen, Horace M. *The Philosophy of William James.* New York: Random House, 1953.

Kammerman, Sheila B., Ralph Dolgoff, George Getzel, and Judith Nelsen. "Knowledge for Practice: Social Science in Social Work." In Alfred J. Kahn, ed., *Shaping the New Social Work*, pp. 97–146. New York: Columbia University Press, 1973.

Kasius, Cora, ed. *Principles and Techniques in Social Casework*. New York: Family Service Association of America, 1950.

Keeney, Bradford P. "Ecosystemic Epistemology: An Alternative Paradigm for Diagnosis." *Family Process* (June 1979), 18:117–129.

Kellog, Angie L. "What Educational Psychology Can Contribute to Casework with the Normal Family." In *Proceedings-National Conference of Social Work, Kansas City, Mo., May 15–22, 1918*, pp. 329–334. Chicago: Rogers and Hall, 1919.

Kellog, Charles D. "Report of the Committee on History of Charity Organizations." In *Proceedings-Conference of Charities and Correction, Chicago, June 8–11, 1893*, pp. 52–93. Boston: Ellis, 1893.

Kellog, Charles D. "Statistics: Their Value in Charity Organization Work." In *Proceedings-National Conference of Charities and Correction, Baltimore, Md., May 14–21, 1890*, pp. 31–35. Boston: Ellis, 1890.

Kellog, D. O. "The Principle and Advantage of Association in Charities." *Journal of Social Science* (December 1880), 12:84–90.

Kerlinger, Frederick N. *Foundations of Behavioral Research*. New York: Holt, Rinehart and Winston, 1973.

Kernberg, Otto. *Borderline Conditions and Pathological Narcissism*. New York: Jason Aronson, 1975.

Kirk, Stuart A., and Aaron Rosenblatt. "New Applications of Research in Clinical Practice." In Aaron Rosenblatt and Diana Waldfogel, eds., *Handbook of Clinical Social Work*, pp. 549–559. San Francisco: Jossey-Bass, 1983.

Kirkpatrick, Clifton. "Community of Interest and the Measurements of Marriage Adjustment." *The Family* (June 1937), 18:133–137.

Kleinbaum, David G. "A Generalization of the Growth Curve Model Which Allows Missing Data." *Journal of Multivariate Analysis* (March 1973), 3: 117–124.

Koch, Sigmund, ed. *Psychology: A Study of Science*. New York: McGraw-Hill, 1959.

Kogan, Leonard S., and Benjamin H. Brown. "Two Year Study of Casework Uses." *Social Casework* (June 1954), 35:252–257.

Kogan, Leonard S., J. McVicker Hunt, and Phyllis F. Bartelme. *A Follow-up Study of the Results of Social Casework*. New York: Family Service Association of America, 1953.

Kohut, Heinz. *The Restoration of the Self*. New York: International Universities Press, 1977.

Kratochwill, Thomas R., ed. *Single Subject Research: Strategies for Evaluating Change*. New York: Academic Press, 1978.

Krause, Merton S. "Predicting Client Discontinuance at Intake." *Social Casework* (June 1962), 43:308–312.

Krill, Donald F. "Existential Social Work." In Francis J. Turner, ed., *Social Work Treatment: Interlocking Theoretical Approaches*, 1st ed., pp. 276–313; 2d ed., pp. 147–176. New York: Free Press, 1974, 1979.

Kuhn, Thomas S. *The Essential Tension: Selected Studies in Scientific Tradition and Change*. Chicago: University of Chicago Press, 1977.

Kuhn, Thomas S. *The Structure of Scientific Revolutions*, 2d ed. Chicago: University of Chicago Press, 1970.

Kutash, Irving, and Louis B. Schlesinger et al. *Handbook on Stress and Anxiety.* San Francisco: Jossey-Bass, 1980.

Laird, Nan M., and James H. Ware. "Random Effects Models for Longitudinal Data." *Biometrics* (December 1982), 38:963–974.

Lakatos, Imre. *Philosophical Papers.* Vol. 1: *The Methodology of Scientific Research Programmes;* vol. 2: *Mathematics, Science and Epistemology.* John Worral and Gregory Currie, eds. Cambridge: Cambridge University Press, 1977, 1978.

Lakatos, Imre, and A. Musgrove. *Criticism and the Growth of Knowledge.* Cambridge: Cambridge University Press, 1970.

Lambert, Karel, and Gordon G. Brittange. *An Introduction to the Philosophy of Science.* Englewood Cliffs, N.J.: Prentice-Hall, 1970.

Lane, Gerry, and Tom Russell. "Systemic Therapy: An Alternative to Social Control for Violent Couples." Paper presented in part at the Ninth Annual Family Therapy Network Symposium, Washington, D.C., March 1986.

Laudan, Larry. *Progress and Its Problems.* Berkeley, Cal.: University of California Press, 1977.

Laudan, Larry. *Science and Hypothesis.* Dordrecht, Holland: Reidel, 1981.

Laudan, Larry. *Science and Values.* Berkeley, Cal.: University of California Press, 1984.

Leader, Arthur L. "The Role of Intervention in Family Group Treatment." *Social Casework* (June 1964), 45:327–332.

Lee, Porter R. "The Fabric of the Family." In *Proceedings-National Conference of Social Work, Atlantic City, N.J., June 1–8, 1919,* pp. 319–326. Chicago: Rogers and Hall, 1919.

Levine, Baruch. "Factors Related to Interpersonal Balance in Social Work Treatment Groups." Ph.D. dissertation, University of Chicago, 1968.

Levinger, George. "Continuance in Casework and Other Helping Relationships: A Review of Current Research." *Social Work* (July 1960), 5:40–51.

Levitt, Eugene E. "The Results of Psychotherapy with Children: An Evaluation." *Journal of Consulting Psychology* (June 1957), 21:189–196.

Levitt, John L., and William J. Reid. "Rapid-Assessment Instruments for Practice." *Social Work Research and Abstracts* (Spring 1981), 17:13–19.

Levy, Rona L. "Overview of Single-Case Experiments." In Aaron Rosenblatt and Diana Waldfogel, eds., *Handbook of Clinical Social Work,* pp. 583–602. San Francisco: Jossey-Bass, 1983.

Lewin, Kurt. "Group Decision and Social Change." In Theodore M. Newcomb and Eugene L. Hartley, eds., *Readings in Social Psychology,* pp. 459–473. New York: Henry Holt, 1947.

Lewis, Harold. *The Intellectual Base of Social Work Practice.* New York: Haworth Press, 1982.

Lieberman, Florence. *Social Workers as Psychotherapists.* New York: Gardner Press, 1982.

Maas, Henry S., ed. *Five Fields of Social Service: Reviews of Research.* New York: National Association of Social Workers, 1966.

Maas, Henry S. *People and Contexts.* Englewood Cliffs, N.J.: Prentice-Hall, 1984.

Maas, Henry S., ed. *Research for the Social Services: A Five Year Review.* New York: National Association of Social Workers, 1971.

Maas, Henry S. "Research in Social Work." In *Social Work Encyclopedia,* 17th ed., pp. 1183–1194. Washington, D.C.: National Association of Social Workers, 1977.

Maas, Henry S., ed. *Social Service Research: Reviews of Studies*. Washington, D.C.: National Association of Social Workers, 1978.

McBroom, Elizabeth. "Socialization and Social Casework." In Robert W. Roberts and Robert H. Nee, eds., *Theories of Social Casework*, pp. 315–351. Chicago: University of Chicago Press, 1970.

McCall, George J. and J. L. Simmons, eds. *Issues in Participant Observation*. Reading, Mass.: Addison-Wesley, 1969.

M'Culloch, Oscar C. "The Organization of Charities." Report of the Standing Committee. In *Proceedings-National Conference of Charities and Correction, San Francisco, September 11–18, 1889*, pp. 10–35. Boston: Ellis, 1889.

MacDonald, Mary E. "Social Work Research: A Perspective." In Norman A. Polansky, ed., *Social Work Research*, pp. 1–23. Chicago: University of Chicago Press, 1960.

M'Dowell, Mary E. "The Settlement and Organized Charity." In *Proceedings-National Conference of Charities and Correction, Grand Rapids, Michigan, June 4–10, 1896*, pp. 123–127. Boston: Ellis, 1896.

McMullin, Ernan. "Panel Discussion of Explanation of Historical Discoveries." In Thomas Nickles, ed., *Scientific Discovery: Case Studies*, pp. 28–33. Dordrecht, Holland: Reidel, 1980.

Mahler, Margaret S., Fred Pine, and Anni Bergman. *The Psychological Birth of the Human Infant*. New York: Basic Books, 1975.

Malisoff, William Marias. *Meet the Sciences*. Baltimore: Williams and Wilkins, 1934.

Malisoff, William Marias. "What is Science?" *Philosophy of Science* (January 1934), 1:1.

Malthus, Thomas Robert. *An Essay on the Principle of Population*, vol. 2. First American ed., from the 3d. London ed. Washington City: Roger Chew Weightman, 1809.

Maluccio, Anthony. "Promoting Competence Through Life Experiences." In Carel B. Germain, ed., *Social Work Practice: People and Environments*, pp. 282–302. New York: Columbia University Press, 1979.

Martin, Patricia Yancey, and Barry K. Turner. "Grounded Theory and Organizational Research." *Journal of Applied Behavioral Science* (November 1986), 22:141–157.

Maslow, Abraham. *The Psychology of Science: A Reconnaissance*. South Bend, Ind.: Gateway Editions, 1966.

Masterson, James F. *Psychotherapy of the Borderline Adult*. New York: Brunner/Mazel, 1976.

Meier, Elizabeth G. *A History of the New York School of Social Work*. New York: Columbia University Press, 1954.

Method and Process in Social Casework. Report of a Staff Committee, Community Service Society of New York. New York: Family Service Association of America, 1958.

Meyer, Carol H. "Direct Services in New and Old Contexts." In Alfred J. Kahn, ed., *Shaping the New Social Work*, pp. 26–54. New York: Columbia University Press, 1973.

Meyer, Carol H. "Purposes and Boundaries: Casework Fifty Years Later." *Social Casework* (May 1973), 54:268–275.

Meyer, Carol H. "The Search for Coherence." In Carol H. Meyer, ed., *Clinical Social*

Work in the Eco-Systems Perspective, pp. 5–34. New York: Columbia University Press, 1983.

Meyer, Carol H. "Selecting Appropriate Practice Models." In Aaron Rosenblatt and Diana Waldfogel, eds., *Handbook of Clinical Social Work*, pp. 731–749. San Francisco: Jossey-Bass, 1983.

Meyer, Carol H. *Social Work Practice: A Response to the Urban Crisis.* New York: Free Press, 1970.

Meyer, Carol H. "Trends and Issues in Direct Social Work Practice." In Miriam Dinerman, ed. *Social Work Futures*, pp. 225–236. New Brunswick, N.J.: Rutgers University Press, 1983.

Meyer, Carol H., ed. *Clinical Social Work in the Eco-Systems Perspective.* New York: Columbia University Press, 1983.

Meyer, Henry J. "Professionalization and Social Work." In Alfred J. Kahn, ed., *Issues in American Social Work*, pp. 319–340. New York: Columbia University Press, 1959.

Meyer, Henry J. "Social Worker-Social Scientist." In Jeanette Regensberg, ed., *Some Educational Patterns in Doctoral Programs in Schools of Social Work*, pp. 87–106. New York: Council on Social Work Education, 1966.

Meyer, Henry J., Edgar F. Borgatta, and Wyatt C. Jones. *Girls of Vocational High: An Experiment in Social Work Intervention.* New York: Russell Sage Foundation, 1965.

Miles, Mathew B., and A. Michael Huberman. *Qualitative Data Analysis.* Beverly Hills, Cal.: Sage, 1984.

Miller, Henry, and James Bieri. "An Informational Analysis of Clinical Judgment." *Journal of Abnormal and Social Psychology* (October 1963), 67:317–325.

Miller, James G. "Living Systems: Basic Concepts" in William Gray et al., eds., *General Systems Theory and Psychiatry*, pp. 51–133. Boston: Little, Brown, 1969.

Miller, Roger. "Observations on a Clinical Doctorate." In Aaron Rosen and John J. Stretch, eds., *Doctoral Education in Social Work*, pp. 78–81. St. Louis: Group for the Advancement of Doctoral Education in Social Work, 1982.

Minuchin, Salvador. *Families and Family Therapy.* Cambridge, Mass.: Harvard University Press, 1974.

Mitroff, Ian I., and Richard O. Mason. *Creating a Dialectical Social Science: Concepts, Methods and Models.* Dordrecht, Holland: Reidel, 1981.

Morick, Harold, ed. *Challenges to Empiricism.* Indianapolis: Hackett, 1980.

Mostwin, Danuta. *Social Dimensions of Family Treatment.* Washington, D.C.: National Association of Social Workers, 1980.

Moustakas, Clark. "Heuristic Research." In James F. T. Bugental, ed., *Challenges of Humanistic Psychology*, pp. 101–107. New York: McGraw-Hill, 1967.

Mullen, Edward J. "Casework Communication." *Social Casework* (November 1968), 49:546–551.

Mullen, Edward J. "Casework Treatment Procedures as a Function of Client Diagnostic Variables." D.S.W. dissertation, Columbia University, 1968.

Mullen, Edward J. "Differences in Worker Style in Casework." *Social Casework* (June 1969), 50:345–353.

Mullen, Edward J. "Methodological Dilemmas in Social Work Research." *Social Work Research and Abstracts* (Winter 1985), 21:12–20.

Mullen, Edward J. "Personal Practice Models." In Aaron Rosenblatt and Diana Waldfogel, eds., *Handbook of Clinical Social Work*, pp. 623–649. San Francisco: Jossey-Bass, 1983.

Mullen, Edward J. "The Relation Between Diagnosis and Treatment in Casework." *Social Casework* (April 1969), 50:210–226.

Mullen, Edward J., Robert M. Chazin, and David M. Feldstein. *Preventing Chronic Dependency.* New York: Community Service Society of New York, 1970.

Mullen, Edward J., James R. Dumpson et al., eds. *Evaluation of Social Intervention.* San Francisco: Jossey-Bass, 1972.

Myrick, Helen L. "Psychological Processes in Interviewing." *The Family* (March 1926), 7:25–29.

Nagel, Ernest. *The Structure of Science: Problems in the Logic of Scientific Explanation.* New York: Harcourt, Brace and World, 1961.

NASW Policy Statement I: Code of Ethics, Silver Spring, Md.: National Association of Social Workers, July 1, 1980.

Nelsen, Judith C. *Family Treatment: An Integrative Approach.* Englewood Cliffs, N.J.: Prentice-Hall, 1983.

Nelsen, Judith C. "Issues in Single-Subject Research for Nonbehaviorists." *Social Work Research and Abstracts* (Summer 1981), 17:31–37.

Neurath, Otto, Rudolf Carnap, and Charles Morris, eds. *International Encyclopedia of Unified Science.* Chicago: University of Chicago Press, 1938.

Newcomb, Theodore M., and Eugene L. Hartley, eds. *Readings in Social Psychology.* New York: Henry Holt, 1947.

Nickles, Thomas, ed. *Scientific Discovery: Case Studies.* Dordrecht, Holland: Reidel, 1980.

Northen, Helen. *Clinical Social Work.* New York: Columbia University Press, 1982.

Northen, Helen. "Evaluating Movement of Individuals in Social Group Work." In *Group Work Papers in 1957,* pp. 28–37. New York: National Association of Social Workers, 1958.

Nowicki, Stephen, Jr., and Bonnie R. Strickland. "A Locus of Control Scale for Children." *Journal of Consulting and Clinical Psychology* (1973), 40(1):148–154.

O'Connor, Richard. "Clients' Reactions to Brief Treatment." Ph.D. dissertation, University of Chicago, 1983.

O'Connor, Richard, and William J. Reid. "Dissatisfaction with Brief Treatment." *Social Service Review* (December 1986), 60:526–537.

Orcutt, Ben A. "Casework Intervention and the Problems of the Poor." *Social Casework* (February 1973), 54:85–95.

Orcutt, Ben A. "Poverty on the American Scene." In Ben A. Orcutt, ed., *Poverty and Social Casework Services.* Metuchen, N.J.: Scarecrow Press, 1974.

Orcutt, Ben A. "Process Analysis of the First Phase of Treatment." In Pauline Cohen and Merton Krause, eds., *Casework with Wives of Alcoholics,* pp. 147–164. New York: Family Service Association of America, 1971.

Orcutt, Ben A., ed. *Poverty and Social Casework Services.* Metuchen, N.J.: Scarecrow Press, 1974.

Orcutt, Ben A. "A Study of Anchoring Effects in Clinical Judgment." *Social Service Review* (December 1964), 38:408–417.

Orcutt, Ben A., and Paul R. Mills, Jr. "The Doctoral Practice Laboratory," *Social Service Review* (December 1979), 53:633–643.

Orcutt, Ben A., and Paul R. Mills, Jr. "Education for Doctoral Social Work Clinical Practice in the 1980's." *Social Thought* (Fall 1982), 8:38–49. Also in Aaron Rosen and John J. Stretch, eds., *Doctoral Education in Social Work,* pp. 109–117. St. Louis: Group for the Advancement of Doctoral Education in Social Work, 1982.

Orcutt, Ben A., and Paul R. Mills, Jr. "A Model of Doctoral Education: Practice Dimensions." In Aaron Rosen and John J. Stretch, eds., *Doctoral Education in Social Work*, pp. 100–108. St. Louis: Group for the Advancement of Doctoral Education in Social Work, 1982.

Otis, Lillian L. "Unemployment and Its Treatment in Non-resident Families: A Study of Fifty Non-resident White Families Known to the Cleveland Associated Charities." *The Family* (June 1933), 14:136–143.

Overton, Alice, and Katherine H. Tinker. *Casework Notebook*. St. Paul, Minn.: Greater St. Paul United Fund and Council, 1959.

Palmer, Richard E. *Hermeneutics: Interpretation Theory in Schleiermacher, Dilthey, Heidegger, and Gadamer*. Evanston, Ill.: Northwestern University Press, 1969.

Papp, Peggy. *The Process of Change*. New York: Guilford Press, 1983.

Parad, Howard J., ed. *Ego Psychology and Dynamic Casework*. New York: Family Service Association of America, 1958.

Parad, Howard J., and Roger Miller, eds. *Ego-Oriented Casework: Problems and Perspectives*. New York: Family Service Association of America, 1963.

Parsons, Bruce V., and James F. Alexander. "Short-term Family Intervention: A Therapy Outcome Study," *Journal of Consulting and Clinical Psychology* (1973), 41:195–201.

Patchner, Michael A. "A Decade of Social Work Doctoral Graduates: Their Characteristics and Educational Programs." *Journal of Education for Social Work* (Spring 1982), 18:35–41.

Patti, Rino J. "The Prospects for Social R & D: An Essay Review." *Social Work Research and Abstracts* (Summer 1981), 17:38–44.

Pearl, Arthur, and Frank Riesmann. *New Careers for the Poor*. New York: Free Press, 1965.

Pearson, Karl. *The Grammar of Science*. New York: Meridian Books, 1957.

Pearson, Karl. *The Life, Letters and Labors of Francis Galton*. Cambridge: Cambridge University Press, 1914–1930.

Pearson, Karl, ed. *Tables for Statisticians and Biometricians*. Cambridge: Cambridge University Press, 1930–31.

Peirce, Charles Sanders. *Collected Papers of Charles Sanders Peirce*. 8 vols. Vols. 1–6, Charles Hartshorne and Paul Weiss, eds. Cambridge, Mass.: Harvard University Press, Belknap Press, 1965. Vols. 7–8, Arthur W. Burks, ed. Cambridge, Mass.: Harvard University Press, Belknap Press, 1966.

Perlman, Helen H. *Casework: A Problem Solving Process*. Chicago: University of Chicago Press, 1957.

Perlman, Helen H. "Casework and the Case of Chemung County." In Gordon E. Brown, ed., *The Multiproblem Dilemma*, pp. 47–50. Metuchen, N.J.: Scarecrow Press, 1968.

Perlman, Helen H. *Perspectives on Social Casework*. Philadelphia: Temple University Press, 1971.

Perlman, Helen H. "Social Work Method: A Review of the Decade 1955–65." In Helen H. Perlman, *Perspectives on Social Casework*, pp. 99–124. Philadelphia: Temple University Press, 1971.

Perlman, Helen H. "Social Work Method: A Review of the Past Decade," *Social Work* (October 1965), 10:166–178.

Phelps, Harold A. "The Case Record and Scientific Method." *The Family* (June 1927), 8:103–109.

Pieper [Piper], Martha Heineman. "Author's Reply," *Social Service Review* (March 1982), 56:146–148; (June 1982), 56:312.

Pieper, Martha Heineman. "Comments on 'Scientific Imperatives in Social Work Research: Pluralism is not Skepticism.' " *Social Service Review* (June 1987), 61:368–370.

Pieper, Martha Heineman. "The Future of Social Work Research." *Social Work Research and Abstracts* (Winter 1985), 21:3–11.

Piers, Ellen V. *Manual for the Piers-Harris Children's Self-Concept Scale.* Nashville: Counselor Recordings and Tests, 1969.

Pincus, Allen, and Anne Minahan, eds. *Social Work Practice.* Itasca, Ill.: Peacock, 1973.

Pinkus, Helen. "Casework Techniques Related to Selected Characteristics of Clients and Workers," D.S.W. dissertation, Columbia University, 1968.

Pinsoff, William M. "Family Therapy Process Research." In Alan S. Gurman and David P. Kniskern, eds., *Handbook of Family Therapy*, pp. 699–741. New York: Brunner/Mazel, 1981.

Polansky, Norman A. "Research in Social Work: Social Treatment." In *Social Work Encyclopedia*, 17th ed., pp. 1206–1213. Washington, D.C.: National Association of Social Workers, 1977.

Polansky, Norman A., ed. *Social Work Research.* Chicago: University of Chicago Press, 1960.

Polansky, Norman A., and Jacob Kounin. "Clients' Reactions to Initial Interviews: A Field Study." *Human Relations* (August 1956), 9:237–264.

Polanyi, Michael. *Personal Knowledge: Toward a Post-Critical Philosophy.* Chicago: University of Chicago Press, 1958.

Polanyi, Michael. *Science, Faith, and Society.* Chicago: University of Chicago Press, 1964.

Polanyi, Michael. *The Tacit Dimension.* Garden City, N.Y.: Doubleday, 1966.

Popper, Karl R. *Conjectures and Refutations: The Growth of Scientific Knowledge.* New York: Basic Books, 1962.

Popper, Karl R. *The Logic of Scientific Discovery.* New York: Basic Books, 1959.

Postman, Leo, and G. A. Miller. "Anchoring of Temporal Judgments," *American Journal of Psychology* (January 1945), 58:43–53.

Psychoanalytic Studies of the Personality. London: Routledge and Kegan Paul, 1981.

Pumphrey, Paul E., and Muriel W. Pumphrey. *The Heritage of American Social Work.* New York: Columbia University Press, 1961.

Quine, Willard Van Orman. *From a Logical Point of View: 9 Logico-Philosophical Essays.* Cambridge, Mass.: Harvard University Press, 1953; 2d rev. ed. 1980.

Quine, Willard Van Orman. *Methods of Logic*, 4th ed. Cambridge, Mass.: Harvard University Press, 1982.

Quine, Willard Van Orman. *Ontological Relativity and Other Essays.* New York: Columbia University Press, 1969.

Quine, Willard Van Orman. *Theories and Things.* Cambridge, Mass.: Harvard University Press, 1981.

Quine, Willard Van Orman. "Two Dogmas of Empiricism." *The Philosophical Review* (January 1951), 60:20–43; also in Harold Morick, ed., *Challenges to Empiricism*, pp. 46–70. Indianapolis: Hackett, 1980.

Rabin, Claire."Matching the Research Seminar to Meet Practice Needs: A Method for Integrating Research and Practice." *Journal of Social Work Education* (Winter 1985), 21:5–12.

Radnitzky, Gerald. *Contemporary Schools of Metascience.* Chicago: Regnery, 1973.

Rank, Otto. *The Trauma of Birth.* London: Paul French, Gruber; New York: Harcourt Brace and World, 1929.

Rank, Otto. *Will Therapy and Truth and Reality.* New York: Knopf, 1947.

Rapoport, Lydia. "Creativity in Social Work." *Smith College Studies in Social Work* (June 1968), 38:141–161.

Rapoport, Lydia. "Crisis Intervention as a Mode of Brief Treatment." In Robert W. Roberts and Robert H. Nee, eds., *Theories of Social Casework*, pp. 265–311. Chicago: University of Chicago Press, 1970.

Reason, Peter, and John Rowan, eds. *Human Inquiry.* New York: Wiley, 1981.

Reason, Peter, and John Rowan. "Issues of Validity in New Paradigm Research." In Peter Reason and John Rowan, eds., *Human Inquiry*, pp. 238–250. New York: Wiley, 1981.

Redl, Fritz. "Strategy and Technique in the Life Space Interview." *American Journal of Orthopsychiatry* (January 1959), 29:1–18.

Reed, Cherry. "Family Dependency Roles." *The Family* (April 1931), 12:64–70.

Regensberg, Jeannette. "Social Implications of Mental Testing." *The Family* (February 1927), 7:295–300.

Regensberg, Jeannette, ed. *Some Educational Patterns in Doctoral Programs in Schools of Social Work.* New York: Council on Social Work Education, 1966.

Reichenbach, Hans. *Experience and Prediction.* Chicago: University of Chicago Press, 1938.

Reichenbach, Hans. *The Rise of Scientific Philosophy.* Berkeley: University of California Press, 1951.

Reid, William J. "Characteristics of Casework Intervention." *Welfare in Review* (1967), 5:11–19.

Reid, William J. "Developing Intervention Methods Through Experimental Designs." In Aaron Rosenblatt and Diana Waldfogel, eds., *Handbook of Clinical Social Work*, pp. 650–672. San Francisco: Jossey-Bass, 1983.

Reid, William J. *Family Problem Solving.* New York: Columbia University Press, 1985.

Reid, William J. "The Model Development Dissertation." *Journal of Social Service Research* (Winter 1979), 3:215–225.

Reid, William J. "Practice Research: A Focus for Doctoral Programs in Social Work." Paper presented at annual meeting for Advancement of Doctoral Education, St. Louis, Mo., November 1978.

Reid, William J. "Research Developments." *1983–84 Supplement to the Encyclopedia of Social Work*, 17th ed., pp. 126–134. Silver Spring, Md.: National Association of Social Workers, 1983.

Reid, William J. "Research in Social Work." *Encyclopedia of Social Work*, 18th ed., pp. 474–487. Silver Spring, Md.: National Association of Social Workers, 1987.

Reid, William J. "Research Strategies for Improving Individualized Services." In David Fanshel, ed., *Future of Social Work Research*, pp. 38–52. New York: National Association of Social Workers, 1980.

Reid, William J. "Some Reflections on the Practice Doctorate." *Social Service Review* (September 1978), 52:449–455.

Reid, William J. "Target Problems, Time Limits, Task Structure." *Journal of Education for Social Work* (Spring 1972), 8:58–68.

Reid, William J. *The Task-Centered System.* New York: Columbia University Press, 1978.

Reid, William J. "Task-Centered Treatment." In Francis J. Turner, ed., *Social Work Treatment: Interlocking Theoretical Approaches,* 2d ed., pp. 479–497. New York: Free Press, 1979.

Reid, William J. "A Test of a Task-Centered Approach." *Social Work* (January 1975), 20:3–9.

Reid, William J., and Laura Epstein, *Task-Centered Casework.* New York: Columbia University Press, 1972.

Reid, William J., and Laura Epstein, eds. *Task-Centered Practice.* New York: Columbia University Press, 1977.

Reid, William J., and Patricia Hanrahan. "Recent Evaluations of Social Work: Grounds for Optimism." *Social Work* (July 1982), 27:328–340.

Reid, William J., and Ann W. Shyne. *Brief and Extended Casework.* New York: Columbia University Press, 1969.

Reid, William J., and Audrey D. Smith. *Research in Social Work.* New York: Columbia University Press, 1981.

Resnik, Michael. *Frege and the Philosophy of Mathematics.* Ithaca, N.Y.: Cornell University Press, 1980.

Reynolds, Paul D. *Primer in Theory Construction.* Indianapolis: Bobbs-Merrill, 1971.

Reynolds, Rosemary. "They Have Neither Money Nor Work." *The Family* (April 1931), 12:35–39.

Richey, Cheryl A., Betty J. Blythe, and Sharon B. Berlin. "Do Social Workers Evaluate Their Practice?" *Social Work Research and Abstracts* (Summer 1987), 23:14–20.

Richmond, Mary E. "The Social Caseworker in a Changing World." In *Proceedings-National Conference of Charities and Correction, Baltimore, Md., May 12–19, 1915,* pp. 43–49. Chicago: Hildmann, 1915.

Richmond, Mary E. *Social Diagnosis.* New York: Russell Sage Foundation, 1917.

Ricoeur, Paul. *Freud and Philosophy: An Essay on Interpretation.* D. Savage, trans. New Haven: Yale University Press, 1970.

Riehman, Lynne. "Beginning Where the Client Is: Social Casework Intervention in Direct Work with Families Who are Poor." In Ben A. Orcutt, ed., *Poverty and Social Casework Services,* pp. 73–107. Metuchen, N.J.: Scarecrow Press, 1974.

Riessman, Frank, Jerome Cohen, and Arthur Pearl, eds. *Mental Health of the Poor.* New York: Free Press of Glencoe, 1974.

Ripple, Lillian. "Factors Associated with Continuance in Casework Service." *Social Work* (January 1957), 2:87–94.

Ripple, Lillian. *Report of the Task Force on Structure and Quality in Social Work Education.* New York: Council on Social Work Education, 1974.

Ripple, Lillian, Ernestina Alexander, and Bernice W. Polemis. *Motivation, Capacity, and Opportunity: Studies in Casework Theory and Practice.* Chicago: University of Chicago Press, 1964.

Roberts, Robert W., and Robert H. Nee, eds. *Theories of Social Casework.* Chicago: University of Chicago Press, 1970.

Roberts, Robert W., and Helen Northen. *Theories of Social Work With Groups.* New York: Columbia University Press, 1976.

Robinson, Nancy. "Current Issues for Social Casework in the Provision of Services to Lower Socio-economic Groups." In Ben A. Orcutt, ed., *Poverty and Social Casework Services,* pp. 39–58. Metuchen, N.J.: Scarecrow Press, 1974.

Robinson, Virginia P. "Analysis of Processes in the Records of Family Caseworking Agencies." *The Family* (July 1921), 2:101–106.

Robinson, Virginia P. "Case Studies of the Family for Research Purposes." *The Family* (February 1926), 6:298–300.

Robinson, Virginia P. *A Changing Psychology in Social Casework.* Chapel Hill: University of North Carolina Press, 1930.

Robinson, Virginia P. *The Dynamics of Supervision Under Functional Controls.* Philadelphia: University of Pennsylvania Press, 1950.

Rogers, Carl. "A Theory of Therapy, Personality, and Interpersonal Relationships as Developed in the Client-Centered Framework." In Sigmund Koch, ed., *Psychology: A Study of Science*, pp. 184–256. New York: McGraw-Hill, 1959.

Rogers, Carl. "Toward More Human Science of the Person." *Journal of Humanistic Psychology* (Fall 1985), 25:7–24.

Rose, Sheldon D., and Ronald A. Feldman, eds. *Research in Social Group Work.* New York: Haworth Press, 1986.

Rosen, Aaron, and John J. Stretch, eds. *Doctoral Education in Social Work.* St. Louis: Group for the Advancement of Doctoral Education in Social Work, 1982.

Rosenau, Nathaniel S. "Report of the Committee on Charity Organization." In *Proceedings-National Conference of Charities and Correction, May 14–21, 1890, Baltimore, Md.*, pp. 25–31. Boston: Ellis, 1890.

Rosenblatt, Aaron. "The Practitioner's Use and Evaluation of Research." *Social Work* (January 1968), 13:53–59.

Rosenblatt, Aaron. "The Utilization of Research in Social Work Practice." In Neil Gilbert and Harry Specht, eds., *Handbook of the Social Services*, pp. 548–559. Englewood Cliffs, N.J.: Prentice-Hall, 1981.

Rosenblatt, Aaron, and James Mayer. "Client Disengagement and Alternative Treatment Resources." *Social Casework* (October 1966), 47:515–519.

Rosenblatt, Aaron, and Diana Waldfogel, eds. *Handbook of Clinical Social Work.* San Francisco: Jossey-Bass, 1983.

Rothman, Beulah and Bert Kaplan. "The Practice Internship in Clinical Doctoral Education." In Aaron Rosen and John J. Stretch, eds., *Doctoral Education in Social Work*, pp. 82–88. St. Louis, Mo.: Group for the Advancement of Doctoral Education in Social Work, 1982.

Rothman, Jack. "Harnessing Research to Enhance Practice: A Research and Development Model." In David Fanshel, ed., *Future of Social Work Research*, pp. 75–90. Washington, D.C.: National Association of Social Workers, 1980.

Rothman, Jack. *Research and Development in the Human Services.* Englewood Cliffs, N.J.: Prentice-Hall, 1979.

Rowan, John. "A Dialectical Paradigm for Research." In Peter Reason and John Rowan, eds., *Human Inquiry*, pp. 93–112. New York: Wiley, 1981.

Rubin, Allen, and Aaron Rosenblatt, eds. *Sourcebook on Research Utilization.* New York: Council on Social Work Education, 1979.

Ruse, Michael. "Ought Philosophers Consider Scientific Discovery? A Darwinian Case Study." In Thomas Nickles, ed., *Scientific Discovery: Case Studies*, pp. 131–149. Dordrecht, Holland: Reidel, 1980.

Russell, Bertrand. *Introduction to Mathematical Philosophy.* London: George Allen and Unwin; New York: Macmillan, 1919.

Russell, Bertrand. *Principles of Mathematics.* New York: Norton, 1938.

Sager, Clifford J., and Helen S. Kaplan, eds. *Progress in Group and Family Therapy.* New York: Brunner/Mazel, 1972.

Salmon, Wesley C. "The Foundations of Scientific Inference." In Robert Colodny, ed., *Mind and Cosmos*, pp. 135–275. Pittsburgh: University of Pittsburgh Press, 1966.

Salmon, Wesley C. *Logic*, 3d ed. Englewood Cliffs, N.J.: Prentice-Hall, 1984.

Sanborn, F. B., ed. *Proceedings of the Sixth Annual Conference of Charities, Chicago, June 1879.* Boston: Williams, Sept. 1879.

Sanborn, F. B. "The Work of Social Science, Past and Present." *Journal of Social Science* (May 1876), 8:23–39.

Sanford, Nevitt. "A Model for Action Research." In Peter Reason and John Rowan, eds., *Human Inquiry*, pp. 173–181. New York: Wiley, 1981.

Satir, Virginia. *Conjoint Family Therapy*. Palo Alto, Cal.: Behavior Books, 1964.

Satir, Virginia, James Stachowiak, and Harvey A. Taschman. *Helping Families to Change*. New York: Aronson, 1975.

Schafer, Roy. *Language and Insight*. New Haven: Yale University Press, 1978.

Schaffner, Kenneth F. "Discovery in the Biomedical Sciences: Logic or Irrational Intuition?" In Thomas Nickles, ed., *Scientific Discovery: Case Studies*, pp. 171–205. Dordrecht, Holland: Reidel, 1980.

Schensul, Stephen L. "Science, Theory, and Application in Anthropology." *American Behavioral Scientist* (November/December 1985), 29:164–185.

Scheurman, John R. "The Obsolete Scientific Imperative in Social Work Research." *Social Service Review* (March 1982), 56:144–146.

Schiller, F. C. S. "Scientific Discovery and Logical Proof." In C. Singer, ed., *Studies in the History and Methods of the Sciences*, vol. 1, pp. 235–289. Oxford: Clarendon Press, 1917.

Schlick, Moritz. "Positivism and Realism." David Rynin, trans. In Alfred Jules Ayer, ed., *Logical Positivism*, pp. 82–107. New York: Free Press, 1959.

Schön, Donald S. *The Reflective Practitioner*. New York: Basic Books, 1983.

Schwartz, William. "Neighborhood Centers and Group Work." In Henry S. Maas, ed., *Research for the Social Services: A Five Year Review*, pp. 130–191. New York: National Association of Social Workers, 1971.

Schweinitz, Karl de. "Sickness as a Factor in Poverty." *Proceedings-National Conference of Social Work, Atlantic City, N.J., June 1–8, 1919*, pp. 156–164. Chicago: Rogers and Hall Co., 1919.

Scope and Methods of the Family Service Agency. Report of the Committee on Methods and Scope. New York: Family Service Association of America, 1953.

Scriven, Michael. "A Possible Distinction Between Traditional Scientific Disciplines and the Study of Human Behavior." In Herbert Feigl and Michael Scriven, eds., *Minnesota Studies in the Philosophy of Science*, vol. 1, pp. 330–339. Minneapolis: University of Minnesota Press, 1956.

Scriven, Michael. *The Logic of Evaluation*. Point Reyes,Cal.: Edge Press, 1981.

Seinfeld, Jeffrey. *The Bad Object: Handling the Negative Therapeutic Reaction*. New York: Aronson, 1989.

Seinfeld, Jeffrey. "An Object Relations Theoretical Contribution to the Understanding of the Psychopathology and Intensive Psychotherapy of the Borderline Personality Organization." Ph.D. dissertation, New York University, 1987.

Selltiz, Claire, Marie Jahoda, Morton Deutsch, and Stuart Cook. *Research Methods in Social Relations*, rev. ed. New York: Holt, Rinehart and Winston, 1963.

Shalinsky, William. "The Effect of Group Composition on Aspects of Group Functioning." D.S.W. dissertation, Case Western Reserve University, 1967.

Shapiro, Deborah. *Agencies and Foster Children.* New York: Columbia University Press, 1976.

Shapiro, Gary, and Alan Sicada, eds. *Hermeneutics: Questions and Prospects.* Amherst, Mass.: University of Massachusetts Press, 1984.

Sherman, Corrine A. "The Caseworker and Social Research." *The Family* (June 1925), 6:100–102.

Shore, Barbara. "The Future of Doctoral Education in Social Work." Paper presented at the National Conference on Social Welfare, Chicago, May 17, 1977.

Shoshani, Batya Schneider. "Gordon Hamilton: An Investigation of Core Ideas." D.S.W. dissertation, Columbia University, 1984.

Shyne, Ann W. "Casework Research: Past and Present." *Social Casework* (November 1962), 43:467–473.

Shyne, Ann W., ed. *Use of Judgments as Data in Social Work Research.* New York: National Association of Social Workers, 1959.

Shyne, Ann W., and Leonard S. Kogan. "A Study of Components of Movement," *Social Casework* (June 1958), 39:333–342.

Siegal, Deborah H. "Effective Teaching of Empirically Based Practice." *Social Work Research and Abstracts* (Spring 1985), 21:40–47.

Siegel, Sidney. *Nonparametric Statistics for the Behavioral Sciences.* New York: McGraw-Hill, 1956.

Silverman, David. *Qualitative Methodology and Sociology.* Brookfield, Vt.: Gower, 1985.

Silverman, Marvin. "Knowledge in Social Group Work: A Review of the Literature." *Social Work* (July 1966), 11:56–62.

Simon, Herbert A. "Does Scientific Discovery Have a Logic?" *Philosophy of Science* (December 1973), 40:471–480.

Simon, Herbert A. *Models of Discovery.* Dordrecht, Holland: D. Reidl, 1977.

Simon, Herbert A. "Scientific Discovery and Psychology of Problem Solving." In Robert G. Colodny, ed., *Mind and Cosmos*, pp. 22–40. Pittsburgh: University of Pittsburgh Press, 1966.

Simon, Herbert A. "Thinking by Computers." In Robert G. Colodny, ed., *Mind and Cosmos*, pp. 3–21. Pittsburgh: University of Pittsburgh Press, 1966.

Simpson, Richard L. "Is Research Utilization for Social Workers?" *Journal of Social Service Research* (Winter 1978), 2:142–157.

Singer, C., ed. *Studies in the History and Methods of the Sciences.* Oxford: Clarendon Press, 1917.

Sinsheimer, Robert L. "The Presumptions of Science." *Daedalus* (Spring 1978), 107:23–35.

Siporin, Max. "Current Social Work Perspectives on Clinical Practice." *Clinical Social Work Journal* (Fall 1985), 13:198–217.

Siporin, Max. "Doctoral Education for Direct Service Practice in Social Work." *Journal of Education for Social Work* (Fall 1973), 9:78–86.

Siporin, Max. *Introduction to Social Work Practice.* New York: Macmillan, 1975.

Smalley, Ruth E. "Social Casework: The Functional Approach." *Encyclopedia of Social Work*, 16th ed., pp. 1195–1206. New York: National Association of Social Workers, 1971.

Smalley, Ruth E. *Theory for Social Work Practice.* New York: Columbia University Press, 1967.

Smith, Norman Kemp. *A Commentary to Kant's 'Critique of Pure Reason',* 2d ed.

London: Macmillan, 1923; repr. Atlantic Highlands, N.J.: Humanities Press, 1962.

Smith, Norman Kemp. *The Philosophy of David Hume: A Critical Study of its Origins and Central Doctrines*. London: Macmillan, 1941.

Smith, Zilpha. "Report of the Committee on the Organization of Charity." In *Proceedings-National Conference of Charities and Correction, July 5–11, 1888, Buffalo, N.Y.*, pp. 120–130. Boston: Ellis, 1888.

Snow, Richard E., "Representative and Quasi-representative Designs for Research in Teaching," *Review of Educational Research* (Summer 1974), 44:265–292.

Sobey, Francine. *The Nonprofessional Revolution in Mental Health*. New York: Columbia University Press, 1970.

Sobey, Francine, ed. *Changing Roles in Social Work Practice*. Philadelphia: Temple University Press, 1977.

"Social Forces," *Charities and the Commons* (October 1906–April 1907), 17:1. Editor's foreword.

Social Work Education in the Post-Master's Program. New York: Council on Social Work Education.
   Monograph 1: *Guiding Principles*. January 1953.
   Monograph 2: *Approaches to Curriculum Content*. April 1954.
   Monograph 3: *Field Work and Related Issues*. June 1955.

Social Work Encyclopedia, 17th ed. Washington, D.C.: National Association of Social Workers, 1977; 18th ed. Silver Spring, Md.: National Association of Social Workers, 1987.

Southard, E. E. "The Kingdom of Evil: Advantages of an Orderly Approach in Social Case Analysis." In *Proceedings-National Conference of Social Work, May 15–22, 1918*, pp. 334–340. Chicago: Rogers and Hall, 1919.

Spiegelberg, Herbert. *The Phenomenological Movement: A Historical Introduction*. The Hague: Nijhoff, 1960.

Stamm, Isabel L. "Ego Psychology in Casework." In Alfred J. Kahn, ed., *Issues in American Social Work*, pp. 80–109. New York: Columbia University Press, 1959.

Stanton, M. Duncan, and Thomas C. Todd. "A Critique of the Wells and Dezen Review of the Results of Non-behavioral Family Therapy." *Family Process* (June 1980), 19:169–178.

Steele, R. S. "Psychoanalysis and Hermeneutics." *International Review of Psychoanalysis* (1979), 6:389–411.

Stein, Herman D. "Social Science in Social Work Practice and Education." *Social Casework* (March 1955), 36:147–155.

Strean, Herbert S. *Clinical Social Work*. New York: Free Press, 1978.

Swerdloff, Esther S. "The Effect of the Depression on Family Life." *The Family* (January 1933), 13:310–334.

Taft, Jessie. "A Conception of the Growth Process Underlying Social Casework Practice." *Social Casework* (October 1950), 31:311–318. In Cora Kasius, ed., *Principles and Techniques in Social Casework*, pp. 247–259. New York: Family Service Association of America, 1950.

Taft, Jessie. "The Effect on an Unsatisfactory Mother-Daughter Relationship Upon the Development of Personality." *The Family* (March 1926), 7:10–17.

Taft, Jessie. "Function as the Basis of Development in Social Work Processes." Paper presented at meeting of American Association of Psychiatric Social Workers, June, 1939.

Taft, Jessie. "Qualifications of the Psychiatric Social Worker." In *Proceedings-National Conference of Social Work, Atlantic City, N.J., June 1–8, 1919*, pp. 593–599. Chicago: Rogers and Hall, 1919.

Taft, Jessie. "The Relation of Function to Process in Social Casework." *Journal of Social Work Process* (1937), 1:23–31.

Tallant, Steven H. "Meta-Analysis: Statistical Considerations and Applications in Small Group Treatment Research." In Sheldon D. Rose and Ronald A. Feldman, eds., *Research in Social Group Work*, pp. 43–53. New York: Haworth Press, 1986.

Taylor, Alfred E. *Elements of Metaphysics*, 12th ed. London: Methuen, 1946.

Thayer, Horace S. *Meaning and Action: A Critical History of Pragmatism.* Indianapolis: Bobbs-Merrill, 1968.

Theis, Sophie Van Senden. *How Foster Children Turn Out.* New York: State Charities Aid Association, 1924.

Thomas, Edwin J. "Behavioral Modification and Casework." In Robert W. Roberts and Robert H. Nee, eds., *Theories of Social Casework*, pp. 181–218. Chicago: University of Chicago Press, 1970.

Thomas, Edwin J. "Beyond Knowledge Utilization in General Human Service Technology." In David Fanshel, ed., *Future of Social Work Research*, pp. 91–103. Washington, D.C.: National Association of Social Workers, 1980.

Thomas, Edwin J. *Designing Interventions for the Helping Professions.* Beverly Hills, Cal.: Sage, 1984.

Thomas, Edwin J. "Mousetraps, Developmental Research, and Social Work Education." *Social Service Review* (September 1978), 52:468–483.

Thomas, Edwin J. "Research and Service in Single-Case Experimentation: Conflicts and Choices." *Social Work Research and Abstracts* (Winter 1978), 14:20–31.

Thomas, Edwin J. "Uses of Research Methods in Interpersonal Practice." In Norman A. Polansky, ed., *Social Work Research*, pp. 254–283. Rev. ed. Chicago: University of Chicago Press, 1975.

Thurz, Daniel. "Professional Education for Expected Political Action by Social Workers." *Journal of Education for Social Work* (Fall 1973), 9:87–93.

Tice, Terrence N., and Thomas P. Slavens. *Research Guide to Philosophy.* Chicago: American Library Association, 1983.

Timberlake, Elizabeth M., and Lewis Carr. "Research and the Social Work Practitioner." *Social Thought* (Fall 1982), 8:22–37.

Tinker, Katherine H. *Patterns of Family-Centered Treatment: A Descriptive Study of 30 FCP Closed Cases.* St. Paul, Minn.: Greater St. Paul United Fund and Council, 1959.

Todd, Arthur James. *The Scientific Spirit and Social Work.* New York: Macmillan, 1920.

Tolson, Eleanor R., and William J. Reid, eds. *Models of Family Treatment.* New York: Columbia University Press, 1981.

Toulmin, Stephen. "From Form to Function: Philosophy and History of Science in the 1950's and Now." *Daedalus* (Summer 1977), 106:143–162.

Trattner, William I. *From Poor Law to Welfare State*, 2d rev. ed. New York: Free Press, 1979.

Tripodi, Tony. *Evaluative Research for Social Workers.* Englewood Cliffs, N.J.: Prentice-Hall, 1983.

Tripodi, Tony, and James Bieri. "Information Transmissions in Clinical Judgments as a Function of Stimulus Dimensionality and Cognitive Complexity." *Journal of Personality* (March 1964), 32:119–137.

Tripodi, Tony, and Irwin Epstein. *Research Techniques for Clinical Social Workers*. New York: Columbia University Press, 1980.

Tripodi, Tony, and Henry Miller. "The Clinical Judgment Process: A Review of the Literature." *Social Work* (July 1966), 11:63–69.

Turk, Austin T. "The Sociological Relevance of History: A Footnote to Research on Legal Control in South Africa." In Michael Armer and Allen D. Grimshaw, eds., *Comparative Social Research: Methodological Problems and Strategies*, pp. 285–300. New York: Wiley, 1973.

Turner, Francis J. "A Comparison of Procedures in the Treatment of Clients with Two Different Value Orientations." *Social Casework* (May 1964), 45:273–277.

Turner, Francis J. *Differential Diagnosis and Treatment in Social Work*, 3d ed. New York: Free Press, 1983.

Turner, Francis J. "Ethnic Difference and Client Performance." *Social Service Review* (March 1970), 44:1–10.

Turner, Francis J. "Social Work Treatment and Value Differences." D.S.W. dissertation, Columbia University, 1963.

Turner, Francis J., ed. *Social Work Treatment: Interlocking Theoretical Approaches*, 1st, 2d, 3d eds. New York: Free Press, 1974, 1979, 1986.

Videka-Sherman, Lynn. "Research on the Effect of Parental Bereavement: Implications for Social Work Intervention." *Social Service Review* (March 1987), 61:102–116.

Videka-Sherman, Lynn, and Morton Lieberman. "The Effects of Self-Help and Psychotherapy Intervention on Child Loss: The Limits of Recovery." *American Journal of Orthopsychiatry* (January 1985), 55:70–82.

Volkman, John. "The Anchoring of Absolute Scales." *Psychological Bulletin* (November 1936), 33:743–744.

Walker, Helen M. "Some Data Regarding 162 Families Affected by Unemployment Known to the Cleveland Associated Charities." *The Family* (June 1933), 14:131–135.

Wallace, David. "The Chemung County Evaluation of Casework Service to Dependent Multiproblem Families." *Social Services Review* (December 1967), 41:379–389.

Wallis, W. Allen, and Harry V. Roberts. *Statistics*. Glencoe, Ill.: Free Press, 1956.

Warner, Amos G. *American Charities: A Study in Philanthropy and Economics*. New York and Boston: Thomas Y. Crowell, 1894.

Wartofsky, Marx W. *Conceptual Foundations of Scientific Thought: An Introduction to the Philosophy of Science*. New York: Macmillan Co., 1968.

Wartofsky, Marx W. "Scientific Judgment: Creativity and Discovery in Scientific Thought." In Thomas Nickles, ed., *Scientific Discovery: Case Studies*, pp. 1–16. Dordrecht, Holland: Reidel, 1980.

Webster's Collegiate Dictionary, 5th ed. Springfield, Mass.: Merriam-Webster, 1947.

Weinbach, Robert W., and Allen Rubin, eds. *Teaching Social Work Research: Alternative Programs and Strategies*. New York: Council on Social Work Education, 1980.

Welch, Gary John. "Will Graduates Use Single-Subject Designs to Evaluate Their Case Work Practice?" *Journal of Education for Social Work* (Spring 1983), 19:42–47.

Wells, Richard A. "The Empirical Base of Family Therapy: Practice Implications."

In Eleanor R. Tolson and William J. Reid, eds. *Models of Family Treatment*, pp. 248–305. New York: Columbia University Press, 1981.

Wells, Richard A., and Alan E. Dezen. "The Results of Family Therapy Revisited: The Non-Behavioral Methods," *Family Process* (September 1978), 17:251–274.

Wells, Richard A., Thomas C. Dilkes, and Nina Trivelli. "The Results of Family Therapy: A Critical Review of the Literature." *Family Process* (June 1972), 11:189–207.

White, R. Clyde. "The Relative Value of Case Study and Statistics." *The Family* (January 1930), 10:259–265.

Whitehead, Alfred North, and Bertrand Russell. *Principia Mathematica*, vols. 1, 2, and 3. Cambridge: Cambridge University Press, 1910, 1911, 1913.

Wiehe, Vernon R. "Scientific Technology and the Human Condition." *Journal of Sociology and Social Welfare* (March 1986), 13:88–97.

Wilensky, Harold L., and Charles N. Lebeaux. *Industrial Society and Social Welfare*. New York: Russell Sage Foundation, 1958.

Wimsatt, William. "Reductionistic Research Strategies and Their Biases in the Units of Selection Controversy." In Thomas Nickles, ed., *Scientific Discovery: Case Studies*, pp. 213–259. Dordrecht, Holland: Reidl, 1980.

Winslow, C. E. A. "Poverty as a Factor in Disease." In *Proceedings-National Conference of Social Work, Atlantic City, N.J., June 1–8, 1919*, pp. 153–166. Chicago: Rogers and Hall, 1919.

Witkin, Stanley L. "Toward a Scientific Social Work." *Journal of Social Service Research* (Spring 1989), 12:83–98.

Wittgenstein, Ludwig. *Tractatus Logico-Philosophicus*. D. F. Pears and B. F. McGuiness, trans. London: Routledge and Kegan Paul, 1961.

Wodarski, John S. *The Role of Research in Clinical Practice*. Baltimore: University Park Press, 1981.

Woodroofe, Kathleen. *From Charity to Social Work in England and the United States*. London: Routledge and Kegan Paul, 1962.

Woodrow, Richard D. "Casework: A Psychosocial Therapy." In Carol H. Meyer, ed., *Clinical Social Work in the Eco-Systems Perspective*, pp. 81–116. New York: Columbia University Press, 1983.

Wright, Albert O. "The New Philanthropy." In *Proceedings-National Conference of Charities and Correction, Grand Rapids, Michigan, June 4–10, 1896*, pp. 1–10. Boston: Ellis, 1896.

Wynne, Lyman C. "Communication Disorders and the Quest for Relatedness in Families of Schizophrenics." In Clifford J. Sager and Helen S. Kaplan, eds., *Progress in Group and Family Therapy*, pp. 595–615. New York: Brunner/Mazel, 1972.

Zald, Mayer N., ed. *Social Welfare Institutions: A Sociological Reader*. New York: Wiley, 1965.

Zimbalist, Sidney E. *Historic Themes and Landmarks in Social Welfare Research*. New York: Harper and Row, 1977.

Zimbalist, Sidney E. "The Single Case Clinical Research Design in Developmental Perspective: Mainstream or Tangent." *Journal of Education for Social Work* (Winter 1983), 19:61–66.

Index